WHITE
LINES

WHITE LINES

WRITERS ON COCAINE

EDITED BY

STEPHEN HYDE AND GENO ZANETTI

THUNDER'S MOUTH PRESS
NEW YORK

White Lines: *Writers on Cocaine*

© 2002 by Stephen Hyde and Geno Zanetti

Published by
Thunder's Mouth Press
An Imprint of Avalon Publishing Group Incorporated
161 William St., 16th Floor
New York, NY 10038

Library of Congress Cataloging-in-Publication Data

White lines: writers on cocaine / edited by Stephen Hyde and Geno Zanetti
    p. cm.
  ISBN 1-56025-378-9 (trade paper)
  1. American literature—20th century.   2. Cocaine habit—Literary collections.
3. English literature—20th century.   4. Cocaine—Literary collections.
I. Hyde, Stephen. II. Zanetti, Geno

PS509.C587 W48   2002
810.9'355—dc21

                         2002018065

9 8 7 6 5 4 3 2 1

Designed by Kathleen Lake, Neuwirth and Associates, Inc.
Printed in the United States of America
Distributed by Publishers Group West

Contents

Contents

"I snorted cocaine for about 15 years . . . with my dumb ass. I must have snorted up Peru. I could have bought Peru all the shit I snorted.

"I started off snorting little tiny pinches. I said, "I know I ain't gonna get hooked. Not on no coke! You can't get hooked." My friends, they've been snorting for 15 years. They're not hooked.

"Somebody told me if you put it on your dick, you could fuck all night. They shouldn't have told me that! My dick had a jones. $600 a day, just to get my dick hard." —RICHARD PRYOR

'Coke for fuel, coke for energy. Have a coke and a smile. Coking coal. This is white, not black; clean, not filth. You never eat coke. You snort it up. —IRVINE WELSH

From *Filth*

(Ooooh . . . White Lines) Vision dreams of passion
(Blowin through my mind) And all the while I think of you
(Pipe cries) A very strange reaction
(For us to unwind) The more I see the more I do
(Something like a phenomenon) Baby
(Tellin your body to come along, but white line . . . blow away)
(Blow! Rock it! Blow!)
Ticket to ride white line highway
Tell all your friends, they can go my way
Pay your toll, sell your soul
Pound for pound costs more than gold
The longer you stay the more you pay
My white lines go a long way
Either up your nose or through your vein
With nothin to gain except killin your brain

— *White Lines*
BY GRANDMASTER FLASH AND MELLE MEL

Editors' Note

IN THE ESSAY that opens this book, "Drugs and the Writer", Terry Southern writes, "Almost no one kicks a major junk habit: only super-artists, whose work is even stronger than the drug itself: Burroughs and Miles Davis are rather obvious examples. Mere mortals, however, beware." In the course of compiling this book we have stood then as mere editorial mortals before such super-artists as Burroughs and Davis, as well as Robert Louis Stevenson, Freud, Conan Doyle, Stephen King, Richard Price and J. G. Ballard. For them cocaine had been a dark muse — both inspiration and torment along the arduous path to becoming one of Southern's super-artists. Their pain, however, has been in some respects our pleasure as we have trawled the literature of cocaine from its Victorian origins to its latest manifestations. It has also been a pleasure working with Neil Ortenberg, Dan O'Connor, Ghadah Alrawi and Michelle Rosenfield at Thunder's Mouth Press who have provided us with a happy literary home to assemble this book. We should also like to thank Ana and Tony Hyde, Paul Long, Clive Ashenden, the Zanetti family, Bernard McKenna, Catherine Bromley and Stefanie Ameres, all of whom have given their support on the way to this book's completion.

Drugs and the Writer

by Terry Southern

Terry kept company with some of the most notorious "heads" of the twenti-eth century: John Lennon, Harry Nilsson, Timothy Leary, William Bur-roughs; and he was often asked by journalists about the role of drugs in literature.

I THINK BIG Chuck Bukowski (if, indeed, that is his name) is proba-bly right that drink brings good luck to writers. God (certainly) knows it brings warmth and companionship—to an otherwise absurdly forlorn sit-uation. Faulkner always liked to say: "A writer without a bottle of whiskey is like a chicken without a goddamn head." And Hemingway, of course, enjoyed nothing more than eulogizing the "Godly Brothers Gordon" for hours on end. Joyce would "knock back a whopper" at every opportunity. In fact, one would be hard-pressed to name more than five writers of first account who were not drinkers. For whatever reason, this does not appear to be the case with women. Indeed, there is (almost) nothing worse than a drunken woman writer. Exceptions abound, up to a point. Simone de Beauvoir, whom I knew during her Nelson Algren period, worked very well behind absinthe, or its substitute, Pernod, sipping it for hours at the Flore and turning out her typical top-of-the-shelf stuff. But whenever

1

Nels got her on to Boiler Makers she would soon be totally wrecked, and start singing Piaf. This was not bad in itself but she would apply her creative gifts towards 'improving' on these grand old *La Vie En Rose*–type favorites, and would end up rendering some kind of grotesque distortion. Nels had to give her a snappy *"Tais-toi*, cherie!" on more than one terse occasion.

Dot Parker was no stranger to the grape, nor indeed to the double belt by all accounts. But she could handle it, according to Benchley ("She may have stumbled, but she never fell"), and there's every reason to believe she did some of her best work under the steadying influence of a certain *Monsieur Courvoisier*, V.S.O.P.

This is not to suggest that any of these writers were alcoholics. I don't believe that a serious writer is in danger of becoming an alcoholic, because, after a certain point, one would not be working *behind* it, but directly in front of it, at peril of getting wiped out blotto, thereby defeating its purpose—which is, after all, motivational and as a hedge against the desolation of such a lonely endeavor. Good writers have so much (dare one say 'beauty and excitement'?) to come back to that they are not likely to go very far afield for any great length of time. It may be that addiction to alcohol exists among writers only as a psychological painkiller for the *'manqués,'* who had set great store by the potential ID value of it.

I think this may be said for other recreational drugs as well—with the notable exception of heroin, the effect of which is to reduce everything to a single glow, where it is no longer a question of doing or becoming— one is. A difficult package for anyone to resist. Almost no one kicks a major junk habit; only super-artists, whose work is even stronger than the drug itself: Burroughs and Miles Davis are rather obvious examples. Mere mortals, however, beware.

But, as Dr. Leary advises, "Don't just say 'No,' say 'No thanks.' "
—1990s

from

The Encyclopedia of Psychoactive Substances

by Richard Rudgley

Coca

THE COCA PLANT (*Erythroxylum coca*) is a bush or shrub that grows
to a typical height of about 1m. The chewing of its leaves is a traditional
practice in a wide area from Central America and throughout the Andes
and into the Amazon region. There are fourteen different alkaloids that
are contained in the leaves of the coca plant, the most famous, of course,
being cocaine (nicotine is also present in smaller quantities). The 'chewing' of the coca leaf is something of a misnomer but since the use of the
term is so widespread, I have retained it. Whilst the leaves of the coca
plant may be chewed when first put in the mouth (in order to make them
form a quid), after that it is placed between the cheek and gums and not
really chewed as such. Invariably an alkaline substance is added to the
quid in order to facilitate the release of the psychoactive properties of the
leaves. A wide variety of sources of these alkalis are known and they
include a woody cactus, the bark of trees, shells and plant stalks. The alkaline mixture is carefully put in the quid so that it does not burn the inside
of the mouth. What is remarkable is that the various stimulating plants
that are chewed in various disparate parts of the world almost all contain
alkaline additives. This is true of the traditional chewing of tobacco on

3

the Pacific north-west coast of North America, the tobacco and *pituri* chewing in Aboriginal Australia, and the chewing of betel in India, south-east Asia and Melanesia.

According to the archaic indigenous beliefs, coca 'chewing' is essentially harmless. This was given a modern scientific vindication by the Peruvian pharmacologist, Fernando Cabieses Molina, who wrote just after the end of the Second World War that traditional coca consumption has certain features that distinguish it markedly from cocaine abuse. The amount of the cocaine alkaloid is, of course, far lower than in chemically pure extracts from the plant. By introducing the coca leaf orally its psychoactive properties are absorbed slowly and without ill-effects by the digestive system. It is a stimulant and used to suppress hunger, to increase physical endurance and, in the Andes, to help cope with high altitudes. Distinguished visitors to Bolivia, including Pope John Paul II and Princess Anne have drunk coca tea (*mate de coca*) as it is the traditional way of avoiding altitude sickness. Impartial and scientific investigations have shown that regular use of coca is not harmful and no major social problems are known to have resulted from its traditional, and millennia-long, use in the Andes. This contradicts the claims of its ill-effects contained in reports by the United Nations and other official bodies, which seem to be based more on prejudice, ethnocentric bias, and the desire to portray the natural source of cocaine as negatively as possible in order to justify plans for eradicating coca in its homeland.

The ethnobotanist Richard Martin has eloquently highlighted the plight of the coca-using Indians when confronted by the irrational forces of Western civilisation:

> confusion about the effects of crude coca leaves and those of cocaine has caused many people to regard the chewing of coca leaves as practised by the Indians of South America as merely an addictive vice, with the result that coca is now being suppressed even in the areas where the Indians have relied on its stimulating and medicinal properties for thousands of years, and where it has formed a significant part of their religious and cultural heritage . . . to deny the use of coca to the Indians is as serious a disregard for human rights as would be an attempt to outlaw beer in Germany, coffee in the near east or betel chewing in India. The recent attempts to sup-

press and control the use of coca can be interpreted only as the latest step in the white man's attempt to exterminate the Indian way of life and make him completely dependent on the alien society and economy which has gradually surrounded him.

There is archaeological evidence for the ancient use of coca. At a burial site in the Chilean Andes a frozen mummy of an Inca boy was discovered, accompanied by a number of articles including a feathered pouch containing coca leaves. Peruvian Mochican ceramics from around AD 500 are often decorated with motifs clearly indicating the use of coca. Many such vessels show people with their cheeks bulging in the place where the coca quid is held inside the mouth. To the Incas, coca was the entheogen *par excellence* and the places where it grew were considered to be holy places. In the heyday of their empire coca use was largely restricted to priests and nobles. Court orators also used it to stimulate their powers of memory whilst reciting incredibly long oral histories. The sacrifice of coca accompanied almost all of their rites and ceremonies. Coca leaves were placed on fires and the way that they burned was interpreted by diviners. Scrying (divination by the visual appearance of things) is a custom reported throughout the world and can be considered to be one of the foundations of magic. The Inca reading of the coca leaves is analogous to the reading of tea leaves so widely practised in Europe, although the latter practice is debased. When the Spanish invaders brought the Inca empire and its hierarchy to its knees, coca use was no longer restricted to the elite and it became widely used throughout Andean society. Its entheogenic status nevertheless remained intact and it is still venerated as such today. The Quechua Indians make offerings of it to Mother Earth and the dead are not only believed to rest better with a coca quid in their mouths but also to attain paradise by this means.

The Colombian anthropologist Gerardo Reichel-Dolmatoff dedicated most of his professional life to the study of the use of psychoactive substances in native South American cultures. In addition to his highly influential work on the use of *ayahuasca* in the Amazon, he also conducted fieldwork among the coca-using Kogi Indians of the Sierra Nevada de Santa Marta, Colombia, who were later to reach an international audience when a BBC film crew came to hear their dire warnings concerning the destruction of Mother Earth by the world powers, whom the Kogi condescendingly called 'younger brothers', on account of their own superior wisdom. Reichel-Dolmatoff gives the following account of the Kogi views concerning their chosen entheogen:

> Upon the effect of the coca, the Kogi emphasises in the first place that its consumption brings a certain mental clarity which one ought to take advantage of for ceremonial gatherings and any religious act in general, being conversations, personal rites, or group rites. Evidently the coca causes a euphoric state which lasts for a long period and is prolonged by the gradual consumption of larger and larger quantities. The individual turns into an animated speaker, and says that he feels an agreeable sensation of tingling over all the body and that his memory is considerably refreshed which permits him to speak, sing, and recite during the following hours. In the second place the Kogi say that coca appeases hunger. According to them, however, this never is the object of consuming coca but only an agreeable consequence, seeing that during the ceremonies or ceremonial conversations the consumption of food is prohibited and the assistants ought to fast. Another effect which is attributed to coca is insomnia. Here again the Kogi see an advantage since the ceremonial conversations should be carried on at night and individuals who can speak and sing for one or several nights without sleep, merit high prestige. The Kogi ideal would be to never eat anything beside coca, to abstain totally from sex, to never sleep, and to speak all of his life of the 'Ancients', that is to say, to sing, to dance and to recite.

According to tests carried out by Svetla Balabanova on ancient Egyptian mummies, some of them show traces of cocaine. Although her tests have been widely criticised (many critics suggesting contamination of the samples in question) others have seen this as strengthening the possibility of transatlantic links between Egyptian voyagers and the inhabitants of the New World, as no plants native to the Old World are known to contain cocaine.

In those Indian societies where coca has been regularly used its beneficial effects in various aspects of life are taken for granted as manifestly obvious. There are abundant accounts of the powerful stimulating effects of coca. So intimately is it connected with the indigenous lifestyle of the Indians of the Peruvian Sierra that long journeys are calculated in units called *cocada*. Each *cocada* represents the distance that can be covered whilst chewing a single quid of coca. Since the distance that can be traversed depends on the terrain the *cocada* is as much a unit of time as of space. One visitor to the Andes has recorded the powerful effects of coca on a sixty-two-year-old man he hired to undertake some very strenuous digging work. The labourer worked almost continually for five days and nights, averaging two hours of sleep per night. Throughout this period he ate no food but simply chewed a coca quid every three hours. As if this wasn't enough he then proceeded, having finished digging, to accompany his employer on a two-day-long journey, all the time keeping up on foot whilst his employer rode a mule!

Coca's reception in the modern urban-based world has been a mixed one. In Bolivia and Peru, where coca is legal, it is used in toothpaste, chewing gum, wine and, most widely in the form of a tea (*mate de coca*). The cultural story of coca was radically different from that of the crass glitzy beginnings and subsequently sordid short life of its extract cocaine. Increasing demand for cocaine in North America and Europe has caused an inevitable increase in supply from the Andes. Since 1989 the US has sought to take the War on Drugs to the source and attempt to cut down the cultivation of coca; this has failed because, as an anonymous writer for the Catholic Institute for International Relations put it:

> The Andean strategy has failed because the premises upon which it is based are flawed. Most critically it assumes that it is possible significantly to reduce cocaine supply from the Andes while demand in the US remains high. Indeed it relies on supply reduction as the chief method of reducing demand. The Bush administration hoped that by curtailing supply they could force up the price of cocaine on the streets, making it prohibitively expensive for users and thus forcing a drop in actual demand. In doing so the Bush administration overestimated its capacity to impede traffickers and underestimated the power of the first law of the free market: demand elicits supply.

The long and seemingly golden age of traditional coca use has been rudely interrupted by the prostituting of *mama coca* (as the plant is known to the Indians) to the rich hedonists of the West and the pimps of crack.

In 1992 the Bolivian President Jaime Paz Zamora began his campaign to have coca use (but not cocaine use) made legal throughout the world. Not only would this preserve the rights of Andean people to pursue their ancient traditions of coca use unimpeded by foreign powers but would provide a legitimate world market for products containing coca and thus divert at least some coca cultivation away from the production of cocaine. Unless there are radical changes in the West away from the cultural shadow-boxing of the War on Drugs then such practical and economically sound ideas will continue to fall on deaf ears.

Sources: Andrews and Solomon 1975, Anon 1993, Antonil 1978, Grinspoon and Bakalar 1985, Martin 1970, Mortimer 1974.

Cocaine

IN 1860 ALBERT Niemann of the University of Göttingen discovered the way to isolate a psychoactive alkaloid from the leaf of the coca plant and he named it cocaine. Carl Koller discovered its use as a local anaesthetic and from then on cocaine became an important medicinal drug. From the 1860s onwards the stimulating and pleasurable qualities of both coca and cocaine resulted in a number of diverse preparations being launched on the international market. These included cocaine cigarettes, ointments, nasal sprays, and most popular of all, alcoholic drinks laced with coca and cocaine. The most famous of these was Vin Mariani, developed by the Corsican Angelo Mariani. Mariani was enraptured with coca and its lore. He wrote a book in its honour, tended it in his garden and avidly collected Inca artefacts and other paraphernalia relating to the plant. Vin Mariani was launched in 1863, and made by steeping selected coca leaves in wine. Despite many imitators Mariani's wine reigned supreme. In the British Library there are thirteen *de luxe* volumes of comments made by the rich and famous extolling the virtues of his drink. Vin Mariani was enthusiastically quaffed by a great many eminent individuals, including among royalty Queen Victoria, King Alphonse XIII of Spain, Albert I Prince of Monaco, George I King of Greece and the Shah of Persia. Leading religious figures also admired it very much, as their comments written in the various volumes of the book make abundantly clear. The Grand Rabbi of France Zadoc Kahn wrote: 'My conversion is complete. Praise be to Mariani's wine!' Pope Pius X was also an enthusiast and Leo XIII gave Mariani a gold medal in thanks. Cardinal Lavigerie wrote the somewhat perverse compliment: 'your coca from America gave my European priests the strength to civilise Asia and Africa.' Its stimulating properties made it a favourite of Louis Blériot, the first man to fly across the English Channel, who took a flask of Mariani wine with him on the flight. Dr Jean Charcot, who led the French Antarctic Expedition of 1903, expressed his plan to take a supply of it with him on the arduous journey. Vin Mariani had many advocates in the world of letters, Alexandre Dumas, Anatole France, Edmond Rostand, Jules Verne, H.G. Wells and Henrik Ibsen among them. There is even a communication from the secretary of William McKinley, the President of the United States, which reads:

Executive Mansion, June 14, 1898.

My dear Sir,

Please accept thanks on the President's behalf and on my own for your courtesy in sending a case of the celebrated Vin Mariani, with whose tonic virtues I am already acquainted, and will be happy to avail myself of in the future as occasion may require.

Very truly yours,

John Addison Porter,
Secretary to the President.

This missive displays a rather different attitude to coca than that of either Reagan or Bush! Even inventors such as Thomas Edison (the inventor of the gramophone) and the Lumière brothers (who invented the cinema) were regular drinkers of Vin Mariani. Both Vin Mariani and cocaine were used by opera singers to relieve sore throats, an occupational hazard.

Coca-Cola was originally developed by a pharmacist from Georgia named Styth Pemberton in 1886. The most famous carbonated soft drink in the world, Coca-Cola contained cocaine until 1906. Sigmund Freud, in his 1884 paper 'On Coca', eulogised the drug as a harmless panacea. The celebrated fictional detective, Sir Arthur Conan Doyle's Sherlock Holmes, was portrayed by his creator as resorting to injecting himself with cocaine when his mind was not working on a case. Legend has it that Robert Louis Stevenson wrote the famous story Dr Jekyll and Mr Hyde under the influence of cocaine. Stevenson is known to have written this 60,000-word book in six days and nights in October 1885. This achievement is doubly impressive since after three days he destroyed the manuscript and started again from scratch! It has even been suggested that the story is an allusion to the cocaine abuse that by this time had begun to appear among members of the medical profession. Although it had been widely used in the treatment of alcoholism and opiate addiction (as suggested by Freud and other leading figures of the time) this effectively ceased when its own habit-forming properties became known. One of the early critics of the use of cocaine in this way was Louis Lewin, one of the founders of ethnopharmacology, whose book Phantastica: Narcotic and Stimulating Drugs is still a very useful work today. In his final publication on the drug in 1887 (Craving for and Fear of Cocaine) Freud retracted his support for the use of cocaine in treating opiate addiction but denied that cocaine itself was addictive. Freud himself used cocaine sporadically but does not seem to have had any problems with it; his chosen drug seems to have been nicotine administered in the form of cigars.

It is in the 1880s that the historian of cocaine, David Courtwright, sees the rise of the first cocaine 'epidemic' in the United States that continued until the 1920s. The press had, by the 1890s, begun to associate the drug with the fringes of society—with criminals, prostitutes, pimps, gamblers and racial minorities. The use of the word 'coke' as an abbreviation for cocaine goes back at least to the turn of the century. A well-known prostitute working in Fort Worth, Texas at this time was called 'Queen Coke Fiend'. Legal restrictions in the US around the turn of the century meant that doctors and druggists could no longer supply many of those who were reselling it. Not surprisingly, this led to an expansion of the black market which would ultimately lead to the development of the Colombian drug cartels. Cocaine's popularity waned in the 1930s, in part because of the readily available amphetamines which provided users with an alternative and similarly potent stimulant drug. Nevertheless there were still many users in Europe, particularly in Germany. Among the most notable consumers of the drug was Hermann Goering, who was also a morphine addict.

The revival of cocaine as a leading recreational drug took place in the 1970s. The image of cocaine at this time was one of glamour, sophistication and class. It was portrayed as a rich man's drug and was popular in media and modern musical circles. Songs such as J.J. Cale's 'Cocaine' (later covered by Eric Clapton) demonstrate the easy-going attitude towards the drug at this time. The solid silver cocaine-sniffing spoons of the era epitomise the acceptance of the drug in certain chic circles of society; they are a type of artefact akin to the snuff-boxes and paraphernalia of a more genteel time. Whilst cocaine was reborn with a silver spoon in its nose its image was soon to be shattered by the powerful media images of the crack baby. Cocaine prices dropped dramatically from 1980 onwards as the drug cartels successfully expanded their client base, bringing in many people who previously could not afford to use the 'champagne drug'.

The changing face of cocaine and its economic anatomy is epitomised in the career of the most famous of the South American drug barons— Pablo Escobar. Pablo Emilio Escobar Gaviria was born in 1949, his father was a peasant farmer and his mother a primary school teacher. He was raised in Medellín which was to become, in the words of Escobar's biographer Simon Strong, 'the epicentre of the world's cocaine industry'. As a teenager Pablo was already involved in petty crime, serving his apprenticeship in car theft and protection. Escobar was fond of marijuana and the occasional drink but apparently did not use the cocaine which was to make him his fortune. Despite his ascending the ranks of the criminal classes to the high status of kidnapper, smuggler and murderer, Escobar nevertheless managed to convince himself that he was a Robin Hood figure. More particularly he identified himself with the famous Mexican bandit Pancho Villa and collected rare paraphernalia and bibliographic items relating to his chosen exemplar.

Escobar began a business partnership with Carlos Lehder, the son of a beauty queen and a German immigrant, who hero-worshipped Hitler. Lehder was able to bring to the negotiating table an established network that led directly, among other places, into the heart of Hollywood.

According to Escobar's brother-in-law, the partners in crime were fully aware not only of the economic power that could be gained through the cocaine industry but also its political potential. The political effects were to be diverting billions of dollars out of America and into the coffers of the cartel, the reduction of US influence on the internal affairs of Latin American states and the enfeebling of the American youth by their craving for cocaine. Escobar's personal fortune became vast, it is estimated that by 1983 he was worth $5 billion dollars. By this time he had already established business links with the Mafia and in deference to them he named his 3,000-hectare ranch *Nápoles*. Besides Pancho Villa artefacts, he also collected vintage cars made in the 1920s and 1930s with an unsurprising penchant for those models most closely identified with the infamous Chicago gangsters. In order to complete the effect he is said to have shot through a vintage Chevrolet with bullet holes and left it beside the driveway at *Nápoles*. Getting his livestock on the black market he set up a zoo, open to the public and boasting elephants, zebras and hippopotamuses.

In 1984 there was the first real crackdown by the Colombian authorities against the drug lords; Escobar was forced to flee the country and the Medellín cartel had to switch its headquarters to Panama. This new arrangement soon ran into problems when the US forced the Panamanian authorities to send the army in to destroy the cartel's illegal laboratory in the jungle close to the Colombian border. It was not only the Colombian, Panamanian and American authorities that were bearing down on Escobar's empire; relations with the rival Cali cartel had degenerated to the point of no return and Escobar's own home was bombed by them in 1987. Meanwhile the Colombian government were in pursuit but, apparently due to a tip off, Escobar narrowly escaped a pre-dawn raid which involved 1,000 soldiers backed up with tanks and helicopters. This was only the first of several embarrassing incidents for the authorities and Escobar escaped two similar attempts to catch him in 1989. Escobar fought back by paying hitmen $4,000 for every policeman killed in Medellín. The situation was now escalating on all fronts with the Cali cartel upping the stakes by offering a $1.5 million bounty for his head.

By 1992 Escobar was running out of options and turned himself in. He was placed in a special jail along with fourteen of his accomplices. Accounts of life in the jail suggest that it was hardly the punishment it was supposed to be—64″TVs adorned every room and jacuzzis were installed especially for the prisoners' comfort. This farcical state of affairs had its more sinister side and there were reports of Escobar and his entourage torturing *their* prisoners within the confines of this most open of prisons. The outrage against this lenient treatment of Escobar meant that his being moved to a top-security location was on the cards. He decided to escape, which, considering his criminal status, was achieved in a ludicrously simple fashion. He bribed a guard and went through a hole in the perimeter fence, taking his brother with him. This final humiliation for the Colombian authorities impelled them to track him down and finish the job. The financial stakes reached a new height with an official jackpot of nearly $7 million (much of it being put up by Interpol, the CIA, the FBI and the DEA) offered for his capture, closely followed by the 'black market' Cali bid of $5 million. The final act took place on 2 December 1993 when Escobar phoned his family from a hideaway, was tracked down by scanners and shot dead by order of the authorities.

Needless to say the death of Escobar did little to alter the cocaine trade; others eager for riches and power took his place. Although it was an operation somewhat overshadowed by cocaine production, during the 1980s the drug barons were investing heavily in the cultivation of the opium poppy in Colombia. Chemists who had been working in the heroin business on the Indian subcontinent were hired to oversee production. So successful was the operation that official sources estimate that by 1992 Colombia had replaced Mexico as the world's third largest producer of heroin. The profits that can be gained from heroin production far exceed those derived from cocaine.

The widespread use of freebase and crack also radically alter the image of cocaine. Freebasing seems to have begun in California in 1974. It is a process by which adulterated powder cocaine is converted into cocaine freebase. By heating cocaine hydrochloride in a water solution with ether and ammonia a pure crystalline form of cocaine can be made. This can then be smoked in a pipe and gives the user a stronger 'hit' than powder cocaine. In 1980 the comedian Richard Pryor had a near fatal accident, catching on fire in the process of making freebase. In practical terms most of the freebase (also called 'base' or 'rock') made in the 1970s was not made by any sophisticated means that produced a 'pure' product, it was made using baking soda and was crack in everything but name. The simple technique used in the preparation of crack consists of heating cocaine hydrochloride in a baking soda and water solution and smoking the resultant cocaine residue. Crack gets its name from the crackling sounds made by the 'rocks' (i.e. lumps of the drug) when they are smoked in a pipe. Thus, crack appeared much earlier than its discovery by the media would suggest. The word crack seems to have been first used in the media in the *New York Times* on 17 November 1985. In its post-glamour phase the image of cocaine has been projected as intimately connected with social deviance, the polar extremes being the tycoons of the cocaine trade on the one hand and the crack fiend of the streets on the other. The media has had a field day with stories relating to crack cocaine and despite the inaccuracies and scare-mongering in such tales there are, unfortunately, many stories from real life to show the human degradation and suffering that is caused by the drug.

In the tradition of earlier ethnographic reports of urban drug use (such as those on PCP), a series of anthropological field studies was conducted on crack use and the subordination of women who sell themselves for crack. In these studies, which were undertaken in major American cities, including New York, Chicago, Los Angeles, Miami and San Francisco, a common theme emerged in which an underground economy exists in which (mainly) female habitual crack users prostituted themselves not for money in order to buy the drug but for the drug itself. In this way crack acts as a currency, a sinister but economically ideal product akin to William Burroughs' descriptions of heroin. Dr James Inciardi, Director of the Centre for Drug and Alcohol Studies at the University of Delaware, who has been studying crack use in Miami since 1986, describes an all too typical scene:

> My first direct exposure to the sex-for-crack market came in 1988, during an initial visit to a North Miami crack house. I had gained entry through a local drug dealer, who had been a key informant of mine for almost a decade. He introduced me to the crack house door man as someone 'straight but OK'. After the door man checked us for weapons, my guide proceeded to show me around. Upon entering a room in the rear of the crack house (what I later learned was called a freak room), I observed what appeared to be the gang-rape of an unconscious child. Emaciated, seemingly comatose, and likely no

older than fourteen years of age, she was lying spread-eagled on a filthy mattress while four men in succession had vaginal intercourse with her. After they had finished and left the room, however, it became readily clear that it had not been forcible rape at all. She opened her eyes and looked about to see if anyone was waiting. When she realised that our purpose there was not for sex, she wiped her groin with a ragged beach towel, covered herself with half of a tattered sheet affecting a somewhat peculiar sense of modesty, and rolled over in an attempt to sleep . . . upon leaving the crack house a few minutes later, the dealer/informant explained that she was a house girl, a person in the employ of the crack house owner. He gave her food, a place to sleep, and all the crack she wanted in return for her providing sex—any type and amount of sex—to his crack house customers.

Many similar horror stories from crack culture are told by the other ethnographers involved in the study. Crack use affects those of all ages, even foetuses in the womb. Foetuses, newly born babies and children can be directly affected by powder cocaine or crack (putting aside all the family problems that will arise in a cocaine-using household) if the mother has used either during pregnancy or if the father has in the week before conception. The extent of the problem in the United States is difficult to assess. Government figures from 1989 state that some 375,000 children were affected as a result of alcohol or other drug use by their mothers during pregnancy. This figure may be far too low; some estimates suggest that 400,000 babies per year are born affected by cocaine abuse. Among the catalogue of problems that occur as a consequence of cocaine and crack use are damage to neurotransmitters which effects the workings of their nervous system, strokes, brain damage, genital deformities, cerebral palsy, addiction withdrawal symptoms and a number of disorders which interfere with the process of bonding such as 'gaze aversion' (when the baby avoids eye contact) and 'touch aversion'. A whole new series of problems may confront the crack-affected child as he or she grows—hyperactivity, incontinence, eating and sleeping disorders, learning problems and alienation.

With such a horrific social scenario it is hardly surprising that many people approve of the War on Drugs and believe that it can achieve its goal of reducing drug-related harm. But, whether or not one approves of the War on Drugs, it does not appear to be working and there is a growing movement that seeks to seriously explore other options, including the legalisation of hard drugs. The rationale behind this is basically to distinguish between the medical and social problems caused by the drug itself and the problems resulting from its illegal status. Criminal activity may be divided into two types—the drug trade itself and criminal acts committed by users seeking to sustain their habits. Obviously the two are not entirely distinct, but those who call for the legalisation of the hard drugs argue that the extreme violence associated with the black market trade in these substances would be eliminated if the drugs were available legally, and if they were legal and affordable there would be no need for habitual users to resort to theft and prostitution to guarantee a continual supply of the drug. Since the illegality of various drugs dissuades their users from seeking medical or social help to deal with their problems (fearing arrest) the rise in addiction and habituation continues unabated. Another point often stressed by those who wish to see an end to the War on Drugs is that the police and other law enforcement agencies would save a great deal of time and money and could therefore pursue other aspects of their work more effectively. Furthermore it is argued that taxes derived from the sale of such drugs could provide funds to deal with the enormous health problems arising from their use. Finally it is argued that legalisation would result in quality control of the drugs in question and eliminate dangerous adulterants that are so common in street drugs. Clearly there are objections to such plans for a 'cease fire'. The counter-arguments to this suggest that to legalise is to condone or even encourage (clearly if such drugs were legally manufactured and marketed by pharmaceutical companies there would be advertising, even if it were of the restricted kind, as in the case of tobacco products). Such a drastic change in legislation could result in an explosion of drug abuse on a scale hitherto unknown and at present contained only by legal sanctions. There is, of course, no simple answer but present policies do not seem to be working, no victory against the 'evil' of drugs seems imminent.

The American academic David Lenson has made a strong case for a radical review of current drug policy in the United States. He argues that the War on Drugs with its battle cries 'Just Say No' and 'Zero Tolerance' put all presently illegal substances into a single group without differentiating them in regard to their potency, addictive or non-addictive properties or psychoactive effects. He sees the War on Drugs having come into its own in the 1980s as a monolithic enemy needed to replace a waning Communism. The strategies and tactics that were used in the anti-Communist propaganda of the Cold War period were recycled in order to vilify the new enemy that was 'infecting' the body politic. As Lenson puts it the new: 'scapegoat could . . . be totally Other (Colombian, Peruvian, Panamanian, Bolivian) and at the same time as close as one's own bloodstream' and 'as close and distant as Bolshevism, with a needle and pipe instead of a hammer and sickle'. With a large percentage of the American population using illicit substances, Lenson also questions the wisdom of criminalising citizens purely on the basis of their use of drugs. He sees important civil liberties threatened in an uncomfortably intimate way: 'What crosses the blood-brain barrier is now open to the same surveillance as what crosses international borders. There is a customs in the cranium, a Checkpoint Consciousness.'

Recent research conducted by the Scottish Cocaine Research Group has shown how inaccurate a picture of the typical cocaine user is painted when the polar images of the cocaine yuppie and the crack ghetto child are taken as the starting point. The Group make the very obvious, but highly important, point that the users of cocaine (and, by implication, other illicit drugs) who are usually made the subjects of the social studies that generate meaningful statistics are, almost invariably, made up of individuals who have either been caught by the police or sought out medical assistance. But what about all the other users who do not appear in these statistics, the invisible majority? That is whom the Group sought out through confidential interviews. At least as far as Scotland goes they found these users were not: 'particularly young, particularly delinquent, particularly poor or deprived, nor particularly wealthy.' In fact, the typical cocaine-using Scottish man is in his mid-twenties, has a university degree and a job at which he earns £10,000–£15,000 a year. He takes cocaine occasionally as one of a number of drugs of choice that he uses. He takes it because it makes him relaxed and self-assured but complains that it is expensive and causes insomnia. Despite these rather minor reservations about the drug, he doesn't worry about getting hooked to cocaine.

The research team that undertook this survey of cocaine users felt that the 'psycho-pharmacological witch-hunting' of present drugs policies are rather inappropriate, particularly as so many of those users interviewed were clearly rather 'normal' citizens. The message of this study is that the silent majority of users of illicit substances are integrated in mainstream society and cannot be pigeonholed simply as medical patients or anti-social criminals.

Sources: Andrews and Solomon 1975, Courtwright 1995, Ditton and Hammersley 1996, Grinspoon and Bakalar 1985, Lenson 1995, Lewin 1964, Mortimer 1974, Ratner 1993, Strong 1995, Waller 1993.

Dr Lanyon's Narrative

by Robert Louis Stevenson

ON THE NINTH of January, now four days ago, I received by the evening delivery a registered envelope, addressed in the hand of my colleague and old school-companion, Henry Jekyll. I was a good deal surprised by this; for we were by no means in the habit of correspondence; I had seen the man, dined with him, indeed, the night before; and I could imagine nothing in our intercourse that should justify the formality of registration. The contents increased my wonder; for this is how the letter ran:

10th December 18—

Dear Lanyon,—You are one of my oldest friends; and although we may have differed at times on scientific questions, I cannot remember, at least on my side, any break in our affection. There was never a day when, if you had said to me, "Jekyll, my life, my honour, my reason, depend upon you," I would not have sacrificed my fortune or my left hand to help you. Lanyon, my life, my honour, my reason, are all at your mercy; if you fail me to-night, I am lost. You might suppose, after this preface, that I am going to ask you for something dishonourable to grant. Judge for yourself.

I want you to postpone all other engagements for to-night—ay, even if you were summoned to the bedside of an emperor; to take a cab, unless your carriage should be actually at the door; and, with this letter in your hand for consultation, to drive straight to my house. Poole, my butler, has his orders; you will find him waiting your arrival with a locksmith. The door of my cabinet is then to be forced; and you are to go in alone; to open the glazed press (letter E) on the left hand, breaking the lock if it be shut; and to draw out, *with all its contents as they stand,* the fourth drawer from the top or (which is the same thing) the third from the bottom. In my extreme distress of mind, I have a morbid fear of misdirecting you; but even if I am in error, you may know the right drawer by its contents: some powders, a phial, and a paper book. This drawer I beg of you to carry back with you to Cavendish Square exactly as it stands.

That is the first part of the service: now for the second. You should be back, if you set out at once on the receipt of this, long before midnight; but I will leave you that amount of margin, not only in the fear of one of those obstacles that can neither be prevented nor foreseen, but because an hour when your servants are in bed is to be preferred for what will then remain to do. At midnight, then, I have to ask you to be alone in your consulting-room, to admit with your own hand into the house a man who will present himself in my name, and to place in his hands the drawer that you will have brought with you from my cabinet. Then you will have played your part and earned my gratitude completely. Five minutes afterwards, if you insist upon an explanation, you will have understood that these arrangements are of capital importance; and that by the neglect of one of them, fantastic as they must appear, you might have charged your conscience with my death or the shipwreck of my reason.

Confident as I am that you will not trifle with this appeal, my heart sinks and my hand trembles at the bare thought of such a possibility. Think of me at this hour, in a strange place, labouring under a blackness of distress that no fancy can exaggerate, and yet well aware that, if you will but punctually serve me, my troubles will roll away like a story that is told. Serve me, my dear Lanyon, and save

Your friend,

H. J.

PS.—I had already sealed this up when a fresh terror struck upon my soul. It is possible that the post office may fail me, and this letter not come into your hands until to-morrow morning. In that case, dear Lanyon, do my errand when it shall be most convenient for you in the course of the day; and once more expect my messenger at midnight. It may then already be too late; and if that night passes without event, you will know that you have seen the last of Henry Jekyll.

Upon the reading of this letter, I made sure my colleague was insane; but till that was proved beyond the possibility of doubt, I felt bound to do as he requested. The less I understood of this farrago, the less I was in a position to judge of its importance; and an appeal so worded could not be set aside without a grave responsibility. I rose accordingly from table, got into a hansom, and drove straight to Jekyll's house. The butler was awaiting my arrival; he had received by the same post as mine a registered letter of instruction, and had sent at once for a locksmith and a carpenter. The tradesmen came while we were yet speaking; and we moved in a body to old Dr Denman's surgical theatre, from which (as you are doubtless aware) Jekyll's private cabinet is most conveniently entered. The door was very strong, the lock excellent; the carpenter avowed he would have great trouble, and have to do much damage, if force were to be used; and the locksmith was near despair. But this last was a handy fellow, and after two hours' work, the door stood open. The press marked E was unlocked; and I took out the drawer, had it filled up with straw and tied in a sheet, and returned with it to Cavendish Square.

Here I proceeded to examine its contents. The powders were neatly enough made up, but not with the nicety of the dispensing chemist; so that it was plain they were of Jekyll's private manufacture; and when I opened one of the wrappers, I found what seemed to me a simple crys-

talline salt of a white colour. The phial, to which I next turned my attention, might have been about half-full of a blood-red liquor, which was
highly pungent to the sense of smell, and seemed to me to contain phos-
phorus and some volatile ether. At the other ingredients I could make no
guess. The book was an ordinary version book, and contained little but a
series of dates. These covered a period of many years, but I observed that
the entries ceased nearly a year ago and quite abruptly. Here and there a
brief remark was appended to a date, usually no more than a single word:
'double' occurring perhaps six times in a total of several hundred entries;
and once very early in the list and followed by several marks of exclamation, 'total failure!!!' All this, though it whetted my curiosity, told me little
that was definite. Here were a phial of some tincture, a paper of some salt,
and the record of a series of experiments that had led (like too many of
Jekyll's investigations) to no end of practical usefulness. How could the
presence of these articles in my house affect either the honour, the sanity,
or the life of my flighty colleague? If his messenger could go to one place,
why could he not go to another? And even granting some impediment,
why was this gentleman to be received by me in secret? The more I
reflected, the more convinced I grew that I was dealing with a case of cerebral disease; and though I dismissed my servants to bed, I loaded an old
revolver, that I might be found in some posture of self-defence.

Twelve o'clock had scarce rung out over London, ere the knocker
sounded very gently on the door. I went myself at the summons, and
found a small man crouching against the pillars of the portico.

'Are you come from Dr Jekyll?' I asked.

He told me 'yes' by a constrained gesture; and when I had bidden him
enter, he did not obey me without a searching backward glance into the
darkness of the square. There was a policeman not far off, advancing with
his bull's eye open; and at the sight, I thought my visitor started and made
greater haste.

These particulars struck me, I confess, disagreeably; and as I followed
him into the bright light of the consulting-room, I kept my hand ready on
my weapon. Here, at last, I had a chance of clearly seeing him. I had
never set eyes on him before, so much was certain. He was small, as I
have said; I was struck besides with the shocking expression of his face,
with his remarkable combination of great muscular activity and great
apparent debility of constitution, and—last but not least—with the odd,

subjective disturbance caused by his neighbourhood. This bore some resemblance to incipient rigor, and was accompanied by a marked sinking of the pulse. At the time, I set it down to some idiosyncratic, personal distaste, and merely wondered at the acuteness of the symptoms; but I have since had reason to believe the cause to lie much deeper in the nature of man, and to turn on some nobler hinge than the principle of hatred.

This person (who had thus, from the first moment of his entrance, struck in me what I can only describe as a disgustful curiosity) was dressed in a fashion that would have made an ordinary person laughable; his clothes, that is to say, although they were of rich and sober fabric, were enormously too large for him in every measurement—the trousers hanging on his legs and rolled up to keep them from the ground, the waist of the coat below his haunches, and the collar sprawling wide upon his shoulders. Strange to relate, this ludicrous accoutrement was far from moving me to laughter. Rather, as there was something abnormal and misbegotten in the very essence of the creature that now faced me— something seizing, surprising and revolting—this fresh disparity seemed but to fit in with and to reinforce it; so that to my interest in the man's nature and character there was added a curiosity as to his origin, his life, his fortune and status in the world.

These observations, though they have taken so great a space to be set down in, were yet the work of a few seconds. My visitor was, indeed, on fire with sombre excitement.

'Have you got it?' he cried. 'Have you got it?' And so lively was his impatience that he even laid his hand upon my arm and sought to shake me.

I put him back conscious at his touch of a certain icy pang along my blood. 'Come, sir,' said I. 'You forget that I have not yet the pleasure of your acquaintance. Be seated, if you please.' And I showed him an example, and sat down myself in my customary seat and with as fair an imitation of my ordinary manner to a patient, as the lateness of the hour, the nature of my pre-occupations, and the horror I had of my visitor would suffer me to muster.

'I beg your pardon, Dr Lanyon,' he replied, civilly enough. 'What you say is very well founded; and my impatience has shown its heels to my politeness. I come here at the instance of your colleague, Dr Henry Jekyll, on a piece of business of some moment; and I understood . . . ' he

paused and put his hand to his throat, and I could see, in spite of his collected manner, that he was wrestling against the approaches of the hysteria—'I understood, a drawer . . .'

But here I took pity on my visitor's suspense, and some perhaps on my
own growing curiosity.

'There it is, sir,' said I, pointing to the drawer where it lay on the floor
behind a table, and still covered with the sheet.

He sprang to it, and then paused, and laid his hand upon his heart; I
could hear his teeth grate with the convulsive action of his jaws; and his
face was so ghastly to see that I grew alarmed both for his life and reason.

'Compose yourself,' said I.

He turned a dreadful smile to me, and, as if with the decision of
despair, plucked away the sheet. At sight of the contents, he uttered one
loud sob of such immense relief that I sat petrified. And the next
moment, in a voice that was already fairly well under control, 'Have you
a graduated glass?' he asked.

I rose from my place with something of an effort, and gave him what
he asked.

He thanked me with a smiling nod, measured out a few minims of the
red tincture and added one of the powders. The mixture, which was at
first of a reddish hue, began, in proportion as the crystals melted, to
brighten in colour, to effervesce audibly, and to throw off small fumes of
vapour. Suddenly, and at the same moment, the ebullition ceased, and
the compound changed to a dark purple, which faded again more slowly
to a watery green. My visitor, who had watched these metamorphoses
with a keen eye, smiled, set down the glass upon the table, and then
turned and looked upon me with an air of scrutiny.

'And now,' said he, 'to settle what remains. Will you be wise? will you
be guided? will you suffer me to take this glass in my hand, and to go forth
from your house without further parley? or has the greed of curiosity too
much command of you? Think before you answer, for it shall be done as
you decide. As you decide, you shall be left as you were before, and neither richer nor wiser, unless the sense of service rendered to a man in
mortal distress may be counted as a kind of riches of the soul. Or, if you
shall so prefer to choose, a new province of knowledge and new avenues
to fame and power shall be laid open to you, here, in this room, upon the

instant; and your sight shall be blasted by a prodigy to stagger the unbelief of Satan.'

'Sir,' said I, affecting a coolness that I was far from truly possessing, 'you speak enigmas, and you will perhaps not wonder that I hear you with no very strong impression of belief. But I have gone too far in the way of inexplicable services to pause before I see the end.'

'It is well,' replied my visitor. 'Lanyon, you remember your vows: what follows is under the seal of our profession. And now, you who have so long been bound to the most narrow and material views, you who have denied the virtue of transcendental medicine, you who have derided your superiors—behold!'

He put the glass to his lips, and drank at one gulp. A cry followed; he reeled, staggered, clutched at the table and held on, staring with injected eyes, gasping with open mouth; and as I looked, there came, I thought, a change—he seemed to swell—his face became suddenly black, and the features seemed to melt and alter—and the next moment I had sprung to my feet and leaped back against the wall, my arm raised to shield me from that prodigy, my mind submerged in terror.

'O God!' I screamed, and 'O God!' again and again; for there before my eyes—pale and shaken, and half fainting, and groping before him with his hands, like a man restored from death—there stood Henry Jekyll!

What he told me in the next hour I cannot bring my mind to set on paper. I saw what I saw, I heard what I heard, and my soul sickened at it; and yet, now when that sight has faded from my eyes, I ask myself if I believe it, and I cannot answer. My life is shaken to its roots; sleep has left me; the deadliest terror sits by me at all hours of the day and night; I feel that my days are numbered, and that I must die; and yet I shall die incredulous. As for the moral turpitude that man unveiled to me, even with tears of penitence, I cannot, even in memory, dwell on it without a start of horror. I will say but one thing, Utterson, and that (if you can bring your mind to credit it) will be more than enough. The creature who crept into my house that night was, on Jekyll's own confession, known by the name of Hyde and hunted for in every corner of the land as the murderer of Carew.

HASTIE LANYON

Über Coca

by Sigmund Freud

In his vividly written earliest article on the coca plant, Freud offers the reader a wealth of material on the history of its use in South America, its spread to Western Europe, its effects on humans and animals and its manifold therapeutic uses. Investigations by a host of authors are reported in detail. There are, at this stage, various hints towards the anesthetizing property of the drug and promises are held out in this respect, but no specific area of application is advocated.

The author's attitude toward the use of coca is favorable and comes near occasionally to being enthusiastic.

In the later Addenda to the paper, Freud mentions Koller's use of cocaine to anesthetize the cornea in eye operations, a practice which since then has become famous. Anna Freud

I. The Coca Plant

THE COCA PLANT, Erythroxylon coca, is a bush four to six feet in height, similar to our blackthorn. It is cultivated extensively in South America, in particular in Peru and Bolivia. It thrives best in the warm valleys on the eastern slopes of the Andes, 5000–6000 feet above sea level, in a rainy climate free from extremes of temperature. The leaves, which provide an indispensable stimulant for some 10 million people, are egg-shaped, 5–6 cm long, stalked, undivided, and pruinose. They are distinguished by two linear folds, especially prominent on the lower surface of the leaf, which, like lateral nerves, run along the medial nerve from the base of the leaf to its point in a flat arc. The bush bears small white flowers in lateral clusters of two or three, and produces red egg-shaped fruits. It can be propagated either by seed or by cuttings; the young plants are transplanted after a year and yield their first crop of leaves after eighteen months. The leaves are considered ripe when they have become so stiff that their stalks break upon being touched.

They are then dried rapidly, either in the sun or with the aid of fire, and sewn into sacks (*cestos*) for transport. In favorable conditions a coca bush yields four or five leaf crops annually and will continue to produce a yield for between thirty and forty years. The large-scale production (allegedly 30 million pounds annually) makes coca leaves an important item of trade and taxation in the countries where they are grown.

II. The History and Uses of Coca in its Country of Origin

WHEN THE SPANISH conquerors forced their way into Peru they found that the coca plant was cultivated and held in high esteem in that country; and indeed that it was closely connected with the religious customs of the people. Legend held that Manco Capac, the divine son of the Sun, had descended in primeval times from the cliffs of Lake Titicaca, bringing his father's light to the wretched inhabitants of the country; that he had brought them knowledge of the gods, taught them the useful arts, and given them the coca leaf, this divine plant which satiates the hungry, strengthens the weak, and causes them to forget their misfortune. Coca leaves were offered in sacrifice to the gods, were chewed during religious ceremonies, and were even placed in the mouths of the dead in order to assure them of a favorable reception in the beyond. The historian of the Spanish conquest, himself a descendant of the Incas, reports that coca was at first a scarce commodity in the land and its use a prerogative of the rulers; by the time of the conquest, however, it had long since become accessible to everyone. Garcilasso endeavored to defend coca against the ban which the conquerors laid upon it. The Spaniards did not believe in the marvelous effects of the plant, which they suspected as the work of the devil, mainly because of the role which it played in the religious ceremonial. A council held in Lima went so far as to prohibit the use of the plant on the ground that it was heathenish and sinful. Their attitude changed, however, when they observed that the Indians could not perform the heavy labor imposed upon them in the mines if they were forbidden to partake of coca. They compromised to the extent of distributing coca leaves to the workers three or four times daily and allowing them short periods of respite in which to chew the beloved leaves. And so the coca plant has maintained its position among the natives to the present day; there even remain traces of the religious veneration which was once accorded to it.

The Indian always carries a bundle of coca leaves (called *chuspa*) on his wanderings, as well as a bottle containing plant ash (*llicta*). In his mouth he forms the leaves into a ball, which he pierces several times with a thorn dipped in the ash, and chews slowly and thoroughly with copious secretion of saliva. It is said that in other areas a kind of earth, *tonra*, is added to the leaves in place of the plant ash. It is not considered immoderate to chew from three to four ounces of leaves daily. According to Mantegazza, the Indian begins to use this stimulant in early youth and continues to use it throughout his life. When he is faced with a difficult journey, when he takes a woman, or, in general, whenever his strength is more than usually taxed, he increases the customary dose.

(It is not clear what purpose is achieved through the admixture of the alkalis contained in the ash. Mantegazza claims to have chewed coca leaves both with and without *llicta* and to have noticed no difference. According to *Martius* and Demarle, the cocaine, probably held in compound with tannic acid, is released by the action of the alkalis. A *llicta* analyzed by Bibra consisted of 29% carbonate of lime and magnesia, 34% potassium salts, 3% argillaceous earth and iron, 17% insoluble compounds of argillaceous earth, siliceous earth and iron, 5% carbon and 10% water.)

There is ample evidence that Indians under the influence of coca can withstand exceptional hardships and perform heavy labor, without requiring proper nourishment during that time. Valdez y Palacios claims that by using coca the Indians are able to travel on foot for hundreds of hours and run faster than horses without showing signs of fatigue. Castelnau, Martius, and Scrivener confirm this, and Humboldt speaks of it in connection with his trip to the equatorial regions as a generally known fact. Often quoted is Tschudi's report concerning the performance of a *cholo* (half-breed) whom he was able to observe closely. The man in question carried out laborious excavation work for five days and nights, without sleeping more than two hours each night, and consumed nothing but coca. After the work was completed he accompanied Tschudi on a two-day ride, running alongside his mule. He gave every assurance that he would gladly perform the same work again, without eating, if he were given enough coca. The man was sixty-two years old and had never been ill.

In the *Journey of the Frigate 'Novara'*, similar examples are recounted of increased physical powers resulting from the use of coca. Weddell, von Meyen, Markham, and even Poeppig (whom we have to thank for many of the slanderous reports about coca) can only confirm this effect of the leaf, which, since it first became known, has continued to be a source of astonishment throughout the world.

Other reports stress the capacity of the *coqueros* (coca chewers) to abstain from food for long periods of time without suffering any ill effects. According to Unanué, when no food was available in the besieged city of La Paz in the year 1781, only those inhabitants survived who partook of coca. According to Stewenson, the inhabitants of many districts of Peru fast, sometimes for days, and with the aid of coca are still able to continue working.

In view of all this evidence, and bearing in mind the role which coca has played for centuries in South America, one must reject the view sometimes expressed, that the effect of coca is an imaginary one and that through force of circumstances and with practice the natives would be able to perform the feats attributed to them even without the aid of coca. One might expect to learn that the *coqueros* compensate for abstention from food by eating correspondingly more during the intervals between their fasts, or that as a result of their mode of life they fall into a rapid decline. The reports of travelers on the former point are not conclusive; as for the latter, it has been denied emphatically by reliable witnesses. To be sure, Poeppig painted a terrible picture of the physical and intellectual decadence which are supposed to be the inevitable consequence of the habitual use of coca. But all other observers affirm that the use of coca in moderation is more likely to promote health than to impair it, and that the *coqueros* live to a great age. Weddell and Mantegazza too, however,

point out that the immoderate use of coca leads to a cachexia characterized physically by digestive complaints, emaciation, etc., and mentally by
moral depravity and a complete apathy toward everything not connected
with the enjoyment of the stimulant. White people sometimes succumb
as well to this state, which bears a great similarity to the symptoms of
chronic alcoholism and morphine addiction. It is not taken in wholly
immoderate quantities, and never from a presumptive disproportion
between the amount of nourishment taken and the amount of work performed by the *coqueros*.

III. Coca Leaves in Europe—Cocaine

ACCORDING TO DOWDESWELL, the earliest recommendation for
coca is contained in an essay by Dr. Monardes (Seville, 1569) which
appeared in English translation in 1596. Like the later reports of the
Jesuit Father Antonio Julian, and the doctor Pedro Crespo, both of Lima,
Monardes' essay extols the marvelous effect of the plant in combating
hunger and fatigue. Both of the former authors had great hopes for the
introduction of coca into Europe. In 1749 the plant was brought to Europe; it was described by A. L. de Jussieu and classed with the genus Erythroxylon. In 1786 it appeared in Lamarck's *Encyclopédie Méthodique
Botanique* under the name of *Erythroxylon coca*. Reports of travelers such
as Tschudi and Markham, among others, provided proof that the effect of
coca leaves is not confined to the Indian race.

In 1859, Paolo Mantegazza, who had lived for a number of years in
South America's coca regions, published his discoveries about the physiological and therapeutic effects of coca leaves in both hemispheres. Mantegazza is an enthusiastic eulogist of coca and illustrated the versatility of
its therapeutic uses in reports of case histories. His report aroused much
interest but little confidence. However, I have come across so many correct observations in Mantegazza's publication that I am inclined to
accept his allegations even when I have not personally had an opportunity to confirm them.

In 1859, Dr. Scherzer, a member of the expedition in the Austrian
frigate *Novara*, brought a batch of coca leaves to Vienna, some of which
he sent to Professor Wöhler for examination. Wöhler's pupil Niemann

isolated the alkaloid cocaine from them. After Niemann's death, Lossen, another pupil of Wöhler, continued the investigation of the substances contained in coca leaves.

Niemann's cocaine crystallizes in large, colorless, 4–6-sided prisms of the monoclinic type. It has a somewhat bitter taste and produces an anesthetic effect on the mucous membranes. It melts at a temperature of 98°C, is difficult to dissolve in water but is easily soluble in alcohol, ether, and dilute acids. It combines with platinum chloride and gold chloride to form double salts. On heating with hydrochloric acid it breaks down into benzoic acid, methyl alcohol, and a little-studied base called ecgonin. Lossen established the following formula for cocaine: $C_{17}H_{24}NO_4$. Because of their high degree of solubility in water, the salts which it forms with hydrochloric acid and acetic acid are particularly suitable for physiological and therapeutic uses.

In addition to cocaine, the following substances have been found in coca leaves: cocatannic acid, a peculiar wax, and a volatile base, hygrine, which has a smell reminiscent of trimethylamine, and which Lossen isolated in the form of a viscous light yellow oil. Judging by reports from chemists, there are still more substances contained in coca leaves which have not yet been discovered.

Since the discovery of cocaine numerous observers have studied the effects of coca on animals as well as on healthy and sick human beings; they sometimes used a preparation described as cocaine, and sometimes the coca leaves themselves, either in an infusion or after the manner of the Indians. In Austria, Schroff senior carried out the first experiments on animals in 1862; other reports on coca have come from Frankl (1860), Fronmüller (1863), and Neudörfer (1870). As for work carried out in Germany, the therapeutic recommendations of Clemens (1867), von Anrep's experiments on animals (1880) and Aschenbrandt's experiments on exhausted soldiers (1883) may be mentioned.

In England A. Bennett carried out the first experiments on animals in 1874; in 1876 the reports of the president of the British Medical Association, Sir Robert Christison, created a considerable stir; and when a correspondent of the British Medical Journal claimed that a Mr. Weston (who had astonished scientific circles in London by his remarkable walking feats) chewed coca leaves, coca became, for a time, a subject of general interest. In the same year (1876) Dowdeswell published the results of a completely ineffective experiment carried out in the laboratory of University College, after which coca seems to have found no one in England willing to undertake further research.

From the French literature on the subject, the following should be mentioned: Rossier (1861), Demarle (1862), Gosse's monograph on Erythroxylon coca (1862), Reiss (1866), Lippmann's *Etude sur la coca du Pérou* (1868), Moréno y Maïz (1868), who provided certain new facts about cocaine, Gazeau (1870), Collins (1877), and Marvaud in the book *Les aliments d'épargne* (1874), the only of the above essays at my disposal.

In Russia Nikolsky, Danini (1873), and Tarkhanov (1872) concentrated particularly on studying the effects of cocaine on animals. Many reports, all of which have been published in the *Detroit Therapeutic Gazette,* have emerged from North America in recent years on the the successful therapeutic use of cocaine preparations.

The earlier of the investigations referred to here led, on the whole, to great disillusionment and to the conviction that effects from the use of coca such as had been reported so enthusiastically from South America could not be expected in Europe. Investigations such as those carried out by Schroff, Fronmüller, and Dowdeswell produced either negative or, at the most, insignificant results. There is more than one explanation for these failures. Certainly the quality of the preparations used was largely to blame. In a number of cases the authors themselves express doubt as to the quality of their preparations; and to the extent that they believe the reports of travelers on the effects of coca, they assume that these effects must be attributed to a volatile component of the leaf. They base this assumption on the report of Poeppig, among others, that even in South America leaves which have been stored for a long time are considered worthless. The experiments carried out recently with the cocaine prepared by Merk [sic] in Darmstadt alone justify the claim that cocaine is the true agent of the coca effect, which can be produced just as well in Europe as in South America and turned to good account in dietetic and therapeutic treatment.

IV. The Effect of Coca on Animals

WE KNOW THAT animals of different species—and even individuals of the same species—differ most markedly from one another in those chemical characteristics which determine the organism's receptivity to foreign substances. We would, therefore, as a matter of course, not expect to find that the effect of coca on animals in any way resembled the effects which it has been described to have on man. We may be satisfied with the results of our inquiry to the extent that we can comprehend the way cocaine affects both man and animals from a unified standpoint.

We are indebted to von Anrep for the most exhaustive experiments regarding the effects of coca on animals. Before him, such experiments were carried out by Schroff senior, Moréno y Maïz, Tarkhanov, Nikolsky, Danini, A. Bennett, and Ott. The majority of these authors introduced the alkaloid either orally or subcutaneously.

The most general result of such experiments is that, in small doses, coca has a stimulating, and in larger doses a paralyzing, effect on the nervous system. In the case of cold-blooded animals the paralyzing effect is particularly noticeable, while in warm-blooded animals symptoms of stimulation are the most apparent.

According to Schroff, cocaine produces in frogs a soporific condition accompanied by paralysis of the voluntary muscles. Moréno y Maïz, Danini, Nikolsky, and Ott made fundamentally the same discovery; Moréno y Maïz alleges that the general paralysis ensuing from moderate doses is preceded by tetanus; under the same conditions Nikolsky describes a stage of excitation of the muscular system, while Danini, on the other hand, never observed any spasms.

Von Anrep likewise reports a paralyzing effect of cocaine on frogs after a short period of excitation. At first the sensory nerve endings and later the sensory nerves themselves are affected; breathing is at first accelerated and then brought to a standstill; and the functioning of the heart is slowed down until the point of diastolic failure is reached. Doses of 2mg suffice to provoke symptoms of poisoning.

According to Schroff's accounts of his experiments with rabbits (which in detail are fraught with contradictions), coca produces multiple spasms in rabbits, increased respiration and pulse rate, dilation of the pupils, and convulsive death. The effectiveness of the poisoning depended to a large extent on the mode of application. According to Danini, cocaine poisoning in warm-blooded animals produces at first agitation, which manifests itself in continuous jumping and running, then paralysis of the muscular functions, and finally spasmodic (clonic) cramps. Tarkhanov discovered an increase of mucous secretion in dogs dosed with coca, and also sugar in the urine.

In von Anrep's experiments, the effect of cocaine, even in large doses, on warm-blooded animals manifested itself first of all in powerful psychic agitation and an excitation of the brain centers which control voluntary movement. After doses of 0.01g of cocaine per kg, dogs show obvious signs of happy excitement and a maniacal compulsion to move. From the character of these movements von Anrep sees evidence that all nerve centers are affected by the stimulation, and he interprets certain swinging motions of the head as an irritation proceeding from the semi-circular canals. Further manifestations of cocaine intoxication are accelerated respiration, a great increase in the pulse rate owing to early paralysis of the N. vagi, dilation of the pupils, an acceleration of intestinal movement, a great increase in blood-pressure, and diminution of secretions. Even after doses large enough to produce eventual convulsions, symptoms of paralysis and death due to paralysis of the respiratory center, the striated muscle substance remains intact. Von Anrep does not establish the lethal dose for dogs; for rabbits it is 0.10g and for cats 0.02g per kg.

When the spinal cord is severed from the oblongata, cocaine produces neither cramps nor a rise in blood-pressure (Danini); when the dorsal portion of the spinal cord is severed, cocaine spasms occur in the front but not in the rear extremities (von Anrep). Danini and von Anrep assume, therefore, that cocaine affects primarily the vital area of the medulla oblongata.

I should add that only the elder Schroff refers to cocaine as a narcotic and classes it with opium and cannabis, while almost everyone else ranks it with caffeine, etc.

V. The Effect of Coca on the Healthy Human Body

I HAVE CARRIED out experiments and studied, in myself and others, the effect of coca on the healthy human body; my findings agree fundamentally with Mantegazza's description of the effect of coca leaves.

The first time I took 0.05g. of *cocaïnum muriaticum* in a 1% water solution was when I was feeling slightly out of sorts from fatigue. This solution is rather viscous, somewhat opalescent, and has a strange aromatic smell.

At first it has a bitter taste, which yields afterwards to a series of very pleasant aromatic flavors. Dry cocaine salt has the same smell and taste, but to a more concentrated degree.

A few minutes after taking cocaine, one experiences a sudden exhilaration and feeling of lightness. One feels a certain furriness on the lips and palate, followed by a feeling of warmth in the same areas; if one now drinks cold water, it feels warm on the lips and cold in the throat. On other occasions the predominant feeling is a rather pleasant coolness in the mouth and throat.

During this first trial I experienced a short period of toxic effects, which did not recur in subsequent experiments. Breathing became slower and deeper and I felt tired and sleepy; I yawned frequently and felt somewhat dull. After a few minutes the actual cocaine euphoria began, introduced by repeated cooling eructation. Immediately after taking the cocaine I noticed a slight slackening of the pulse and later a moderate increase.

I have observed the same physical signs of the effect of cocaine in others, mostly people of my own age. The most constant symptom proved to be the repeated cooling eructation. This is often accompanied by a rumbling which must originate from high up in the intestine; two of the people I observed, who said they were able to recognize movements of their stomachs, declared emphatically that they had repeatedly detected such movements. Often, at the outset of the cocaine effect, the subjects alleged that they experienced an intense feeling of heat in the head. I noticed this in myself as well in the course of some later experiments, but on other occasions it was absent. In only two cases did coca give rise to dizziness. On the whole the toxic effects of coca are of short duration, and much less intense than those produced by effective doses of quinine or salicylate of soda; they seem to become even weaker after repeated use of cocaine.

Mantegazza refers to the following occasional effects of coca: temporary erythema, an increase in the quantity of urine, dryness of the conjunctiva and nasal mucous membranes. Dryness of the mucous membrane of the mouth and of the throat is a regular symptom which lasts for hours. Some observers (Marvaud, Collan) report a slight cathartic effect. Urine and feces are said to take on the smell of coca. Different observers give very different accounts of the effect on the pulse rate.

According to Mantegazza, coca quickly produces a considerably
increased pulse rate which becomes even higher with higher doses;
Collin, too, noted an acceleration of the pulse after coca was taken, while
Rossier, Demarle, and Marvaud experienced, after the initial acceleration, a longer lasting retardation of the pulse rate. Christison noticed in
himself, after using coca, that physical exertion caused a smaller increase
in the pulse rate than otherwise; Reiss disputes any effect on the pulse
rate. I do not find any difficulty in accounting for this lack of agreement;
it is partly owing to the variety of the preparations used (warm infusion of
the leaves, cold cocaine solution, etc.), and the way in which they are
applied, and partly to the varying reactions of individuals. With coca this
latter factor, as Mantegazza has already reported, is in general of very
great significance. There are said to be people who cannot tolerate coca
at all; on the other hand, I have found not a few who remained unaf-
fected by 5cg, which for me and others is an effective dose.

The psychic effect of *cocaïnum muriaticum* in doses of 0.05–0.10g
consists of exhilaration and lasting euphoria, which does not differ in any
way from the normal euphoria of a healthy person. The feeling of excitement which accompanies stimulus by alcohol is completely lacking; the
characteristic urge for immediate activity which alcohol produces is also
absent. One senses an increase of self-control and feels more vigorous
and more capable of work; on the other hand, if one works, one misses
that heightening of the mental powers which alcohol, tea, or coffee
induce. One is simply normal, and soon finds it difficult to believe that
one is under the influence of any drug at all.

This gives the impression that the mood induced by coca in such doses
is due not so much to direct stimulation as to the disappearance of elements in one's general state of well-being which cause depression. One
may perhaps assume that the euphoria resulting from good health is also
nothing more than the normal condition of a well-nourished cerebral
cortex which "is not conscious" of the organs of the body to which it
belongs.

During this stage of the cocaine condition, which is not otherwise distinguished, appear those symptoms which have been described as the
wonderful stimulating effect of coca. Long-lasting, intensive mental or
physical work can be performed without fatigue; it is as though the need
for food and sleep, which otherwise makes itself felt peremptorily at cer-

tain times of the day, were completely banished. While the effects of cocaine last one can, if urged to do so, eat copiously and without revulsion; but one has the clear feeling that the meal was superfluous. Similarly, as the effect of coca declines it is possible to sleep on going to bed, but sleep can just as easily be omitted with no unpleasant consequences. During the first hours of the coca effect one cannot sleep, but this sleeplessness is in no way distressing.

I have tested this effect of coca, which wards off hunger, sleep, and fatigue and steels one to intellectual effort, some dozen times on myself; I had no opportunity to engage in physical work.

A very busy colleague gave me an opportunity to observe a striking example of the manner in which cocaine dispels extreme fatigue and a well justified feeling of hunger; at 6:00 P.M. this colleague, who had not eaten since the early morning and who had worked exceedingly hard during the day, took 0.05g of *cocaïnum muriaticum*. A few minutes later he declared that he felt as though he had just eaten an ample meal, that he had no desire for an evening meal, and that he felt strong enough to undertake a long walk.

This stimulative effect of coca is vouched for beyond any doubt by a series of reliable reports, some of which are quite recent.

By way of an experiment, Sir Robert Christison—who is seventy-eight years old—tired himself to the point of exhaustion by walking fifteen miles without partaking of food. After several days he repeated the procedure with the same result; during the third experiment he chewed 2 drams of coca leaves and was able to complete the walk without the exhaustion experienced on the earlier occasions; when he arrived home, despite the fact that he had been for nine hours without food or drink, he experienced no hunger or thirst, and woke the next morning without feeling at all tired. On yet another occasion he climbed a 3000-foot mountain and arrived completely exhausted at the summit; he made the descent upon the influence of coca, with youthful vigor and no feeling of fatigue.

Clemens and J. Collan have had similar experiences—the latter after walking for several hours over snow; Mason calls coca "an excellent thing for a long walk"; Aschenbrandt reported recently how Bavarian soldiers, weary as a result of hardships and debilitating illnesses, were nevertheless capable, after taking coca, of participating in maneuvers and marches. Moréno y Maïz was able to stay awake whole nights with the aid of coca;

Mantegazza remained for forty hours without food. We are, therefore, justified in assuming that the effect of coca on Europeans is the same as that which the coca leaves have on the Indians of South America.

The effect of a moderate dose of coca fades away so gradually that, in normal circumstances, it is difficult to define its duration. If one works intensively while under the influence of coca, after from three to five hours there is a decline in the feeling of well-being, and a further dose of coca is necessary in order to ward off fatigue. The effect of coca seems to last longer if no heavy muscular work is undertaken. Opinion is unanimous that the euphoria induced by coca is not followed by any feeling of lassitude or other state of depression. I should be inclined to think that after moderate doses (0.05–0.10g) a part at least of the coca effect lasts for over twenty-four hours. In my own case, at any rate, I have noticed that even on the day after taking coca my condition compares favorably with the norm. I should be inclined to explain the possibility of a lasting gain in strength, such as has often been claimed for coca by the totality of such effects.

It seems probable, in the light of reports which I shall refer to later, that coca, if used protractedly but in moderation, is not detrimental to the body. Von Anrep treated animals for thirty days with moderate doses of cocaine and detected no detrimental effects on their bodily functions. It seems to me noteworthy—and I discovered this in myself and in other observers who were capable of judging such things—that a first dose or even repeated doses of coca produce no compulsive desire to use the stimulant further; on the contrary, one feels a certain unmotivated aversion to the substance. This circumstance may be partly responsible for the fact that coca, despite some warm recommendations, has not established itself in Europe as a stimulant.

The effect of large doses of coca was investigated by Mantegazza in experiments on himself. He succeeded in achieving a state of greatly increased happiness accompanied by a desire for complete immobility; this was interrupted occasionally, however, by the most violent urge to move. The analogy with the results of the animal experiments performed by von Anrep is unmistakable. When he increased the dose still further he remained in a *sopore beato*: His pulse rate was extremely high and there was a moderate rise in body temperature; he found that his speech was impeded and his handwriting unsteady; and eventually he experienced the most splendid and colorful hallucinations, the tenor of which was frightening for a short time, but invariably cheerful thereafter. This coca intoxication, too, failed to produce any state of depression, and left no sign whatsoever that the experimenter had passed through a period of intoxication. Moréno y Maïz also experienced a similar powerful compulsion to move after taking fairly large doses of coca. Even after using 18 drams of coca leaves Mantegazza experienced no impairment of full consciousness. A chemist who attempted to poison himself by taking 1.5g of cocaine became sick and showed symptoms of gastroenteritis, but there was no dulling of the consciousness.

VI. The Therapeutic Uses of Coca

IT WAS INEVITABLE that a plant which had achieved such a reputation for marvelous effects in its country of origin should have been used to treat the most varied disorders and illnesses of the human body. The first Europeans who became aware of this treasure of the native population were similarly unreserved in their recommendation of coca. On the basis of wide medical experience, Mantegazza later drew up a list of the therapeutic properties of coca, which one by one received the acknowledgment of other doctors. In the following section I have tried to collate the recommendations concerning coca, and, in doing so, to distinguish between recommendations based on successful treatment of illnesses and those which relate to the psychological effects of the stimulant. In general the latter outweigh the former. At present there seems to be some promise of widespread recognition and use of coca preparations in North America, while in Europe doctors scarcely know them by name. The failure of coca to take hold in Europe, which in my opinion is unmerited, can perhaps be attributed to reports of unfavorable consequences attendant upon its use, which appeared shortly after its introduction into Europe; or to the doubtful quality of the preparations, their relative scarcity and consequent high price. Some of the evidence which can be found in favor of the use of coca has been proved valid beyond any doubt, whereas some warrants at least an unprejudiced investigation. Merk's [sic] cocaine and its salts are, as has been proved, preparations which have the full or at least the essential effects of coca leaves.

a) *Coca as a stimulant*. The main use of coca will undoubtedly remain that which the Indians have made of it for centuries: it is of value in all cases where the primary aim is to increase the physical capacity of the body for a given short period of time and to hold strength in reserve to meet further demands—especially when outward circumstances exclude the possibility of obtaining the rest and nourishment normally necessary for great exertion. Such situations arise in wartime, on journeys, during mountain climbing and other expeditions, etc.—indeed, they are situations in which the alcoholic stimulants are also generally recognized as being of value. Coca is a far more potent and far less harmful stimulant than alcohol, and its widespread utilization is hindered at present only by its high cost. Bearing in mind the effect of coca on the natives of South America, a medical authority as early as Pedro Crespo (Lima, 1793) recommended its use by European navies; Neudörfer (1870), Clemens (1867) and Surgeon-Major E. Charles recommended that it should be adopted by the armies of Europe as well; and Aschenbrandt's experiences should not fail to draw the attention of army administrators to coca. If cocaine is given as a stimulant, it is better that it should be given in small effective doses (0.05–0.10g) and repeated so often that the effects of the doses overlap. Apparently cocaine is not stored in the body; I have already stressed the fact that there is no state of depression when the effects of coca have worn off.

At present it is impossible to assess with any certainty to what extent coca can be expected to increase human mental powers. I have the impression that protracted use of coca can lead to a lasting improvement if the inhibitions manifested before it is taken are due only to physical causes or to exhaustion. To be sure, the instantaneous effect of a dose of coca cannot be compared with that of a morphine injection; but, on the good side of the ledger, there is no danger of general damage to the body as is the case with the chronic use of morphine.

Many doctors felt that coca would play an important role by filling a gap in the medicine chest of the psychiatrists. It is a well-known fact that psychiatrists have an ample supply of drugs at their disposal for reducing the excitation of nerve centers, but none which could serve to increase the reduced functioning of the nerve centers. Coca has consequently been prescribed for the most diverse kinds of psychic debility—hysteria, hypochondria, melancholic inhibition, stupor, and similar maladies. Some successes have been reported: for instance, the Jesuit, Antonio Julian (Lima, 1787) tells of a learned missionary who was freed from severe hypochondria; Mantegazza praises coca as being almost universally effective in improving those functional disorders which we now group together under the name of neurasthenia; Fliessburg reports excellent results from the use of coca in cases of "nervous prostration"; and according to Caldwell, it is the best tonic for hysteria.

E. Morselli and G. Buccola carried out experiments involving the systematic dispensation of cocaine, over a period of months, to melancholics. They gave a preparation of cocaine, as prescribed by Trommsdorf, in subcutaneous injections, in doses ranging from 0.0025–0.10g per dose. After one or two months they confirmed a slight improvement in the condition of their patients, who became happier, took nourishment, and enjoyed regular digestion.

On the whole, the efficacy of coca in cases of nervous and psychic debility needs further investigation, which will probably lead to particularly partially favorable conclusions. According to Mantegazza coca is of no use, and is sometimes even dangerous, in cases of organic change and inflammation of the nervous system.

b) *The use of coca for digestive disorders of the stomach.* This is the oldest and most firmly founded use of coca, and at the same time it is the most comprehensible to us. According to the unanimous assertions of the oldest as well as the most recent authorities (Julian, Martius, Unanuè, Mantegazza, Bingel, Scrivener, Frankl, and others) coca in its most various forms banishes dyspeptic complaints and the disorders and debility associated therewith, and after protracted use results in a permanent cure. I have myself made a series of such observations.

Like Mantegazza and Frankl, I have experienced personally how the painful symptoms attendant upon large meals—viz, a feeling of pressure and fullness in the stomach, discomfort and a disinclination to work—disappear with eructation following small doses of cocaine (0.025–0.05). Time and again I have brought such relief to my colleagues; and twice I observed how the nausea resulting from gastronomic excesses responded in a short time to the effects of cocaine, and gave way to a normal desire to eat and a feeling of bodily well-being. I have also learned to spare myself stomach troubles by adding a small amount of cocaine to salicylate of soda.

My colleague, Dr. Josef Pollak, has given me the following account of an astonishing effect of cocaine, which shows that it can be used to treat not merely local discomfort in the stomach but also serious reflex reactions; one must therefore assume that cocaine has a powerful effect on the mucous membrane and the muscular system of this organ.

"A forty-two-year-old, robust man, whom the doctor knew very well, was forced to adhere most strictly to a certain diet and to prescribed mealtimes; otherwise he could not avoid the attacks about to be described. When traveling or under the influence of any emotional strain he was particularly susceptible. The attacks followed a regular pattern: They began in the evening with a feeling of discomfort in the epigastrium, followed by flushing of the face, tears in the eyes, throbbing in the temples and violent pain in the forehead, accompanied by a feeling of great depression and apathy. He could not sleep during the night; toward morning there were long painful spasms of vomiting which lasted for hours. Round about midday he experienced some relief, and on drinking a few spoonfuls of soup had a feeling 'as though the stomach would at last eject a bullet which had lain in it for a long time.' This was followed by rancid eructation, until, toward evening, his condition returned to normal. The patient was incapable of work throughout the day and had to keep to his bed.

"At 8:00 PM on the tenth of June the usual symptoms of an attack began. At ten o'clock, after the violent headache had developed, the patient was given 0.075g *cocaïnum muriaticum*. Shortly thereafter he experienced a feeling of warmth and eructation, which seemed to him to be 'still too little.' At 10:30 a second dose of 0.075g of cocaine was given; the eructations increased; the patient felt some relief and was able to write a long letter. He alleged that he felt intensive movement in the stomach; at twelve o'clock, apart from a slight headache, he was normal, even cheerful, and walked for an hour. He could not sleep until 3:00 AM, but that did not distress him. He awoke the next morning healthy, ready for work, and with a good appetite."

The effect of cocaine on the stomach—Mantegazza assumes this as well—is two-fold: stimulation of movement and reduction of the organ's sensitivity. The latter would seem probable not only because of the local sensations in the stomach after cocaine has been taken but because of the analogous effect of cocaine on other mucous membranes. Mantegazza claims to have achieved the most brilliant successes in treatments of gastralgia and enteralgia, and all painful and cramping afflictions of the stomach and intestines, which he attributes to the anesthetizing properties of coca. On this point I cannot confirm Mantegazza's experiences; only once, in connection with a case of gastric catarrh, did I see the sensitivity of the stomach to pressure disappear after the administration of coca. On other occasions I have observed myself, and also heard from other doctors, that patients suspected of having ulcers or scars in the stomach complained of increased pain after using coca; this can be explained by the increased movement of the stomach.

Accordingly, I should say that the use of coca is definitely indicated in cases of atonic digestive weakness and the so-called nervous stomach disorders; in such cases it is possible to achieve not merely a relief of the symptoms but a lasting improvement.

c) *Coca in cachexia.* Long-term use of coca is further strongly recommended—and allegedly has been tried with success—in all diseases which involve degeneration of the tissues, such as severe anemia, phthisis, long-lasting febrile diseases, etc.; and also during recovery from such diseases. Thus McBean noted a steady improvement in cases of typhoid fever treated with coca. In the case of phthisis, coca is said to have a limiting effect on the fever and sweating. Peckham reports with regard to a case of definitely diagnosed phthisis that after fluid extract of coca had been used for seven months there was a marked improvement in the patient's condition. Hole gives an account of another rather serious case in which chronic lack of appetite had led to an advanced condition of emaciation and exhaustion; here, too, the use of coca restored the patient to health. R. Bartholow observed, in general, that coca proved useful in treating phthisis and other "consumptive processes." Mantegazza and a number of other authorities attribute to coca the same invaluable therapeutic quality: that of limiting degeneration of the body and increasing strength in the case of cachexia.

One might wish to attribute such successes partly to the undoubted favorable effect of coca on the digestion, but one must bear in mind that a good many of the authors who have written on coca regard it as a "source of savings"; i.e., they are of the opinion that a system which has absorbed even an extremely small amount of cocaine is capable, as a result of the reaction of the body to coca, of amassing a greater store of vital energy which can be converted into work than would have been possible without coca. If we take the amount of work as being constant, the body which has absorbed cocaine should be able to manage with a lower metabolism, which in turn means a smaller intake of food.

This assumption was obviously made to account for the, according to von Voit, unexplained effect of coca on the Indians. It does not even necessarily involve a contradiction of the law of conservation of energy. For labor which draws upon food or tissue components involves a certain loss, either in the utilization of assimilated food or in the conversion of energy into work; this loss could perhaps be reduced if certain appropriate steps were taken. It has not been proved that such a process takes place, however. Experiments designed to determine the amount of urine eliminated with and without the use of coca have not been altogether conclusive; indeed, these experiments have not always been conducted in such conditions that they could furnish conclusive results. Moreover, they seem to have been carried out on the assumption that the elimination of urine—which is known not to be effected by labor—would provide a measure of metabolism in general. Thus Christison noted a slight reduction in the solid components of his urine during the walks on which he took coca; Lippmann, Demarle, Marvaud, and more recently Mason similarly concluded from their experiments that the consumption of coca reduces the amount of urine elimination. Gazeau, on the other hand, established an *increase* of urine elimination of 11–24% under the influence of coca. A better availability of materials already stored in the body explains, in his opinion, the body's increased working power and ability to do without food when under the influence of coca. No experiments have been carried out with regard to the elimination of carbon dioxide.

Voit proved that coffee, which also rated as a "source of savings," had no influence on the breakdown of albumen in the body. We must regard the conception of coca as a "source of savings" as disproven after certain experiments in which animals were starved, both with and without cocaine, and the reduction of their body weight and the length of time they were able to withstand inanition were observed. Such experiments were carried out by CI. Bernard, Moréno y Maïz, Demarle, Gazeau, and von Anrep. The result was that the animals to which cocaine had been administered succumbed to inanition just as soon—perhaps even sooner—than those which had received no cocaine. The starvation of La Paz—an experiment carried out by history itself, and reported by Unanuè—seems to contradict this conclusion, however, for the inhabitants who had partaken of coca are said to have escaped death by starvation. In this connection one might recall the fact that the human nervous system has an undoubted, if somewhat obscure, influence on the nourishment of tissues; psychological factors can, after all, cause a healthy man to lose weight.

The therapeutic quality of coca which we took as our argument at the outset does not, therefore, deserve to be rejected out of hand. The excitation of nerve centers by cocaine can have a favorable influence on the nourishment of the body afflicted by a consumptive condition, even though that influence might well not take the form of a slowing down of metabolism.

I should add here that coca has been warmly praised in connection with the treatment of syphilis. R. W. Taylor claims that a patient's tolerance of mercury is increased and the mercury cachexia kept in check when coca is administered at the same time. J. Collan recommends it as the best remedy for *stomatitis mercurialis* and reports that Pagvalin always prescribes it in conjunction with preparations of mercury.

d) *Coca in the treatment of morphine and alcohol addiction.* In America the important discovery has recently been made that coca preparations possess the power to suppress the craving for morphine in habitual addicts, and also to reduce to negligible proportions the serious symptoms of collapse which appear while the patient is being weaned away from the morphine habit. According to my information (which is largely from the *Detroit Therapeutic Gazette*), it was W. H. Bentley who announced, in May 1878, that he had substituted coca for the customary alkaloid in the case of a female morphine addict. Two years later, Palmer, in an article in the *Louisville Medical News*, seems to have aroused the greatest general interest in this treatment of morphine addiction; for the next two years "*Erythroxylon coca* in the opium habit" was a regular heading in the reports of the *Therapeutic Gazette*. From then on information regarding successful cures became rarer: whether because the treatment became established as a recognized cure, or because it was abandoned, I do not know. Judging by the advertisements of drug dealers in the most recent issues of American papers, I should rather conclude that the former was the case.

There are some sixteen reports of cases in which the patient has been successfully cured of addiction; in only one instance is there a report of failure of coca to alleviate morphine addiction, and in this case the doctor wondered why there had been so many warm recommendations for the use of coca in cases of morphine addiction. The successful cases vary in their conclusiveness. Some of them involve large doses of opium or morphine and addictions of long standing. There is not much information on the subject of relapses, as most cases were reported within a very short time of the cure having been effected. Symptoms which appear during abstention are not always reported in detail. There is especial value in those reports which contain the observation that the patients were able to dispense with coca after a few weeks without experiencing any further desire for morphine. Special attention is repeatedly called to the fact that morphine cachexia gave way to excellent health, so that the patients were scarcely recognizable after their cure. Concerning the method of withdrawal, it should be made clear that in the majority of cases a gradual reduction of the habitual dose of the drug, accompanied by a gradual increase of the coca dose, was the method chosen; however, sudden discontinuation of the drug was also tried. In the latter case Palmer prescribes that a certain dose of coca should be repeated as often during the day as the desire for morphine recurs. The daily dose of coca is lessened gradually until it is possible to dispense with the antidote altogether. From the very beginning the attacks experienced during abstinence were either slight or else became milder after a few days. In almost every case the cure was effected by the patient himself, whereas the cure of morphine addiction without the help of coca, as practiced in Europe, requires surveillance of the patient in a hospital.

I once had occasion to observe the case of a man who was subjected to the type of cure involving the sudden withdrawal of morphine, assisted by the use of coca; the same patient had suffered severe symptoms as a result of abstinence in the course of a previous cure. This time his condition was tolerable; in particular, there was no sign of depression or nausea as long as the effects of coca lasted; chills and diarrhea were now the only permanent symptoms of his abstinence. The patient was not bedridden, and could function normally. During the first days of the cure he consumed 3dg of *cocaïnum muriaticum* daily, and after ten days he was able to dispense with the coca treatment altogether.

The treatment of morphine addiction with coca does not, therefore, result merely in the exchange of one kind of addiction for another—it does not turn the morphine addict into a *coquero;* the use of coca is only temporary. Moreover, I do not think that it is the general toughening effect of coca which enables the system weakened by morphine to withstand, at the cost of only insignificant symptoms, the withdrawal of morphine. I am rather inclined to assume that coca has a directly antagonistic effect on morphine, and in support of my view I quote the following observations of Dr. Josef Pollak on a case in point:

"A thirty-three-year-old woman has been suffering for years from severe menstrual migraine which can be alleviated only by morphia injections. Although the lady in question never takes morphia or experiences any desire to do so when she is free of migraine, during the attacks she behaves like a morphine addict. A few hours after the injection she suffers intense depression, biliousness, attacks of vomiting, which are stopped by a second morphine injection; thereupon, the symptoms of intolerance recur, with the result that an attack of migraine, along with all its consequences, keeps the patient in bed for three days in a most wretched condition. Cocaine was then tried to combat the migraine, but the treatment proved unsuccessful. It was necessary to resort to morphine injections. But as soon as the symptoms of morphine intolerance appeared, they were quickly relieved by 1dg of cocaine, with the result that the patient recovered from her attack in a far shorter time and consumed much less morphine in the process."

Coca was tried in America for the treatment of chronic alcoholism at about the same time as it was introduced in connection with morphine addiction, and most reports dealt with the two uses conjointly. In the treatment of alcoholism, too, there were cases of undoubted success, in which the irresistible compulsion to drink was either banished or alleviated, and the dyspeptic complaints of the drinkers were relieved. In general, however, the suppression of the alcohol craving through the use of coca proved to be more difficult than the suppression of morphomania; in one case reported by Bentley the drinker became a *coquero.* One need only suggest the immense economic significance which coca would acquire as a "source of savings" in another sense, if its effectiveness in combating alcoholism were confirmed.

e) *Coca and asthma.* Tschudi and Markham report that by chewing coca leaves they were spared the usual symptoms of the so-called mountain sickness while climbing in the Andes; this complex of symptoms includes shortness of breath, pounding of the heart, dizziness, etc. Poizat reports that the asthmatic attacks of a patient were arrested in every case by coca. I mention this property of coca because it appears to admit of a physiological explanation. Von Anrep's experiments on animals resulted in early paralysis of certain branches of the vagus; and altitude asthma, as well as the attacks characteristic of chronic bronchitis, may be interpreted in terms of a reflex excitation originating in the pulmonary branches of the vagus. The use of coca should be considered for the treatment of other vagus neuroses.

f) *Coca as an aphrodisiac.* The natives of South America, who represented their goddess of love with coca leaves in her hand, did not doubt the stimulative effect of coca on the genitalia. Mantegazza confirms that the *coqueros* sustain a high degree of potency right into old age; he even reports cases of the restoration of potency and the disappearance of functional weaknesses following the use of coca, although he does not believe that coca would produce such an effect in all individuals. Marvaud emphatically supports the view that coca has a stimulative effect; other writers strongly recommend coca as a remedy for occasional functional weaknesses and temporary exhaustion; and Bentley reports on a case of this type in which coca was responsible for the cure.

Among the persons to whom I have given coca, three reported violent sexual excitement which they unhesitatingly attributed to the coca. A young writer, who was enabled by treatment with coca to resume his work after a longish illness, gave up using the drug because of the undesirable secondary effects which it had on him.

g) *Local application of coca.* Cocaine and its salts have a marked anesthetizing effect when brought in contact with the skin and mucous membrane in concentrated solution; this property suggests its occasional use as a local anesthetic, especially in connection with affections of the mucous membrane. According to Collin, Ch. Fauvel strongly recommends cocaine for treating diseases of the pharynx, describing it as *"le tenseur par excellence des chordes vocales."* Indeed, the anesthetizing properties of cocaine should make it suitable for a good many further applications.

from

The Sign of Four

Arthur Conan Doyle

SHERLOCK HOLMES TOOK his bottle from the corner of the mantelpiece, and his hypodermic syringe from its neat morocco case. With his long, white nervous fingers he adjusted the delicate needle, and rolled back his left shirt-cuff. For some little time his eyes rested thoughtfully upon the sinewy forearm and wrist, all dotted and scarred with innumerable puncture-marks. Finally, he thrust the sharp point home, pressed down the tiny piston and sank back into the velvet-lined armchair with a long sigh of satisfaction.

Three times a day for many months I had witnessed this performance, but the custom had not reconciled my mind to it. On the contrary, from day to day I had become more irritable at the sight, and my conscience swelled nightly within me at the thought that I had lacked the courage to protest. Again and again I had registered a vow that I should deliver my soul upon the subject; but there was that in the cool, nonchalant air of my companion which made him the last man with whom one would care to take anything approaching to a liberty. His great powers, his masterly manner, and the experience which I had had of his many extraordinary qualities, all made me diffident and backward in crossing him.

Yet upon that afternoon, whether it was the Beaune which I had taken with my lunch, or the additional exasperation produced by the extreme deliberation of his manner, I suddenly felt that I could hold out no longer.

"Which is it today," I asked "morphine or cocaine?"

He raised his eyes languidly from the old black-letter volume which he had opened.

"It is cocaine," he said, "a seven-per-cent solution. Would you care to try it?"

"No, indeed," I answered, brusquely. "My constitution has not got over the Afghan campaign yet. I cannot afford to throw any extra strain upon it."

He smiled at my vehemence. "Perhaps you are right, Watson," he said. "I suppose that its influence is physically a bad one. I find it, however, so transcendingly stimulating and clarifying to the mind that its second action is a matter of small moment."

"But consider!" I said, earnestly. "Count the cost! Your brain may, as you say, be roused and excited, but it is a pathological and morbid process, which involves increased tissue-change, and may at last leave a permanent weakness. You know, too, what a black reaction comes upon you. Surely the game is hardly worth the candle. Why should you, for a mere passing pleasure, risk the loss of those great powers with which you have been endowed? Remember that I speak not only as one comrade to another, but as a medical man to one for whose constitution he is to some extent answerable."

He did not seem offended. On the contrary, he put his finger-tips together, and leaned his elbows on the arms of his chair, like one who has a relish for conversation.

"My mind," he said, "rebels at stagnation. Give me problems, give me work, give me the most abstruse cryptogram, or the most intricate analysis, and I am in my own proper atmosphere. I can dispense then with artificial stimulants. But I abhor the dull routine of existence. I crave for mental exaltation. That is why I have chosen my own particular profession, or rather created it for I am the only one in the world."

"The only unofficial detective?" I said, raising my eyebrows.

"The only unofficial consulting detective," he answered. "I am the last and highest court of appeal in detection. When Gregson, or Lestrade, or Athelney Jones are out of their depths—which, by the way, is their normal state—the matter is laid before me. I examine the data, as an expert, and pronounce a specialist's opinion. I claim no credit in such cases. My name figures in no newspaper. The work itself, the pleasure of finding a field for my peculiar powers, is my highest reward. But you have yourself had some experience of my methods of work in the Jefferson Hope case."

"Yes indeed," said I, cordially. "I was never so struck by anything in my life. I even embodied it in a small brochure, with the somewhat fantastic title of 'A Study in Scarlet.'"

He shook his head sadly.

"I glanced over it," said he. "Honestly, I cannot congratulate you upon it. Detection is, or ought to be, an exact science, and should be treated in the same cold and unemotional manner. You have attempted to tinge it with romanticism, which produces much the same effect as if you worked a love-story or an elopement into the fifth proposition of Euclid."

"But the romance was there," I remonstrated. "I could not tamper with the facts."

"Some facts should be suppressed, or, at least, a just sense of proportion should be observed in treating them. The only point in the case which deserved mention was the curious analytical reasoning from effects to causes, by which I succeeded in unravelling it."

I was annoyed at this criticism of a work which had been specially designed to please him. I confess, too, that I was irritated by the egotism which seemed to demand that every line of my pamphlet should be devoted to his own special doings. More than once during the years that I had lived with him in Baker Street I had observed that a small vanity underlay my companion's quiet and didactic manner. I made no remark, however, but sat nursing my wounded leg. I had had a Jezail bullet through it some time before, and, though it did not prevent me from walking, it ached wearily at every change of the weather.

"My practice has extended recently to the Continent," said Holmes, after a while, filling up his old briar-root pipe. "I was consulted last week by François le Villard, who, as you probably know, has come rather to the front lately in the French detective service. He has all the Celtic power of quick intuition, but he is deficient in the wide range of exact knowledge which is essential to the higher developments of his art. The case was concerned with a will, and possessed some features of interest. I was able to refer him to two parallel cases, the one at Riga in 1857, and the other at St Louis in 1871, which have suggested to him the true solution. Here is the letter which I had this morning acknowledging my assistance."

He tossed over, as he spoke, a crumpled sheet of foreign notepaper. I glanced my eyes down it, catching a profusion of notes of admiration, with stray *'magnifiques'*, *'coup-de-maitres'*, and *'tours de force'*, all testifying to the ardent admiration of the Frenchman.

"He speaks as a pupil to his master," said I.

"Oh, he rates my assistance too highly," said Sherlock Holmes lightly. "He has considerable gifts himself. He possesses two out of the three qualities necessary for the ideal detective. He has the power of observation and that of deduction. He is only wanting in knowledge, and that may come in time. He is now translating my small works into French."

"Your works?"

"Oh, didn't you know?" he cried, laughing. "Yes, I have been guilty of several monographs. They are all upon technical subjects. Here, for example, is one 'Upon the Distinction between the Ashes of the Various Tobaccos.' In it I enumerate a hundred and forty forms of cigar, cigarette, and pipe tobacco, with coloured plates illustrating the difference in the ash. It is a point which is continually turning up in criminal trials, and which is sometimes of supreme importance as a clue. If you can say definitely, for example, that some murder had been done by a man who was smoking an Indian lunkah, it obviously narrows your field of search. To the trained eye there is as much difference between the black ash of a Trichinopoly and the white fluff of bird's-eye as there is between a cabbage and a potato."

"You have an extraordinary genius for minutiae," I remarked.

"I appreciate their importance. Here is my monograph upon the tracing of footsteps, with some remarks upon the uses of plaster of Paris as a preserver of impresses. Here, too, is a curious little work upon the influence of a trade upon the form of the hand, with lithotypes of the hands of slaters, sailors, cork-cutters, compositors, weavers, and diamond-polishers. That is a matter of great practical interest to the scientific detective—especially in cases of unclaimed bodies, or discovering the antecedents of criminals. But I weary you with my hobby."

"Not at all," I answered, earnestly. "It is of the greatest interest to me especially since I have had the opportunity of observing your practical application of it. But you spoke just now of observation and deduction. Surely the one to some extent implies the other."

"Why hardly," he answered, leaning back luxuriously in his armchair, and sending up thick blue wreaths from his pipe. "For example, observation shows me that you have been to the Wigmore Street Post Office this morning, but deduction lets me know that when there you dispatched a telegram."

"Right!" said I. "Right on both points! But I confess that I don't see how you arrived at it. It was a sudden impulse upon my part, and I have mentioned it to no one."

"It is simplicity itself," he remarked, chuckling at my surprise—"so absurdly simple that an explanation is superfluous; and yet it may serve to define the limits of observation and of deduction. Observation tells me that you have a little reddish mould adhering to your instep. Just opposite the Wigmore Street office they have taken up the pavement and thrown up some earth, which lies in such a way that it is difficult to avoid treading in it in entering. The earth is of the peculiar reddish tint which is found, as far as I know, nowhere else in the neighbourhood. So much is observation. The rest is deduction."

"How, then, did you deduce the telegram?"

"Why, of course I knew that you had not written a letter, since I sat opposite to you all morning. I see also in your open desk there that you have a sheet of stamps and a thick bundle of postcards. What could you go into the post-office for, then, but to send a wire? Eliminate all other factors, and the one which remains must be the truth."

"In this case it certainly is so," I replied, after a little thought. The thing, however, is, as you say, of the simplest. Would you think me impertinent if I were to put your theories to a more severe test?"

"On the contrary," he answered; "it would prevent me from taking a second dose of cocaine. I should be delighted to look into any problem which you might submit to me."

"I have heard you say that it is difficult for a man to have any object in daily use without leaving the impress of his individuality upon it in such a way that a trained observer might read it. Now, I have here a watch which has recently come into my possession. Would you have the kindness to let me have an opinion upon the character or habits of the late owner?"

I handed him over the watch with some slight feeling of amusement in my heart, for the test was, as I thought, an impossible one, and I intended it as a lesson against the somewhat dogmatic tone which he occasionally assumed. He balanced the watch in his hand, gazed hard at the dial, opened the back, and examined the works, first with his naked eyes and then with a powerful convex lens. I could hardly keep from smiling at his crestfallen face when he finally snapped the case to and handed it back.

"There are hardly any data," he remarked. "The watch has been recently cleaned, which robs me of my most suggestive facts."

"You are right," I answered. "It was cleaned before being sent to me."

In my heart I accused my companion of putting forward a most lame and impotent excuse to cover his failure. What data could he expect from an uncleaned watch?

"Though unsatisfactory, my research has not been entirely barren," he observed, staring up at the ceiling with dreamy, lack-lustre eyes. "Subject to your correction, I should judge that the watch belonged to your elder brother who inherited it from your father."

"That you gather, no doubt, from the H.W. on the back?"

"Quite so. The W. suggests your own name. The date of the watch is nearly fifty years back, and the initials are as old as the watch; so it was made for the last generation. Jewellery usually descends to the eldest son, and he is most likely to have the same name as the father. Your father has, if I remember right, been dead for many years. It has, therefore, been in the hands of your eldest brother."

"Right, so far," said I. "Anything else?"

"He was a man of untidy habits—very untidy and careless. He was left with good prospects, but threw away his chances, lived for some time in poverty with occasional short intervals of prosperity, and, finally, taking to drink, he died. That is all I can gather."

I sprang from my chair and limped impatiently about the room with considerable bitterness in my heart.

"This is unworthy of you, Holmes," I said. "I could not have believed that you would have descended to this. You have made inquiries into the history of my unhappy brother, and you now pretend to deduce this knowledge in some fanciful way. You cannot expect me to believe that you have read all this from his old watch! It is so unkind, and to speak plainly, has a touch of charlatanism in it."

"My dear Doctor," said he, kindly, "pray accept my apologies. Viewing the matter as an abstract problem, I had forgotten how personal and painful a thing it might be to you. I assure you, however, that I never even knew that you had a brother until you handed me the watch."

"Then how in the name of all that is wonderful did you get these facts? They are absolutely correct in every particular."

"Ah, that is good luck. I could only say what was the balance of probability. I didn't at all expect to be so accurate."

"But it was not mere guess-work?"

"No, no; I never guess. It is a shocking habit—destructive to the logical faculty. What seems strange to you is only because you do not follow my train of thought or observe the small facts upon which large inferences may depend. For example, I began by stating that your brother was careless. When you observe the lower part of that watch-case you will notice that it is not only dinted in two places, but it is cut and marked all over from the habit of keeping other hard objects, such as coins or keys, in the same pocket. Surely, it is no great feat to assume that a man who treats a fifty-guinea watch so cavalierly must be a careless man. Neither is it a very far-fetched inference that a man who inherits one article of such value is pretty well provided for in other respects."

I nodded, to show that I followed his reasoning.

"It is very customary for pawnbrokers in England, when they take a watch, to scratch the number of the ticket with a pin-point upon the inside of the case. It is more handy than a label, as there is no risk of the number being lost or transposed. There are no less than four such numbers visible to my lens on the inside of this case. Inference—that your brother was often at low water. Second inference—that he had occasional bursts of prosperity, or he could not have redeemed the pledge. Finally, I ask you to look at the inner plate which contains the keyhole. What sober man's key could have scored those grooves? But you will never see a drunkard's watch without them. He winds it at night, and he leaves these traces of his unsteady hand. Where is the mystery to all this?"

"It is as clear as daylight," I answered. "I regret the injustice which I did you. I should have had more faith in your marvellous faculty. May I ask whether you have any professional inquiry on foot at present?"

"None. Hence the cocaine. I cannot live without brain-work. What else is there to live for? Stand at the window here. Was there ever such a dreary, dismal, unprofitable world? See how the yellow fog swirls down the street and drifts across the dun-coloured houses. What could be more hopelessly prosaic and material? What is the use of having powers, Doctor, when one has no field upon which to exert them? Crime is commonplace, existence is commonplace, and no qualities save those which are commonplace have any function upon earth."

I had opened my mouth to reply to this tirade, when, with a crisp knock, our landlady entered, bearing a card upon the brass salver.

"A young lady for you, sir," she said, addressing my companion.

"Miss Mary Morstan," he read. "Hum! I have no recollection of her name. Ask the young lady to step up. Mrs. Hudson. Don't go, Doctor. I should prefer that you remain."

from

Novel with Cocaine

M. Ageyev

DURING THE LONG nights and long days I spent under the influence of cocaine in Yag's room I came to see that what counts in life is not the events that surround one but the reflection of those events in one's consciousness. Events may change, but insofar as the changes are not reflected in one's consciousness their result is nil. Thus, for example, a man basking in the aura of his riches will continue to feel himself a millionaire so long as he is unaware that the bank where he keeps his capital has gone under; a man basking in the aura of his offspring will continue to feel himself a father until he learns that his child has been run over. Man lives not by the events surrounding him, therefore, but by the reflection of those events in his consciousness.

All of a man's life — his work, his deeds, his will, his physical and mental prowess — is completely and utterly devoted to, fixed on bringing about one or another event in the external world, though not so much to experience the event in itself as to experience the reflection of the event on his consciousness. And if, to take it all a step further, everything a man does he does to bring about only those events which, when reflected in his consciousness, will make him feel happiness and joy, then what he spontaneously reveals thereby is nothing less than the basic mechanism behind his life and the life of every man, evil and cruel or good and kind.

One man does everything in his power to overthrow the tsar, another to overthrow the revolutionary junta; one man wishes to strike it rich, another gives his fortune to the poor. Yet what do these contrasts show but the diversity of human activity, which serves at best (and not in every case) as a kind of individual personality index. The *reason* behind human activity, as diverse as that activity may be, is always one: man's need to bring about events in the external world which, when reflected in his consciousness, will make him feel happiness.

So it was in my insignificant life as well. The road to the external event was well marked: I wished to become a rich and famous lawyer. It would seem I had only to take the road and follow it to the end, especially since I had much to recommend me (or so I tried to convince myself). But oddly enough, the more time I spent making my way towards the cherished goal, the more often I would stretch out on the couch in my dark room and imagine I was what I intended to become, my penchant for sloth and reverie persuading me that there was no point in laying out so great an expenditure of time and energy to bring the external events to fruition when my happiness would be all the stronger if the events leading up to it came about rapidly and unexpectedly.

But such was the force of habit that even in my dreams of happiness I thought chiefly of the event rather than the feeling of happiness, certain that the event (should it but occur) would lead to the happiness I desired. I was incapable of divorcing the two.

The problem was that before I first came in contact with cocaine I assumed that happiness was an entity, while in fact all human happiness consists of a clever fusion of two elements: 1) the physical feeling of happiness, and 2) the external event providing the psychic impetus for that feeling. Not until I first tried cocaine did I see the light; not until then did I see that the external event I had dreamed of bringing about—the result I had been slaving day and night for and yet might never manage to achieve—the external event was essential only insofar as I needed its reflection to make me feel happy. What if, as I was convinced, a tiny speck of cocaine could provide my organism with instantaneous happiness on a scale I had never dreamed of before? Then the need for any event whatever disappeared and, with it, the need for expending great amounts of work, time, and energy to bring it about.

Therein lay the power of cocaine—in its ability to produce a feeling of physical happiness psychically independent of all external events, even when the reflection of the events in my consciousness would otherwise have produced feelings of grief, depression, and despair. And it was that property of the drug that exerted so terribly strong an attraction on me that I neither could nor would oppose or resist it. The only way I could have done so was if the feeling of happiness had come less from bringing about the external event than from the work, the effort, the energy invested in bringing it about. But that was a kind of happiness I had never known.

OF COURSE, EVERYTHING I have said thus far about cocaine must be understood only as the opinion of someone who has only just begun to take the drug and not as a general statement. The neophyte does indeed believe that the main property of cocaine is its ability to make him feel happy, much as the mouse, before it is caught, believes that the main property of mousetraps is to provide him with lard.

The most awful aftereffect of cocaine, and one that followed the hours of euphoria without fail, was the agonizing reaction which doctors call depression and which took hold of me the instant I finished the last grain of powder. It would go on for what seemed an eternity—though by the clock it was only three or four hours—and consisted of the deepest, darkest misery imaginable. True, my mind knew that it would be over in a few hours, but my body could not believe it.

It is a well-known fact that the more a person is ruled by his emotions the less capable he is of lucid observation. The feelings I experienced under the spell of cocaine were so potent that my power of self-observation dwindled to a state found only in certain of mental illnesses; my "feeling I" grew to such proportions that my "self-observing I" all but ceased operation. There being nothing left to bridle my feelings, they poured out with total abandon—in my face, in my movements, in everything I did. But the moment the cocaine was gone and the misery took over, I began to see myself for what I was; indeed, the misery consisted largely in seeing myself as I had been while under the influence of the drug.

Slumped over as if nauseous, the nails of one hand digging into the palm of the other, I recalled every sinister, shameful detail. Standing frozen by the door of Yag's silent room at night, trembling with the idiotic but insuperable fear that someone was creeping along the passageway about to burst in on me and peer into my frightful eyes. And stealing slowly, ever so slowly, up to the dark, blindless window, certain that the moment I turned my back someone would glower at me through it, yet perfectly aware it was on the second floor. And turning off the lamp and its almost audible glare, which seemed to invite intruders. And lying on the couch, straining my neck to keep my head from touching the pillow and waking the entire house with the racket. And staring into the vibrating red darkness, my eyes aching with terror at the imminent prospect of being gouged. And striking match after match, my hand so numb with cold and horror that the effort appeared doomed until, after a long hiss, one would indeed take fire, and my body recoiled as the match dropped to the couch. And pulling myself up every ten minutes for a new fix, feeling for the packet, scraping the cocaine with the dull end of a steel pen-point, though even when quivering directly beneath my nostril (lifted there in the dark by a hand growing scrawnier with every night) the pen-point failed to give me my sniff: still wet from the last time round, it had moistened the cocaine, which then hardened, and all that came through was an acrid smell of rust. And answering countless calls of the bladder, forcing myself each time to overcome the panic-stricken immobility of my body and use the chamber pot there in the room, gritting my chattering teeth as I listened to the monstrous sound I made for all the building to hear, and then, sticky from a particularly pungent, fetid sweat, climbing back on the frozen mountain of a couch and falling into a state of stupefaction until the next urgent call roused me. And watching day break and objects take on shapes again, a process that did not in the least relax the muscles, which, longing for the protective covering of night and shunning the light that exposes face and eyes, contracted even more. And licking off the rusty pen-point by the morning light, delighting in the dry rush of a fresh fix from a new packet—the slight dizzy spell, the nausea-cum-bliss—then grieving at the first sounds of people in other flats awakening. And, finally, the knock at the door, returning at long, rhythmic intervals, a cough, which, though it racked the body, was necessary to dislodge the tongue, and then my voice quaking with happiness (despite the anguish) as I muttered through my teeth, "Who's there?

What do you want? Who's there?" and suddenly another knock, insistent, implacable, but from a new direction: it was the sound of wood being chopped in the courtyard.

Each time I came to the end of a session I would have visions, fanciful reconstructions of what I had just been through, how I had looked and behaved, and with the visions grew the certainty that soon, very soon—if not tomorrow then next week, if not next week then next month or year—I would end up in an insane asylum. And yet I kept increasing the dose, taking as many as three and a half grams and prolonging the effect for periods of over twenty-four hours. On the one hand, I had an insatiable desire for the drug; on the other, I merely desired to postpone its ever more ominous aftereffects.

Whether because I had increased the dosage or because any poison gives the organism a rude shock—and perhaps for both reasons—the shell my cocaine bliss presented to the world eventually began to crumble. I was possessed by the strangest of manias within an hour of the first sniff. Sometimes I would run out of matches and start searching for another box, moving the furniture away from the walls, emptying out all the drawers, carrying on with great pleasure for hours at a stretch, yet knowing all the while there was not a match in the room; at other times I would be obsessed with some dire apprehension, yet have no idea what or whom I so dreaded, and crouch in abject fear, crouch—again, for hours—by the door, torn between the unbearable need for a new fix, which meant going back to the couch, and the terrible risk involved in leaving the door unguarded for even a moment; at yet other times—and these had begun to grow in frequency lately—I would be set upon by all my manias at once, and then my nerves would be strained to the breaking point.

One night, while everyone was asleep and I had my ear to the door keeping vigil, I heard a sudden resonant noise—the sort of bang one sometimes hears in the night—followed immediately by a long wail. It was a moment or two before I realized that it was I who had wailed and *my* hand that was clamped over my mouth.

Au Pays de Cocaine

Aleister Crowley

I CAN'T REMEMBER any details of our first week in Paris. Details had ceased to exist. We whirled from pleasure to pleasure in one inexhaustible rush. We took everything in our stride. I cannot begin to describe the blind, boundless beatitude of love. Every incident was equally exquisite.

Of course, Paris lays herself out especially to deal with people in just that state of mind. We were living at ten times the normal voltage. This was true in more senses than one. I had taken a thousand pounds in cash from London, thinking as I did so how jolly it was to be reckless. We were going to have a good time, and damn the expense!

I thought of a thousand pounds as enough to paint Paris every colour of the spectrum for a quite indefinitely long period; but at the end of the week the thousand pounds was gone, and so was another thousand pounds for which I had cabled to London; and we had absolutely nothing to show for it except a couple of dresses for Lou, and a few not very expensive pieces of jewellery.

We felt that we were very economical. We were too happy to need to spend money. For one thing, love never needs more than a pittance, and I had never before known what love could mean.

What I may call the honeymoon part of the honeymoon seemed to occupy the whole of our waking hours. It left us no time to haunt Montmartre. We hardly troubled to eat, we hardly knew we were eating. We didn't seem to need sleep. We never got tired.

The first hint of fatigue sent one's hand to one's pocket. One sniff which gave us a sensation of the most exquisitely delicious wickedness, and we were on fourth speed again!

The only incident worth recording is the receipt of a letter and a box from Gretel Webster. The box contained a padded kimono for Lou, one of those gorgeous Japanese geisha silks, blue like a summer sky with dragons worked all over it in gold, with scarlet eyes and tongues.

Lou looked more distractingly, deliriously glorious than ever.

I had never been particularly keen on women. The few love affairs which had come my way had been rather silly and sordid. They had not revealed the possibilities of love; in fact, I had thought it a somewhat overrated pleasure, a brief and brutal blindness with boredom and disgust hard on its heels.

But with cocaine, things are absolutely different.

I want to emphasise the fact that cocaine is in reality a local anæsthetic. That is the actual explanation of its action. One cannot feel one's body. (As every one knows, this is the purpose for which it is used in surgery and dentistry.)

Now don't imagine that this means that the physical pleasures of marriage are diminished, but they are utterly etherealised. The animal part of one is intensely stimulated so far as its own action is concerned; but the feeling that this passion is animal is completely transmuted.

I come of a very refined race, keenly observant and easily nauseated. The little intimate incidents inseparable from love affairs, which in normal circumstances tend to jar the delicacy of one's sensibilities, do so no longer when one's furnace is full of coke. Everything soever is transmuted as by "heavenly alchemy" into a spiritual beatitude. One is intensely conscious of the body. But as the Buddhists tell us, the body is in reality an instrument of pain or discomfort. We have all of us a subconscious intuition that this is the case; and this is annihilated by cocaine.

Let me emphasise once more the absence of any reaction. There is where the infernal subtlety of the drug comes in. If one goes on the bust in the ordinary way on alcohol, one gets what the Americans call "the morning after the night before." Nature warns us that we have been breaking the rules; and Nature has given us common sense enough to know that although we can borrow a bit, we have to pay back.

We have drunk alcohol since the beginning of time; and it is in our racial consciousness that although "a hair of the dog" will put one right after a spree, it won't do to choke oneself with hair.

But with cocaine, all this caution is utterly abrogated. Nobody would be really much the worse for a night with the drug, provided that he had the sense to spend the next day in a Turkish bath, and build up with food and a double allowance of sleep. But cocaine insists upon one's living upon one's capital, and assures one that the fund is inexhaustible.

As I said, it is a local anæsthetic. It deadens any feeling which might arouse what physiologists call inhibition. One becomes absolutely reckless. One is bounding with health and bubbling with high spirits. It is a blind excitement of so sublime a character that it is impossible to worry about anything. And yet, this excitement is singularly calm and profound. There is nothing of the suggestion of coarseness which we associate with ordinary drunkenness. The very idea of coarseness or commonness is abolished. It is like the vision of Peter in the Acts of the Apostles in which he was told, "There is nothing common or unclean."

As Blake said, "Everything that lives is holy." Every act is a sacrament. Incidents which in the ordinary way would check one or annoy one, become merely material for joyous laughter. It is just as when you drop a tiny lump of sugar into champagne, it bubbles afresh.

Well, this is a digression. But that is just what cocaine does. The sober continuity of thought is broken up. One goes off at a tangent, a fresh, fierce, fantastic tangent, on the slightest excuse. One's sense of proportion is gone; and despite all the millions of miles that one cheerily goes out of one's way, one never loses sight of one's goal.

While I have been writing all this, I have never lost sight for a moment of the fact that I am telling you about the box and the letter from Gretel.

We met a girl in Paris, half a Red Indian, a lovely baby with the fascination of a fiend and a fund of the foulest stories that ever were told. She lived on cocaine. She was a more or less uneducated girl; and the way she put it was this: "I'm in a long, lovely garden, with my arms full of parcels, and I keep on dropping one; and when I stoop to pick it up, I always drop another, and all the time I am sailing along up the garden."

So this was Gretel's letter.

"My Darling Lou,—I could not *begin* to tell you the other day how delighted I was to see you My Lady and with such a *splendid* man for your husband. I don't blame you for getting married in such a hurry; but, on the other hand, you mustn't blame your old friends for not being prophets! So I could not be on hand with the goods. However, I have lost no time. You know how poor I am, but I hope you will value the little present I am sending you, not for its own sake, but as a token of my *deep affection* for the loveliest and most charming girl I know. A word in your ear, my dear Lou: *the inside is sometimes better than the outside*. With my *very kindest* regards and best wishes to dear Sir Peter and yourself, though I can't expect you to know that I even exist at the present,

"Yours ever devotedly,
"Gretel."

Lou threw the letter across the table to me. For some reason or no reason, I was irritated. I didn't want to hear from people like that at all. I didn't like or trust her.

"Queer fish," I said rather snappily.

It wasn't my own voice; it was, I fancy, some deep instinct of self-preservation speaking within me.

Lou, however, was radiant about it. I wish I could give you an idea of the sparkling quality of everything she said and did. Her eyes glittered, her lips twittered, her cheeks glowed like fresh blown buds in spring. She was the spirit of cocaine incarnate; cocaine made flesh. Her mere existence made the Universe infinitely exciting. Say, if you like, she was possessed of the devil!

Any good person, so-called, would have been shocked and scared at her appearance. She represented the siren, the vampire, Melusine, the dangerous, delicious devil that cowards have invented to explain their lack of manliness. Nothing would suit her mood but that we should dine up there in the room, so that she could wear the new kimono and dance for me at dinner.

We ate gray caviare, spoonful by spoonful. Who cared that it was worth three times its weight in gold? It's no use calling me extravagant; if you want to blame any one, blame the Kaiser. He started the whole fuss; and when I feel like eating gray caviare, I'm going to eat gray caviare.

We wolfed it down. It's silly to think that things matter.

Lou danced like a delirious demon between the courses. It pleased her to assume the psychology of the Oriental pleasure-making woman. I was her Pasha-with-three-tails, her Samurai warrior, her gorgeous Maharaja, with a scimitar across my knee, ready to cut her head off at the first excuse.

She was the Ouled Naïl with tatooed cheeks and chin, with painted antimony eyebrows, and red smeared lips.

I was the masked Toureg, the brigand from the desert, who had captured her.

She played a thousand exquisite crazy parts.

I have very little imagination, my brain runs entirely to analysis; but I revel in playing a part that is devised for me. I don't know how many times during that one dinner I turned from a civilised husband in Bond Street pyjamas into a raging madman.

It was only after the waiters had left us with the coffee and liqueurs—which we drank like water without being affected—that Lou suddenly threw off her glittering garment.

She stood in the middle of the room, and drank a champagne glass half full of liqueur brandy. The entrancing boldness of her gesture started me screaming inwardly. I jumped up like a crouching tiger that suddenly sees a stag.

Lou was giggling all over with irrepressible excitement. I know "giggling all over" isn't English; but I can't express it any other way.

She checked my rush as if she had been playing full back in an International Rugger match.

"Get the scissors," she whispered.

I understood in a second what she meant. It was perfectly true—we had been playing it a bit on the heavy side with that snow. I think it must have been about five sniffs. If you're curious, all you have to do is to go back and count it up—to get me to ten thousand feet above the poor old Straits of Dover, God bless them! But it was adding up like the price of the nails in the horse's shoes that my father used to think funny when I was a kid. You know what I mean—Martingale principle and all that sort of thing. We certainly had been punishing the snow.

Five sniffs! it wasn't much in our young lives after a fortnight.

Gwendolen Otter says:—

> "Heart of my heart, in the pale moonlight,
> Why should we wait till to-morrow night?"

And that's really very much the same spirit.

> "Heart of my heart, come out of the rain,
> Let's have another go of cocaine."

I know I don't count when it comes to poetry, and the distinguished authoress can well afford to smile, if it's only the society smile, and step quietly over my remains. But I really have got the spirit of the thing.

> "Always go on till you have to stop,
> Let's have another sniff, old top!"

No, that's undignified.

> "Carry on! over the top!"

would be better. It's more dignified and patriotic, and expresses the idea much better. And if you don't like it, you can inquire elsewhere.

No, I won't admit that we were reckless. We had substantial resources at our command. There was nothing whatever of the "long firm" about us.

You all know perfectly well how difficult it is to keep matches. Perfectly trivial things, matches—always using them, always easy to replace them, no matter at all for surprise if one should find one's box empty; and I don't admit for one moment that I showed any lack of proportion in the matter.

Now don't bring that moonlight flight to Paris up against me. I admit I was out of gas; but every one knows how one's occupation with one's first love affair is liable to cause a temporary derangement of one's ordinary habits.

What I liked about it was that evidently Gretel was a jolly good sport, whatever people said about her. And she wasn't an ordinary kind of good old sport either. I don't see any reason why I shouldn't admit that she is what you may call a true friend in the most early Victorian sense of the word you can imagine.

She was not only a true friend, but a wise friend. She had evidently foreseen that we were going to run short of good old snow.

Now I want all you fellows to take it as read that a man, if he calls himself a man, isn't the kind of man that wants to stop a honeymoon with a girl in a Japanese kimono of the variety described, to have to put on a lot of beastly clothes and hunt all around Paris for a dope peddler.

Of course, you'll say at once that I could have rung for the waiter and have him bring me a few cubic kilometres. But that's simply because you don't understand the kind of hotel at which we were unfortunate enough to be staying. We had gone there thinking no harm whatever. It was right up near the Étoile, and appeared to the naked eye an absolutely respectable first-class family hotel for the sons of the nobility and gentry.

Now don't run away with the idea that I want to knock the hotel. It was simply because France had been bled white; but the waiter on our floor was a middle-aged family man and probably read Lamartine and Pascal and Taine and all those appalling old bores when he wasn't doing shot drill with the caviare. But it isn't the slightest use my trying to conceal from you the fact that he always wore a slightly shocked expression, especially in the way he cut his beard. It was emphatically not the thing whenever he came into the suite.

I am a bit of a psychologist myself, and I know perfectly well that that man wouldn't have got us cocaine, not if we'd offered him a Bureau de Tabac for doing it.

Now, of course, I'm not going to ask you to believe that Gretel Webster knew anything about that waiter—beastly old prig! All she had done was to exhibit wise forethought and intelligent friendship. She had experience, no doubt, bushels of it, barrels of it, hogsheads of it, all those measures that I couldn't learn at school.

She had said to herself, in perfectly general terms, without necessarily contemplating any particular train of events as follows:—

"From one cause or another, those nice kids may find themselves shy on snow at a critical moment in their careers, so it's up to me to see that they get it."

While these thoughts were passing through my mind, I had got the manicure scissors, and Lou was snipping the threads of her kimono lining round those places where those fiercely fascinating fingers of hers had felt what we used to call in the hospital a foreign body.

Yes, there was no mistake. Gretel had got our psychology, we had got her psychology, everything was going as well as green peas go with a duck.

Don't imagine we had to spoil the kimono. It was just a tuck in the quilting. Out comes a dear little white silk bag ; and we open that, and there's a heap of snow that I'd much rather see than Mont Blanc.

Well, you know, when you see it, you've got to sniff it. What's it for? Nobody can answer that. Don't tell me about "use in operations on the throat." Lou didn't need anything done to her throat. She sang like Melba, and she looked like a peach; and she was a Pêche-Melba, just like two and two makes four.

You bet we sniffed! And then we danced all round the suite for several years—probably as much as eight or nine minutes by the clock—but what's the use of talking about clocks when Einstein has proved that time is only another dimension of space? What's the good of astronomers proving that the earth wiggles round 1000 miles an hour, and wiggles on 1000 miles a minute, if you can't keep going?

It would be absolutely silly to hang about and get left behind, and very likely find ourselves on the moon, and nobody to talk to but Jules Verne, H. G. Wells, and that crowd.

Now I don't want you to think that that white silk packet was very big.

Lou stooped over the table, her long thin tongue shot out of her mouth like an ant-eater in the Dictionary of National Biography or whatever it is, and twiddled it round in that snow till I nearly went out of my mind.

I laughed like a hyena, to think of what she'd said to me. "Your kiss is bitter with cocaine." That chap Swinburne was always talking about bitter kisses. What did he know, poor old boy?

Until you've got your mouth full of cocaine, you don't know what kissing is. One kiss goes on from phase to phase like one of those novels by Balzac and Zola and Romain Rolland and D. H. Lawrence and those chaps. And you never get tired! You're on fourth speed all the time, and the engine purrs like a kitten, a big white kitten with the stars in its whiskers. And it's always different and always the same, and it never stops, and you go insane, and you stay insane, and you probably don't know what I'm talking about, and I don't care a bit, and I'm awfully sorry for you, and you can find out any minute you like by the simple process of getting a girl like Lou and a lot of cocaine.

What did that fellow Lamus say?

> "Stab your demoniac smile to my brain,
> Soak me in cognac, kisses, cocaine."

Queer fish, that chap Lamus! But seems to me that's pretty good evidence he knew something about it. Why, of course he did. I saw him take cocaine myself. Deep chap! Bet you a shilling. Knows a lot. That's no reason for suspicion. Don't see why people run him down the way they do. Don't see why I got so leary myself. Probably a perfectly decent chap at bottom. He's got his funny little ways—man's no worse for that.

Gad, if one started to get worried about funny little ways, what price Lou! Queerest card in the pack, and I love her.

"Give me another sniff off your hand."

Lou laughed like a chime of bells in Moscow on Easter morning. Remember, the Russian Easter is not the same time as our Easter. They slipped up a fortnight one way or the other—I never can remember which—as long as you know what I mean.

She threw the empty silk bag in the air, and caught it in her teeth with a passionate snap, which sent me nearly out of my mind again. I would have loved to be a bird, and have my head snapped off by those white, small, sharp incisors.

Practical girl, my Lady Pendragon! Instead of going off the deep end, she was cutting out another packet, and when it was opened, instead of the birds beginning to sing, she said in shrill excitement, "Look here, Cockie, this isn't snow."

I ought to explain that she calls me Cockie in allusion to the fact that my name is Peter.

I came out of my trance. I looked at the stuff with what I imagine to have been a dull, glazed eye. Then my old training came to my rescue.

It was a white powder with a tendency to form little lumps rather like chalk. I rubbed it between my finger and thumb. I smelt it. That told me nothing. I tasted it. That told me nothing, either, because the nerves of my tongue were entirely anæsthetised by the cocaine.

But the investigation was a mere formality. I know now why I made it. It was the mere gesture of the male. I wanted to show off to Lou. I wished to impress upon her my importance as a man of science; and all the time I knew, without being told, what it was.

So did she. The longer I have known Lou, the more impressed I am with the extent and variety of her knowledge.

"Oh, Gretel is too sweet," she chirped. "She guessed we might get tired of coco, 'grateful and comforting' as it is. So the dear old thing sent us some heroin. And there are still some people who tell us that life is not worth living!"

"Ever try it?" I asked, and delayed the answer with a kiss.

When the worst was over, she told me that she had only taken it once, and then, in a very minute dose, which had had no effect on her as far as she knew.

"That's all right," I said, from the height of my superior knowledge. "It's all a question of estimating the physiological dose. It's very fine indeed. The stimulation is very much better than that of morphine. One gets the same intense beatific calm, but without the languor. Why, Lou, darling, you've read De Quincey and all those people about opium, haven't you? Opium's a mixture, you know—something like twenty different alkaloids in it. Laudanum : Coleridge took it, and Clive—all sorts of important people. It's a solution of opium in alcohol. But morphia is the most active and important of the principles in opium. You could take it in all sorts of ways. Injection gives the best results; but it's rather a nuisance, and there's always danger of getting dirt in. You have to look out for blood-poisoning all the time. It stimulates the imagination marvellously. It kills all pain and worry like a charm. But at the very moment when you have the most gorgeous ideas, when you build golden palaces of what you are going to do, you have a feeling at the same time that nothing is really worth doing, and that itself gives you a feeling of terrific superiority to everything else in the world. And so, from the objective point of view, it comes to nothing. But heroin does all that morphia does. It's a derivative of morphia, you know— Diacetyl-Morphine is the technical name. Only instead of bathing you in philosophical inertia, you are as keen as mustard on carrying out your ideas. I've never taken any myself. I suppose we might as well start now."

I had a vision of myself as a peacock strutting and preening. Lou, her mouth half open, was gazing at me fascinated with enormous eyes; the pupils dilated by cocaine. It was just the male bird showing off to his mate. I wanted her to adore me for my little scraps of knowledge; the fragments I had picked up in my abandoned education.

Lou is always practical; and she puts something of the priestess into everything she does. There was a certain solemnity in the way in which she took up the heroin on the blade of a knife and put it on to the back of her hand.

"My Knight," she said, with flashing eyes, "your Lady arms you for the fight."

And she held out her fist to my nostrils. I snuffed up the heroin with a sort of ritualistic reverence. I can't imagine where the instinct came from. Is it the sparkle of cocaine that excites one to take it greedily, and the dullness of the heroin which makes it seem a much more serious business?

I felt as if I were going through some very important ceremony. When I had finished, Lou measured a dose for herself. She took it with a deep, grave interest.

I was reminded of the manner of my old professor at U.C.H. when he came to inspect a new case ; a case mysterious but evidently critical. The excitement of the cocaine had somehow solidified. Our minds had stopped still, and yet their arrest was as intense as their previous motion.

We found ourselves looking into each other's eyes with no less ardour than before; but somehow it was a different kind of ardour. It was as if we had been released from the necessity of existence in the ordinary sense of the word. We were both wondering who we were and what we were and what was going to happen; and, at the same time, we had a positive certainty that nothing could possibly happen.

It was a most extraordinary feeling. It was of a kind quite unimaginable by any ordinary mind. I will go a bit further than that. I don't believe the greatest artist in the world could invent what we felt, and if he could he couldn't describe it.

I'm trying to describe it myself, and I feel that I'm not making out very well. Come to think of it, the English language has its limitations. When mathematicians and men of science want to exchange thoughts, English isn't much good. They've had to invent new words, new symbols. Look at Einstein's equations.

I knew a man once that knew James Hinton, who invented the fourth dimension. Pretty bright chap, he was, but Hinton thought, on the most ordinary subjects, at least six times as fast as he did, and when it came to Hinton's explaining himself, he simply couldn't do it.

That's the great trouble when a new thinker comes along. They all moan that they can't understand him; the fact annoys them very much; and ten to one they persecute him and call him an Atheist or a Degenerate or a Pro-German or a Bolshevik, or whatever the favourite term of abuse happens to be at the time.

Wells told us a bit about this in that book of his about giants, and so does Bernard Shaw in his *Back to Methuselah*. It's nobody's fault in particular, but there it is, and you can't get over it.

And here was I, a perfectly ordinary man, with just about the average allowance of brains, suddenly finding myself cut off from the world, in a class by myself—I felt that I had something perfectly tremendous to tell, but I couldn't tell even myself what it was.

And there was Lou standing right opposite, and I recognised instinctively, by sympathy, that she was just in the same place.

We had no need of communicating with each other by means of articulate speech. We understood perfectly; we expressed the fact in every subtle harmony of glance and gesture.

The world had stopped suddenly still. We were alone in the night and the silence of things. We belonged to eternity in some indefinable way; and that infinite silence blossoms inscrutably into embrace.

The heroin had begun to take hold. We felt ourselves crowned with colossal calm. We were masters; we had budded from nothingness into existence! And now, existence slowly compelled us to action. There was a necessity in our own natures which demanded expression and after the first intense inter-penetration of our individualities, we had reached the resultant of all the forces that composed us.

In one sense, it was that our happiness was so huge that we could not bear it; and we slid imperceptibly into conceding that the ineffable mysteries must be expressed by means of sacramental action.

But all this took place at an immense distance from reality. A concealed chain of interpretation linked the truth with the obvious commonplace fact that this was a good time to go across to Montmartre and make a night of it.

We dressed to go out with, I imagine, the very sort of feeling as a newly made bishop would have the first time he puts on his vestments.

But none of this would have been intelligible to, or suspected by, anybody who had seen us. We laughed and sang and interchanged gay nothings while we dressed.

When we went downstairs, we felt like gods descending upon earth, immeasurably beyond mortality.

With the cocaine, we had noticed that people smiled rather strangely. Our enthusiasm was observed. We even felt a little touch of annoyance at everybody not going at the same pace; but this was perfectly different. The sense of our superiority to mankind was constantly present. We were dignified beyond all words to express. Our own voices sounded far, far off. We were perfectly convinced that the hotel porter realised that he was receiving the orders of Jupiter and Juno to get a taxi.

We never doubted that the chauffeur knew himself to be the charioteer of the sun.

"This is perfectly wonderful stuff," I said to Lou as we passed the Arc de Triomphe. "I don't know what you meant by saying the stuff didn't have any special effect upon you. Why, you're perfectly gorgeous!"

"You bet I am," laughed Lou. "The king's daughter is all-glorious within; her raiment is of wrought gold, and she thrusts her face out to be kissed, like a comet pushing its way to the sun. Didn't you know I was the king's daughter?" she smiled, with such seductive sublimity that something in me nearly fainted with delight.

"Hold up, Cockie," she chirped. "It's all right. You're it, and I'm it, and I'm your little wife."

I could have torn the upholstery out of the taxi. I felt myself a giant. Gargantua was a pigmy. I felt the need of smashing something into matchwood, and I was all messed up about it because it was Lou that I wanted to smash, and at the same time she was the most precious and del-

icate piece of porcelain that ever came out of the Ming dynasty or whatever the beastly period is.

The most fragile, exquisite beauty! To touch her was to profane her. I
had a sudden nauseating sense of the bestiality of marriage.

I had no idea at the time that this sudden revulsion of feeling was due
to a mysterious premonition of the physiological effects of heroin in
destroying love. Definitely stimulating things like alcohol, hashish and
cocaine give free range to Cupid. Their destructive effect on him is simply due to the reaction. One is in debt, so to speak, because one has out-
run the constable.

But what I may call the philosophical types of dope, of which morphine
and heroin are the principal examples, are directly inimical to active emotion and emotional action. The normal human feelings are transmuted
into what seem on the surface their spiritual equivalents. Ordinary good
feeling becomes universal benevolence; a philanthropy which is infinitely
tolerant because the moral code has become meaningless for it. A more
than Satanic pride swells in one's soul. As Baudelaire says: "Hast thou not
sovereign contempt, which makes the soul so kind?"

As we drove up the Butte Montmartre towards the Sacré Cœur, we
remained completely silent, lost in our calm beatitude. You must understand that we were already excited to the highest point. The effect of the
heroin had been to steady us in that state.

Instead of beating passionately up the sky with flaming wings, we were
poised aloft in the illimitable ether. We took fresh doses of the dull soft
powder now and again. We did so without greed, hurry or even desire.
The sensation was of infinite power which could afford infinite deliberation. Will itself seemed to have been abolished. We were going nowhere
in particular, simply because it was our nature so to do. Our beatitude
became more absolute every moment.

With cocaine, one is indeed master of everything; but everything matters intensely.

With heroin, the feeling of mastery increases to such a point that nothing matters at all. There is not even the disinclination to do what one
happens to be doing which keeps the opium smoker inactive. The body is
left to itself so perfectly that one is not worried by its natural activities.

Again, despite our consciousness of infinity, we maintained, concur-
rently, a perfect sense of proportion in respect of ordinary matters.

Coke Bugs

William Burroughs

THE SAILOR'S GREY felt hat and black overcoat hung twisted in atrophied yen-wait. Morning sun outlined The Sailor in the orange-yellow flame of junk. He had a paper napkin under his coffee cup—mark of those who do a lot of sitting over coffee in the plazas, restaurants, terminals and waiting rooms of the world. A junky, even at the Sailor's level, runs on junk Time and when he makes his importunate irruption into the Time of others, like all petitioners, he must wait. (How many coffees in an hour?)

A boy came in and sat at the counter in broken lines of long, sick junk-wait. The Sailor shivered. His face fuzzed out of focus in a shuddering brown mist. His hands moved on the table, reading the boy's Braille. His eyes traced little dips and circles, following whorls of brown hair on the boy's neck in a slow, searching movement.

The boy stirred and scratched the back of his neck: "Something bit me, Joe. What kinda creep joint you run here?"

"Coke bugs, kid," Joe said, holding eggs up to the light. "I was travelling with Irene Kelly and her was a sporting woman. In Butte, state of Montany, her got the coke horrors and run through the hotel screaming Chinese coppers chase her with meat cleavers. I knew this cop in Chi sniff coke used to come in form of crystals, blue crystals. So he go nuts and start screaming the Federals is after him and run down this alley and stick his head in the garbage can. And I said, 'What you think you are doing?' and her say, 'Get away or I shoot you! I got myself hid good!' When the roll is called up yonder we'll be there, right?"

Joe looked at the Sailor and spread his hands in the junky shrug. The Sailor spoke in his feeling voice that reassembles in your head, spelling out the words with cold fingers: "Your connection is broken, kid."

The boy shied. His street-boy face, torn with black scars of junk, retained a wild, broken innocence; shy animals peering out through grey arabesques of terror.

"I don't dig you, Jack."

The Sailor leapt into sharp, junky focus. He turned back his coat lapel, showing a brass hypo needle covered with mold and verdigris. "Retired for the good of the service. . . . Sit down and have a blueberry crumb pie on the expense account. Your monkey loves it. . . . Make his coat glossy."

The boy felt a touch on his arm across eight feet of morning lunch room. He was suddenly siphoned into the booth, landing with an inaudible shlup. He looked into the Sailor's eyes, a green universe stirred by cold black currents.

"You are agent, mister?"

"I prefer the word . . . vector." His sounding laughter vibrated through the boy's substance.

"You holding, man? I got the bread. . . ."

"I don't want your money, Honey: I want your Time."

"I don't dig."

"You want fix? You want straight? You wanta, nooood?"

The Sailor cradled something pink and vibrated out of focus.

"Yeah."

"We'll take the Independent. Got their own special heat, don't carry guns only saps. I recall, me and the Fag fell once in Queen's Plaza. Stay away from Queen's Plaza, son . . . evil spot . . . fuzz haunted. Too many levels. Heat flares out from the broom closet high on ammonia like burning lions . . . fall on poor old lush worker, scare her veins right down to the bone. Her skin pop a week or do that five-twenty-nine kick handed out free and gratis by NYC to jostling junkies. . . . So Fag, Beagle, Irish, Sailor beware, Look down, look down along that line before you travel there. . . ."

The subway sweeps by with a black blast of iron.

A Night with Captain Cocaine

Charles Nicholls

IT WAS A Saturday night. I had no particular company. The back room had been empty since Nancy left. There were few tourists in town. It was April, the hot, slack month before the brief rainy season. Soon after dark I left the Fruit Palace and made for the sea-front, thinking to get a beer or two at the Pan-American, where they usually had a band playing on Saturday nights. A fat orange moon, two days past the full, squatted over the low hills inland.

As I crossed the Parque Bolívar I could hear the music already, but by a habit swiftly acquired in this small, predatory town, I crossed over the main beach-drag and walked under the tall palms of the promenade. Thus separated from the sea-front cafés, one could observe who was drinking where and select one's watering-hole accordingly.

The Pan-American was Santa Marta's smartest café. It had white tables laid out under a blue awning, and the legend 'Aire condicionado' emblazoned in scrolly red neon. Featuring that night on the little stage in the corner was a Barranquilla trio, Bruno y su Jazz. Bruno was a squat, check-shirted costeño with an old Gibson electric guitar. He played fast, upper-register licks somewhat in the manner of Carlos Santana. His combo consisted of a ferrety bass-man in beret and sunglasses, and an energetic black drummer in a sleeveless blue singlet already soaked in sweat.

Slightly off to one side, self-invited, an old black in a hat was playing the wooden rhythm stick called a *guacharaca*. The waiters wanted to get rid of him, but he stood just inside the charmed circle of the music and they couldn't touch him.

Sitting alone at one of the tables was a gringo I didn't recognize—a 'pure' gringo from the United States, I guessed, as opposed to the hybrid European variety. He was smartly dressed in lightweight gear, mustachioed, bulky, balding, age indeterminate. He was sitting over a beer with his back to the music. He glanced fitfully over the magazine in front of him—doubtless *Time* or *Newsweek*—but it was obvious he was waiting for someone. I took a seat at the next table, and when the song finished we got talking. He was from New York City, I learned. No, he'd never been in Colombia before, in fact he'd never been further south than Phoenix, Arizona, before yesterday. Yes, he was just here on vacation. He wore beige slacks and canvas beach shoes. They looked bought the day before yesterday. He had spilt something on one of them, and now he was spilling a bit of beer as he drank, and wiping the drips off his walrus moustache. He had a high-pitched voice, aggressive in the New York way, and rather catarrhal. He seemed to want to talk, but was anxious to keep a lookout for whoever he was waiting for. Quite a crowd had gathered for the music, and he craned nervously for a view of the sidewalk.

'You're waiting for someone?' I asked.

'Goddamn right I am,' he replied, with another irritated check at his watch. 'And it looks like he ain't going to show. He said he'd be here at 6. Lahs says. That's 6 o'clock, right?'

I agreed that it was. His watch said nearly 8. 'At a guess,' I bantered, 'you're waiting for a Colombian. They're not the best time-keepers in the world.'

'*Mañana*, huh?'

He drummed his fingers on the table, drained his beer, said 'Aw, shit!' and dismissed with a wave the sidewalk and the person who wasn't hoving into view along it. I ordered two more beers. We formalized our meeting with a handshake. His palm was cold and damp. His name was Harvey. He had been in Santa Marta twenty-four hours, he said, and the whole goddamn place seemed crazy.

We drank and smoked, discussed Colombia, and eyed the *costeñas*, the stunning local girls, in their Saturday best. I was showing off rather, full of tips and lore and knowing the ropes. I would get my comeuppance soon enough. Harvey ordered more beers, in English. One of the things he didn't like about Colombia, he implied, was the Spanish language. Just a minor hassle, like the bad water, but someone back home should have warned him about it. He was getting a bit drunk now. He had been through three bottles of Aguila beer before I arrived. An unhealthy dew of sweat lay on his forehead. He looked pale and egg-headed among these laughing Samarios.

Bruno brought a long guitar solo to a climax of high, gull-like notes, then a dramatic pause before the final bar. This was spoilt somewhat by the old man with the *guacharaca*, who kept on hammering the stick on the neck of his rum bottle, dancing away with his eyes tight shut and a huge, oblivious grin on his face.

It was in the lull after this number that Harvey leaned conspiratorially across the table. He was glad he had met me, he said, because he had this problem.

This did not entirely surprise me. In Santa Marta two and two do not infallibly make four, but a nervous, catarrhal gringo fresh into town almost certainly spells 'cocaine'. Sure enough. 'I'm not really here on vacation,' he explained. 'I've come down for a bit of business. You know—' he touched the side of his nose with his finger—'Cousin Charlie.'

I nodded understandingly, but said nothing.

'Just a quick in and out job,' he added sharply. His look suggested that the way out was not at this moment quite clear.

'So there's a problem?' I said. He nodded, looked around, and leant still closer. In anticipation of a long and delicate story I said, 'Why don't we pay, and go for a walk along the beach?'

THE STORY HARVEY told me as we walked along the beach was simple enough. For a couple of years now, since arriving in New York from some backwood in Wisconsin, he had been doing a bit of small-time cocaine dealing. He loved the stuff dearly, and the dealing was mainly to keep himself in 'candy' and make back the money his habit was costing him. He was living up in Queens, which has a large population of Colombian immigrants. Connections were easy. He would buy an ounce at a time, step on it a little with mannite, and knock it out in grams among his friends. He was vaguely connected with the music business, so selling it was no problem.

'For a time it was great,' he said wistfully. 'Plenty of candy, plenty of bread. Then you start getting greedy. You're doing two, three grams a night, seven nights a week. When you start getting greedy, it's trouble time. You can't walk away from it any more. That's when you're going to take a fall.'

Harvey indeed took a fall. He started selling larger quantities, and one day a Lexington Avenue street dealer 'pulled out a piece and spat in my eye'—robbed him, in other words, at gunpoint. Net result: half a kilo of cocaine, as yet unpaid for, 'down the john'. Fortunately for Harvey, the owner of the cocaine did not exact any violent retribution—'like they drop you in the river twice and pull you out once'. Instead he offered Harvey an arrangement. He needed someone to take care of a shipment from the Colombian end. If Harvey would look after it for him, he would forget about this unpleasant business of the missing half-kilo.

'I was fifteen adrift, man,' Harvey whined. Fifteen thousand dollars was what a half-kilo was worth in New York in the early seventies. 'I had no way of paying up. The man could cut me up into any shape he liked. He offers me a deal. No way I could refuse.

'It all seemed pretty tight. He gives me Air Florida tickets, New York—Miami—Barranquilla—Santa Marta. He tells me where to go and who to deal with. He gives me a false-bottom valise with a stack of hundreds in it, plenty of spending money, and an ounce of free candy over the top when I get home. All I got to do is deliver the money, check the gear for quantity and quality, and see it on to the boat. Then I fly home, clean as a bone.'

We reached one end of the town beach. In the sand near the water's edge were black drifts of mica. Specks of pyrites, fool's gold, glinted in the diffuse, mauvish light of the town. A station-wagon lurched noisily off the beach-drag into 22nd Street. It stopped outside a lit doorway where a knot of people were lounging. Two men got out and lifted a third, wrapped in a blanket, out of the back of the car. Another patient was being admitted to the emergency ward of the town's hospital.

Harvey asked what was going on. When I told him he said, 'Christ Jesus!' softly, and rubbed his hands up and down his white arms as if he were cold. We set off back up the beach.

Everything had gone fine, he said, till he got to 'this shit-yard Santa Marta' yesterday afternoon. He was supposed to meet his contact in the bar of his hotel in Rodadero—Santa Marta's tourist complex, a couple of miles out of town—at 6 o'clock. The contact, he had been assured, would have everything arranged, and he spoke perfect English. Harvey waited, but no one came. Then the barman brought him the phone—'a call for you, *señor*'—and someone was jabbering at him in Spanish. The caller eventually got the gist of the message across. Harvey's contact was no longer in on the deal; Harvey was to take a taxi into town the next morning; he was to go to the Hotel Venezuela and ask for someone called Manolo.

The following morning, the morning of this Saturday, Harvey did as he had been instructed. He met Manolo, 'a little jerk in shades', at the Venezuela. (I later looked over this establishment from the outside: a poky little clip-joint with barred windows up near the *mercado popular*.) Manolo told him the coke would be ready that night, and wanted to see the money. Harvey said the money was back at his hotel in Rodadero. Manolo said to bring all his stuff over from Rodadero, there was a room for him here at the Venezuela, the *portero* would look after him, and so on. Harvey did not like this arrangement, 'a back-to-the-wall set-up'. Manolo, on the other hand, refused to bring the *coco* over to Rodadero. Communication was difficult. They made a truce arrangement, to meet at the Pan-American at six. Already fearing a rip-off, Harvey sped back to Rodadero. His money-bag was still there. He sat guard over it all day, smoking cigarettes and listening to the clatter of the air-conditioner.

Harvey's second 6 o'clock in Colombia came and went like the first, waiting for a 'friend' who did not come, and so it was that a couple of hours later I had seen this balding gringo, casting a worried eye up and down the sidewalk outside the Pan-American.

This, broadly, was Harvey's account of the business so far. From what I knew about the cocaine racket, it sounded like the usual cloak-and-dagger stuff. So why was he telling me? And what exactly was the 'problem' he had mentioned, the problem that I—I suspected—was in some way supposed to solve? I asked him.

'The problem?' he snapped. 'The goddamn problem is that I got to *do* it!'

'I'm sorry, I don't understand.'

'Look, Charlie. Everything about this score smells wrong. First my connection vanishes and I'm dealing with this little hood Manolo instead. Now *he* doesn't show. I've been sitting here scratching since yesterday afternoon and I haven't even had a taste yet. It all smells wrong. OK, ninety-nine times out of a hundred you walk away. No score, no nothing. Don't need a weatherman to know which way the wind blows, right? But this one's different. Number one hundred. I owe it to the man. I'm plumbed right into it.'

I murmured sympathy. We were sitting with our backs to a beach hut. The lighthouse on Morro Island was lit: they must have mended it, I thought. Harvey was looking at me thoughtfully. 'So what's your next move?' I asked.

'It's all a question of how we handle Manolo . . . '

'Just a minute, Harvey, *we* aren't . . . '

'I can read that guy like a clock, man! He's just aching to finger the money. What I got to do is make sure I get the candy in return. If he can't take the money and run, he'll come up with the gear. I'm sure of it. What I need is muscle.'

'Well, don't look at me, chum,' I said firmly. I am not what you would call 'muscle'. Surely Harvey could see that.

'I don't mean strong-arm stuff, man. I mean negotiating muscle.' He gripped my arm. The cards, at last, were landing on the table. 'I need two things, Charlie, and you can supply them both. First thing, I need space. I'm not doing any deal at the Venezuela. That's Manolo's patch. This place of yours, this Fruit Castle, sounds just about right. There'll be you, me and that guy of yours, Julio, all nice and cosy, and little Manolo with *his* back to the wall. We'll put the flake on the table, the money on the table, five-o five-o and no monkey business.

'The second thing I need is someone who can speak the lingo. Shit, man. Manolo and me were just talking like babies at each other back there. You can't do this sort of business when you're talking like babies. I need an interpreter, Charlie, someone to whisper sweet nothings in that little cock-sucker's ear. What you say, man?'

Harvey was glinting and glistening at me. Whether or not he had convinced me, he had certainly convinced himself. He was riding high on his own hip talk. He was Harvey the street-wise superfly, the veteran of a hundred daring deals. I could see the fantasy gleam in his bulbous eye. All right, I thought: he wants to play Captain Cocaine, but do I want to play his bloody batman? Sitting here years later, with the benefit of hindsight, it is easy to say I should have told Harvey politely but firmly to go and find someone else to talk him through his cocaine deal. But the night was hot, and these things have a logic of their own. There were risks, of course, but there were undeniable attractions. First, the carrot: $250 on the nail for me, the same for Julio. Second, the story: I was supposed to be some kind of journalist, wasn't I? Third, the general scenario: suitcases stuffed with bank-notes, lashings of someone else's cocaine. In short, greed battled with fear, and greed won. 'Why not?' I said, and thus with a handshake I became the smallest of small-time accomplices in the cocaine trade.

From that point on everything clicked ominously into place. We headed back for the Pan-American. I skulked on the beach while Harvey scanned the tables from the promenade. He loped back clumsily through the sand. 'He's there, man!' he hissed, 'we're in business.' The next step was for me to consult with Julio. Harvey would meanwhile 'keep the little creep happy' at the Pan-American. Back at the Fruit Palace Julio listened patiently. He then said he didn't like *coco*, he didn't like Manolo, he didn't want trouble with the Mafia or the F-2, and consequently he couldn't let his place be used for a trifling 250. He wanted 500.

Back I toiled to the Pan-American. Manolo rose suavely to shake hands, a little man with a thin smile and gold in his teeth. His slicked-back hair shone like wet coal. I was relieved to see he was unaccompanied and, judging from the trim fit of his clothes, unarmed. I told Harvey of Julio's price. He grumbled but, as Julio had doubtless divined, he was in no position to refuse.

'OK, OK,' he said. 'Now, Charlie. I want you to explain it all to our friend here, nice and gentle. You tell him he does the deal our way or not at all. We meet at the Fruit Palace at'—he checked his watch—'at midnight. He comes alone, with the gear. Five kilos, as arranged. Any monkey business and the deal's off. OK?'

Manolo listened blandly to my polite schoolboy Spanish. It's all right, I thought. He'll simply say 'No' and the whole business will be over. But it was a night for wrong decisions, and what he finally said, with a last lingering look at both of us and a light shrug, was: 'OK, I'll be there.'

The arrangements confirmed, Manolo slipped away through the crowd like a lizard. Harvey let out a long sigh of relief and ran his hand up through his hair. Bruno launched into an up-tempo samba shuffle, and my heart raced along in time to it.

MIDNIGHT FOUND THE four of us—Julio, Harvey, Manolo and myself—sitting round the 'private table' at the Fruit Palace. The air was hot and sweet. A single light shone down on the table: coffee cups, ashtrays, a half-empty bottle of Medellín rum. The street door was shut and bolted. A passer-by might have seen the light under the door, but he would have kept on walking, because at midnight on 10th Street the rule was always to keep on walking.

Harvey had arrived by taxi an hour before, stumbling in with two suitcases, one of them containing $50,000. While we waited Julio tried to sell him some emeralds, but Harvey's mind was elsewhere and his palms were sweating, and he kept on dropping the stones. Now Manolo had just turned up—without the 5 kilos, but with a small *muestra*, a sample, instead.

Harvey did not like this. 'Where's the deal, man?' he whinged. 'I want to see the deal.'

I translated, nervously formal. '*Harvey quiere ver toda la mercancia.*'

'I can get it. No problem. Half an hour.' Manolo spoke smoothly, with flashes of gold from his teeth. 'Doesn't Señor Harvey trust me?'

Harvey said, 'Shit, man. I can't afford to trust anyone. He knows that. I don't even trust myself.'

'Harvey is a little nervous,' I relayed reassuringly.

'Why doesn't he try the *muestra*? It's real good stuff. Ninety-eight per cent pure.'

Harvey caught the last phrase, '*pureza de noventa y ocho por ciento*', and snorted tetchily. 'I've heard *that* up in Spanish Harlem. I didn't believe it then and I don't believe it now.'

I told him to cool down and try the sample. Manolo pushed the small, rectangular fold of paper over to him. It was cheap lined paper from a letter pad. Harvey took it. Grumpily, but with gentle care, he opened it up and inspected the small, flattened heap of cream-coloured cocaine inside. He nodded abstractedly. It seemed to please him. He dabbed a bit on to the end of his forefinger and tasted it. Again he nodded. Now he wet his finger and took another dab, and watched while the powder dissolved.

He held the finger out to me. There was a trace of grey, fluffy dust on it. 'The cut,' he murmured. This is a fallible test, I'm told—many 'cuts', or adulterants, are quite as soluble as the coke itself—but right then it seemed impressive enough. Harvey looked every inch the professional. He was on home ground at last.

Julio, slightly out of the arc of light, rocked back on the thin-legged café chair. He looked poised and philosophical, as always, but his brown eyes didn't miss a trick. Hardly moving a muscle, he called out for coffee. '*Hay tinto, Miriam?*' A sulky, droned '*Sí*' came out of the bedroom, and Miriam plodded kitchenwards, scraping her flip-flop sandals on the floor. She did not look at us as she passed. She did not approve of *narcotráfico*.

'Looks OK to me,' said Harvey. He took out a small Stanley knife with a retractable blade, and began to dice up some of the cocaine on the table. He cursed when grains of crystal jumped away from the blade. I saw that his hands were trembling. He fashioned a small pile of coke into thin lines. Manolo unhooked a coke-spoon from a silver neck-chain under his shirt, but Harvey shook his head—'Uh-uh'—and took out a crisp $100 bill. He rolled it neatly into a thin pipe. 'I take it Wonder Warthog style,' he chuckled. The imminent pleasure of the cocaine-hit was sweeping aside all his grumbles and paranoias, clearing his mind like a runway for take-off. He hunched over the table and hoovered up a line through the bill with a single deep snort. He winced a little and jerked his head back. His nose stuck up like a shark's fin. He emitted a long, slow hiss of pleasure, as if the cocaine had gone in like a spike and let out all the stale air in him. He opened his eyes but kept staring up at the ceiling. 'Nice,' he sighed, 'nice,' then 'Hmmmm,' and an odd, girlish giggle. He bent back down to repeat the procedure via the other nostril, then pressed some leftover dust off the melamine table-top, and massaged it into his gums.

He handed me the little pipe. I took a hit, rather smaller than Harvey's. I felt my nostril scorch, my mouth freeze, my veins hum all the way down to my feet. I had tasted coke before, but this felt lethal. Simple case of motor stimulation, I reminded myself. Heart racing, adrenal secretions, everything hastening to some unknown crescendo. Purely pharmaceutical, of course. Not *really* on a big dipper at all. Not falling, not flying, not swooping through the room like a white owl over a dark field.

My hand was waving the rolled-up bill at Julio. He shook his head. 'I'm thinking of getting some sleep tonight.' Manolo also declined it. Instead he stuck his coke-spoon straight into the *muestra*, and sniffed up two level spoonfuls with a practised, haughty movement, like a coffee-house fop taking snuff. Harvey lit a cigarette with trembling hands. The smoke eddied under the light. His face had a sheen, a chilly polish. He looked like he had a gum-shield in his mouth.

'Pheeee-ew!' he went. 'White line fever!' I felt the first bitter tang of mucus coming down the back of my throat, and Miriam came in with a trayful of *tintos*.

IT MUST HAVE been about three in the morning when Manolo at last came back with 'the deal'. It was in a big cardboard box tied up with packing-string. Harvey's eyes were out on stalks by now. He was chain-smoking and jiggling his knees up and down under the table. He had seen off the rest of the *muestra* more or less single-handed, with rum and coffee on the side. He had talked till he was hoarse and now he was apparently trying to grind all the enamel off his teeth. I had urged caution, but Manolo's *coco* was the first nice thing that had happened to him in Colombia and, deal or no deal, he was going to savour it.

The box was on the table, Manolo's jewelled fingers resting on it. 'So this is it, huh?' said Harvey, with a pitiful, lockjawed attempt at a smile. 'Let's take a look.' He moved to take the box, but Manolo's pressure on it hardened.

'*La plata?*' he said politely.

Harvey sat back. 'The silver?' he said, with a baffled, half-focused stare at Manolo. He knew the word because he had bought a silver ring from a hawker at the Pan-American.

'He means the money, Harvey,' I hissed. 'He wants to see the colour of your money.'

The money—a good touch—was in the smaller, flimsier suitcase, the tartan zip-up rather than the stouter Revelation piece. Harvey fumbled up the top section—shirts, socks, sponge-bag—and there they were. Ten neat wads, so fresh you could almost smell the ink, each one containing fifty $100 bills.

'There she blows, man! Fifty grand. Five kilos at nine apiece makes forty-five, and five over for the boat.'

I stored these figures away and later worked on them. Harvey's man would sell on his merchandise pretty quickly, but he would almost certainly 'step on' it a little before he did so. Even if he only put a light hit on it—turned 5 kilos of pure into 7 or 8 of adulterated—he still stood to clear, I reckoned, something approaching $200,000. Not a bad margin from one fairly modest run, with someone else doing all the sweating.

The stakes are high, but it is all or nothing, and right now his investment was on a fulcrum between the two. Harvey held open the tartan money-bag, Manolo nursed the box of cocaine. Like swapping captured agents on a frontier, neither party wanted to be the first to surrender its bargaining piece.

The money had straightened Harvey up. 'I want to check the stuff he's brought,' he said.

'*Quiere verlo.*'

Manolo shrugged and smiled. He took a thin, black-handled switchblade from his back pocket, held it thoughtfully in his delicate fingers. The blade sprang out like a snake's tongue. He cut the string around the carton and sliced down the adhesive tape along the top flaps. Inside were folds of sacking, and under them the kilo bags, polythene, each about the size of a small pillow. 'Which one?' he asked. Harvey shrugged. Manolo tossed one of the bags on to the table and nicked a slit in it to expose the cocaine inside. Harvey took some on to his knife and, as before, he poked and sifted, tasted and tested, and finally snorted some of the specimen, frowning all the while with concentration. He said nothing.

We waited in the silence, the smoke, the hot, stale air of the small hours cloying with the rank smell of fruit. Manolo inspected his fingernails, wrinkled his brow, a study in quiet confidence. I wished fervently I was somewhere else, not in this stuffy little room with two knives sitting on the table.

Harvey had digested his hit. He said softly, 'You goddam little creep!' Manolo, still attending to his manicure, raised an inquiring eyebrow at me. I felt Julio stiffen beside me.

Harvey's voice was low and fierce. 'Tell him, Charlie. Tell him this shit's been stepped on so hard it's flat as a fucking frisbee.'

'God, Harvey, are you sure?'

'Sure I'm sure. Looks different, tastes different. It's the oldest trick in the book, the beginner's rip-off. They hit you with a sample of heavy and sell you a crock of shit while you're flying. You tell him, man.'

I told Manolo, as if he didn't know, that Harvey did not like the *coco*. He stiffened into an exaggerated air of surprise and regret, shoulders up in a shrug, eyebrows up towards the brilliantined hair-line, can this be true *señor*? He actually said nothing.

'Tell him it's crap, Charlie.'

'No, no,' said Manolo. 'It's real good *perica*, very pure.'

'Ask him if it's the same stuff as before.'

Manolo chose his words with care. 'No. It is not the same. It is better!' I groaned inwardly. He can go on lying all night, I thought. I hardly had the heart to tell Harvey of this latest pitch. 'The very best,' Manolo urged. 'Fresh in from Bucaramanga tonight.'

Harvey was looking very bad now. His face was white as paper and wet with sweat. His cigarette, one of Julio's untipped Pielrojas, was falling apart as he smoked it. He began to rock up and down, spitting flakes of tobacco off his lips and saying, 'Oh no! Oh no!' He turned straight to Manolo and said two of his few words of Spanish: *'No quiero.'* I do not want it.

'Si,' said Manolo steelily. 'It is all agreed.' They glared at one another across the table.

It was at this moment of impasse that things began to get seriously out of control. Out of the silence, with just a faint rustle of warning, came a sudden loud knock at the street door. Harvey leapt up, a gargle of fear in his throat. 'It's the cops!' he shouted. 'It's a fucking burn!' Julio and Manolo were both up too. Julio shot a questioning look at Manolo, Manolo shook his head. Briskly they began clearing away the cocaine. There was more knocking and a muffled shout. 'No way, man!' cried Harvey. He grabbed the tartan case and, holding it under his arm, blundered past me into, the back-yard. I called after him, but he raced down to the end, pushing aside my hammock, looking for a way out. Seeing none, he made a flying leap on to the hen-house and began to scale the end wall. The hen-house promptly collapsed, with much indignant squawking from within. 'Oh Jesus, God, please,' Harvey wailed. He now started scrambling up the side wall by the kitchen door, but the guard dog on the neighbour's roof came snarling and snapping at him from the other side of the parapet. I had heard it many times but never seen it before — it was a sleek black alsatian, and this was the first piece of action it had seen in months. Harvey let go with a yelp and crashed back down, splintering wood and scattering feathers. He lurched across to the other wall. He jumped to grab the top of it and screamed in pain as his hands closed over a serried line of broken glass, put there for some such occasion as this. He crumpled back into the hen-house and lay still, whimpering faintly, clutching his money-bag to him like a teddy bear.

'Tell him to shut up,' said Julio. They had stowed the drugs in Julio's bedroom. The Fruit Palace was just a room full of smoke and rum glasses: a quiet evening among friends. He went to the door and called, 'Who is it?' A voice answered from the other side. Julio swore softly, and called back to us to relax. He unbolted the door and a very drunken negro swayed in. It was the old *guacharacero* who had been playing down at the Pan-American.

'What the hell do you want, Jo-jo?'

'Breakfast,' said the old-timer, and tacked across to a table.

SOON THERE CAME a sudden dawn, and then it was Sunday morning in Santa Marta, another hot day on the way. Julio told Manolo to push off, and in accordance with some imperceptible Samario pecking-order, Manolo meekly left with his carton of low-grade *coco*. Miriam washed the chicken shit off Harvey's face and shirt, cleaned up his bleeding hands and bandaged them with strips of cloth. Jo-jo fell asleep at a table, his head on his forearms, his hat still on. There were two *papagallo* feathers in his hat-band, one blue, one orange.

Julio mixed us a morning-after *jugo*—papaya, lemon-water and crushed ice. It was always a pleasure to watch him at work. Even after this night of fiasco he attended to it with the same casual, tender care, choosing just the right fruit from the glass-fronted case, chopping and shredding, assiduously observing as he blended it up in the antique Kenwood with Art Deco fluting round the base. In a trance-like calm Harvey paid us our fees. Struck with pity and remorse I made to refuse, but Julio swiftly reminded me of monies owed for food and board.

The last I saw of Harvey was when I put him in a taxi on the beach-drag. He was going to the airport, going home. His immediate task, unenviable and unprofitable, was carrying $50,000 *back* into the United States—not actually illegal, but prone to awkward questions. Then there was the music to face in New York. But as he sank back into the taxi, I could see that just being in a car, even in a jalopy like this, was making him feel better already. Whatever the music back in New York, it would be better than Colombia's crazy syncopations. We made to shake hands, but he winced and drew back his bandaged hand.

'Sorry it didn't work out, Harvey.'

'That's showbiz,' said Captain Cocaine. The taxi moved off, and I walked on down to the French Corner for some breakfast.

from

Snowblind

Robert Sabbag

ZACHARY SWAN IS not a superstitious man, but he is a very careful one. Like any professional gambler, he has survived by taking only calculated risks. So, in October of 1972, when he decided to throw a party to celebrate his most recent return to New York, he decided to throw a small one, and his caution was inspired less by the fact that it was Friday the thirteenth than by the compelling reality that on the mantelpiece above his suitcase there were three and a half kilograms of 89-percent-pure cocaine.

The cocaine had entered the United States that morning in the hollows of three Colombian souvenirs fashioned out of Madeira wood. They included a long, colorfully painted rolling pin, the symbol of marital bliss in Colombia; one rough-hewn statue, twenty inches high, of the Blessed Virgin; and a hand-wrought effigy of an obscure tribal head, about the size of a coconut. The fill had been made a week earlier in Bogotá. The load had passed U.S. Customs at Kennedy Airport, New York. It was carried through and declared: 'Souvenirs.'

The arrival of these artifacts at Zachary Swan's beach house in East Hampton, Long Island, launched a celebration which would not end until the following morning. It began at eight p.m. when the Madeira head was cleaved top-dead-center across the parietal lobe with the cold end of a chisel. Within minutes of this exotic lobotomy—a procedure reminiscent in equal measure of desperation combat surgery and a second-rate burglary attempt—the skull yielded up 500 grams of high-grade uncut cocaine, double-wrapped in clear plastic.

By the time the skull, which looked like that of a shrapnel victim, was reduced to ashes around the andirons of the fireplace, the celebration had assumed ceremony and the coke was performing fabulous and outlawed miracles in the heads for which it had been ultimately intended. They belonged to Swan himself; his girlfriend Alice Haskell, twenty-four, a children's fashion designer; Charles Kendricks, thirty, an Australian national and sometime employee of Swan; and Kendricks's girlfriend Lillian Giles, twenty-three, also an Australian. The Bolivian brain food they had ingested was only one course in a sublime international feast which featured French wine, English gin, Lebanese hashish, Colombian cannabis, and a popular American synthetic known pharmacologically as methaqualone.

It is difficult to verify at exactly what point in the proceedings (possibly over dessert) Swan's originally calculated risk became a long shot. The party went out of control somewhere in the early hours before dawn, and the steps he had taken in the beginning to minimize his losses were eventually undermined by the immutable laws of chemistry—his mind, simply, had turned to soup. He was up against the law of averages with a head full of coke. The smart money pulled out, and the odds mounted steadily. By sunrise, Swan was beaten by the spread.

AMAGANSETT, NEW YORK, is situated 120 miles due east of Manhattan on the coastal underbelly of Long Island. One of several ocean-front resorts on the fringes of Long Island's potato belt, it owes its maritime climate to the temperate waters in the leeward drift of the Gulf Stream. The region was abandoned by Algonquins in the wake of colonial sprawl, a mounting overture to Manifest Destiny which brought New England to the outer reaches of the Empire State, and Amagansett, a tribute to the Indians in name only, is the custodian of a Puritan heritage. The whales are gone but the weathervanes remain. An occasional widow's walk acknowledges the debt to the sea. Anchors and eagles abound. George Washington would have been proud to sleep here.

In the off-season, order prevails. Time struggles to stand still. But when the weather breaks and the trade winds come in, the elders of Amagansett, like their colonial predecessors and the Algonquins before them, find themselves volunteers in a counterassault on cultural blight—minutemen knee-deep in the onslaught of souvenirs, fast-food and ersatz antiques. A kind of thug capitalism asserts itself. The tourists who come screeching down upon the town and the local retail sharks who surface to feed on them provoke an embarrassing display of provincial paranoia; and every summer, the town fathers, helpless, unhinged, watch their community move one irreversible step closer to the dark maw of the twentieth century, visibly shaken by what they consider to be a pronounced threat to Amagansett's Puritan soul.

Their dread has taken an inevitable turn. Amagansett has become a working model for an aggression/response approach to municipal government. Symptomatic of such an approach is a curious brand of frontier law enforcement, characterized by an allegiance to the principle that ' . . . we got a nice quiet community here, son . . . ,' dialogue resonant of hanging judges, pistol whippings, and the application of rifle butts to the dental work. You've got until sundown, as it were. In Amagansett the Wyatt Earp spirit runs especially high between the months of May and September, but a residual strain lingers through late autumn, tapering off appropriately around Thanksgiving, after which only the locals have an opportunity to break the law.

This is what Zachary Swan, forty-six, a pioneer whose embrace of the Puritan ethic had never been an all-encompassing one, would come up against on the morning of October 14. He and his friends would be arrested on the beach at sunrise and charged with public intoxication. And out of this circumstantial confrontation between the energetic bounty hunters of Amagansett, still juiced on adrenalin generated in the summer tourist-haunts, and a man who in six months had spent more money on cocaine alone than he had paid in state and local income taxes in twenty years—out of this head-on collision would grow a Federal investigation spanning at least two continents, twice as many international boundaries, and criminal jurisdictions as diverse as those covered by the United States Department of the Treasury and the traffic division of the East Hampton, Long Island, Police Department.

✳   ✳   ✳

AT FIVE A.M. Zachary Swan, surrounded by $100,000 worth of cocaine, was smiling. He was smiling at the Madonna over his fireplace and dreaming of an island off the coast of Ceylon. Sprawled on the floor athwart three sleeping dogs, struggling to stay conscious, he looked like a besotted country squire out of the pages of an eighteenth-century novel.

Dawn was approaching. The room was quiet. The party had downshifted dramatically. All motor activity not essential to life had been suspended in the interest of the cardiac muscles. The body, in the grip of the downs, was making sacrifices.

Somebody had an idea (remarkable under the circumstances).

'Let's go to the beach and watch the sunrise.'

A response, identifiable only in the deepest methaqualone funk, struggled to solitary life somewhere across the room. It contained many vowels. It was affirmative. Call it a sentence. A phrase. Someone had answered.

(We are on the threshold of human interchange here, speech, verbal commerce along the barren avenues of Quaalude City. Communication at this level, although sophisticated in its own way, can best be described as haphazard. It is a kind of space-age remodeling of traditional counterintelligence techniques—scrambled messages, predistorted transmissions, sympathetically programmed transceivers—a kind of mojo cryptography which contains no universal cipher and is efficient only when two people are doing the same kind of dope.)

Out of the chance marriage between this one remarkably conceived idea and the crypto-response which followed, there blossomed, like a flower in time-lapse motion, what was soon to be a legitimate conversation. It was force-bloomed according to the principle governing the first law of psychogravitational dynamics: *The quickest way to come off downs is to do some* ups. Follow the Quaalude with two or three lines of coke and you can throw even the most desultory dialogue into high gear. There is order in the Universe.

Monosyllables became murmurs:

'The . . . sun.'

An odds-on favorite to rise.

Murmurs became phrases:

'See . . . the . . . sun.'

But nothing was taken for granted.

That the sun would not rise was a remote possibility, but one which nevertheless marshalled a certain amount of attention. Unnecessary risks, such as standing up, were postponed while an analysis of the odds for and against the sun's coming up at all was made. This delay was characteristic of severe psychochemical shock, but surprisingly it provided the first hard evidence of progress. (It marked the appearance of key polysyllabic words—participles, certain adjectives, an occasional predicate nominative—and diphthongs. A subordinate clause was pending.) The Quaaludes were still throwing their weight around, but it was a futile display of power; their defeat was imminent, and signaled moments later:

'We haven't got much time,' someone said.

A clear, audible statement. The cocaine was closing in. A decision, the final factor in the psychogravitational equation, was inevitable now. It would lead to activity and thus certify the successful application of Newton's first law to the infinite possibilities of drug abuse. In fact the decision came almost immediately, a tribute to the quality of this particular blow of coke:

'Let's go,' someone decided.

And so, at the zenith of the cocaine ecliptic, activity was resumed. Status quo. What goes up must come down; what goes down must come up. Q.E.D. Physics, man. But now, with four people behind some heavy coke (one of them a certified Frank Sinatra fan), anything was possible.

Phase II . . . Overdrive. Out-and-out mobilization. Tide tables were checked. Weather information from around the world gathered. Analyzed. Data was collated and patterns were charted. An expeditionary force was provisioned.

'We'll need plenty of drugs.'

Yes. Of course. Consider the possibilities. Imagine the appropriateness of it. Standing in the Atlantic tide, welcoming the sun back to the United States of America. We, the people, bent, holding enough dope to fix three Kentucky Derbies. Enough to capture the imagination of . . . yes . . . even the Miami Dolphins. How fitting. How just. (How dangerous.)

THEY CHOSE THE Volkswagen because it was aimed at the beach, not unanimously unaware, certainly, that they were also choosing the only car in the driveway that could float. With their ranks bolstered, and their oxygen supply severely depleted, by the added company of three hyper-

ventilating Labrador retrievers, a total, then, of twenty legs, each jockey-
ing for position, any two feet at the ends of which might have been operating the accelerator and the clutch (the brake, reportedly, was used
rarely, if at all), Swan and his friends reached the ocean through the com-
bined application of dead reckoning and the gratuitous hand of God. (It
is whispered in the cloakrooms of America's drug underground that *He*
looks out for the heavy user.)

A joint, eighty-dollar Colombian, passing clockwise around the cock-
pit, outlined their efforts in a surreal, purple haze, and acting as a sort of
gyroscope it provided slight, but presumably adequate, stabilization. It
also pushed everyone's carboxy-hemoglobin level to the red line, bringing on that shameful and subversive Reefer Madness (manifest only in
the Labradors, however) hinted at in arcane government manuscripts. It
was quality dope, and its sharers were suffused with the magnificence and
intergalactic splendor of star travelers. But at their energy/output ratio,
given the specific gravity of their load and the negligible horsepower of
the Volkswagen, they looked more like the Joads leaving Oklahoma.

> Hark, hark,
> The dogs do bark,
> The beggars are coming to town;
> Some in rags,
> And some in jags,
> And one in a velvet gown.
>
> 'Hark, Hark,'
> from *Mother Goose*

They erupted like circus clowns out of the overstuffed automobile and
onto the beach, a tumbling agglomeration of weird, multicolored raga-
muffins. For a moment it was hard to tell the humans from the
quadrupeds. And then the dogs hit the water. It was not long before the
idea caught on, and within minutes they were all stripped down, ready to
celebrate the Rites of Spring—late.

THE SUN WAS on the horizon and all seven were bobbing in the surf
when in the distance an intruder appeared. A jogger. He approached,

moving at an even pace along the waterline, his face flushed, his breathing steady, his body drenched with sweat and glory, radiating that all-American, infinite faith in the cardiovascular benefits of discomfort. He was about fifty-five and well-fed. Swan recognized him as the owner of a local nursery. It looked as if he were going to pass by, until he saw the strange variety of clothing, like a forbidden invitation, leading to the water. He stopped. And then he looked. When his eyes met Swan's, chivalry was dead. He did not return the smile—admittedly a bizarre one, glassy at best, but everything Swan could muster—he simply stared, squinting against the sun, saying nothing. He was still, and he remained that way, in mute confrontation.

And now Swan, forsaking the smile, staring back in mute defiance, returning the look . . . *yes, we're out here swimming . . . stoned . . . Immaculate . . . spawning on the current . . . all of us . . . breeding tiny and rebellious monsters . . . the Enemy . . . us . . . go on, . . . lock up your daughters . . . scream . . . you sad and friendless man . . . you'll dream of us tonight . . . I know you're going to turn us in, you son of a bitch.*

Without a word, the man left. He continued along the beach and out of sight.

'He's going to turn us in,' Swan said.

And he was right.

SOMEWHERE IN THE accumulated misspending of what was someday to become known as his youth, Zachary Swan was taken aside by a man much older than he and confronted with what, at the time, was quaintly referred to as the cold truth about life. 'Son,' he was told, 'there's no free lunch.' He did not believe it then, and now, for the first time in forty-six years, Zachary Swan had hard evidence to show in support of his opinion.

'Mine was rare without the pickles,' he said, 'and give me a side of fries with that . . .'

The chow wagon moved rapidly along the cell block, and Swan was left with Suffolk County's answer to winning the hearts and minds of the people.

' . . . hold the ketchup,' he mumbled.

Three days in Riverhead and he was as close as he had ever come in his life to an overdose . . . *another jailbird, DOA/HAMBURGERS, poor bastard didn't even get the tourniquet off, cover him up, nurse* . . . the mayor must be from Texas, Swan thought, cow country; a Hindu would starve here . . . *Hare Krishna, pardner.*

Swan washed the dry lump down with a calculated intake of jail coffee, a 70-percent solution of refined sugar, viscous, the consistency of syrup. A diabetic would not last an hour in the slammer—one shot of this coffee in the right place and you could throw an eight-cylinder Chevy onto the scrap heap forever. Swan swallowed the slush and felt the soft embolus of the hamburger suzette skidding down his esophagus into that vast wasteland once remembered as his stomach.

ON SATURDAY AFTERNOON, just prior to its second ration of ground beef, that same stomach had taken the punch that was to slow it down for the next two years. It was delivered by a police officer in plain clothes. He was looking at Swan:

'We found drugs in your house,' he said.

Swan's established digestive patterns changed radically and forever at that moment. It was the beginning of a progress report. One that would grow tedious. He would become indignant at what the same detective delivered in the way of an uppercut:

'The word is out that you carry a gun.'

The word is out? This cop either watches a lot of television or he reads *The Daily News.* I'm an executive, for Christ's sake. I belong to the Westchester Country Club. Charlie, I own stock in some of the largest corporations in the world. My wife was on the Dick Cavett Show. What is this guy talking about? The air duct, Charlie, drop it down the fucking air duct.

While Zachary Swan was parting with his stomach, Charles Kendricks, code name the Hungarian, was parting with a sterling silver coke spoon of great sentimental value. He dropped it through the grill of the air shaft that ventilated his cell on the second floor of the Suffolk County courthouse. His nose twitched goodbye. Where had he gone wrong, he wondered.

They had been busted on the beach. Two patrol cars. That was understandable. It was a slow night and the thought of two young women swimming in the nude must have appealed to the boys on the night shift. Kendricks tried to imagine them spilling their coffee when the carburetors kicked in. They got there fast, but not before the Volkswagen was under way . . . *the Volkswagen, the latest reincarnation of the Dachau boxcar, the unimpeachable symbol of the Fatherland's relentless effort to demonstrate that the Devil himself prefers canned food.* Lillian, at the wheel, had just lost the game of musical laps that began when the four shivering getaways paused in their escape to fight over the three warm-blooded dogs, a regrettable delay under the circumstances, he thought, but then, too, it had taken them a while to get into their clothes. At the time Kendricks blamed it on the earth—spinning so fast, while at the same time . . . *if you can believe it, revolving around the bloody sun.* He remembered Swan trying to get both feet into his pants at once—cutting corners this way, he supposed . . . *but not standing up, man!* He recalled that Swan mumbled a lot . . . *yes, officer, the Kendrickses here, our friends from down under, are members of the Australian Olympic Team, swimmers, you see, and they have just crawled in from Sydney . . . my wife and I were not expecting them until tomorrow, of course . . . but then the Gulf Stream and what not . . . Gibraltar tomorrow, isn't it, Charles . . .* then, 'Follow us . . . public intoxication . . . stick around . . . ' and now the gun . . . all that dope . . . it all came back to Kendricks, whose nose had started running. The spoon disappeared with a forlorn rattle.

Fingerprints and photographs. More hamburgers. Then the handcuffs. At one a.m. the four prisoners were reunited before a judge and arraigned. The men and women were then driven separately to Riverhead, home of the Suffolk County Jail. They were disinfected and wardrobed. And then they were confined. The Ides of October. Sunday mornin', comin' down.

On the night of the party, Swan had loaned Kendricks some clothes, clearly a mistake, for when they were discovered to be wearing matching briefs, the processing officer ordered the guard on duty to 'put these guys on different floors.' They saw each other only once in the four days that Swan was there. On that occasion Swan learned his first lesson in prison discipline. Kendricks was standing four places ahead of him in the physical examination lineup, and Swan, who had been out of boot camp for at least thirty years, started forward to talk to him. He was rescued by his fellow inmates . . . *where you goin', man, they're gonna smack you . . .* who were obliged to demonstrate the series of casual pirouettes by which forward and backward progress along a supervised line is correctly achieved . . . *see, man, you're just talkin' to me for a minute here, and we're just shufflin' our feet, right? and then just like magic you're lookin' that way and I'm lookin' this way, and there you are, and your friend's comin' this way, see that.* And you've both got all your teeth. It took them about three minutes to get together.

'How are you holding up, Charlie?'

'The coffee sucks.'

'What did they tell you about phone calls?'

'I reckon they're going to let me make one after lunch. Jesus, if it's another bloody hamburger I'll shit.'

'Call Seymour,' Swan said.

'Where's your beard gone?' Charlie asked him.

'They made me shave it.'

'The bastards.'

'There's something wrong with these people, Charlie. They take a mug shot of me with a full beard. And then they shave it off. Can you figure that out? I can't figure it out.'

'You're near fifty. You've brought the average age in here up to approximately twenty-two. You tell me why they have to play Frank Sinatra and Tony Bennett on the fucking Muzak.'

'You call Seymour. Give him Sandy's name. I'll get us a lawyer.'

Kendricks yawned. He nodded and turned around.

'Charlie, watch out for this guy, I hear he goes for fellas your age. Keep an eye on him. Don't let the stethoscope fool you; if he smiles, you're in trouble. I'll write soon.'

Charlie made the call. Sandy never came through.

SWAN OPENED HIS eyes. Another bad night. The man in the cell next to his had been masturbating again. Late. Their beds were each part of the same bunk, one elongated bedspring built into and passing through the concrete wall that separated them—the man had been at it again, and with every stroke Swan's bed shook. Jail, he decided, was miserable.

The library boys came around. They preceded the hamburger by about an hour.

'Bookmobile.'

'Terrific.'

'What are you in for?' they wanted to know.

Swan told them. They looked at one another.

'Don't stand trial here,' was all they could say.

A black prisoner who occupied the cell opposite Swan's overheard the conversation with the library boys and felt obliged to say something to Swan. It amounted to:

'Hey, man, you didn't happen to get any of that stuff in here, did you?'

The hamburger came.

WHILE ZACHARY SWAN was washing his hamburger suzette down in the Riverhead Jail, a young Canadian man with blond hair and a horse-latitudes tan was stepping from a jet onto the runway at Kennedy Airport. He was traveling alone and traveling light. And he was traveling on a false passport. And in addition to his expense money, the young man was carrying $5,000 in cold American cash. Within an hour, Swan, by way of his Constitutional rights, would have a lawyer and have his bail reduced. Within two hours, by way of a noble gesture, Swan would have $1,000 in cash in his hand, and the young Canadian, who had come from nowhere, would be booking a flight south.

'WHO WAS THAT?' his lawyer asked when the four prisoners were released and eating their first lunch together in five days.

'A friend of mine,' Swan said.

'He must be a very good friend.'

'He is. We're in the same business. We've known each other for about two years now.'

'What's his name?'

'Canadian Jack.'

'What's his real name?'

'Your guess is as good as mine. I've known him pretty well for about two years, and for two years I've known him only as Canadian Jack. In my business you don't ask your friends a lot of questions. And you especially don't ask them, "What's your real name?" '

Swan's lawyer smiled.

Ernie Peace, of Peace, Lehrman & Gullo, Mineola, Long Island, had been recommended to Swan by a personal friend. It was only a coincidence, according to Swan, that the friend was, by profession, a narcotics detective. Swan had had to assume that there was no one better qualified to rate a lawyer than a cop, and he was right. Ernie Peace was one of the best. A lot of narcotics detectives thought so, and many of them had found out the hard way. Peace sat across from Swan dressed in an unimpressive double-knit suit, a white shirt and a blue tie. He was a shorter man than Swan, about the same age. His build was average, his hair was short, and all in all he was a very unprepossessing fellow. He was one of those people who seemed always to be thinking about anything but what you were saying, looking here, looking there, taking it easy, preoccupied with everything else but you—he was also one of those people who five minutes later would quote verbatim what you had just said. He was smiling now, a kind of smile Swan had seen many times. Swan was pleased. It was a gambler's smile, pleasant, shy, and not a few parts lethal. Ernie Peace was measuring his man.

What Ernie Peace had on his hands was a middle-aged cloak-and-dagger freak, a man who betrayed a wealth of information on bugging devices, police technique, international drug traffic, Customs procedure, organized crime, pseudo-tribal FBI newspeak, and every other contingency covering his work; Zachary Swan was a man who possessed an encyclopedic knowledge of every conceivable high-level money transaction in the world. He even knew how to beat the phone company out of a dime.

Zachary Swan was tall and trim. His posture would have embarrassed his father. He had a strong handshake, an engaging smile, and a gentle voice an octave below middle C. He had liar's eyes. They were bright blue, cool, and very hard to ignore. He had a small birthmark on his left cheekbone. His hair was short—prison-length—and thick, going from brown to gray. He looked his age. It was because he did not act his age that he was here today. He was wearing about $600 worth of clothes; he was drinking a Martini and chain-smoking Kools. He handled himself well for a man under the gun.

'O.K.,' Peace said, 'the way it's going to work is like this. I can get the rest of you off. The DA's not really concerned about you anyway. But I want the whole truth. Everything. And then,' he said to Swan, 'we'll see what we can do about getting *you* out of this mess. Now, they are going to get cooperation from the Federal authorities, so I want you to tell me what the Feds know.'

'I don't think they can make a smuggling charge stick. I covered myself pretty well.'

'How?'

'Well,' he said, 'smuggling's easy.' He lit a cigarette. 'Anybody can do it, and a lot of people do, believe me. They do it a million ways. Some are smart, some are very stupid—for instance there are people who still get busted with false-bottom suitcases, which I want to say right now is something I never used. It is absolutely the worst way to smuggle anything. It's a sucker move. It's the first thing a Customs agent looks for—before he even takes anything out. He puts one finger inside and one finger outside, and if his fingers don't find each other you're in trouble. He's got a ruler and he measures. If the math goes against you, forget it.

'If you've got any brains at all, smuggling is easy. It's covering yourself every step of the way that's tough. If one of my carriers gets busted, he walks away. He's got excuses down the line. No way they can break his story. And that's the trick. You've got to prop up your carriers, because if they talk, you're both finished. My people stand up because they know they are going to walk. Is the smoke bothering you?'

'No, go ahead.'

'Most smugglers use mules, usually a girl, and she gets paid $1,000 a kilo to walk the load through Customs. Now, tell me, how are you going to say it's not yours if it's strapped to your back? And when the mule gets busted, nothing she can say is going to help her. She's finished, because her man's disappeared. It's really sad, but it happens all the time. And that's the way most smugglers operate. Say you're carrying. He's paid you a thousand and given you an airline ticket. You're broke, you want to get home. One of his lieutenants follows the load through Customs—if you get tossed, it's you and the lions. He's gone. I don't operate that way. If you carry for me, you're guaranteed to walk away.'

Peace sat back in his chair and looked around the table. It was apparent that the others had heard the sales pitch before. He did not pursue the Federal question any further. He simply nodded and leaned forward.

'Now, they found a lot of cocaine in your house. And they found a gun.

I'd be interested to know why you told them where the gun was buried. Apparently all they found in the house were the bullets.'

'That's right. The gun was buried under the pebbles of the patio.'

'And you told them that.'

'Right.'

'Did they threaten you?'

'No.'

'What happened?'

'They said if I didn't tell them, they were going to take the house apart board by board until they found it.'

'So?'

Swan looked at his friends. Then he looked back at his lawyer.

'Well, you see, they missed the load.'

'What do you mean they missed the load?'

'You said they found a lot of cocaine in the house.'

'They did.'

'How much?'

'The police say several ounces.'

'Yeah, that's what the judge said when he arraigned us. I wasn't sure.'

'That's what it is. And that's how the charge reads.'

Swan put his fork down. He looked at his attorney:

'Yeah, well, they missed the load, then. You see, on the mantelpiece, in the house, right now, there are three kilos of cocaine that they *didn't* find. And if the police lab is right, it's about 89 percent pure.'

from

Panama

Thomas McGuane

THIS IS THE first time I've worked without a net. I want to tell the truth. At the same time, I don't want to start a feeding frenzy. You stick your neck out and you know what happens. It's obvious.

The newspaper said that the arrests were made by thirty agents in coordinated raids "early in the a.m." and that when the suspects were booked, a crowd of three hundred gathered at the Monroe County Courthouse and applauded. The rest of the page had to do with the charges against the men, which were neither here nor there. Most people I heard talking thought it, was just too Cuban for words.

I stepped out onto the patio as the city commissioner was taken to the unmarked car in handcuffs. He was in his bathrobe and lottery tickets were blowing all over the place. Last week they picked up my dog and it cost me a five. The phone number was on her collar and they could have called. I knew how badly they had wanted to use the gas. But then, they're tired of everything. The wind blows all winter and gets on your nerves. It just does. They have nothing but their uniforms and the hopes of using the gas.

Out on the patio, I could see the horizon. The dog slept in the wedge of sun. There were no boats, the sea was flat, and from here, there was not a bit of evidence of the coordinated raids, the unmarked cars. The lottery—the bolita—was silent; it was always silent. And behind the wooden shutters, there was as much cocaine as ever. I had a pile of scandal magazines to see what had hit friends and loved ones. There was not one boat between me and an unemphatic horizon. I was home from the field of agony or whatever you want to call it; I was home from it. I was dead.

I WENT UP to the Casa Marina to see my stepmother. The cats were on the screen above the enclosed pool and the grapefruits were rotting in the little grove. Ruiz the gardener was crawfishing on the Cay Sal bank and the bent grass was thick and spongy and neglected. I was there five minutes when she said, "You were an overnight sensation." And I said, "Gotta hit it, I left the motor running." And she said, "You left the motor running?" and I said, "That's it for me, I'm going." And she tottered after me with the palmetto bugs scattering in the foyer and screamed at me as I pulled out: "You left the motor running! You don't have a car!" I actually don't know how smart she is. What could she have meant by that? I believe that she was attacking my memory.

She is a special case, Roxy; she is related to me three different ways and in some sense collects all that is dreary, sinister, or in any way glorious about my family. Roxy is one of those who have technically died; was in fact pronounced dead, then accidentally discovered still living by an alert nurse. She makes the most of this terrible event. She sometimes has need of tranquilizers half the size of Easter eggs. She drinks brandy and soda with them; and her face hollows out everywhere, her eyes sink, and you think of her earlier death. Sometimes she raises her hand to her face thinking the drink is in it. Roxy can behave with great charm. But then, just at the wrong time, pulls up her dress or throws something. I time my visits with extreme caution. I watch the house or see if her car has been properly parked. I used to spy but then I saw things which I perhaps never should have; and so I stopped that. When she thinks of me as an overnight sensation, she can be quite ruthless, flinging food at me or, without justification, calling the police and making false reports. I tolerate that because, under certain circumstances, I myself will stop at nothing. Fundamentally though, my stepmother is a problem because she is disgusting.

I guess it came to me, or maybe I just knew, that I have not been remembering things as clearly as I could have. For instance, Roxy is right, I don't have a car. I have a memory problem. The first question—look, you can ask me this—is exactly how much evasive editing is part of my loss of memory. I've been up against that one before. My position with respect to anyone else's claims for actuality has always been: it's you against me and may the best man win.

I'm not as stupid as I look. Are you? For instance, I'm no golfer. I did have a burst, and this is the ghastly thing which awaits each of us, of creating the world in my own image. I removed all resistance until I floated in my own invention. I creamed the opposition. Who in the history of ideas has prepared us for creaming the opposition? This has to be understood because otherwise . . . well, there is no otherwise; it really doesn't matter.

THE FIRST TIME I ran into Catherine, coming from the new wing of the county library, I watched from across the street noting that her Rhonda Fleming, shall we say, *grandeur* had not diminished. It seemed a little early in the present voyage to reveal myself. I sat on the wall under the beauty parlor, just a tenant in my self, or a bystander, eyes flooded, pushing my fingers into my sleeves like a nun. I thought, *When I find the right crooked doctor, I'm going to laugh in your face.*

I followed her for two blocks and watched her turn up the blind lane off Caroline where the sapodilla tree towers up from the interior of the block as though a piece of the original forest were imprisoned there. This spring they dug up the parking lot behind some clip joint on lower Duval and found an Indian grave, the huge skull of a Calusa seagoing Indian staring up through four inches of blacktop at the whores, junkies, and Southern lawyers.

So I sent her flowers without a note and two days later a note without flowers; and got this in return, addressed "Chester Hunnicutt Pomeroy, General Delivery": "Yes Chet I know you're home. But don't call me now, you flop you.—Catherine." I went into the garden and opened the toolshed, bug life running out among the rake tines. I got the big English stainless-steel pruning shears and came, you take it from me, *that* close to sending Catherine the finger I'd lost in her darkness so many thousands of times. The palmetto bugs are translucent as spar varnish and run over your feet in the shed. The sea has hollowed the patio into resonant chambers and when the wind has piped up like today you hear its moiling, even standing in the shed with the rakes and rust and bugs.

I felt better and lost all interest in mutilating myself, even for Catherine. Tobacco doves settled in the crown-of-thorns and some remote airplane changed harmonics overhead with a soft pop like champagne, leaving a pure white seam on the sky. I was feeling better and better and better. On stationery from my uncle's shipyard, I wrote, "There is no call for that. I'm just here with respect of healing certain injuries. Catherine, you only hurt hurt hurt when you lash out like that. I don't believe you try to picture what harm you do.—Chet." I traced my finger on the back of the sheet with a dotted line where the shears would have gone through. I said nothing as to the dotted line. It seemed to me with some embarrassment that it might have looked like a request for a ring.

I dialed Information and asked for Catherine Clay. The operator said it was unpublished. I told her it was a matter of life or death; and the operator said, I know who you are, and clicked off. They wouldn't treat Jesse James like that.

WHEN THEY BUILD a shopping center over an old salt marsh, the seabirds sometimes circle the same place for a year or more, coming back to check daily, to see if there isn't some little chance those department stores and pharmacies and cinemas won't go as quickly as they'd come. Similarly, I come back and keep looking into myself, and it's always steel, concrete, fan magazines, machinery, bubble gum; nothing as sweet as the original marsh. Catherine knows this without looking, knows that the loving child who seems lost behind the reflector Ray-Bans, perhaps or probably really is lost. And the teeth that were broken in schoolyards or spoiled with Cuban ice cream have been resurrected and I am in all respects the replica of an effective bright-mouthed coastal omnivore, as happy with spinach salads as human flesh; and who snoozing in the sun of his patio, inert as any rummy, Rolex Oyster Chronometer imbedding slightly in softened flesh, teeth glittering with ocean light like minerals, could be dead; could be the kind of corpse that is sometimes described as "fresh."

"I am a congestion of storage batteries. I'm wired in series. I've left some fundamental components on the beach, and await recharging, bombardment, implanting, *something*, shall we say, very close to the bone. I do want to go on; but having given up, I can't be expected to be very sympathetic."

"That's all very pretty," Catherine Clay said. "But I don't care. Now may I go?"

"There's more."

"I don't care. And above all, I don't want you stalking me like this in the supermarket. I can't have you lurking in the aisles."

"It's still the same."

"It's not, you liar, you flop!"

Slapping me, crying, yelling, oh God, clerks peering. I said, "You're prettiest like this." She chunks a good one into my jaw. The groceries were on the floor. Someone was saying, "Ma'am? Ma'am?" My tortoise-shell glasses from Optique Boutique were askew and some blood was in evidence. My lust for escape was complete. Palm fronds beat against the air-conditioned thermopane windows like my own hands.

Two clerks were helping Catherine to the door. I think they knew. Mrs. Fernandez, the store manager, stood by me.

"Can I use the crapper?" I asked.

She stared at me coolly and said, "First aisle past poultry."

I stood on the toilet and looked out at my nation through the ventilator fan. Any minute now, and Catherine Clay, the beautiful South Carolina wild child, would appear shortcutting her way home with her groceries.

I heard her before I could see her. She wasn't breathing right. That scene in the aisles had been too much for her and her esophagus was constricted. She came into my view and in a very deep and penetrating voice I told her that I still loved her, terrifying myself that it might not be a sham, that quite apart from my ability to abandon myself to any given moment, I might in fact still be in love with this crafty, amazing woman who looked up in astonishment. I let her catch no more than a glimpse of me in the ventilator hole before pulling the bead chain so that I vanished behind the dusty accelerating blades, a very effective slow dissolve.

I put my sunglasses back on and stood in front of the sink, staring at my blank reflection, scrutinizing it futilely for any expression at all and committing self-abuse. The sunglasses looked silvery and pure in the mirror, showing twins of me, and I watched them until everything was silvery and I turned off the fan, tidied up with a paper towel, and went back out through poultry toward the electric doors. Mrs. Fernandez, the store manager, smiled weakly and I said, "Bigger even than I had feared." The heat hit me in the street and I started . . . I think I started home. It was to feed the dog but I was thinking of Catherine and I had heartaches by the million.

MY FATHER WAS a store detective who was killed in the Boston subway fire, having gone to that city in connection with the Bicentennial. He had just left Boston Common, where we have kin buried. Everything I say about my father is disputed by everyone. My family have been shipwrights and ship's chandlers, except for him and me. I have been as you know in the Svengali business; I saw a few things and raved for money. I had a very successful show called *The Dog Ate The Part We Didn't Like*. I have from time to time scared myself. Even at the height of my powers, I was not in good health. But a furious metabolism preserves my physique and I am considered a tribute to evil living.

Those who have cared for me, friends, uncles, lovers, think I'm a lost soul or a lost cause. When I'm tired and harmless, I pack a gun, a five-shot Smith and Wesson .38. It's the only .38 not in a six-shot configuration I know of. How the sacrifice of that one last shot makes the gun so flat and concealable, so deadlier than the others. Just by giving up a little!

As to my mother, she was a flash act of the early fifties, a bankrolled B-girl who caught cancer like a bug that was going around; and died at fifty-six pounds. There you have it. The long and the short of it. And I had a brother Jim.

The money began in a modest way in the 1840's. A grandfather of minor social bearing, who had fought a successful duel, married a beautiful girl from the Canary Islands with two brothers who were ship's carpenters. They built coasters, trading smacks, sharpie mailboats, and a pioneer lightship for the St. Lucie inlet. The Civil War came and they built two blockade runners for the rebellion, the *Red Dog* and the *Rattlesnake*; went broke, jumped the line to Key West again while Stephen Mallory left town to become Secretary of the Confederate Navy. At what is now the foot of Ann Street, they built a series of deadly blockade boats, light, fast, and armed. They were rich by then, had houses with pecan wood dining-room tables, crazy chandeliers, and dogwood joists pinned like the ribs of ships. Soon they were all dead; but the next gang were solid and functional and some of them I remember. Before our shipyard went broke in the Depression, they had built every kind of seagoing conveyance that could run to Cuba and home; the prettiest, a turtle schooner, the *Hillary B. Cates*, was seen last winter off Cap Haitien with a black crew, no masts, and a tractor engine for power, afloat for a century. She had been a yacht and a blockade runner, and her first master, a child Confederate officer from the Virginia Military Institute, was stabbed to death by her engineer, Noah Card, who defected to the North and raised oranges at Zephyrhills, Florida, until 1931. He owed my grandfather money; but I forget why.

My grandfather was a dull, stupid drunk; and the white oak and cedar and longleaf pine rotted and the floor fell out of the mold loft while he filed patents on automobiles and comic cigarette utensils. I recall only his rheumy stupor and his routine adoration of children.

Let me try Catherine again.

"One more and I go to the police for a restraining order."

No sense pursuing that for the moment.

MY STEPMOTHER HAD a suitor. He was an attorney-at-law and affected argyle socks and low blue automobiles. He screamed when he laughed. What I think he knew was that the shipyard was a world of waterfront property and that when the Holiday Inn moved in where the blockade boats and coasters had been built, Roxy got all the money. His name was Curtis Peavey and he was on her case like a man possessed, running at the house morning noon and night with clouds of cheap flowers. Roxy had been known to fuck anything; and I couldn't say she ever so much as formed an opinion of Peavey. I noticed though that she didn't *throw* the flowers away, she pushed them into the trash, blossoms forward, as if they'd been involved in an accident. In this, I pretended to see disgust. I myself didn't like Peavey. His eyes were full of clocks, machinery, and numbers. The curly head of hair tightened around his scalp when he talked to me and his lips stuck on his teeth. But he had a devoted practice. He represented Catherine. No sense concealing that. If Peavey could, he'd throw the book at me. He said I was depraved and licentious; he said that to Roxy. Whenever I saw him, he was always about to motivate in one of the low blue cars. Certain people thought of him as a higher type; he donated Sandburg's life of Lincoln to the county library with his cornball bookplate in every volume, a horrific woodcut of a sturdy New England tree; with those dismal words: Curtis G. Peavey. As disgusting as Roxy was, I didn't like to see her gypped; which is what Peavey clearly meant to do. I didn't care about the money at all. I have put that shipyard up my nose ten times over.

I DON'T THINK Peavey was glad to see me hunker next to him on the red stool. The fanaticism with which he slurped down the bargain quantities of ropa vieja, black beans, and yellow rice suggested a speedy exit.

I said, "Hello, Curtis."

"How long are you back for—"

"Got a bit of it on your chin there, didn't you."

"Here, yes, pass me one of those."

"How's Roxy holding up?" I asked.

"She's more than holding up. A regular iron woman."

"A regular what?"

"Iron woman."

"You want another napkin?"

"Get out of here you depraved pervert."

I said, "You'll never get her money."

"I'd teach you a lesson," said Curtis Peavey, rising to his feet and deftly thumbing acrylic pleats from his belt line, "but you're carrying a gun, aren't you?"

"Yes," I said, "to perforate your duodenum."

"You have threatened me," he said softly. "Did you hear that, shit-for-brains? It won't do." Peavey strolled into the heat and wind. I stopped at the cash register and paid for his slop.

I went for a walk.

Something started the night I rode the six-hundred-pound Yorkshire hog into the Oakland auditorium; I was double-billed with four screaming soul monsters and I shut everything down as though I'd burned the building. I had dressed myself in Revolutionary War throwaways and a top hat, much like an Iroquois going to Washington to ask the Great White Father to stop sautéing his babies. When they came over the lights, I pulled a dagger they knew I'd use. I had still not replaced my upper front teeth and I helplessly drooled. I was a hundred and eighty-five pounds of strangely articulate shrieking misfit and I would go too god damn far.

At the foot of Seminary I stopped to look at a Czech marine diesel being lowered into a homemade trap boat on a chain fall. It was stolen from Cuban nationals, who get nice engines from the Reds. The police four-wheel drifted around the corner aiming riot guns my way. Getting decency these days is like pulling teeth. Once the car was under control and stopped, two familiar officers, Nylon Pinder and Platt, put me up against the work shed for search.

"Drive much?" I asked.

"Alla damn time," said Platt.

"Why work for Peavey?" I asked.

Platt said, "He's a pillar of our society. When are you gonna learn the ropes?"

Nylon Pinder said, "He don't have the gun on him."

Platt wanted to know, "What you want with the .38 Smith?"

"It's for Peavey's brain pan. I want him to see the light. He's a bad man."

"Never register a gun you mean to use. Get a cold piece. Peavey's a pillar of our society."

"Platt said that."

"Shut up, you. He's a pillar of our society and you're a depraved pervert."

"Peavey said that."

"Nylon said for you to shut your hole, misfit."

"I said that, I said 'misfit.' "

Platt did something sudden to my face. There was blood. I pulled out my bridge so if I go trounced I wouldn't swallow it. Platt said, "Look at that, will you."

I worked my way around the Czech diesel. They were going to leave me alone now. "Platt," I said, "when you off?"

"Saturdays. You can find me at Rest Beach."

"Depraved pervert," said Nylon, moving only his lips in that vast face. "Get some teeth," he said. "You look like an asshole."

The two of them sauntered away. I toyed with the notion of filling their mouths with a couple of handfuls of bees, splitting their noses, pushing small live barracudas up their asses. The mechanic on the chain fall said, "What did they want with you? Your nose is bleeding."

"I'm notorious," I said. "I'm cheating society and many of my teeth are gone. Five minutes ago I was young. You saw me! What is this? I've given my all and this is the thanks I get. If Jesse James had been here, he wouldn't have let them do that."

The mechanic stared at me and said, *"Right."*

I hiked to my stepmother's, to Roxy's. I stood like a druid in her doorway and refused to enter. "You and your Peavey," I said. "I can't touch my face."

"Throbs?"

"You and your god damn Peavey."

"He won't see me any more. He says you've made it impossible. I ought to kill you. But your father will be here soon and he'll straighten you out."

"Peavey buckled, did he? I don't believe that. He'll be back. —And my father is dead."

"Won't see me any more. Peavey meant something and now he's gone. He called me his tulip."

"His . . . ?"

"You heard me."

I gazed at Roxy. She looked like a circus performer who had been shot from the cannon one too many times.

In family arguments, things are said which are so heated and so immediate as to seem injuries which could never last; but which in fact are never forgotten. Now nothing is left of my family except two uncles and this tattered stepmother who technically died; nevertheless, I can trace myself through her to those ghosts; those soaring, idiot forebears with their accusations, and their steady signal that, whatever I thought I was, I was not the real thing. We had all said terrible things to each other, added insult to injury. My father had very carefully taken me apart and thrown the pieces away. And now his representatives expected me to acknowledge his continued existence.

So, you might ask, why have anything to do with Roxy? I don't know. It could be that after the anonymity of my fields of glory, coming back had to be something better than a lot of numinous locations, the house, the convent school, Catherine. Maybe not Catherine. Apart from my own compulsions, which have applied to as little as the open road, I don't know what she has to do with the price of beans . . . I thought I'd try it anyway. Catherine. Roxy looked inside me.

"Well, you be a good boy and butt out. Somehow, occupy yourself. We can't endlessly excuse you because you're recuperating, I *died* and got less attention. Then, I was never an overnight sensation."

I went home and fed the dog, this loving speckled friend who after seven trying years in my life has never been named. The dog. She eats very little and stares at the waves. She kills a lizard; then, overcome with remorse, tips over in the palm shadows for a troubled snooze.

CATHERINE STUCK IT out for a while. She stayed with me at the Sherry-Netherland and was in the audience when I crawled out of the ass of a frozen elephant and fought a duel in my underwear with a baseball batting practice machine. She looked after my wounds. She didn't quit until late. There was no third party in question.

I COULD THROW a portion of my body under a passing automobile in front of Catherine's house. A rescue would be necessary. Catherine running toward me resting on my elbows, my crushed legs on the pavement between us. All is forgiven. I'll be okay. I'll learn to remember. We'll be happy together.

I had a small sharpie sailboat which I built with my own hands in an earlier life and which I kept behind the A&B Lobster House next to the old cable schooner. I did a handsome job on this boat if I do say so; and she has survived both my intermediate career and neglect. I put her together like a fiddle, with longleaf pine and white-oak frames, fastened with bronze. She has a rabbeted chine and I let the centerboard trunk directly into the keel, which was tapered at both ends. Cutting those changing bevels in hard pine and oak took enormous concentration and drugs; not the least problem was in knowing ahead of time that it would be handy to have something I had made still floating when my life fell apart years later.

She had no engine and I had to row her in and out of the basin. When the wind dropped, I'd just let the canvas slat around while I hung over the transom staring down the light shafts into the depths. Then when it piped up, she'd trim herself and I'd slip around to the tiller and take things in hand. Sailboats were never used in the Missouri border fighting.

I went out today because my nose hurt from Peavey's goons and because I was up against my collapse; and because Catherine wouldn't see me. My hopes were that the last was the pain of vanity. It would be reassuring to think that my ego was sufficiently intact as to sustain injury; but I couldn't bank that yet.

The wind was coming right out of the southeast fresh, maybe eight or ten knots, and I rowed just clear of the jetty and ran up the sails, cleated off the jib, sat back next to the tiller, pointed her up as good as I could, and jammed it right in close to the shrimp boats before I came about and tacked out of the basin. I stayed on that tack until I passed two iron wrecks and came about again. The sharpie is so shoal I could take off cross-country toward the Bay Keys without fear of going aground. I trimmed her with the sail, hands off the tiller, cleated the main sheet, and turned on some Cuban radio. I put my feet up and went half asleep and let the faces parade past.

Immediately east of the Pearl Basin, I found a couple shivering on a sailboard they had rented at the beach. He was wearing a football jersey over long nylon surfing trunks; and she wore a homemade bikini knotted on her brown, rectilineal hips. What healthy people! They had formed a couple and rented a sailboard. They had clean shy smiles, and though they may not have known their asses from a hole in the ground in terms of a personal philosophy, they seemed better off for it, happier, even readier for life and death than me with my ceremonious hours of thought and unparalleled acceleration of experience.

I rigged the board so that it could be sailed again, standing expertly to the lee of them with my sail luffing. I told them they were ready to continue their voyage and she said to the boy, "Hal, it's a bummer, I'm freezing." And Hal asked me if she could ride back in my boat because it was drier. I told them I'd be sailing for a while, that I had come out to think, that I was bad company, and that my father had died in the subways of Boston. They said that was okay, that she would be quiet and not bother me. I let her come aboard, politely concealing my disappointment; then shoved Hal off astern. He was soon underway, with his plastic sailboard spanking on the chop, the bright cigarette advertisement on his sail rippling against the blue sky.

I continued toward the Bay Keys while the girl watched me with cold gray eyes, the shadow of the sail crossing her slowly at each tack. Then she went forward and took the sun with her hands behind her head.

"Your boyfriend a football player?" I asked.

"No, he deals coke."

"I see."

"Do you like coke?"

"Yes, quite a lot."

"Well, Hal has some Bolivian rock you can read your fortune in, I'll tell you that."

"Oh, gee, I—"

"Anybody ever tell you the difference between acid and coke?"

"Nobody ever did."

"Well, with acid you think you see God. With coke you think you *are* God. I'll tell you the honest truth, this rock Hal's got looks like the main exhibit at the Arizona Rock and Gem Show. Did you ever hear a drawl like mine?"

"No, where's it from?"

"It's not from anywhere. I made the god damn thing up out of magazines."

"How much of that rock is left?"

"One o.z. No more, no less. At a grand, it's the last nickel bargain in Florida."

"I'll take it all."

"We'll drop it off. Hey, can you tell me one thing, how come you got hospitalized? The papers said exhaustion but I don't believe everything I read. You don't look exhausted."

"It was exhaustion."

That night, after I had paid them, I asked if the business in the boats that afternoon had been a setup. She said that it had. "Don't tell him that!" giggled the boyfriend. "You coo-coo brain!"

My eyes were out on wires and I was grinding my teeth. When I chopped that shit, it fell apart like a dog biscuit. Bolivian rock. I didn't care. I just made the rails about eight feet and blew myself a daydream with a McDonald's straw. Let them try and stop me now!

By the time I got to Reynolds Street I was in tears. I went down to the park and crossed over to Astro City. The ground was beaten gray and flat and the tin rocketships were unoccupied. I climbed high enough on the monkey bars that no one could look into my eyes and wept until I choked.

I considered changing my name and cutting my throat. I considered taking measures. I decided to walk to Catherine's house again and if necessary nail myself to her door. I was up for the whole shooting match.

I walked over to Simonton, past the old cigar factory, around the schoolyard and synagogue, and stopped at the lumber company. I bought a hammer and four nails. Then I continued on my way. On Eaton Street, trying to sneak, I dropped about a gram on the sidewalk. I knelt with my red and white straw and snorted it off the concrete while horrified pedestrians filed around me. *"It takes toot to tango,"* I explained. Nylon and Platt would love to catch me at this, a real chance to throw the book. I walked on, rubbing a little freeze on my gums and waiting for the drip to start down my throat and signal the advent of white-line fever or renewed confidence.

The wind floated gently into my hair, full of the ocean and maritime sundries from the shipyard. A seagull rocketed all the way from William Street close to the wooden houses, unseen, mind you, by any eyes but mine. A huge old tamarind dropped scented moisture into the evening in trailing veils. Mad fuck-ups running to their newspapers and greasy dinners surged around my cut-rate beneficence. I felt my angel wings unfold. More than that you can't ask for.

Catherine's house with her bicycle on the porch was in a row of wooden cigarmakers' houses grown about with untended vegetation, on a street full of huge mahoganies. I thought to offer her a number of things—silence, love, friendship, departure, a hot beef injection, shining secrets, a tit for a tat, courtesy, a sensible house pet, a raison d'être, or a cup of coffee. And I was open to suggestion, short of "get outa here," in which case I had the hammer and nails and would nail myself to her door like a summons.

I crossed the street to her house, crept Indian style onto the porch, and looked through the front window. Catherine was asleep on the couch in

her shorts and I thought my heart would stop. I studied her from this lux-
urious point, staring at the wildly curly hair on her bare back; her arm
hung down and her fingertips just rested on the floor next to a crammed
ashtray. I had the nails in my shirt pocket, the hammer in the top of my
pants like Jesse James's Colt.

"Catherine," I said, "you let me in." This handsome woman, whom
Peavey had once had the nerve to call my common-law wife, was suddenly on her feet, walking toward me with jiggling breasts, to ram down
the front window and bolt the door. Then she went upstairs and out of
sight. I called her name a couple of more times, got no answer, and
nailed my left hand to the door with Jesse's Colt.

from

After Hours

Edwin Torres

SO COMES THE time of Diane Vargas's birthday. God forbid the question, but I calculated from the effect of gravity on her body, thirty-five, give and take a year. We was still coppin' a pop once in a while but nothin' regular. She was keepin' company with an old Greek that owned a belly dancer joint near the Statler Hilton. Dave Kleinfeld sprung the office staff to a big feed at Sal Anthony's on Irving Place. Me and Pachanga, Dave, Cox, Wadleigh, and Diane. We put Diane at the head of the table. Did the cake and the happy-birthday number. She was good people. Her trouble was she was waitin' on some guy to solve her problem. May as well wait for the Park Avenue bus on a snowy night. Pachanga was mad because they didn't have no red beans, or *gandules* (pigeon peas).

'Pachanga, this is an Italian restaurant,' Dave told him.

'So gwat, they can't make no lousy bean? Wasumata from dem, I ain't gonna eat.'

He ate. Ate out the joint. Wanted a bowl of linguini with clam sauce to take home with him. Kleinfeld liked to play with people, used to put him on. Call Pachanga by his real name, Gremildo.

'Gray-mildew, that is an extraordinary outfit you're wearing. A plaid shirt with a plaid suit. Might start a trend.' What and When thought this was a scream.

'Meester Kleinberg. I'm de kinda guy like different colors. Joo see dees two guy ober here,' pointing at Cox and Wadleigh, 'every day dey got the same suit. You got lotta money, why you don give dem more money so they dress pretty. I don go to no lawyer look gworse dan me.'

Gimme a street guy anytime. In the give or take of repartee you can't beat them (specially if they done time—the greatest school of all).

Pachanga always remind me of that guy in the sarong, used to play bad guy in all the Hawaii movies—guy was always stirrin' up the natives against the old chief then the volcano would blow up on Bora-Bora or Manakora and he would go 'Aiee' when the lava got to him. Look just like him. But Pachanga could get around people. Right away he scooped up two girls from another table and sat them down with us. They weren't sayin' too much to look at, so Kleinfeld passed, but Cox and Wadleigh got interested, and likewise the broads. Plain to see they was the three-button-suit-and-vest type. Pachanga winked at me. He had *cache*.

'Somebody gotta look out for Cox and Watz. *Son pendéjos*,' he said.

About one a.m., Diane insisted on seeing the club. We were all a little high and feelin' good. I called Saso and told him to have a table, that I was bringin' a party of downtown pipples. We drove up to 79th Street. It was early, but the club already had a nice crowd (Saso was rafflin' off a car). We was a party of eight, so we took a long table along the wall. It was a weekday, so we didn't have no band, just the disco, but loud as hell. It was Diane's day, so I had to dance with her. I ain't no rock 'n roller. Hate that noise. As usual the bar was packed. Kleinfeld had come down from his buzz and was acting glum. Saso (big-ass bird) landed at the table. He sighted on Kleinfeld like crosshairs.

'Counselor, I have heard so much about you from Charles. I wanted a career at the bar, but the fortunes of war—'

'What war was this? Six-day war, Ethiopian war?'

Kleinfeld was a ballbuster. But you couldn't faze Saso.

'No. The war in the ghetto. The war against poverty. A war that knows no quarter. I'm with a community organization in the Bronx, and sometimes we recruit lawyers who are interested in helping the community—'

'Mr Saso,' Kleinfeld said. Serious-faced.

'Ron. Call me Ron, Counselor.'

'Am I a member of the community?'

'Of course. We all are, the human community.'

'All right. Then I need help . . . Ron.'

'Help? What kind of help, Mr Kleinfeld?'

'See that little black piece of tail over there on the dance floor . . . ?'

It was Steffie, the barmaid. She was on her relief and she was out on the deck dancin' in a pair of white pants that had been sprayed on her (no drawers either). Kleinfeld was about to pull rank. Lord of the manor.

' . . . I want that, bring it over here . . . Ron.'

Kleinfeld's hair was a little unpressed by now and his eyes were gettin' beadier and beadier. Saso looked at me and said, in Spanish, 'She belongs to Benny Blanco.'

'What happened to Rudy, the waiter? I thought him and her—'

'Benny chased him.'

Now I got hot.

'Fuck Benny Blanco. Bring her over here. She got the rest of the night off.'

So Steffie come over and lit a fire under Kleinfeld's ass. 'You rilly sump'n, Mr Kleinfeld. You puttin' me on, Dave. Man got hisself a Mercedes, got hisself a yacht. Damn, Carlito, where you been hidin' this man?'

She gave him both barrels. Kleinfeld had his tie off, hair standin' straight up, and he's boogeyin' with Steffie. Lovin' it, too, Jack. She's shakin' and turnin' and doin' her thing and Kleinfeld's beads are glued to her ass. Look like somebody hit him in the forehead with a rubber hammer. He's staggerin', but he ain't out. Then they go into that Pendergrass 'Bad Luck' number and Kleinfeld really goes ape. I hadn't had a laugh like that since I come outa jail.

About this time comes Benny Blanco from the Bronx. Along with his two water boys. Three white Puerto Ricans with the short sideburns covering the top of the ear. Roll collars long as the lapels on the suit. Rice and beans mafioso. They was 'boys'. Very uptight about findin' out that they was bad. Like, 'damn people are scared of me.' They took a table facing us on the other side of the dance floor. Steffie still hadn't seen them even after she and Kleinfeld sat down again. Saso turned white (shoulda took his picture).

Pachanga got up and went to the side of the room. Diane's a veteran, so she's already panicked. She can hear a beef comin' up like thunder.

Kleinfeld's got his hands all over Steffie and he's wooin' n' cooin'. Benny is sittin' straight up, with both hands on the table. Then he smiles at me, and waves. I can see the flash of his fancy joolery. He points a long finger at Saso, still smilin'. Saso looks at me. I nod. Saso goes over, talks awhile; then comes back.

'He says he wants to send a bucket of champagne over. He says he wants you to send Steffie over.' Steffie spun quick, saw Benny, and pitched a fit on the spot.

'Saso! Carlito! What—?' She's gaspin'.

I tried to calm her.

'Take it easy, Steffie. There's no problem here. You're with Mr Kleinfeld. Benny will understand.'

Kleinfeld is total stoned now. He's swingin' his head around.

'What Benny? Fuck Benny. C'mon, Steffie, wassa matter, baby?'

So the pot thickens and I ain't lettin' Steffie go nowhere. And Kleinfeld wants to dance. To improve matters, the air conditioning breaks down and the joint is gettin' hot. Wadleigh is dancin' with one of the girls, jumpin' up and down in the same place, bumpin' and knockin' into people. Cox is passed out on the table with his broad puttin' ice on his neck. Fuckin' squares when they get drunk is worse than the hoodlums. Then they go to a wise-guy joint, get outa shape, catch a beatin', then they call the cops, 'hoodlums attacked me from behind.' Diane knows I'm runnin' a game, so she gets real quiet. She got her pocketbook under her arm. She's lookin' for a foxhole.

Rudy, the waiter, brought over a bottle of Piper-Heidsieck in a bucket of ice.

'You know who this is from,' he said.

'Send it back,' I told him.

Rudy was grinnin'. He took the bucket back to the service bar. Now we got both feet out the window.

Kleinfeld jumped up.

'Hey, where's he going with that bottle? Tell him to bring it back, Carlito. Champagne for everybody. Atta baby, Steffie.'

I pulled him back down.

'Wrong table, Dave.'

But he didn't hear me, he's strokin' Steffie. Saso leaned into my ear about this time. Even his moustache was sweatin.'

'Charles, please. Benny spends a lot of money here. Why do we need this? We can't afford another incident.'

'Plus you owe him money, right?'

'I paid him.'

'That's your lookout, Saso. He's just another nickel-bagger to me.'

'Why do you push the kids so much? They bring in the money.'

'I was doin' time. They was out here. That's why.'

'Charles, something's happened to you. You used to be a fun guy. Now you're always in a bad mood. We go back a long time, so I'll tell you. People are talking about you, say you're stir crazy. They're afraid of you. You should see how you look at people. You won't have a drink with anybody. Bad for business. I'm serious.'

'You're serious? You and your phoney community *guiso*—'

'What do you know about my work? I'm down at the Welfare or at Landlord-Tenant every day. You're always putting down my work. What have you done, besides racketeer?'

'Bailed you out, didn't I? You put your sticky hands on it real quick-like, didn't you?'

Saso leaned back. Started sliding his upper plate around in his mouth. The clickin' meant he was thinkin' heavy. Ha.

'It doesn't make sense that you should hate these people. They're what you were twenty years ago . . . And they bring in the money.'

'We gonna do *This Is Your Life* now, right? Look, Saso, you ain't got no diploma, you ain't no shrink, so get off that kick.'

Saso got up.

'He won't back down, Charles. You'll have to kill him.'

'Do that too.'

'What about Walberto?'

'He bleeds.'

'*Me lavo las manos*,' Saso said. He turned and walked toward the bar. Diane got up and followed him, so I knew Benny was crossin' the floor.

Except for his white shirt, he was all in gray. Gray suit, gray tie, gray stickpin, no cufflinks. Lad was clean. He was a smiler, had a little Bronx gold in his teeth. Big nose. His two flunkies were behind him. He came up behind Steffie and Kleinfeld, facin' me. I had my back to the wall. He put his hands on Steffie's shoulders and leaned over her head toward me.

'That's the second time you turned down a drink from me, Carlito.'

I could see a big stone on his left pinkie. Diamond watch, silver bracelet.

Steffie froze in her chair. Kleinfeld turned to look up at Benny.

'Say whatcha gotta say, Benny,' I said.

'I say Steffie's at the wrong table. Right, babe?'

And he pulled her up. Pachanga, Rudy, and two of the bouncers jumped from behind, grabbin' Benny and his boys. They couldn't move. We dragged them into the office. Kleinfeld insisted on comin' along. They only had one gun between the three of them. Musta been on parole. Kleinfeld had a snub nose in his hand. And that room was crowded.

'What the hell you doin', Dave?'

'I'm going to shoot this cock-sucker. Trying to take my girl away.'

He was swacked out of his skull.

'Put that away,' I told him, but I had to laugh.

Dave, the hit man. I didn't want Benny hurt too bad. Out of respect for Rolando.

There was no back door, so we tried to sneak them out past the bar, but people knew what was going on. We went through the first door and had them on the landing. I told Pachanga and the bouncers to put these guys out and they were barred from the club 'for life' (if not sooner). This got Benny hot.

'Carlito, you better fuck me up now, 'cause next time we meet I'm gonna kill you. I swear by my mother—'

I kicked him down the stairs. He went ass over teakettle. It was a long flight and he didn't miss a step. He was sprawled out on the street floor. His punks carried him out. Faggot.

Typical of me. Twice I had to rumble over this black broad and I ain't laid a glove on her yet. But I can see Benny's point. Never was a Latin cat could pass up on a fine black kitty. God invented black and God invented white. But it took the Spanish to invent the mulatto. And the mixture was better with the Latins, softer. Put 'em all in the blender and you get women like the mulatta chorus girls from the Tropicana in Havana (before Fidel). Never seen women like that. The US of A is going that way. We're all mixed up here already. When you see so many white guys walkin' around with kinky hair. This is the wave of the future. In other words, the man of the future is here already, and he's a PR.

The party broke up. No air conditionin' and too much excitement. Diane stayed at the bar with Saso, who was gassin' her to death. Cox was on his ass, we put him in a cab with Wadleigh and the two bimbos. Dave was becomin' a pain in the gazool. Wanted to snort coke. Pachanga scored off a reliable guy upstairs gamblin', and me, Steffie, and Kleinfeld took a blow. Didn't do nothin' for me. Kleinfeld, of course, wouldn't stop talking now.

'Leave your car, Carlito. You drive me and Steffie. I'll bring you back in the morning. I want to show you and her my house. Cohen's Coliseum. Taj Mahal of Little Neck and Manhasset Bay. C'mon. We have to talk. Our boat ride's coming up on Sunday.'

He was talkin' this shit in front of Steffie. Leave it to the candy. So we split the joint. I'm drivin' the Mercedes-Benz out to Kings Point. Kleinfeld and Steffie in the back, like I'm the chauffeur. Didn't bother me none. Dave's m'man.

It was the wee hours, so the roads were clear. Little Dave is smoke-stackin' for Steffie about what a tough guy he was. Booze and coke had him believin' it himself. How he pulled his gun on this big spook in his office and how he was gonna shoot Benny but I stopped him. Everybody wants to be what they ain't. *Paloma por gavilán.*

'I'm getting tired of these hoods coming to my office and pushing me around. I can be rough too, eh, Carlito?'

'Meanwhile, you don't know enough to close the windows when you're in the car wash.'

Dave hesitated, then he remembered.

'Tell Steffie how I stood up to that whole gang on 111th Street.'

'Yeah, but if I ain't there, you ain't here.'

'They would have killed me.'

'For sure. That was Bobbie Duke and some of the Viceroys. That pipe wouldn't done you any good.'

'It was a crowbar. I've kept it as a memento. I showed that rabble I was a man.'

'Nobody ever questioned that. You showed 'em where you was at. You shoulda seen him, Steffie—'

Always puff a man up in front of his ol' lady.

Women get bored when men start macho-trippin' but Steffie was doin' her 'wow, don't tell me' routine. I could hear her wheels schemin', 'this

lil' Jew-boy gonna take care of business, home free.' I looked for her face
in the rear-view mirror, but all I could see were dollar signs. Guys don't
wanna be loved for their money. Wish somebody would love me for my
money. She-it. Dave was funny-lookin', so he would get shook up if you
told him that. He wants to be 'luv-ed'. What he don't know is that them's
the best kinda broads, lookin' out for themselves. Them other kind,
romantic broads, walk around with their own rhythm section in their
head, get you in trouble. And he thinks he's a tough guy.

'Truth is there ain't no tough guys, Dave, only actors. The whole street
is an act. You oughta hear the tough guys scream and cry in the back of a
station house or on New Year's Eve in prison.'

'Actors? What do you think lawyers are? That's all lawyers do, act. I can
laugh, cry, rant, rave, all on cue. Like an Olivier. I can assume any shape
or form. I can adjust to any speed, any psyche. Try pleading for mercy in a
courtroom for some miserable pederast who hasn't even paid your fee—'

I figured a foot doctor.

'If you an actor, recite somethin',' Steffie said.

'OK.'

He musta tickled her because she started laughin' loud. They were
horsin' around awhile, then things got quiet in the back. I figured he had
his face between her legs. Divin' for black pearls, no doubt. Dave, you
dawg. Then I saw the lights behind us. Empty highway and this car's
blinkin' his brights behind us.

'Don't let him pass us, Carlito. Step on the gas.'

I hear Dave. He's sittin' up and scared. I push the car over ninety, but
they were gonna pass. The first bullet is always for the driver, so you know
I was concerned. Tried to squeeze my head through the steerin' wheel.
They were right alongside. Kleinfeld is stretched flat on the floor by now.
He squeaks, 'Don't let them pass on the outside. Keep them on the right.'

He was on the left side, of course. Steffie, dumb broad, is straight up,
she doesn't know what the hell is comin' off. They passed. False alarm.
Couple of kids in a souped-up car. Me and Dave felt stupid for gettin'
excited.

'See what I mean, Dave?' I said.

He kept quiet. As a matter of fact, he kept quiet all the rest of the way
to Kings Point.

Taj Mahal all right, ranch style. House had to go for a quarter mill, easy. Had a giant fireplace maybe twenty feet wide in the middle of the living room. Made out of all kinds and colors of stone. The floor seemed to be made of marble. There were sliding glass walls with wooden panels behind them that went up and down. The place could be sealed up like a shoe box. Coulda had a stickball game easy inside that house. Dave apologized that the new furniture and decorations were not in yet. Steffie came out of the bathroom saying there was a red marble tub she could fit her apartment into. She was dazzled. Doin' all right, Kleinfeld.

'This used to be Woody, my former partner's house. I fixed it up.'

'Too bad about Cohen, huh?'

Tragedy. He was a beautiful guy. Taught me a lot.'

We're sprawled out around the fireplace. Steffie fell out. Dave wanted to talk. His nose was stoked, but he still made a lot of sense. There's no subject he's not into. We got to talkin' about Russia, which I was into heavy because of a buddy I had in Lewisburg, Antinov. He was a Ukrainian, from Canada, in for check forgery. Antinov had been with the Red Army in '41, was captured by the Germans, and switched to the German army under Vlasov. Then he was turned over to the Russians again. He told me his buddies were jumpin' offa rooftops and eating glass so they wouldn't send them back. Stalin sent him to the Gulag. Lost all his teeth (he had iron teeth in his mouth). Guy had wrists like ham hocks. Could do a Pennsylvania winter in an undershirt. Gave me the scoop on the whole war. Talk about a survivor. He's the one turned me on to Solzhenitsyn, the greatest convict in history. Man did eleven years (same as me, altogether), did cancer, and still out there raisin' hell. It was readin' Solzhenitsyn and his troubles that got me to thinkin' about me. In other words, unless you been inside, you ain't ever looked inside yourself . . .

'And examined the infinity of the inner space, which cannot be contemplated without the indispensably purifying, spiritual experience of confinement,' Kleinfeld said.

Exactly. It is a pleasure to talk to an intelligent man. Unfortunately, I mostly only meet these guys inside, because the street these days ain't got nothin' but clowns and stool pigeons.

Then he said, 'Bullshit,' and laughed. Dave was a cynical sombitch.

I had read all of Antinov's books on the war. So me and Kleinfeld got into Stalingrad, Sevastopol, Kursk and the Carel, Werth, and Guy Sajer books. Dave told me he had been to Russia (his mother was from Odessa)

and had stood at the spot where they stopped the Panzers, sixteen kilome-
ters from the Kremlin. Could see the onion domes. Stood in front of the
Winter Palace, where Lenin kicked off the revolution. Dave had been
everywhere. Meanwhile, I had spent my life on a barstool.

It was dawn and I wanted to conk out. He walked me to a bedroom.
Bed was mounted on a platform; you fall off, you'd be killed.

'We go this Sunday, Carlito.'

Damn. Thought we passed on Tony T. I need to bust into Riker's
Island like I need another felony. I musta had some puss, 'cause he
added, 'Think of it as a commando operation, like St Nazaire.'

'You know what you're doin'? I mean I got two felony convictions
already.'

'It's been done before.'

'I don't go for this.'

'Wait a minute. Not too long ago your issue was very much in doubt.
Remember that long trip I made to Lewisburg to see you? Remember
what you said to me?'

'Said a lot of things.'

'You said, "Today for me, tomorrow for you," that's what you said.'

'Yeah, *Hoy por mi, mañana por ti*.'

'I want you to come with me. You're lucky, Carlito. You don't think so,
but you're lucky.'

'How about lights? Dogs?'

'No lights. No dogs.'

'What about patrol boats?'

'A joke. There's no security, the cutbacks. Sunday night. The boat will
be ready. Be here about eight p.m.'

'Fifty large?'

'Plus a bonus.'

'He'll never make it. Tony T is too old, he's sick.'

'What do you care? You still get paid. You can buy out Saso or do whatever you want. Beats selling dope.'

'You got the balls of a flat burglar, Dave.'

'I know. Go to sleep. I have to wake Steffie up now.'

'For a little man you stretch a long way.'

'I'll be up by nine a.m., making phone calls to Geneva.'

'That's where your stash is, eh?'

'Fuck you, Brigante, go to sleep.'

'Oh, before I forget, do me a favor.'

'What?'

'Leave the piece home. You're gonna get hurt or you're gonna get me hurt.'

'Bullshit.'

'Dave, you're gonna wave it at the wrong guy. He's gonna take it from you, and then what?'

'You don't think I'll use it?'

'Something like that, yeah.'

'You may be right, but then again, you may be wrong. Irrespective of which, the gun remains. Good-night, Alexandre.'

'Good-night, Nikita.'

Slept good. Once my mind is made up, I don't sweat for nobody.

from

Miles: The Autobiography

by Miles Davis

AFTER MARGUERITE LEFT, Jackie Battle and I became a team almost. I still went out with other women sometimes, but I was mostly with her. Jackie and I had a great relationship. She was almost in my blood, we were so close. I had never felt this way about a woman other than Frances. But I took her through a lot of things, because I know I was hard to put up with. She was always trying to keep me off coke, and I would stop for a while and then I would start again. One time when we were on a plane in San Francisco, this stewardess walked up and handed me a matchbox full of coke that I just started snorting right there in the seat. Man, sometimes it got so crazy after I had been snorting coke and dropping seven or eight Tuinals (downers), I would think I would hear voices and begin looking under rugs, in the radiators, under the sofas. I would swear that people were in the house.

I used to drive Jackie crazy with this kind of behavior, especially when I ran out of coke. Then I would be looking for it in the car, going through her bag because she would always be throwing it out every time she found some. Once I had run out of coke and we were getting on a plane to go somewhere. I thought Jackie might have hidden the coke in her purse, so I took her purse and started going through it to see if she had it there. I came across this package of Woolite powdered soap and I remember breaking it open and swearing it was cocaine because it was white powder. After I tasted it I knew it was soap and I felt so embarrassed.

In October 1972 I wrecked my car on the West Side Highway. Jackie wasn't with me; she was at home asleep, where I should have been. I think we had just come off the road that night from playing somewhere and everyone was a little tired. I didn't feel like going to sleep although I had taken a sleeping pill. Jackie was staying at my house, and I wanted to go out somewhere, but she just wanted to sleep. So then I left; I think I was going to some after-hours place in Harlem. Anyway, I fell asleep at the wheel and ran my Lamborghini into a divider and broke both my ankles. When they called Jackie and told her, she had a fit when she got to the hospital.

Jackie and my sister, Dorothy, who had flown in from Chicago to help out, cleaned up my house while I was in the hospital. They found these Polaroid snapshots of women doing all kinds of things. I used to just watch these women freak out on themselves. I didn't make them do it or anything like that, they would just do it because they thought it would please me, and they gave me the pictures to look at. I think these pictures upset Jackie and Dorothy a lot. But I was upset that they had come into my house and gone through my private things like that. At that time I liked the house dark all the time; I guess because my mood was dark.

I think that incident had a lot to do with Jackie's getting fed up with me. Women were calling there all the time. And Marguerite lived in the apartment upstairs and would come down to keep the house when Jackie went out on the road with me. I was laid up for almost three months, and when I got home, I had to walk on crutches for a while, which further fucked up my bad hip.

When I came home from the hospital, Jackie made me vow that I would stay off drugs, and I did for a hot minute. Then I got that craving again. I remember one day she had put me out on the patio by the garden in back of my house. It was a nice fall day, not too cold, not too warm. I had this hospital bed I was sleeping in so that I could raise and lower my legs. Jackie had a bed and was sleeping out in the garden next to me when it was nice outside. At night of course we came inside and slept. This particular day we were resting out in the garden, and my sister, Dorothy, was sleeping upstairs in the house. All of a sudden I got a craving for cocaine. I got up on my crutches and called a friend, who came and picked me up to go and score. I did that, and when I got back both Jackie and my sister were hysterical because they figured I had probably gone to buy drugs. They both got really, really angry. But Dorothy, because she is my sister, stayed; Jackie left and went back to her apartment, which she had never given up, and took the phone off the hook so she wouldn't talk to me. When I finally got her on the phone and asked her to come back, she said no. When Jackie said no, she meant no. I knew that it was over and I was sorrier than a motherfucker. I had given her a ring that my mother had given me. I sent Dorothy down to get my mother's ring.

Jackie used to tell me all the right things. Without her, my life for the next two years just went over into the dark zone. It was coke around the clock without any letup and I was in a lot of pain. I started going out with this woman named Sherry "Peaches" Brewer for a while. She was a beautiful woman, too. She had come to New York from Chicago to be in the Broadway musical *Hello Dolly*, with Pearl Bailey and Cab Calloway. We hung out together, and she was a very nice person, a very good actress. Then I was going out with a model named Sheila Anderson, who was another tall, fine-looking woman. But I was keeping more and more to myself.

By this time I was making around a half million dollars a year, but I was also spending a lot of money on all the things I was doing. I was spending a lot on cocaine. Everything had started to blur after I had that car accident.

Columbia released *On the Corner* in 1972, but they didn't push it, so it didn't do as well as we all thought it would. The music was meant to be heard by young black people, but they just treated it like any other jazz album and advertised it that way, pushed it on the jazz radio stations. Young black kids don't listen to those stations; they listen to R & B stations and some rock stations. Columbia marketed it for them old-time jazz people who couldn't get into what I was doing now in the first place. It was just a waste of time playing it for them; they wanted to hear my *old* music that I wasn't playing anymore. So they didn't like *On the Corner*, but I didn't expect that they would; it wasn't made for them. That just became another sore spot in my relationship with Columbia, and the problems were really adding up by this time. A year later, when Herbie Hancock put out his *Headhunters* album and it sold like hotcakes in the young black community, everybody at Columbia said. "Oh. So that's what Miles was talking about!" But that was too late for *On the Corner*, and watching the way *Headhunters* sold just pissed me off even more.

While recovering from my car accident, I studied a lot more of Stockhausen's concepts of music. I got further and further into the idea of performance as a process. I had always written in a circular way and through Stockhausen I could see that I didn't want to ever play again from eight bars to eight bars, because I never end songs; they just keep going on. Some people around this time felt that I was trying to do too much, trying to do too many new things. They felt I should just stay where I was, stop growing, stop trying different kinds of things. But it don't go like that for me. Just because I was forty-seven years old in 1973 didn't mean I was supposed to sit down in some rocking chair and stop thinking about how to keep doing interesting things. I had to do what I was doing if I was going to keep thinking of myself as a *creative* artist.

Through Stockhausen I understood music as a process of elimination and addition. Like "yes" only means something after you have said "no." I was experimenting a lot, for example, telling a band to play rhythm and hold it and not react to what was going on; let me do the reacting. In a way I was becoming the lead singer in my band, and I felt that I had earned that right. The critics were getting on my nerves, saying that I had lost it, that I wanted to be young, that I didn't know what I was doing, that I wanted to be like Jimi Hendrix, or Sly Stone, or James Brown.

But with Mtume Heath and Pete Cosey joining us, most of the European sensibilities were gone from the band. Now the band settled down into a deep African thing, a deep African-American groove, with a lot of emphasis on drums and rhythm, and not on individual solos. From the time that Jimi Hendrix and I had gotten tight, I had wanted that kind of sound because the guitar can take you deep into the blues. But since I couldn't get Jimi or B. B. King, I had to settle for the next best player out there and most of them were white at that time. White guitar players—at least most of them—can't play rhythm guitar like black cats can, but I couldn't find a black guy who could play the way I wanted him to who wasn't leading his own band. (It stayed like this until I got my present guitarist, Foley McCreary.) I tried out Reggie Lucas (who has become a big record producer these days, doing Madonna's records), Pete Cosey (who was close in his playing to Jimi and Muddy Waters), and an African guy named Dominique Gaumont.

I would try exploring one chord with this band, one chord in a tune, trying to get everyone to master these small little simple things like rhythm. We would take a chord and make it work for five minutes with variations, cross rhythms, things like that. Say Al Foster is playing in 4/4, Mtume might be playing in 6/8, or 7/4, and the guitarist might be comping in another time signature, or another rhythm altogether different. That's a lot of intricate shit we were working off this one chord. But music is real mathematical, you know? Counting beats and time: shit like that. And then I was playing over and under and through all of this, and the pianist and bass were playing somewhere else. Everyone had to be alert to what everyone else was doing. At the time, Pete gave me that Jimi Hendrix and Muddy Waters sound that I wanted, and Dominique gave me that African rhythmic thing. I think that could have been a real good band if we had all stayed together, but we didn't. There was too much happening with my health.

I started to think about retiring from music seriously in 1974. I was in São Paulo, Brazil, and had been drinking all this vodka and I smoked some marijuana—which I never did, but I was having such a great time and they had told me it was so good. Plus I took some Percodan and was doing a lot of coke. When I got back to my hotel room, I thought I was having a heart attack. I called the front desk and they sent up a doctor and he put me in the hospital. They had tubes up my nose and IVs attached to me. The band was scared; everyone thought I was going to die. I thought to myself, This is it. But I pulled through that one. Jim Rose, my road manager, told everyone that I was probably just having heart palpitations from all the drugs and that I would be all right the next day, and I was. They had to cancel the show that night and reschedule it the following night. I played and blew everybody's mind I was playing so good.

They just couldn't believe it. One day I looked on the verge of death and then the next day I was playing my ass off. I guess they were looking at me the way I used to look at Bird, in total amazement. But that's the kind of stuff that makes legends. And I had a ball with all those beautiful women down in Brazil. They were all over me and I found them great in bed. They loved to make love.

After we got back from Brazil we started a tour of the United States playing with Herbie Hancock's group. Herbie had a big hit album and he was really well liked among the young black kids. We agreed to be his opening act. Deep down that pissed me off. When we played Hofstra University on Long Island in New York, Herbie—who is one of the nicest people on earth, and I love him—came back to my dressing room just to say hello. I told him that he wasn't in the band and that the dressing room was off limits to anybody who wasn't in the band. When I thought about it later. I realized that I was just angry about having to open up for one of my ex-sidemen. But Herbie understood and we cleaned it up later.

I was touring all over with Herbie and we were killing everybody. Most of the audiences were young and black and that was good. That's what I wanted, and I was finally getting there. My band was getting real hot and tight by this time. But my hip was a mess, and playing amplified was starting to get to me, too. I was just getting sick of everything, and on top of that, I was sick physically, too.

We played New York and a bunch of other cities. Then I went to St. Louis to play a concert and Irene, my children's mother, showed up at the party afterwards. She started just putting me down in front of my family and friends and musicians. It brought tears to my eyes. I remember the look on everybody's faces, like they were waiting for me just to knock Irene out. But I couldn't do that because I knew where her pain was coming from, from the fact that both our sons were failures and she was blaming me for that. Although it was embarrassing for me to hear it like that, I also knew that some of the things she was saying were true. I was crying because I knew I had to accept a lot of blame. It was a very painful experience.

Right after I saw Irene in St. Louis, I collapsed and they rushed me to Homer G. Phillips Hospital. I had a bad bleeding ulcer and a friend of mine, Dr. Weathers, came over and fixed me up. It was all that drinking and the pills and drugs and shit. I had been spitting up blood a lot but I wasn't really thinking about it until I got to St. Louis. I had been in and out of hospitals so much that it was almost becoming routine. I had just had nodes removed from my larynx. Now here I was in the hospital again. We were supposed to play Chicago the next day and so we had to cancel that.

When I finished all the gigs with Herbie and came back to New York in the summer of 1975, I was thinking seriously about quitting. I played Newport in 1975 and then played the Schaefer Music Festival in Central Park. Then I felt so sick that I canceled a concert I was scheduled to play in Miami. By the time I canceled, all my musicians and their equipment were already there and so the promoters of the concert kept all the sound equipment and tried to sue us. Right after this I decided to quit. By this time the band was Al Foster on drums, Pete Cosey on guitar, Reggie Lucas on guitar, Michael Henderson on bass, Sam Morrison (who had just replaced Sonny Fortune) on saxophone, and Mtume on percussions. I was doubling up on keyboards.

I quit primarily because of health reasons, but also because I was spiritually tired of all the bullshit I had been going through for all those long years. I felt artistically drained, tired. I didn't have anything else to say musically. I knew that I needed a rest and so I took one, the first one I had had since I had begun playing professionally. I thought that after I was a little better physically I would probably start to feel better spiritually also. I was sick and tired of going in and out of hospitals and hobbling around, on and off stage. I was beginning to see pity in people's eyes when they looked at me, and I hadn't seen that since I was a junkie. I didn't want that. I put down the thing I loved most in life—my music—until I could pull it all back together again.

I thought I might be gone for maybe six months, but the longer I stayed away the more uncertain I was whether I was going to come back at all. And the more I stayed away, the deeper I sank into another dark world, almost as dark as the one I had pulled myself out of when I was a junkie. Once again it was a long, painful road back to sanity and light. In the end it took almost six years and even then I was doubtful whether I could truly come all the way back.

FROM 1975 UNTIL early 1980 I didn't pick up my horn; for over four years, didn't pick it up once. I would walk by and look at it, then think about trying to play. But after a while I didn't even do that. It just went out of my mind because I was involved in doing other things; other things which mostly weren't good for me. But I did them anyway and, looking back, I don't have any guilt about doing them.

I had been involved in music continuously since I was twelve or thirteen years old. It was all I thought about, all I lived for, all I completely loved. I had been obsessed with it for thirty-six or thirty-seven straight years, and at forty-nine years of age. I needed a break from it, needed another perspective on everything I was doing in order to make a clean start and pull my life back together again. I wanted to play music, but I wanted to play it differently than I had in the past and I also wanted to play in big halls *all* the time instead of in little jazz clubs. For the time being, I was through with playing little jazz clubs because my music and its requirements had just outgrown them.

My health was also a factor, and it was getting harder and harder for me to play constantly like I was because my hip wasn't getting any better. I hated limping around the stage like I was, being in all that pain and taking all them drugs. It was a drag. I have a lot of pride in myself and in the way I look, the way I present myself. So I didn't like the way I was physically, and didn't like people looking at me with all that pity in their eyes. I couldn't stand that shit, man.

I couldn't play two weeks in a club without having to go to the hospital. Drinking so much, snorting all the time, and fucking all night. You can't do all of that and create music like you want to. You got to do one or the other. Artie Shaw told me one time, "Miles, you can't play that third concert in bed." What he meant was that if you do two concerts and you're doing all that other stuff, then that third concert you're supposed to play when you're doing one-nighters is going to be played in bed because you're going to be wasted. After a while, all that fucking ain't nothing but tits and asses and pussy. After a while there is no emotion in it because I put so much emotion into my music. The only reason I didn't get staggering drunk was because when I played all that shit came out of my pores. I never did get drunk when I drank a lot, but I would throw up the next day at exactly twelve noon. Tony Williams would come by some time in the morning and at 11:55 he would say, "Okay, Miles, you got exactly five minutes before it's time for you to throw up." And then he'd leave the room and I would go into the bathroom at exactly twelve o'clock and throw up.

Then there was the business side of the music industry, which is very tough and demanding and racist. I didn't like the way I was being treated by Columbia and by people who owned the jazz clubs. They treat you like a slave because they're giving you a little money, especially if you're black. They treated all their white stars like they were kings or queens, and I just hated that shit, especially since they were stealing all their shit from black music and trying to act black. Record companies were still pushing their white shit over all the black music and they *knew* that they had taken it from black people. But they didn't care. All the record companies were interested in at that time was making a lot of money and keeping their so-called black stars on the music plantation so that their white stars could just rip us off. All that just made me sicker than I was physically, made me sick spiritually, and so I just dropped out.

I had invested my money pretty good and Columbia still paid me for a couple of years while I was out of the music industry. We worked out a deal so that they could keep me on the label, and that was cool enough to keep some money coming from royalties. In the seventies, my deal with Columbia was that I got over a million dollars to deliver albums, plus royalties. Plus I had a few rich white ladies who saw to it that I didn't want for money. Mostly during those four or five years that I was out of music, I just took a lot of cocaine (about $500 a day at one point) and fucked all the women I could get into my house. I was also addicted to pills, like Percodan and Seconal, and I was drinking a lot, Heinekens and cognac. Mostly I snorted coke, but sometimes I would inject coke and heroin into my leg; it's called a speedball and it was what killed John Belushi. I didn't go out too often and when I did it was mostly to after-hours places up in Harlem where I just kept on getting high and living from day to day.

I'm not the best person in the world about picking up after myself and keeping a house clean and neat because I didn't never have to do any of that stuff. When I was young, either my mother or my sister, Dorothy, did it, and later my father had a maid. I've always been clean about my personal hygiene, but the other shit I never learned to do and, frankly, I didn't even think about doing it. When I started living by myself after I broke up with Frances, Cicely, Betty, Marguerite, and Jackie, the maids who I had during this time just stopped coming, I guess because of how crazy I was acting. They were probably afraid to be alone with me. I would have a maid from time to time but I couldn't keep anyone steady because cleaning up after me got to be a very big job. The house was a wreck, clothes everywhere, dirty dishes in the sink, newspapers and magazines all over the floor, beer bottles and garbage and trash everywhere. The roaches had a field day. Sometimes I would get someone to come in or one of my girlfriends would do it, but mostly the house was filthy and real dark and gloomy, like a dungeon. I didn't give a fuck because I never thought about it, except during those very few times that I was sober.

I became a hermit, hardly ever going outside. My only connection with the outside world was mostly through watching television—which was on around the clock—and the newspapers and magazines I was reading. Sometimes I got information from a few old friends who would drop by to see me to see if everything was all right, like Max Roach, Jack DeJohnette, Jackie Battle, Al Foster, Gil Evans (I saw Gil and Al more than anybody else), Dizzy Gillespie, Herbie Hancock, Ron Carter, Tony Williams, Philly Joe Jones, Richard Pryor, and Cicely Tyson. I got a lot of information from them but sometimes I wouldn't even let them come in.

I changed managers again through this period. I hired Mark Rothbaum, who had worked for my former manager Neil Reshen for a while, and later became Willie Nelson's manager. My road manager, Jim Rose, was around. But the person who was around the most after a while and who ran errands for me was a young black guy named Eric Engles, who I knew through his mother. Eric stayed with me most of the time during those silent years. If I didn't cook for myself or if one of my girlfriends didn't, Eric would run up to the Cellar, my friend Howard Johnson's place, and get me some fried chicken. It was good that I had Eric because there were times during this period when I didn't leave my house for six months or more.

When my old friends came by to see how I was living they would be shocked. But they didn't say nothing because I think they were afraid if they had, I would just put them out, which I would have. After a while many of my old musician friends stopped coming by, because a lot of time I wouldn't let them in. They got sick and tired of that shit so they just stopped coming. When all those rumors got out about me doing a lot of drugs during that time they were all on the money, because I was. Sex and drugs took the place that music had occupied in my life until then and I did both of them around the clock.

I had so many different women during this period that I lost track of most of them and don't even remember their names. If I met them on the street today I probably wouldn't even recognize most of them. They were there one night and gone the next day and that was that. Most of them are just a blur. Toward the end of my silent period, Cicely Tyson came back into my love life, although she had always been a friend and I would see her from time to time. Jackie Battle came by to check on me, but we were no longer lovers, just real good friends.

I was interested in what some people would call kinky sex, you know, getting it on in bed sometimes with more than one woman. Or sometimes I would watch them just freaking out on themselves. I enjoyed it, I ain't going to lie about that. It gave me a thrill—and during this period I was definitely into thrills.

Now, I know people reading this will probably think I hated women, or that I was crazy, or both. But I didn't hate women; I loved them, probably too much. I loved being with them—and still do—doing what a lot of men secretly wish they could do with a whole lot of beautiful women. For those men it's a dream, just some kind of fantasy, but I made it real in my life. A lot of women also want to do all these kinds of things, like be in bed with several handsome men—or women—doing everything they ever fantasized about in their secret imaginations. All I was doing was what my imagination told me to do, fulfilling my most secret desires and nothing else. I was doing it in private and wasn't hurting nobody else, and the women I was with loved it as much as or more than I did.

I know what I'm talking about here is disapproved of in a country that is as sexually conservative as the United States. I know that most people will consider all of this a sin against God. But I don't look at it that way. I was having a ball, and I don't regret ever having done it. And I don't have a guilty conscience, either. I would admit that taking all the cocaine that I was probably had something to do with it, because when you're snorting good cocaine your sex drive needs satisfaction. After a while, all of this got routine and boring, but only after I had had my fill of it.

A lot of people thought I had lost my mind, or was real close to losing it. Even my family had their doubts. My relationship with my sons—which was never what it should have been—hit rock bottom during this time, especially with Gregory, who was now calling himself Rahman. He would just cause me all kinds of grief, like getting arrested, getting into accidents, and just generally being a pain in the ass. I know he loved me and really wanted to be like me. He used to try to play trumpet, but he played so bad it was just terrible to listen to, and I would scream at him to stop. He and I were having a lot of arguments, and I know the way I was using drugs wasn't good for him to see. I know I wasn't a proper father, but that just wasn't my thing, never was.

In 1978 I went to jail for non-support. This time it was Marguerite who had me put there because I wasn't giving her any money for Erin. It cost me $10,000 to get out of jail and I have tried not to neglect that duty in my life since then. For the last few years, Erin has been staying and traveling with me, so now I have full responsibility for him.

When I didn't have coke my temper was real short and things would just get on my nerves. I couldn't handle that. I didn't listen to any music or read anything during this period. So I would snort coke, get tired of that because I wanted go to sleep, then take a sleeping pill. Even then, I didn't want to go to sleep, so I'd go out at four A.M. and prowl the streets like a werewolf or Dracula. I'd go to an after-hours joint, snort more coke, get tired of all the simple motherfuckers who hang out in those joints. So I'd leave, come home with a bitch, snort some, take a sleeping pill.

All I was doing was bouncing up and down. That was four people, because being a Gemini I'm already two. Two people without the coke and two more with the coke. I was four different people; two of them people had consciences and two didn't. I would look into the mirror and see a whole fucking movie, a horror movie. In the mirror I would see all those four faces. I was hallucinating all the time. Seeing things that weren't there, hearing shit that wasn't there. Four days without sleeping and taking all those drugs will do that to you.

I did some weird shit back in those days, too many weird things to describe. But I'll tell you a couple. I remember one day when I was really paranoid from snorting and staying up all the time. I was driving my Ferrari up West End Avenue and I passed these policemen sitting in a patrol car. They knew me—all of them knew me in my neighborhood—so they spoke to me. When I got about two blocks away from them, I became paranoid and thought that there was a conspiracy to get me, bust me for some drugs. I look down in the compartment on the door and see this white powder. I never took coke out of the house with me. It's winter and snowing and some snow got inside the car. But I didn't realize that; I thought it was some coke that someone had planted in the car just so I could get busted. I panicked, stopped the car in the middle of the street, ran into a building on West End Avenue, looked for the doorman, but he wasn't there. I ran to the elevator and got on and went up to the seventh floor and hid in the trash room. I stayed up there for hours with my Ferrari parked in the middle of West End Avenue with the keys in it. After a while I came to my senses. The car was still sitting where I had left it.

I did that another time just like that and a woman was on the elevator. I thought that I was still in my Ferrari, so I told her, "Bitch, what are you doing in my goddamn car!" And then I slapped her and ran out of the building. That's the kind of weird sick shit that a lot of drugs will make you do. She called the police and they arrested me and put me in the nut ward at Roosevelt Hospital for a few days before letting me out.

Another time, I had a white woman dealer and sometimes—when nobody was at my house—I would run over to her place to pick up some coke. One time I didn't have no money, so I asked her if I could give it to her later. I had always paid her and I was buying a lot of shit from her, but she told me, "No money, no cocaine, Miles." I tried to talk her into it, but she wasn't budging. Then the doorman calls upstairs and tells her her boyfriend is on his way up. So I ask her one more time, but she won't do it. So I just lay down on her bed, and started to take off my clothes. I know her boyfriend knows I got a reputation for being big with the ladies, so what's he going to think when he sees me on her bed like that? So now she's begging me to leave, right? But I'm just laying there with my dick in one hand and my other hand held out for the dope, and I'm grinning, too, because I know she's going to give it to me and she does. She cursed me like a motherfucker on my way out, and when the elevator opened and her boyfriend passed me, he kind of looked at me funny, you know, like, "Has this nigger been with my old lady?" I never went back by there after that.

After a while this shit got boring. I got tired of being fucked up all the time. When you're high like that all the time, people start taking advantage of you. I didn't never think about dying, like I hear some people do who snort a lot of coke. None of my old friends were coming around, except Max and Dizzy, who would come by just to check on me. Then I started to miss them guys, the old guys, the old days, the music we used to play. One day I put up all these pictures all over the house of Bird, Trane, Dizzy, Max, my old friends.

Around 1978, George Butler, who used to be at Blue Note Records but was now at Columbia, started calling me and dropping by. There had been changes at Columbia since I had left. Clive Davis was no longer there. The company was now run by Walter Yetnikoff, and Bruce Lundvall was over the so-called jazz arm of the company. There were still some old people who had been there when I retired, like Teo Macero and some others. When George started telling them that he would like to see if he could convince me to record again, a lot of them told him it was useless. They didn't believe I would ever play again. But George took it upon himself to convince me to come back. It wasn't easy for him. In the beginning I was so indifferent to what he was talking about that he must have thought I would never do it. But he was so goddamn persistent and so pleasant when he would come by, or call and talk on the telephone. Sometimes we would just sit around watching television and not saying nothing.

He wasn't exactly the kind of guy I had been hanging around with all these years. George is conservative and has a Ph.D. in music. He was an academic kind of guy, reserved, laid back. But he was black, and he seemed honest and really loved the music I had done in the past.

Sometimes we'd talk and then we'd get into when I was going to start playing again. At first I didn't want to talk about it, but the more he came, the more I thought about it. And then one day I started messing around on the piano, fingering out a few chords. It felt good! So more and more I started thinking about music again.

Around this same time, Cicely Tyson started coming to see me again. She had been dropping by throughout all of this, but now she started coming by more often. We had this real tight spiritual thing. She kind of knows when I'm not doing too well, when I'm sick and shit. Every time I would get sick, she would just show up because she could feel something was wrong with me. Even when I got shot that time in Brooklyn she said she knew something had happened to me. I used to always say to myself that if I ever married someone again after Betty, it would be Cicely. She just started coming around and I stopped seeing all those other women. She helped run all those people out of my house; she kind of protected me and started seeing that I ate the right things, and didn't drink as much. She helped get me off cocaine. She would feed me health foods, a lot of vegetables, and a whole lot of juices. She turned me on to acupuncture to help get my hip back in shape. All of a sudden I started thinking clearer, and that's when I really started thinking about music again.

Cicely also helped me understand that I had an addictive personality, and that I couldn't ever be just a social user of drugs again. I understood this, but I still took a snort or two now and then. At least I cut it way down with her help. I started drinking rum and Coke instead of cognac, but the

Heinekens stayed around for a little while longer. Cicely even got me off cigarettes; she taught me that they were a drug, too. She told me she didn't like kissing me with all that cigarette smell on my breath. She said she would stop kissing me if I didn't stop, so I did.

One of the other important reasons that I came back to music was because of my nephew Vincent Wilburn, my sister's son. I had given Vincent a set of drums when he was about seven, and he fell in love with them. When he was about nine I let him play a song with me and the band one time when we played in Chicago. He sounded pretty good for a kid even then. After he came out of high school, he went to the Chicago Conservatory of Music. So he was serious about music most of his life. Dorothy would complain about him and his friends always being down in the basement playing all the time. I just told her to leave him alone, because I was just like that. From time to time I would call and he would play something for me over the telephone. He could always play. But I would give him advice, tell him what to do and what not to do. Then when I didn't play for those four years or so, Vincent came to New York to stay with me. He would always be asking me to play something for him, show him this, show him that. I wasn't into doing that at the time, so I would just tell him, "Naw, Vincent, I don't feel like it." But he would stay on my case. "Uncle Miles"—he always called me "Uncle Miles," even after he was in my band—"Why don't you play something?" Sometimes he would get on my nerves with that shit. But he always kept music in front of me when he was there, and I used to look forward to his visits.

It was hell trying to get off all those drugs, but I eventually did because I have a very strong will to do whatever I put my mind to. That's what helped me to survive. I got it from my mother and father. I had had my rest and a whole lot of fun—and misery and pain—but I was ready to go back to music, to see what I had left. I knew it was there, at least I felt it was in me and had never left, but I didn't really know for sure. I was confident in my ability and my will to move on. During those years people were even saying that I'd been forgotten. Some people just wrote me off. But I ain't never listened to that kind of shit.

I really believe in myself, in my ability to make things happen in music. I never think about not being able to do something, especially music. I *knew* I could pick up my horn again whenever I wanted to, because my horn is as much a part of me as my eyes and hands. I knew it would take time to get back to where I was when I was *really* playing. I knew I had lost my embouchure because I hadn't played in so long. That would take time to build back up to where it was before I retired. But otherwise, I was ready when I gave George Butler a call in early 1980.

from

You'll Never Eat Lunch in This Town Again

Julia Phillips

ONE DAY JACK and I have a fight that precipitates his speedy departure in the middle of the night. I run after him, knock myself solidly into
the retaining wall. The next day my right side is swollen to twice the size
of my left side. Rottweiler and I have dinner and drugs together. It is
inevitable that we end up in bed.

OVO: And did we have fun?

ME: I can't remember . . .

Two days later, Jack calls from Oregon, where he has gone to visit his
daughters. 'We're a family, you and I,' he says. I look at Rottweiler eating
popcorn on the bed. I don't think so . . .

When Jack comes home, Rottweiler splits so I can end it with Jack in
person. He tries to convince me it's just a stage I'm going through, but I
blow him off definitively.

He's right. It is a stage, a downward stage, freebase turning liquid in the
stem of the pipe and melting into the dirty water . . .

WHILE ROTTWEILER IS designing an office, to be constructed
where the garage is, he comes up with the bright idea of a cactus garden,
marry the indoors with the outdoors. Very Hawaiian. I have a friend in

need of an urgent hemorrhoid operation who's in possession of a mutant peyote cactus. It looks like a brain. She wants two grand, but her ass is more painful daily. I get it for fifteen hundred dollars and her two faggot assistants show up that afternoon with plants and dirt. Rottweiler digs out a space in the garage. Basically he ends up building the room around the cactus.

Sometimes, when the water from the pipe is too dirty to recycle, I throw it into the dirt in which the cactus lives. The cactus grows some off-shoots. One looks like a pair of sagging breasts. I think of that offshoot as the female part of the plant. Then the plant starts to grow straight up, a giant dick. Right here, right in this office/drug room, right in my face. A personal affront that threatens to break through the ceiling . . .

THE SEDUCTIVE THING about freebase, for me anyway, is that at first I have the illusion that I am doing substantially less cocaine than if I toot it. My nose is very sore most of the time, and this pipe-smoking seems like a convenient method of intake.

More important, the high is substantially more dynamic.

I learn a rough recipe from a nice Jewish dealer in the Valley that involves dissolving the raw product in water, mixing it with a small amount of any household cleaner that has ammonia in it, then drying and rolling it around in a Melita coffee filter. It makes hard little rocks and we smoke it in water pipes or bongs.

We light it with whatever is around. Matches, a butane lighter. The problem with this method is that the yield is pretty low and it burns the shit out of your lungs. Also, you can tell that you are getting as high from the ammonia fumes as the coke.

IN ONE OF his many alcoholic wanders, Rottweiler finds a fucked-up chemist from northern California who comes over one morning while Rottweiler sleeps off a colossal bender and teaches me how to make elegant crystals that grow up to the sky. This is partially due to the fact that we use my product, reconstituted Miami shit—horrible to toot, but quite pure. Ergo: big yield. But it is also because Walter's method of production is quite different from what I already know.

Walter's recipe is much more complicated than the one I already know. He tells me that making the rock with household ammonia is very dangerous and can give you lesions on your lungs. This makes me fall over with laughter. Imagine these two freaks discussing anything that is bad for your health while we are batching up this noxious brew?

He laughs, too, and reveals horrible dog teeth. (I don't see such bad teeth on an American person again until Oliver North brightens up one day during the Iran Contra hearings on TV.) Walter bears a disturbing resemblance to Tony Bill, actually. A freaked-out, junked-out, weirder, dirtier Tony Bill, if that is possible.

Walter is very serious about this batching up of freebase. Which is the thing that reminds me most about Tony. He is so serious he takes the joy out of basing, which is not dissimilar from the way Tony made me feel about movies.

Walter is into the ceremony and the ritual of the making of the freebase. Extreme Coke Theater. Maybe he is trying to show me he isn't attached. Me, I've always been a results-oriented type. If you're going to fuck, come; if you're going to improve drugs, do it fast. Get to them before you're bored.

Walter sets his gear up in the office on the table that Rottweiler had made out of a sawblade. He has one of those kids' fold-out chemistry sets, with all the test tubes lined up in a wooden holder. I had a friend in college who kept all his pot in such a manner. An anal retentive hedonist, he also kept all his Marvel comic books in files, alphabetized and cross-referenced by subject, month, and year. His pot was labeled by dealer, year copped, and country of origin. It was a measure of how much he liked you, whether you got the Albanian '69 or the Moroccan '72.

Walter takes me through the steps for his method. First dilute the coke in water, a sad moment for me, because I am pretty sure it will never come back. Then add an equal amount of anhydrous ether. Oooh the smell: I have always been fond of ether smell and ether high. It makes a small horizon, like salt water over fresh water. Then the tiniest bit of ammonium hydroxide, to precipitate a reaction. It makes a thin, bright white line that separates the cocaine water from the ether. It reminds me for a second of the way Doug Trumball created the clouds forming over Jillian's house. Just salt over fresh water with some tempera shot through.

Now screw on the cap, and shake it up. He shows me what the mix looks like. Thick, like lamb placenta. Big fat bubbles gurgling around in slow motion.

He unscrews the cap, and the mixture fizzes and rushes to spill over, champagne for coconuts. Hastily he screws the cap on. 'This is why you need these screw-on caps. There's another kind with rubber caps, but they blow out and you lose everything.' He unscrews and rescrews the top several times, until there is no more fizz and the white line is gone. 'Now you just take this dropper and put the liquid above the water line into this petri dish, and let it dry.'

He blows on it lightly and spins the concave disk around on the glass-covered sawblade. Luminescent crystals start to grow. When everything turns white on the plate, and Walter pronounces it dry, he scrapes it with an industrial razor and produces a pipe. This pipe has nine thousand screens in it, to keep the base from melting down the stem when lit. He also produces a propane torch; it will burn cleaner, he proclaims, and lights it for me.

Freebase does not induce good manners, so I am kind of surprised he offers the pipe to me first, even though the product is mine. He holds on to the pipe, like he needs to have it the minute I am done, which adds an unnecessary element of urgency to the entire enterprise. It is already feeling urgent enough.

'Don't suck it so hard,' he says sharply. Whoa, this is a new one. He pulls the pipe away. 'Like this,' he inhales long and slow. The bowl fills with white smoke (there are those clouds again) and he passes the pipe to me. This time I take a nice long yoga breath, and he holds the torch for me. I can see that this is not a traveling kind of a drug. Bummer.

'Hold the smoke as long as you can and let it out slowly through your nose . . . ' Hey, just a minute, buster, who do you think you're dealing with here, Rebecca of Sunnybrook Farm? But I go along with his instructions anyway. Heyyyyyy noooowwwww. This is definitely better than that Melita crap. Makes that stuff like a toy. Ohhhh, bay-bay.

Bells go off in my ears, and UFOs dance in my peripheral vision. I have an impulse to stand up and lie down at the same time. I freeze. My heart is pounding the way it did when I inhaled Freon from a Baggie, and I wonder briefly if this is going to be the Big One. The Ultimate. Death. Trip. I wait . . . Nothing. Except . . .

This is just about the highest I've been, I think, and look around.

Weird to move. Little bells keep going off in my legs, which feel as if they have been painted by Salvador Dali. Puffs of sensation ebb and flow, and here is the real attraction—they all seem in sync with the ebb and flow of the universe, the macro and micro of it all—the heartbeat of the cosmos in concert with mine.

I stand up and the room goes spinning. I spin with it. Since this spinning is not accompanied by nausea, it is a completely pleasant experience.

'Wait. Wait . . . ' Walter's voice comes from far away but clear as a bell. Is he kidding? I'm not going anywhere. Oh, I get it. The pipe. I am still holding the pipe. Walter pulls out a balloon and blows his smoke into it. 'You must always recycle,' he says. I bend down and blow my smoke into his mouth. There's your cheap thrill. He hands me the balloon. 'Let it whoosh into your lungs,' he instructs.

I exhale all the air out of my mouth and suck on the balloon. If I could just figure out how to make this into a traveling light show, I would be sooooo happy. I am getting too little fresh air behind freebase. It is giving me headaches and making me feed on my soul. Couple of years later, when I found Ron Siegel, he told me this was called the Kindling Effect. The fire in your brain.

Walter and I smoke up the product and then he shows me how to burn the residue out of the pipe stem. It comes out gooey amber. Same procedure, only now the crystals are the color of topaz. Cleaner. Stronger. Better tasting. Am I going to have to have someone smoke my product first, a cat tasting food for the emperor, so I can have this niftier buzz? Well, there is always Rottweiler, whom I can hear stirring in the other room. What fresh hell will this be, I wonder, and puff, and do not care . . .

I AM BURNING the residue from the stem of the pipe and recycling cocaine-laced water when Ray Stark calls. David Parks, who has agreed to be my assistant only if I take a movie career seriously, squints at me. His squint says, If you don't take this call, I'm leaving.

'Hi, Ray,' I chirp, and his secretary says, 'I'll put Mr. Stark on.' It's always the same old shit, secretaries outwaiting each other, or putting both their bosses on at the same time; pecking-order bullshit, but I'm not attached. By the time he gets on the phone, I am shaking the cocaine water and the brown residue from the pipe in a little screw-top test tube.

'Hello, Julia,' Ray purrs. Since he usually likes to call me Laurie, I feel the conversation is going well. I add some anhydrous ether and take a whiff. What a great high, the ether. Some dealer has told me that in the late fifties, when Lord Buckley was big out here, and Lenny Bruce was doing bad impressions in strip joints, there was a circle of comedians, mostly, who were ether heads. They'd soak a towel with it and put the towel over their faces until the second before they passed out. Dr. Jekyll and Mr. Hyde.

The great thing about ether is that it whomps you and then it goes away with no perceptible side effects, although Reice Jones informs me years later that there is a high incidence of spontaneous abortion among nurses who work regularly in operating theaters.

'Hi, Ray. Long time no speak . . . '

'Well, not because your name doesn't come up from time to time . . . ' Yeah, as in, That bitch still alive?

'What can I do for you? I'm a little tied up right now . . . ' I add some ammonium hydrochloride, just enough to make a little white rim between the drugged-out water and the soon to be drug-rich ether.

'Well, what are you doing with yourself right now?'

'Taking a breather . . . ' I screw on the cap and shake it over my head, backup in a corny salsa band.

'I just think you're allowing yourself to be a wasted talent.' Ah, there's that phrase again.

'I think I was a wasted talent when I was doing it all . . . '

'How's your health?' You mean: still doing drugs? I watch the fat little bubbles and unscrew the cap gently. The mixture fizzes, and I close the cap again. Open close open close until it settles down. I find an eyedropper and a petri dish and start extracting my favorite brew.

'Never better,' I lie. I cover the mouthpiece and blow on the petri dish. Little amber crystals start to sprout. Ooh, I really love the chemistry of this drug . . .

'I have a little business idea I'd like to discuss with you. Want to come see me?' Is he summoning me? Fuck me . . . fuck you . . .

'I'm never going to Burbank again.' I smile. 'It fucks up my respiratory system for days . . . '

Ray laughs. 'Okay, how about if I come to see you?' Well, this *is* serious. I wonder what he has in mind.

'Okay,' I say, lying again. Ray Stark in my house? Too weird. Too funny not to try, though.

'When . . . '

'Well, I'm on my way out . . . how are you tomorrow?' There is always tomorrow.

'That'd be fine. Say two thirty, three? Right after lunch?' Hey, babe, I don't eat anymore, but whatever turns you on . . .

'I'll look forward to it, then . . . '

'See you tomorrow . . . '

'Tomorrow . . . ' He hangs up. Also part of the pecking order, who hangs up more abruptly. Who's busier. Hey, no contest here.

I look at the receiver, fall inside one of the holes in the mouthpiece for a moment, meander through a billion empty soundbites, return, and then I hang up, too. Hey, a billion isn't what it used to be . . .

'He's coming to see me tomorrow,' I tell David's questioning eyes. 'Phew, that wore me out . . . '

I check my crystals, my little babies. Ready! I find a clean pipe and some Evian, and get ready for the best hit of my life. 'Course, it's only the first hit that's the best hit. All the others are just chasing the memory of the first. The Chinese, whose brains are larger, call it chasing the dragon. For me, it opens up a number of possibilities, most of which lead to chaos. Not a bad place to be if one is contemplating an impending meeting with Ray Stark, who has the insulting proclivity for calling me Laurie when it suits him.

WHEN RAY ARRIVES promptly at two forty-five the next day, I keep him waiting, not out of power games, but because I am still taking that one last hit for the road in my bathroom. When I finally make my entrance, I find him seated in the cramped little anteroom between the kitchen and my bedroom on a far too cute and small wicker sofa. He is dressed a decade behind the times: plaid shirt, jeans, a cowboy belt with a huge turquoise buckle. He looks like a sad old queen.

Further, his jeans are too blue. I fixate on them for a moment, communing with the tightly woven blue-and-white threads. They start to separate and slink around on his thighs. Little snakes on Big Daddy Snake. I close my eyes and take a deep breath and wave them away in my mind.

When I open my eyes, they wave back. I sit next to him on the matching wicker rocking chair. As he talks, I start to rock.

'Miss making movies?' Always . . .

'I make them in my mind . . . ' Ray permits himself an imperceptible upturning of his mouth. I notice all these things, because my brain is goin' ninety.

'I'll get right to the point . . . ' Busy busy Ray. Places to go, people to see. I wonder what Jack is doing right now.

'Please . . . '

'How would you feel about coming to work for me . . . '

'Ray, you've been offering me a job since before *The Sting*. I'm not into a job . . . '

'What then . . . '

'What about a partnership . . . ' That oughtta get him outta here quick. 'You know, with exclusions of previous projects . . . a startup situation . . . ' the whole catastrophe . . .

'That'd be fine with me . . . ' What?! Moving along to Plan B, eh? I don't wanna be in business with anyone, least of all Ray, but it might structure my time. I have been noticing that I am spending more and more of it sucking freebase in my little basement room. On the in-between days, it bothers me. I show more enthusiasm for this concept than I really mean.

'Really? We could call it Ruthless and Ray . . . '

'Not really . . . there is just one condition,' he says, leaning forward and putting his hand on my knee in a gesture that is fatherly and salacious at the same time, 'just don't embarrass me in public . . . ' I take his hand off my knee and replace it on his own. I smile.

'Fine, as long as you don't embarrass me in . . . 'Slamdunk for the white girl! Ray laughs. He looks more feral than ever. Jagged, yellowing teeth emphasize the molelike aspects of his demeanor. How do these people make all this money and never straighten their teeth? In Ray's case, caps would be a better choice. I laugh back and set off little jingles of high-ness in every pore. It feels good, sitting and laughing and rocking with Ray.

The rest we do from memory. My people will call his people. In the pecking order my people make the first call, Ray leaves, ostensibly a happy man. I'm happy, too. Ostensibly. I power back to the basement room and puff away. I call Norman. He is delirious to make the first call.

'Norman, I need an office with an attached bathroom,' I add to his list of deal points, thinking ahead. I will need some place private to smoke my drugs. Norman assumes I want Ray to grant me important person status and thinks it will be no problem. Suck, Suck harder. Be a good girl. Swallow and try not to bite the dick that feeds you.

David Parks is jubilant. It is the first time in a month his cheeks have any color to them . . . he isn't even bothered by Rottweiler hulking, lurking, waiting for me to pass the pipe . . .

'Whaddya think is really going on?' he says, posing the question I've been asking myself. Has he been sent by Herbie Allen Hirschfield to neutralize me? Or were they all sitting around one day wondering out loud if it was time to kill me, and Ray raised his hand like that annoying kid with glasses in the first row in third grade, and said: I'll do it, I'll do it? Jesus, this drug feeds the paranoia. While I sleep, I have the occasional rational flash; it says: You are not that important to them. Probably Ray thinks he is doing me a favor. When I am smoking freebase, I flash: nobody does favors for free in Hollywood . . .

from

Easy Riders, Raging Bulls

Peter Biskind

"We poured all of ourselves into one movie, and if it didn't hit, our whole career went down with it. There are directors who, after certain titles, didn't have anything more left, any more fight."
— MARTIN SCORSESE

BY THE LATE '70s, there was a hard white snow falling on Hollywood. Coke was so widespread that people wore small gold spoons around their necks as jewelry. Drug connections became intimates, friends, and boyfriends. You went out to eat, you'd leave a line of coke on the table for the waitress as a tip. Scorsese, exhausted, in poor health, and fueled by a perpetual coke high, tried to do everything. He promiscuously took on several projects at once. Then, toward the end of *New York, New York*, producer Jonathan Taplin called. The Band was going to break up, and he asked Scorsese to shoot a documentary about the group's final concert on Thanksgiving Day 1976, which would become *The Last Waltz*. Without giving it a second thought, Scorsese agreed. "He never could resist Robbie Robertson and the Band," says Irwin Winkler, who produced *New York, New York*. In the frame of mind he was in, he figured he could cut the film at night while he edited the feature during the day. Adds

Taplin, "Marty was just so wired he could show up at any hour of the day or night, go into the editing room, do a sequence, and go on to the next thing."

After Julia Cameron moved out in January 1977, Robertson left his family to move into Scorsese's Mulholland Drive house. He had delusions about becoming a movie star, and Marty was his ticket. "We were the odd couple—looking for trouble," says Robertson. Reflects Sandy Weintraub, "It was a shame that Marty wasn't gay. The best relationship he ever had was probably with Robbie."

The Mulholland house was barely furnished, and notable for a seventeenth-century wooden crucifix concealing a dagger that hung over Marty's bed. His friends puzzled over the symbolism. The house looked like a hotel for transients, filled with the groupies, visiting filmmakers, musicians, and druggies who made up Scorsese's circle. The regulars, Steve Prince, Mardik Martin, Jay Cocks, and assorted hangers-on, used to gather in Scorsese's projection room in the garage—which doubled as Robertson's bedroom—and watch four or five movies a night. "Marty's house was blacked out with blinds," says Robertson, "soundproofed, and he installed an air system so you could breathe without opening the windows. We only had two problems: the light and the birds."

"We were like vampires," recalls Martin. "It was like, 'Oh no, the sun is coming up.' We never got to sleep before seven, eight A.M., for six months." Marty had also put in an elaborate security system, which invariably malfunctioned, bringing unwelcome visits from rent-a-cops. Outside of watching movies and doing drugs, Marty's only relaxation was playing with his collection of toy soldiers.

Marty had been taking pills since he was three, so by this time it was second nature to him. He took drugs like aspirin. He was still going up and down in weight. Coke depresses the appetite, but after going without food for two or three days, there was a lot of binge eating, a lot of junk food, anything that was at hand. Moreover, he and his friends needed booze to come down, so they knocked back a couple bottles of wine or vodka just to get to sleep. According to Taplin, "They would call the editor of *The Last Waltz*, Yeu-Bun Yee, in the middle of the night with ideas. They were so stoked they thought everyone else was up all night too."

"At first you felt like you could make five films at once," Scorsese recalls. "And then you wound up spending four days in bed every week because you were exhausted and your body couldn't take it." He had been in and out of the hospital a number of times with asthma attacks. "The doctor would say, 'Take these pills. You're suffering from exhaustion,' " says Robertson. "But we had places to go, people to see." The rule was, live-fast-and-leave-a-good-looking-corpse. Scorsese was convinced he wouldn't see forty. "It was a matter of pushing the envelope, of being bad, seeing how much you can do," he continues. "Embracing a way of life to its limit. I did a lot of drugs because I wanted to do a lot, I wanted to push all the way to the very very end, and see if I could die. That was the key thing, to see what it would be like getting close to death." This kind of recklessness lent his work a high passion that hoisted it above the ordinary, but it was dangerous. "I've always felt that there's something self-destructive in directors," says Ned Tanen—himself no slouch in that department—contemplating the sorry spectacle of the New Hollywood directors careening pell-mell down the mountain, arriving in a heap at the bottom, careers shattered, marriages sundered, friendships broken, lives in ruins. "I once asked Howard Hawks, my former father-in-law, about it, and he said, 'The studio system worked because we couldn't be excessive, we couldn't just do what we wanted to do.' "

One day there was a party at Winkler's home. Scorsese, Martin, and Robertson came late, stoned out of their minds, hung out by themselves at the far end of the pool. Scorsese was dressed in the crisp white suit he favored above all others. All of a sudden John Cassavetes walked up, pulled Marty aside, started in on him for doing drugs. "Whatsamatter with you?" he growled. "Why are you doing this, ruining yourself? You're fucking up your talent. Shape up." Scorsese broke out into a sweat. Cassavetes was a notorious drunk himself, but no one could call him on what he said, because they knew it was true.

De Niro had not given up on *Raging Bull.* But he was still having a hard time getting Scorsese's attention. Marty's personal life was in such turmoil he couldn't concentrate on his work. Despite his success, Scorsese was still extremely fragile, emotionally speaking, a state of affairs that doubtless stemmed from the aggravations of his childhood: his diminutive stature, his frailty, his perception of himself as unattractive. His feelings were easily hurt; he was quick to feel slighted and slow to forgive. He nursed grudges for years. He built a wall around himself. "He was lost personally," says Martin. "Secure as he was on a film set, he was very insecure with himself as a man, dealing with people." Martin once invited him to a party. "I said to him, 'We'll have a lot of fun, girls, orgies . . . ' He said, 'Nah . . . somebody will know who I am . . . ' I said, 'You don't have to tell them who you are. Nobody cares.' He said, 'No, no, no, I can't deal with a woman who doesn't know who I am.' He had to be 'Martin Scorsese' for him to deal with a woman, but then he worried she would only like him because he was 'Martin Scorsese.' "

"I was making love to different women, but I didn't find that very interesting," Scorsese recalls. He was doing it more, enjoying it less. He got into a tempestuous relationship with an assistant, and one night he went to a party where he encountered her, Liza Minnelli, and Julia Cameron, all at the same time. She was the kind of woman who always had another man in her life, which drove Marty insane with jealousy. She threatened suicide every other day, which is to say, she was perfect for him. "Marty sort of likes a little bit of drama, and if it's not there, he creates it," says Martin. "It was a typical living-dangerously mentality. She brought out the worst in him." Scorsese could never stand to be alone. One night, he drove her out and then ran naked down Mulholland after her, screaming, "Come back, don't leave me."

Scorsese knew he was acting badly, driving people away from him, but he couldn't help it. He says, "I was always angry, throwing glasses, provoking people, really unpleasant to be around. I always found, no matter what anybody said, something to take offense at. I'd be the host, but at some point during the evening I'd flip out, just like when I'm shooting." He began to have paranoid hallucinations. He'd say, "I think somebody's watching me," or, "Somebody's trying to get in." Marty had a one-night stand with Yeu-Bun Yee's girlfriend, who looked like a model, and was afraid that he would come up in the middle of the night and kill him. One of Steve Prince's jobs was to protect him from real or imagined dangers.

Scorsese and Robertson took *The Last Waltz* to Cannes in the spring of 1978. Fueled by coke, Marty was doing back-to-back interviews, but even he eventually ran out of words. And coke. He joked, "No more coke, no more interviews." He couldn't score in Cannes, so a private plane was dispatched to Paris to bring back more coke.

"It hit me finally, when I was watching the end credits crawl of *The Last Waltz* at the Cinerama Dome, that I didn't enjoy it anymore," says

Scorsese. "There was nothing left. I knew when I broke up the second marriage—I had a child, I knew I was not going to see the child for a while—but I always had a bottom line: the work, and felt good about having been able to say something in a movie, but this one day, it was like rock bottom. I thought, I've lost my voice."

Scorsese kept everyone at bay, just yessing them to death, but refusing to move forward on *Raging Bull*. He was emotionally and spiritually tapped out. "We were just circling the globe constantly, going from party to party, trying to find what it was that would inspire us again to do work," he recalls. "I knew what I wanted to say in *Mean Streets*, like I knew what I wanted to say in *Taxi Driver*. I even knew what I wanted to say in *New York, New York*. But I know I didn't know what the hell *Raging Bull* was about." He had done three straight pictures with De Niro. "After a while, you want to do movies just on your own, especially after the unhappy experience with *New York, New York*," he adds. "I just didn't want to play anymore."

Mardik was already on salary at Winkler's company, in which he was partnered with Robert Chartoff. Winkler told him to go ahead anyway, write a script. Mardik did a draft, which Scorsese couldn't even bring himself to read. One day, after Mardik pestered him for the hundredth time, the director asked, "Okay, whaddya got?"

"I got one good scene that you're gonna like. You have these gladiators, see, just like in Rome, two guys, fighting each other, and you got all these rich people, fur coats, tuxedos, sitting in the front row, and Bobby gets punched in the face, and his nose starts to squirt blood, and it splatters all over these rich people's clothes and furs."

"Whew, that's great, I love that. Lemme read the script." Scorsese read the script, told Mardik, "I wanna make it more personal." His grandfather, who used to live on Staten Island, owned a fine fig tree, and one day he said, "If the fig tree dies, I'm gonna die." And sure enough, the fig tree died, and he died. Recalls Mardik, "He wanted me to put that in the movie, a lot of crazy stuff that had nothing to do with Jake La Motta. I didn't want him to say no, so I catered to his whims and bullshit. It was driving me crazy. I said, 'Marty. I don't think this makes any sense, Bobby's gonna kill me.' " Indeed, De Niro hated it, said, "What's going on? This is not the picture we agreed upon."

Continues Mardik, "One day, Marty said to me, 'Whaddya think of

Paul Schrader coming in for a polish.' Because Marty was not listening to me anymore, he was doing his Godfather bit. I said, 'Sure, why not.' Paul didn't even come to me. He sent somebody to get all my research, all my versions, three of them. I gave it to the guy, said, 'Good luck.' "

SCHRADER TOOK TO coke like mother's milk; he plunged into the drug scene with the enthusiasm of a lapsed fundamentalist. Like Scorsese, he believed coke helped him creatively. He had always been in the habit of writing while intoxicated, so the transition to drugs was easy. "I would write stoned and revise sober," he says. "When you're very, very stoned you have access to fantasies that are harder to get at when you're straight, particularly for somebody like me that didn't have access to that inner life. The prose gets sometimes a little excessive, and the syntax gets a little wacked. But it's basically what you want to say, and often, very, very, very alive. I would write a scene at three o'clock in the morning, and I would be all jacked up, so excited I would be singing and dancing around the room. Substance abuse was the key that opened that door. It would be hypocritical to look back and blame the key."

A gram cost about $100 in the late '70s, which included the packaging and the convenience of delivery. (It was cheaper on the street.) Schrader's dealer supplied grams in little envelopes fashioned from pages torn out of *Playboy* and *Penthouse*, with the grade (the highest was SG— Show Girl), marked on the front. Schrader was doing an ounce (twenty-eight grams) a week, a habit that cost him about $12,000 a month, or $144,000 a year. He bought a quarter of an ounce (seven grams) at a time, never more than nineteen grams, because in a bust, twenty grams could pull down a conviction for dealing, rather than mere possession.

Schrader was working hard and playing hard. He became very much a part of the gay party scene, which he had been flirting with since the *Taxi Driver* days in 1975. "This was a kind of heady period, where for the first time in American culture, gay choices about music, clothes, design were considered to be the future," says Rosenman. "This was the cutting edge, but it was so exciting and gorgeous and glamorous that everybody knew that it was leading toward an abyss. And that was attractive in and of itself. There was a mystic wildness about the partying, the music, the drugs, the clothes, the free sexuality—the interchange of partners, the constant fucking of boys, girls, it was so shocking and exhilarating. People like Schrader were attracted to it because they understood there was something religious in the intertwining of sex, death, and ecstasy."

Schrader's friends wondered how far Schrader went. Although it would be hard to imagine a less sympathetic audience than the gun-crazed Milius, Schrader used to lecture his friend on the importance of the gay aesthetic. "The arbiters of taste in our society are gay. Most of my friends are gay."

"Well, Paul, are you gay?"

"I can't do it, I can't even succeed here."

Says Milius, "Schrader was this character who had fallen from his Calvinist grace, and was really enjoying his time in hell, sampling every part of it. He loved perversion, but all sexuality in some way was a failure for him. One night, when he was making *Hardcore*, I noticed his wrists were marked. He explained, 'I went to Mistress Vicky and she hung me up and cuffed me. I could only take it for three minutes.' Like, he wasn't a true pervert. He couldn't take it for a half an hour like a real-man pervert. The same thing with being gay, he failed at that too, couldn't get it up for boys."

But Schrader's sexual preferences were less interesting than his cultural ones. For a while, at any rate, he was able to anticipate the sudden and not so sudden changes in the cultural weather, and when he joked to Milius that he'd exchanged "violence for design," he was expressing more than a personal inclination. As Kael noted, there was a rising revulsion against violence in movies. Schrader's carefully nurtured reputation as a wild man had run its course and was now a liability. Whereas *Time's* cover story on *Bonnie and Clyde* in December 1967 lauded shockers like *Point Blank*, in October 1980, Schrader was featured on the cover of *Saturday Review* with Scorsese, De Palma, and Walter Hill under the cover line, "The Brutalists: Making Movies Mean and Ugly." He recalls, "I started getting labeled as a filmmaker who was only into violence. I winced at that, realized I really had to change my image." It was part of the backlash against the New Hollywood—and Schrader sensed that what worked for *Taxi Driver* would work no longer.

DURING THE LAST week of *Hardcore*, when De Niro paid a visit to the set, Schrader knew something was up. The actor was not the sort to

casually drop by. He told Schrader that UA wouldn't make *Raging Bull*
with Mardik's script; he asked Schrader to rewrite it. He also told him he
was fed up with Scorsese's indifference to the project. By that time,
Schrader had firmly established himself as a director, and he was not
eager to work on other people's scripts. At a dinner with Bob and Marty at
Musso and Frank's Grill in the summer of 1978, he agreed to do a polish,
but he made sure they knew he was doing them a favor. This did not sit
well with Marty.

After reading Mardik's drafts. Schrader concluded that more was
needed than just a fix. He knew he had to go back to the sources, do his
own research. It was then that he discovered Jake's brother, Joey. Recalls
Schrader, "They were both boxers. Joey was younger, better looking, and
a real smooth talker. It occurred to Joey that he could do better at manag-
ing his brother. He wouldn't have to get beat up, he'd still get the girls,
and he would get the money. And having a brother myself, it was very
easy for me to tap into that tension. I realized there was a movie there."
Raging Bull, among other things, became a version of Schrader's relationship with Leonard.

Meanwhile, the movie was coming together for De Niro. One day, at
Scorsese's suite in the Sherry, La Motta just got up and banged his head
against the wall. Recalls Scorsese, "De Niro saw this movement and suddenly he got the whole character from him, the whole movie. We knew
we wanted to make a movie that would reach a man at the point of making that gesture with the line. 'I'm not an animal.' "

Schrader wrote at Nickodell's, a bar on Melrose next to Paramount
that, in Simpson's words, "was a great place to get fucked up, because it
was dark and cavernous." He remembers Schrader retiring to the bathroom for some moments, then emerging to take a seat at the bar, where
he feverishly scribbled on a napkin. It was a scene in which La Motta, in
jail and at the nadir of his fortunes, tries to masturbate. But he can't get
off, because his mind is flooded with guilt, memories of how terrible he's
been to the various women in his life. This was Schrader at his best, going
places nobody else would go, raw and fearless.

But material of this kind was way too rich for UA. Winkler met with
the executives at Eric Pleskow's apartment on Ocean Avenue in Santa
Monica, near the beach. "We'd just done a boxing movie, *Rocky*," recalls
Medavoy, "and this was a real downer." According to Winkler, the com-

pany wanted no part of *Raging Bull*. Still, the producer had a trump. "We were in a unique position, 'cause we owned the rights to *Rocky*," he says. UA had released *Rocky* in 1976. It was one of the coming crop of post-New Hollywood feel-good films, a throwback to the '50s, and a peek at the '80s, a racist, Great White Hope slap at Muhammad Ali—on whom the character of Rocky's opponent was all too obviously based—and everything he stood for, the generation of uppity black folk and the anti-war, "nigger-loving" white kids who admired him. *Rocky* was a huge success, taking in about $110 million before it played out, making it the fifth highest grossing picture of all time. So all Winkler had to say was, "Want to make *Raging Bull*? No? Want to make *Rocky II*? Yes? Okay, let's make a deal."

Even the writer of *Taxi Driver* found the characters repellent. Schrader told Marty, "We have to give Jake a depth, a stature he does not possess, otherwise he's not worth making a movie about." He says Scorsese didn't get it. For Scorsese, Jake's Neanderthal sensibility was the whole point. "Bob and I sort of pushed each other in terms of how unpleasant a character could be, and still people cared for him," he says. "Because there's something in Bob as an actor, something about his face, that people see the humanity."

Scorsese, De Niro, and Winkler met with Schrader at the Sherry to discuss the script. It was a tense meeting. Marty thought Schrader's new draft was a breakthrough. He too responded to the sibling aspects of the script. Still, both he and De Niro had reservations. Recalls Schrader, "De Niro was balking at a lot of the heavier stuff, the raw, controversial stuff, the cock and the ice and all that, 'Why do we have to do these things?' Marty wasn't going to take on Bob, because he had to work with him, so he was letting me fight those fights. It was a bold, original kind of scene. But looking at it from De Niro's point of view, it was pretty hard to make it work, sitting there with your dick in your hand." To Marty and Bob, Schrader's attitude was, Here's your script, I don't need this, I want to get back to my own projects. At one point, Paul threw the script across the room, yelling. "If you want a secretary to take dictation, hire one. But I'm here to try to write a real story about someone that people care about," and stormed out. Says Scorsese, "I'll do anything and say anything to get what I want on the screen. Throw something at me, curse at me, do what you want to do as long as I get what I want. I sit there and smile and take it and run, which is what I did. He broke the icejam and gave us something special. But I certainly couldn't embrace the person afterward. Not after years of slights and insults, it was just too much."

But Scorsese's world came crashing down around his ears right after Labor Day 1978. He had been living with Isabella Rossellini since early summer. He, Rossellini, De Niro, and Martin, went to the Telluride Film Festival. "We didn't have any coke, somebody gave us some garbage, it made us sick," recalls Mardik. That weekend, Scorsese started coughing up blood, and blacked out for the first time in his life. From Telluride, he went to New York, where he collapsed. "He was bleeding from his mouth, bleeding from his nose, bleeding from his eyes, ass. He was very near death," Martin adds. Rossellini had to go to Italy for work, and when she left, after that weekend, she thought she was never going to see him alive again.

Steve Prince took Scorsese to New York Hospital. A doctor came running down to the ER carrying a sample of his blood, yelling. "Is this your blood?"

"Yeah," Scorsese replied, blankly.

"Do you realize you have no platelets?"

"I don't know what that means."

"It means you're bleeding internally everywhere."

"I want to get back to work."

"You can't go anywhere, you may get a brain hemorrhage any second."

Scorsese's condition appeared to be a result of the interaction among his asthma medication, other prescription drugs, and the bad coke he had taken over the weekend. He was down to 109 pounds. The doctor stopped all the drugs and pumped him full of cortisone. He was put in a palatial room previously occupied by the Shah of Iran, but he couldn't sleep, and the first three nights he stayed up watching movies, among them, *Dr. Jekyll and Mr. Hyde*, appropriately enough. Eventually, the cortisone worked, and his platelet count started to rise, stopping the bleeding.

"Finally," says Robertson, "Marty got a doctor who conveyed the message that either he changed his life or he was going to die. We knew we had to change trains. Our lives were way too rich. The cholesterol level was unimaginable. I went back to my family, hoping they would overlook my fool heart."

De Niro came into Scorsese's room, said, "What's the matter with you,

Marty? Don't you wanna live to see if your daughter is gonna grow up and get married? Are you gonna be one of those flash-in-the-pan directors who does a couple of good movies and it's over for them?" He changed the subject to *Raging Bull*, said, "You know, we can make this picture. We can really do a great job. Are we doing it or not?" Scorsese replied, "Yes." He had finally found the hook: the self-destructiveness, the wanton damage to the people around him, just for its own sake. He thought: I am Jake.

from

High Concept: Don Simpson and the Hollywood Culture of Excess

Charles Fleming

AVOIDING NARCOTICS IN Hollywood in the 1980s was as difficult as avoiding the Southern California sun. Drugs were everywhere, and cocaine was king, the champagne of recreational stimulants. Demand and supply rose dramatically in the early part of the decade, as price fell and availability increased. According to the National Household Survey, the number of occasional users of cocaine rose between 1974 and 1985 from 5.4 million to 22.2 million. Frequent users increased fivefold over the same period. The number of high school students who used cocaine over the same period doubled. By another barometer, cocaine usage was rising at a staggering rate: Emergency room treatments for cocaine-related medical problems increased 200 percent between 1981 and 1985. The rate of cocaine-induced deaths tripled over the same period. The appearance of cocaine at Hollywood parties was as common as chips and guacamole a decade before.

The social uses of cocaine were myriad: It was a terrific icebreaker, an instant pick-me-up and a great come-on. *Everything* went better with coke. It stimulated conversation and intellectual activity, and increased sexual appetite and prowess. It didn't leave telltale odors or next-day hangovers. It wasn't passé, like marijuana or martinis, and it wasn't deadly, like heroin. It was portable and easy to hide. Ingesting it required no "kit," no special equipment. And, as an added bonus, it was just expensive enough that the *hoi polloi* couldn't afford it. Like other staples of the upscale 1980s—the health club membership, the record company jacket, the BMW or Mercedes, the club bouncer who knew your name—cocaine was a status symbol that said its user was young, hip and alive. "It was the ultimate drug for the times, and the ultimate metaphor for the period," said novelist Jay McInerney, whose *Bright Lights, Big City*, among other works, chronicled yuppie cocaine use in the 1980s. "It was the perfect consumer product—the more you get, the more you want. And it was *fun*."

It was also the ultimate high—and the ultimate metaphor—for movies Simpson wanted to make. Like a good cocaine high, Simpson's movies blasted from moment to moment, each scene and stunt and joke a jolt of adrenaline, until the viewer, like the user, was giddy with sensory over-stimulation. There was nothing tangible left when it was over, in either case, and not much memory of what had passed—just the happy, visceral sensation of having had a good time.

Coke was everywhere you wanted to be, too. At trendy restaurants, nightclubs, bars or private parties, any reasonably attentive person could locate cocaine in any reasonably private location—usually the bathroom. "It was impossible to take a piss," remembered producer Joel Silver, a non-drug user who found cocaine's pan-evidence irritating. "There were six people in every bathroom at every party and in every nightclub in town. You'd have to *pretend* you wanted to do drugs just to get into the bathroom."

Simpson wasn't pretending. He fully embraced drugs in the 1980s, turning what had been an aggressively pursued recreational habit into a full-scale addiction. "Don was in trouble with drugs before *anybody* was in trouble with drugs," observed Simpson's longtime friend actor Gary Woods.

In the beginning, for Simpson, as for many users, cocaine was fun. In Hollywood, hanging out with Steve Roth, or in New York, hanging out with McInerney, it was about having a good time. On a typical evening out in Manhattan, McInerney said, he and Simpson would dine, get high and then spend the rest of the night hitting the hot nightclubs. "It was drinking, doing drugs and looking at women—all night long," McInerney said. "Don was enormously entertaining, and we were both rising 'bad boys,' and the idea was to have fun. New York was my town, and I was showing him the fun." McInerney organized the evenings and kept the supply of drugs coming. "It was my role to show Don what was happening, and the places you wanted to go were the places where drugs were always available."

In Hollywood, Simpson already knew where those places were.

"J.R." is a tall, lanky man who wears his dark brown hair in a long ponytail and describes himself as "sort of English Jewish looking, a real music industry type." He resembles the actor Keith Carradine, and he's a cocaine dealer. Now semiretired, J.R. was the coke king of the Sunset Strip in the late 1980s. Simpson was a client.

J.R. had come to Los Angeles intending to hit big as a guitar player. He was good, but he wasn't good enough to distinguish himself among the thousands of other guitar players who'd come to town with the same dream. Many of them got work playing casuals at weddings and bar mitzvahs, playing lounge music at Holiday Inns, doing session work in recording studios or teaching music to younger guitar players whose dreams had not yet yielded to reality. J.R. was broke and had an expensive speed habit when a friend loaned him some cash, gave him a pager and a client list and sent him to work selling drugs.

J.R. had a good head for business and a keen interest in avoiding arrest. He put the two together to form an ingenious sales stratagem. Every afternoon of the week he would meet up with "Frank," a homeless man he'd befriended after a sidewalk encounter. J.R. would give Frank a collection of "bindles," cocaine wrapped in plastic or in glossy magazine paper folded, origami style, into small packets. The bindles came in different sizes and were priced at different rates. Frank would pack twenty-dollar bindles in one pocket, fifty-dollar bindles in another, hundred-dollar bindles in another. Frank took his work seriously and stayed in character: He never bathed, never washed his hair or clothing, and before starting work would assiduously urinate on himself to intensify his homeless-person odor. After sundown Frank would make his way by public bus to the Sunset Strip, where he would park himself on the curb outside the Rainbow Bar & Grill, the famed music industry watering hole.

By 9:00 P.M. J.R. would be at his usual table inside. Working the room with him would be two or three of his "girls," usually music industry groupies who supported their drug habit by helping J.R. deliver the goods. J.R. would sit sipping champagne. A client would drop by his table to ask if J.R. could hook him up. J.R. would tell the client, "Talk to one of my girls," and send the client away from the table. A girl would presently come to J.R.'s table and say, "He needs a fifty." J.R. would tell the girl to get the money. He would then wander outside to the Rainbow parking lot, check for police presence and then stroll out to the curb. He would pretend to make a phone call on the public telephone there. When he was finished, the homeless Frank would ask him for money. J.R. would shout at him loudly, saying, "Fuck off," or "Get a life, you piece of shit," and then give him fifty cents. While passing the money, J.R. would in return be given a fifty-dollar bindle—or a twenty-dollar bindle if he'd given Frank a quarter, or a hundred-dollar bindle if he'd given Frank a dollar bill. J.R. would then walk the fifty feet back into the club and hand the bindle to his girl, who would later give him the cash.

It was a fine system. J.R. himself would only be in possession of drugs for the time it took him to walk from the curb into the club, and he would only be in possession of a small amount. His girls did the actual transaction. The homeless Frank, who looked, acted and smelled the part of a harmless street bum—and who was therefore unlikely to be searched by even the most dedicated policeman—carried all the inventory. J.R. often turned $5,000 in sales in a single night.

His bulk drug business was pretty good, too. Through connections in Texas and New Orleans, J.R. would buy large quantities of cocaine. Through a car shipping business that formed the front for his drug import business, he would have Louisiana associates stuff automobiles with drugs and then ship the cars to Los Angeles. J.R. would pick up the cars, unload the drugs and bill the customer shipping charges on the car. For reasons J.R. cannot explain, his front was never exposed and he himself was never busted. He came close, one night at the Rainbow, when a friend told him the cops were outside looking for a guy with long brown hair who wore a beret and a long black leather trench coat—J.R.'s signature nighttime attire. J.R. dashed into a bathroom, where he found a guy in a ratty leather jacket. He complimented the man on the jacket and then proposed that they switch. The man agreed. J.R. said, "There's this crazy chick here, chasing me. I need to ditch her. I'll trade jackets with you if you'll just put on my coat, walk out to the sidewalk, then turn left. There's $1,000 in cash in the pocket, and that's yours, too, if you'll just do that." The man happily agreed. They switched coats and the man swaggered out of the Rainbow. J.R. waited at the door, watching until the cops noticed the man in the long black leather coat. When they approached him, J.R. dashed across the parking lot and hid in the back of his friend Al the Limo Guy's limousine. The last thing he saw before crawling into the trunk was the unhappy new owner of his trench coat crumpling to the sidewalk as six cops with billy clubs worked him over.

In the early days most of J.R.'s customers were from the music industry. One night a friend named Gina asked if he'd sell $100 worth of cocaine to two friends sitting in a limo outside the Rainbow. The friends were a vastly successful pop siren and her comedienne companion. J.R. went outside and was introduced to them and sat in the back of the limo for a half hour as the two women went through a gram. Then he sold them three more grams and watched as they snorted at that before driving off into the night. Vince Neil, of Mötley Crüe, was a steady customer—but an irritant. Neil would call J.R. and ask him to deliver a gram to the recording studio where, usually in the company of several half-naked women, he and the band were working. A half hour later he'd call back, wanting an eighth of an ounce. He'd then call again for another gram. A frustrated J.R. would plead with him, "Why don't you just buy a whole ounce, so I don't have to keep coming back?" Neil would scream, "Just bring me the fucking stuff—I'll give you an extra $250." Sometimes the entire Guns N' Roses group would sit at the main "Kings Table" at the Rainbow, making steady purchases all night long. Members of the Allman Brothers and Van Halen would stop by. J.R. felt like a celebrity and found that, soon, what was hip in the music industry was becoming hip in the film and TV industries as well.

He sold dope to Kelsey Grammer at the Vampire Room. He dealt to Charlie Sheen, who mostly bought $200 to $300 at a time, at the Rainbow, or at another club J.R. worked called Roxbury. Billy Idol would make his purchases at the Rainbow, a gram at a time, gram after gram, until the early morning hours. At the Viper Club, J.R. would sit at the "Dragon Table" and wait for customers to approach him. River Phoenix bought cocaine, which he mixed with Valium and Xanax.

J.R. wasn't Phoenix's only supplier. A dealer who goes by the name Nicky sold Phoenix speed several times in the years before the young actor died on the sidewalk outside the Viper Room. One night, in fact, four years before that tragedy, Phoenix nearly died in Nicky's apartment. The dealer remembered that Phoenix had stopped by to score some speed. He shot up while Nicky and a friend watched. In a scene stolen from Quentin Tarantino's *Pulp Fiction*, Phoenix overdosed, passing out and, Nicky recalled, "going totally code blue." Nicky and his friend were experienced drug users, though. "We knew what to do," the dealer said. "We packed his genitals in ice and got his heart beating again. When he came to, he said, 'I was gone, wasn't I?' He *knew*, man." An hour later, fully recovered, Phoenix said to Nicky, "I hope you guys would have done the right thing and thrown me in a Dumpster if I hadn't come out of it."

Don Simpson had out-of-town dealers as well and knew where to go for the highest-quality rocket fuel in other cities. In New York, according to a close friend from the early 1980s, he stumbled onto a blow monkey's dream. His regular dealer was about to be busted, so she took a recent Colombian shipment and hid it in a closet in her parents' apartment on the Lower East Side. Then she got busted. She told her mother, "There's something valuable in the closet. If you ever need money, you can sell it." When the family ultimately did need money, her mother went for the cocaine. What she failed to realize was that it was almost pure cocaine and had not yet been "cut" for street sales. For a while, Simpson and his friend got pure, full-strength cocaine at bargain-basement prices.

In Los Angeles J.R. wasn't Simpson's only dealer. J.R.'s principal Sunset Strip competition was Rayce Newman.

Newman was a tall, pale, rangy kid from Ventura, California, who in 1980 had come south to Los Angeles to enter the big-time drug dealing business. He was eighteen years old and had gotten regular bit work as an actor before he discovered cocaine. He'd developed a habit and discovered that dealing drugs was the best way to satisfy it. After dealing out of a Ventura nightclub called Garfield's, he got fired. A high school friend named Belinda invited him down to Los Angeles, where she was hooking for Madam Alex. Soon Newman was escorting Belinda to parties and meeting her clients. One night they attended a wrap party for a movie called *Transylvania 6-500*, starring Jeff Goldblum and Ed Begley Jr., held at a nightclub called Tramps. A producer named Jonathan Axelrod took Rayce into the bathroom for a hit of coke—low-quality coke, as it happened. Newman returned the favor, and Axelrod liked his cocaine better. The pair wound up spending two days at Axelrod's house, partying until

the drugs ran out. By the time he left, everyone at the party had Newman's telephone number, and his career as a Hollywood cocaine dealer
was on.

Newman met Don Simpson at a party thrown by music impresario
Richard Perry, at the Sunset Plaza house Perry had bought from Ronald
and Nancy Reagan. There were music business people like Don Henley
and Rod Stewart, and music mogul-turned-movie producer Ted Field, and
movie producer Joel Silver. After the introduction, Simpson and Newman
would meet on the Strip circuit, at Tramps, Voila, Carlos 'n' Charlie's,
Helena's and Vertigo.

Newman had a rhythm for the circuit. On Monday night he'd be at the
China Club on Beverly, where he'd do drugs with Simpson, Henley,
Stephen Stills and others, in the downstairs bathroom. On Tuesday night it
was Roxbury, where there was a convenient walk-in closet off the kitchen.
Wednesday night was Bar One, at the westernmost end of the Strip, where
there was a convenient upstairs office. Thursday night was Stringfellows,
on Rodeo Drive, in Beverly Hills. Friday night was the big night of the
week, and Newman would serially work Vertigo, Carlos 'n' Charlie's and
Roxbury. Simpson would usually buy a gram at a time, or sometimes an
eighth of an ounce. He'd often ask Newman, "Can I owe you?" but he was
always good for the money. Newman would sometimes drop off cocaine at
Simpson's house or at the studio—once actually pretending to deliver a
script, which he deposited on a silver tray in front of Simpson and several
Paramount executives while Simpson conducted a business meeting. After
1991, Newman recalled, Simpson stopped making the circuit and became
more of a stay-at-home user who didn't socialize.

But Newman was very social, and he was having fun. Unlike J.R., he
partied with the clients. He'd snort cocaine with Charlie Sheen, who'd
return the favor by phoning Heidi Fleiss and having girls sent over for both
of them. He and Robert Downey Jr. and Julian Lennon would rent a suite
at the Mondrian Hotel and stay high for three or four days at a time, snorting or freebasing cocaine. (Newman seemed to specialize in second generations of Hollywood talent. On other occasions he partied with Lou
Rawls Jr., Marvin Gaye Jr. and Chad McQueen.) Downey Jr. stopped by
Newman's apartment on Burton Way, the day after he had come out of his
first extended stay in rehab. He knocked on the door, came inside and
said, "Can I just get a line?" Newman replied, "Man, you just got out of

rehab!" "I know," Downey said, "but it's just a line. One line won't hurt." Two hours later the two men were smoking cocaine and watching television—actually watching Downey's appearance, taped that afternoon, on *The Tonight Show*, where Downey discussed his newfound sobriety.

J.R. hung around with bigger actors, too. While Jack Nicholson was playing the part of the Joker in *Batman*, he and Newman and producer Robert Evans, a longtime Nicholson pal, would hire hookers and stay up all night doing drugs. Nicholson, Newman recalled, would come straight from the set to Evans' house, stay high all night and then go straight back to Warner Bros. the following morning. ("Nothing is as funny as seeing Jack do lines," Newman said. "Watching him put the bill or straw up to his nose and snort always reminds me of the scene in *The Shining* where he breaks through the door and says, 'Here's Johnny!' ") One night at Roxbury, Newman partied with Bobby Brown, Julian Lennon and George Hamilton, and was introduced to Eddie Murphy. (Murphy never did drugs, and told Newman, "I don't care what *you* do, but don't ever bring drugs into my house." Murphy would thereafter always stop at Newman's table to say hello.) Newman partied at Sylvester Stallone's house, after his hooker friend Belinda began sleeping with the star. Other nights he would meet O.J. and Nicole, with Marcus Allen of the Raiders. He met Rick James. He got high with Princess Stephanie of Monaco and Rob Lowe. "The one thing that everyone had in common," Newman said, "was the drugs. Everyone was doing drugs."

One winter he got an emergency call and was asked to make a delivery of a large quantity of cocaine to a party taking place that night in Aspen, Colorado. It was Christmas Eve, 1984. The party was an annual event being thrown by Don Simpson and Jerry Bruckheimer. (Newman only met Bruckheimer once after that night, when, in 1987, he had to leave a Beverly Hills party to score more drugs and discovered that his car was blocked by a black Porsche. High, and impatient, he decided to steal the Porsche, make his run and return it. When he got back to the party the host screamed at him, "You stole Jerry Bruckheimer's car, you asshole." Newman laughed and went back inside with the drugs.) Newman packed a large popcorn bag with cocaine and flew that night to Aspen.

He found a virtual who's-who of chic Hollywood. The minute he arrived he was dragged into a bathroom by Nicholson. Don Henley was next. Then Michael Douglas. George Hamilton was there. Mickey

Rourke and Don Johnson were there with Melanie Griffith, then Johnson's wife. ("Don and Melanie were so damn wasted at that party," Newman said, "that they didn't remember me" when they met weeks later,
back in Los Angeles, at Bar One.) Jean-Claude Van Damme was there.
After he'd "partied out" Nicholson and the other celebrities, Newman
went off to the Paradise Club, then Aspen's hottest nightspot, and partied
some more before flying back, the same night, to Los Angeles.

It was a glamorous life, and Newman played it out until it almost killed
him. By 1991 his six-foot-three frame had shrunk to 137 pounds. He was
living with musician Rick James, who would shortly after be arrested for
imprisoning, torturing and sexually abusing a young woman in the room
where Newman had slept—crimes for which James would ultimately
serve time in a federal prison. James' freebase cocaine habit had driven
him into a $12,000 debt to Newman, who had been his dealer for years.
Newman was broke, so he moved into James' Mulholland Terrace house
to cut his costs and work down James' debt. For a while, this was fine.
James was on a $25,000-a-month allowance from his managers. On pay-
day he and Newman would have drugs delivered and stay up smoking
cocaine for six days straight. Then they'd take Halcion and sleep for two
days. "And then we'd start over, until the money was all gone," Newman
said. Late one night James came into Newman's bedroom and started
rooting around in his closet. When Newman woke, James was cleaning a
freebase pipe—with shaking, junkie hands. He cleaned the pipe with
rubbing alcohol, and then cooked the cocaine and then tried to light the
pipe. But he had spilled rubbing alcohol on his bathrobe, and as he lit the
pipe he also lit himself on fire. Newman leapt from the bed and knocked
James to the floor and put out the flames. James stood up and left the
room, his bathrobe smoldering, still trying to light the pipe, as if nothing
had happened. Newman hit bottom. Newman called his friend Herbie
Hancock and begged for help. Hancock helped Newman get out of Los
Angeles and back to his family in Florida. (Newman later made several
calls to Don Simpson, who had many times, over the years, said to Newman, "If you ever want to clean up, come to me. I'll help you." Now,
clean but needing work, Newman found Simpson would neither take nor
return his calls.) Newman has been drug-free since and now makes his
home in Arkansas. He wrote of his exploits in the 1994 book *The Hollywood Connection*.

J.R.'s bottoming-out took a different form. He got out of the drug business the day after the murders of Ronald Goldman and Nicole Brown Simpson—a crime in which he was nearly implicated.

In addition to chance meetings with O.J. and Nicole Brown Simpson, J.R. had already brushed up against another player in the future Simpson murder story. One night in 1991, outside a club called the Coconut Teaser, when Ice-T was performing, J.R. made some sales and left the club to find his limousine waiting outside. A young woman named Faye Resnick was sitting inside it. They shared a few lines of cocaine. Then Resnick asked him to give her a gram. J.R. said, "How about a blow for that blow?" Resnick seemed shocked and said, "I'm not a prostitute." J.R. answered, "That's a gram, and that's the deal." And, J.R. remembered later, "The next thing you know, she's got a gram and I'm getting a blow job in the limo."

On the night of June 12, 1994, as J.R. remembered it, he was in his motel room watching the basketball play-offs. At about 8:30 his pager buzzed: 777. J.R. claims he packed a bindle and walked to the Burger King. He arrived at 8:45 and found O.J. Simpson's Bentley in the parking lot. Kato Kaelin was driving; O.J. was sitting in the passenger seat. J.R. found Kaelin "very sketched out"—nervous, jumpy. J.R. opened the back door and sat, as Kaelin gave him a hundred-dollar bill and J.R. passed him a gram of speed. Kaelin immediately removed a mirror from his pocket and cut out a line of speed and snorted it. He then passed the mirror to O.J., who shot a nervous glance into the backseat and said, "What the *fuck*, Kato?" Kato laughed nervously and said, "J.R., man; why don't you get us some burgers?" J.R. left the two men in the parking lot. He came back ten minutes later. Simpson was wiping his eyes and nose on a handkerchief and looked stoned. J.R. gave Kaelin the bag of hamburgers and left for his motel room.

The following morning he heard the news about the murders on Bundy Drive, and he panicked. "It was a double murder, and it was O.J., and there were drugs involved," J.R. said later. "I freaked out. My prints were in that Bentley and probably in the Bronco. I thought, 'I gotta get the fuck outta here.' I called a friend in Florida and the next day booked a flight. Then I thought that was too expensive, so I went Amtrak. I didn't contact anyone in Los Angeles for a month. Later I heard O.J. say, 'We went out to McDonald's.' I thought I was fucked for sure."

A panicky J.R. attempted to clear his name, and to cash in on his new celebrity-adjacent status by selling his story to the press. Rumors about O.J. and Kato making a drug run on the night of the murders began to surface. J.R. submitted to polygraph tests for at least one tabloid newspaper. In time, scattered reports made the mainstream media. One report held that an unidentified drug dealer, reportedly in hiding in Florida, had "sold Simpson $100 worth of crystal methamphetamine two hours before the murders." Kaelin himself later insisted to Barbara Walters that he and Simpson did not buy drugs on the night of the killings, and stuck to his story about buying a quick dinner. "No Burger King," he said. "We went to McDonald's."

J.R., now thirty, subsequently returned to Los Angeles, but not to dealing drugs.

For Don Simpson, drugs were still fun, part of his forever-young, do-or-die, bad-boy image. He delighted in taunting his "straight" friends. Once, on a trip to the Toronto Film Festival, he and friend Steve Roth teased agent Michael Ovitz—tossing a vial of cocaine back and forth, doing lines and then tossing the vial to Ovitz, who did not do drugs and was horrified to be around people who did. Roth kept trying to get a snapshot of Ovitz holding the cocaine, but Ovitz would hot-potato the vial back to Simpson each time it was tossed to him.

Among friends straight or not, Simpson was entirely open about his affection for drugs. Paul Schrader, who wrote the Academy Award–winning *Taxi Driver* and *Raging Bull,* and directed movies like *American Gigolo, Cat People* (both produced by Simpson's partner, Bruckheimer), *Patty Hearst* and *The Comfort of Strangers,* was a close Simpson friend from his days as a Paramount executive, where Simpson was responsible for *American Gigolo.* He and Simpson were part of a group Schrader referred to as "that whole Scarfiotti circle," a social set that swirled around the famed production designer Ferdinando Scarfiotti, who had created the look for award-winning films like *The Conformist* and *Last Tango in Paris,* and who in Hollywood had created the enigmatic, erotic looks for *Cat People* and *American Gigolo.* Regular set members were producers Sean Daniel, Mark Rosenberg, Paula Weinstein and Howard Rosenman, film executives Barry Diller and Thom Mount, music mogul David Geffen, composer Paul Jasmine and others.

"It was a very glamorous, hip world," according to Schrader, "and those were very cokey times." He and Simpson, who both came from strict religious backgrounds, were the kind of people who "would get very stoned and sit around talking about God. After several hours, Don and I would be the only people left in the room," Schrader said. One night Schrader and Simpson left a party, because Simpson wanted to show off his new Porsche. They sat in the front seat, snorting lines of cocaine. "All of a sudden," Schrader said, "it was five hours later. We went back inside and no one was there. For five hours we had talked—serious, deep stuff about aesthetics and morality and ideas about God—and to this day I have no memory of what we actually *talked* about. It was one of those college dorm sorts of conversations which, even if they are sort of jejune, are not that easy to find in Los Angeles." Producer Lynda Obst, a friend to both men, said, "That was the best Los Angeles had to offer—Simpson and Schrader holding court."

Obst recalled that it was during these legendary all-nighters that Simpson began to create, in Obst's memory, what was to become the "high-concept movie"—what Obst calls Simpson's one real contribution to the world of cinema. "Don *did* create this," Obst said. "He created the three-act structure that we all use, the one that Robert McKee and Syd Field use and take credit for. Don made up this logarithm. There is the hot first act with an exciting incident, and the second act with the crisis and the dark bad moments in which our hero is challenged, and the third act with the triumphant moment and the redemption and the freeze-frame ending. Don created the framework for the high-concept movie."

It goes almost without saying that Simpson was running on an almost perpetual cocaine high while he created that framework. A host of Simpson assistants, colleagues and friends recalled that within Simpson's late-night, coke-fueled, tape-recorded "memos" were the seeds of his real brilliance. The memos themselves were rambling and unfocused, but within their manic maelstrom were always bits and pieces of true genius, the crystallized flakes of story and character that would ultimately turn into blockbuster movies.

Simpson's Porsche would feature heavily in a similar episode that eventually made print. In his 1986 short fiction collection *A Hollywood Education: Tales of Movie Dreams and Easy Money*, writer David Freeman barely disguised Simpson in a story called "The Burning Porsche."

In the story, Freeman tells of "Teddy," a movie business hotshot who had left his native South America for Hollywood "carrying a change of clothes and three pounds of creamy, flaked Bolivian cocaine." He'd studied briefly at UCLA, sold some cocaine and gotten hooked up with Hollywood executives with a taste for the Bolivian powder. He'd parlayed those relationships into a studio executive slot, until "the corporate bosses in New York got wind of his nocturnal activities" and fired him. So Teddy became a producer, "took a script called *City Boy* off the shelf, hired four writers, and started dictating changes. [*City Boy*] grossed $65 million and Teddy never looked back."

As the story opens, the narrator and Teddy are attending a bachelor party for a friend, eating at the legendary Beverly Hills Chinese restaurant Mr. Chow's. Teddy "was hot enough to burn," at that stage of his career, and his life was "like a fevered movie dream. The man was breathing hits and wrapping Porsches around trees. He'd wreck one, stagger away, and order another. He'd gone through five of the damn things. Live hard, live fast, make millions." He was also doing a lot of cocaine. Through the evening at Mr. Chow's, Teddy "kept jumping up to go to the bathroom. After the fifth trip to the loo in two hours, he had white dust dribbling from his nostrils." Everyone else was ready to go home by eleven, but "Teddy boy . . . however, was ready for more." He and the narrator went outside Mr. Chow's and sat in Teddy's black Porsche, talking deals and Hollywood.

"Teddy kept the engine running and the cocaine coming," Freeman wrote. "Despite his altered state, the discussion was pertinent—casting, directors, budget, script problems. He talked fast all the time, and when he was on coke, his words rushed out, blurred but not confused. Watching him shovel the stuff into his nose made me feel as if I was watching the scene from across the street. The more loaded Teddy got, the farther away I felt."

The two men sat for hours, snorting cocaine, rambling on about Hollywood. The narrator was working on a script set against the backdrop of life on a daily newspaper. Teddy analyzed it for him: "He's sixteen. She's twenty. Her father's the publisher of a newspaper and he's a copy boy or delivery boy. Why does it have to be a newspaper, anyway? Nobody cares about that shit. Fuck this movie. I want to do one about dope. Put it on a marijuana farm. Two thousand cannibas sativa plants in Oregon and the National Guard comes down with choppers and flame-throwers. Search

and seize. Scorch the earth and nuke the dopers. Your boy rises up, orga-
nizes the kids, and offs the Guard. Put in the romance if you want. I don't
give a shit."

In an earlier conversation, Teddy had told the narrator how to run his
life and, at the same time, how to write screenplays that would electrify
American audiences. "Start fast and hard and loud and then stay that
way," he said. "Don't let up for two hours. Story problem? Character
logic? Fuck it. Turn up the music and dance. I know what America
wants."

"What does the country want, Teddy? Educate me."

"Sex. Loud music. Hot clothes. Drugs. Fast cars. Did I say sex? We'll
open two movies. Side by side. One's called *Sex, Drugs and Death*, the
other's called *Mom and Dad Go for a Walk*. Now, where you going to put
your money, white boy? You do movies about milking the cow. I'll do
ones about fucking and getting loaded. See you at the finish line."

Later, after four o'clock in the morning, Teddy and the narrator part.
An hour later, the narrator learns, Teddy was speeding his Porsche
through Encino, "doing ninety down Balboa Boulevard. He clipped six
parked cars, bounced off a telephone pole, and went through the display
window of a lighting store. His Porsche flipped over, bounced off a wall,
and slammed into a display of floor lamps and chandeliers, all of which
were as lit up as Teddy was. Ripping through all that wiring set the shop
on fire. The car burned too, just like in the movies. There were drugs and
alcohol in his system and a lot of second- and third-degree burns on his
body. The police arrested him and took him to the Sherman Oaks Burn
Center."

Freeman captured a real incident accurately. According to Rusty
Cook, the custom car designer who worked on Simpson's automobiles,
the Encino accident happened just as Freeman described it. And, as
Freeman wrote, it was only one of many. On one occasion Simpson and
Bruckheimer were racing their Mustangs, and Simpson lost control of his
car and "wound up in someone's front yard. He tore the suspension right
off the car." Cook bought that Mustang for parts. Simpson would rou-
tinely "hit curbs too fast and tear the front bumper off" of his older-style
Ferrari 308, Cook said. In another San Fernando Valley accident, Cook
recalled, "Simpson was doing one-hundred-plus down Reseda Boulevard
and made a right turn onto Ventura. He didn't make it. He spun out and

went over the curb and took out a fire hydrant. The car filled with water, and the water damage totaled it. The car went right to the salvage yard, and Don walked away from the accident before the police got there."

For Simpson the accidents were only about money. One of his assistants was saddled with the duty of "settling" his moving violations. Most cost $1,000 to fix, until, at one point, Simpson had racked up so many that not even his skillful lawyer could get one removed from his record. The assistant relayed the lawyer's message that Simpson would have to go to court and answer the charges. Simpson fired the assistant and found a new lawyer.

Less Than Zero

Brett Easton Ellis

As I predicted, Kim's party is tonight. I follow Trent to the party. Trent's wearing a tie when he comes to my house and he tells me to wear one and so I put a red one on. When we stop at Santo Pietro's to get something to eat before the party, Trent catches his reflection in one of the windows and grimaces and takes his tie off and tells me to take mine off, which is just as well since no one at the party is wearing one.

At the house in Holmby Hills I talk to a lot of people who tell me about shopping for suits at Fred Segal and buying tickets for concerts and I hear Trent telling everyone about how much fun he's having at the fraternity he joined at U.C.L.A. I also talk to Pierce, some friend from high school, and apologize for not calling him when I got in and he tells me that it doesn't matter and that I look pale and that someone stole the new BMW his father bought him as a graduation present. Julian is at the party and he doesn't look as fucked up as Alana said: still tan, hair still blond and short, maybe a little too thin, but otherwise looks good. Julian tells Trent that he's sorry he missed him at Carney's the other night and that he's been really busy and I'm standing next to Trent, who has just finished his third gin and tonic, and hear him say, "That's just really fucking irresponsible of you," and I turn away, wondering if I should ask Julian what he wanted when he called and left the message, but when our eyes meet and we're about to say hello, he looks away and walks into the living room. Blair dances over to me, singing the words to "Do You Really Want to Hurt Me?" probably stoned out of her mind, and she says that I look happy and that I look good and she hands me a box from Jerry Magnin and whispers "Merry Christmas, you fox," in my ear, and kisses me.

I open the box. It's a scarf. I thank her and tell her that it's really nice. She tells me to put it on and see if it fits and I tell her that scarves usually fit all people. But she insists and I put the scarf on and she smiles and murmurs "Perfect" and goes back to the bar to get a drink. I stand alone with the scarf wrapped around my neck in the corner of the living room and then spot Rip, my dealer, and am totally relieved.

Rip's wearing this thick, bulky white outfit he probably bought at Parachute, and an expensive black fedora, and Trent asks Rip, as he makes his way toward me, if he's been going parachuting. "Going Parachuting? Get it?" Trent says, giggling. Rip just stares at Trent until Trent stops giggling. Julian comes back into the room and I'm about to go over and say hello, but Rip grabs the scarf around my neck and pulls me into an empty room. I notice that there's no furniture in the room and begin to wonder why; then Rip hits me lightly on the shoulder and laughs.

"How the fuck have you been?"

"Great," I say. "Why is there no furniture in here?"

"Kim's moving," he says. "Thanks for returning my phone call, you dick."

I know that Rip hasn't tried to call me, but I say, "Sorry, I've only been back like four days and . . . I don't know . . . But I've been looking for you."

"Well, here I am. What can I do for you, dude?"

"What have you got?"

"What did you take up there?" Rip asks, not really interested in answering me. He takes two small folded envelopes out of his pocket.

"Well, an art course and a writing course and this music course—"

"Music course?" Rip interrupts, pretending to get excited. "Did you write any music?"

"Well, yeah, a little." I reach into my back pocket for my wallet.

"Hey, I got some lyrics. Write some music. We'll make millions."

"Millions of what?"

"Are you going back?" Rip asks, not missing a beat.

I don't say anything, just stare at the half gram he's poured onto a small hand mirror.

"Or are you gonna stay . . . and play . . . in L.A." Rip laughs and lights a cigarette. With a razor he cuts the pile into four big lines and then he hands me a rolled up twenty and I lean down and do a line.

"Where?" I ask, lifting my head up, sniffing loudly.

"Jesus," Rip says, leaning down. "To school, you jerk."

"I don't know. I suppose so."

"You suppose so." He does both his lines, huge, long lines, and then hands me the twenty.

"Yeah," I shrug, leaning back down.

"Cute scarf. Real cute. Guess Blair still likes you," Rip smiles.

"I guess," I say, doing the other long line.

"You guess, you guess," Rip laughs.

I smile and shrug again. "It's good. How about a gram?"

"Here you go, dude." He hands me one of the small envelopes.

I give him two fifties and a twenty and he hands me the twenty back and says, "Christmas present, okay?"

"Thanks a lot, Rip."

"Well, I think you should go back," he says, pocketing the money. "Don't fuck off. Don't be a bum."

"Like you?" I regret saying this. It comes out wrong.

"Like me, dude," Rip says, missing a beat.

"I don't know if I want to," I begin.

"What do you mean, you don't know if you want to?"

"I don't know. Things aren't that different there."

Rip is getting restless and I get the feeling that it doesn't matter a whole lot to Rip whether I stay or go.

"Listen, you've got a long vacation, don't you? A month, right?"

"Yeah. Four weeks."

"A month, right. Think about it."

"I'll do that."

Rip walks over to the window.

"Are you deejaying anymore?" I ask, lighting a cigarette.

"No way, man." He runs his finger over the mirror and rubs it over his teeth and gums, then slips the mirror back into his pocket. "The trust is keeping things steady for now. I might go back when I run out. Only problem is, I don't think it's ever gonna run out," he laughs. "I got this totally cool penthouse on Wilshire. It's fantastic."

"Really?"

"Yeah. You gotta stop by."

"I will."

Rip sits on the windowsill and says, "I think Alana wants to fuck me. What do you think?"

I don't say anything. I can't understand why since Rip doesn't look anything like David Bowie, he's not left-handed and doesn't live in the Colony.

"Well, should I fuck her or what?"

"I don't know," I say. "Sure, why not?"

Rip gets off the windowsill and says, "Listen, you've got to come over to the apartment. I got *Temple of Doom* bootleg. Cost me four hundred dollars. You should come over, dude."

"Yeah, sure, Rip." We walk to the door.

"You will?"

"Why not."

When the two of us enter the living room these two girls who I don't remember come up to me and tell me I should give them a call and one of them reminds me about the night at The Roxy and I tell her that there have been a lot of nights at The Roxy and she smiles and tells me to call her anyway. I'm not sure if I have this girl's number and just as I'm about to ask her for it, Alana walks up to me and tells me that Rip has been bothering her and is there anything I can do about it? I tell her I don't think so. And as Alana starts to talk about Rip, I watch Rip's roommate dance with Blair next to the Christmas tree. He whispers something into her ear and they both laugh and nod their heads.

There's also this old guy with longish gray hair and a Giorgio Armani sweater and moccasins on who wanders past Alana and me and he begins to talk to Rip. One of the boys from U.S.C. who was at Blair's party is also here and he looks at the old man, guy maybe forty, forty-five, and then turns to one of the girls who met me at The Roxy and makes a face. He notices me looking at him when he does this and he smiles and I smile back and Alana keeps going on and on and luckily someone turns the volume up and Prince starts to scream. Alana leaves once a song she wants to dance to comes on, and this guy from U.S.C., Griffin, comes up to me and asks if I want some champagne. I tell him sure and he goes to the bar and I look for a bathroom to do another line.

I have to go through Kim's room to get to it, since the lock on the one downstairs is broken, and as I get to her door, Trent comes out and closes it.

"Use the one downstairs," he says.

"Why?"

"Because Julian and Kim and Derf are fucking in there."

I just stand there. "Derf's here?" I ask.

"Come with me," Trent says.

I follow Trent downstairs and out of the house and over to his car.

"Get in," he says.

I open the door and get into the BMW.

"What do you want?" I ask him as he gets in on the driver's side.

He reaches into his pocket and pulls out a small vial.

"A little co-kaine," he says in a fake southern drawl.

I don't tell him I already have some and he takes out a gold spoon and presses the spoon into the powder and then holds it up to his nose and does this four times. He then pushes the same tape that is on at the party into the car's stereo and hands me the vial and the spoon. I do four hits also and my eyes water and I swallow. It's different coke than Rip's and I wonder if he got it from Julian. It's not as good.

"Why don't we go to Palm Springs for a week while you're back," he suggests.

"Yeah. Palm Springs. Sure," I tell him. "Listen, I'm going back in."

I leave Trent alone in the car and walk back to the party and over toward the bar, where Griffin is standing, holding two glasses of champagne. "I think it's a little flat," he says.

"What?"

"I said your champagne's flat."

"Oh." I pause, confused for a minute. "That's all right."

I drink it anyway and he pours me another glass.

"It's still pretty good," he says after finishing his glass and pouring himself another. "Want some more?"

"Sure." I finish my second glass and he pours me a third. "Thanks."

"The girl I came with just left with that Japanese guy in the English Beat T-shirt and tight white pants. You know who he is?"

"No."

"Kim's hairdresser."

"Wild," I say, finishing the glass of champagne and looking at Blair from across the room. Our eyes meet and she smiles and makes a face. I smile back, don't make a face. Griffin notices this and says loudly, over the din of the music, "You're the guy who's going out with Blair, right?"

"Well, used to go out with her."

"I thought you still were."

"Maybe we are," I say, pouring another glass of champagne. "I don't know."

"She talks about you a lot."

"Really? Well . . ." My voice trails off.

We don't say anything for a long time.

"Like your scarf," Griffin says.

"Thanks." I drain the glass and pour myself another, and wonder what time it is and how long I've been here. The coke is wearing off and I'm starting to get a little drunk.

Griffin takes a deep breath and says, "Hey, you wanna go to my house? Parents are in Rome for Christmas." Someone changes a tape and I sigh and look at the glass of champagne he's holding, then finish my glass fast and say sure, why not.

GRIFFIN STANDS BY his bedroom window, looking out into the backyard, at the pool, only wearing a pair of jockey shorts and I'm sitting on the floor, my back leaning against his bed, bored, sober, smoking a cigarette. Griffin looks at me and slowly, clumsily, pulls off his underwear and I notice that he doesn't have a tan line and I begin to wonder why and almost laugh.

from

Bright Lights, Big City

Jay McInerney

YOU ARE NOT the kind of guy who would be at a place like this at this time of the morning. But here you are, and you cannot say that the terrain is entirely unfamiliar, although the details are fuzzy. You are at a night-club talking to a girl with a shaved head. The club is either Heartbreak or the Lizard Lounge. All might come clear if you could just slip into the bathroom and do a little more Bolivian Marching Powder. Then again, it might not. A small voice inside you insists that this epidemic lack of clar-ity is a result of too much of that already. The night has already turned on that imperceptible pivot where two A.M. changes to six A.M. You know this moment has come and gone, but you are not yet willing to concede that you have crossed the line beyond which all is gratuitous damage and the palsy of unraveled nerve endings. Somewhere back there you could have cut your losses, but you rode past that moment on a comet trail of white powder and now you are trying to hang on to the rush. Your brain at this moment is composed of brigades of tiny Bolivian soldiers. They are tired and muddy from their long march through the night. There are holes in their boots and they are hungry. They need to be fed. They need the Boli-vian Marching Powder.

A vaguely tribal flavor to this scene—pendulous jewelry, face paint, ceremonial headgear and hair styles. You feel that there is also a certain

Latin theme—something more than the piranhas cruising your bloodstream and the fading buzz of marimbas in your brain.

You are leaning back against a post that may or may not be structural
with regard to the building, but which feels essential to your own mainte-
nance of an upright position. The bald girl is saying this used to be a good
place to come before the assholes discovered it. You don't want to be talking to this bald girl, or even listening to her, which is all you are doing,
but just now you do not want to test the powers of speech or locomotion.

How did you get here? It was your friend, Tad Allagash, who powered
you in here, and he has disappeared. Tad is the kind of guy who would be
at a place like this at this time of the morning. He is either your best self
or your worst self, you're not sure which. Earlier in the evening it seemed
clear that he was your best self. You started on the Upper East Side with
champagne and unlimited prospects, strictly observing the Allagash rule
of perpetual motion: one drink per stop. Tad's mission in life is to have
more fun than anyone else in New York City, and this involves a lot of
moving around, since there is always the likelihood that where you aren't
is more fun than where you are. You are awed by his strict refusal to
acknowledge any goal higher than the pursuit of pleasure. You want to be
like that. You also think he is shallow and dangerous. His friends are all
rich and spoiled, like the cousin from Memphis you met earlier in the
evening who would not accompany you below Fourteenth Street
because, he said, he didn't have a lowlife visa. This cousin had a girlfriend with cheekbones to break your heart, and you knew she was the
real thing when she steadfastly refused to acknowledge your presence.
She possessed secrets—about islands, about horses, about French pro-
nunciation—that you would never know.

You have traveled in the course of the night from the meticulous to the
slime. The girl with the shaved head has a scar tattooed on her scalp. It
looks like a long, sutured gash. You tell her it is very realistic. She takes
this as a compliment and thanks you. You meant as opposed to romantic.

"I could use one of those right over my heart," you say.

"You want I can give you the name of the guy that did it. You'd be surprised how cheap."

You don't tell her that nothing would surprise you now. Her voice, for
instance, which is like the New Jersey State Anthem played through an
electric shaver.

The bald girl is emblematic of the problem. The problem is, for some reason you think you are going to meet the kind of girl who is not the kind of girl who would be at a place like this at this time of the morning. When you meet her you are going to tell her that what you really want is a house in the country with a garden. New York, the club scene, bald women — you're tired of all that. Your presence here is only a matter of conducting an experiment in limits, reminding yourself of what you aren't. You see yourself as the kind of guy who wakes up early on Sunday morning and steps out to cop the *Times* and croissants. Who might take a cue from the Arts and Leisure section and decide to check out an exhibition — costumes of the Hapsburg Court at the Met, say, or Japanese lacquerware of the Muromachi period at the Asia Society. The kind of guy who calls up the woman he met at a publishing party Friday night, the party he did not get sloppy drunk at. See if she wants to check out the exhibition and maybe do an early dinner. A guy who would wait until eleven A.M. to call her, because she might not be an early riser, like he is. She may have been out late, perhaps at a nightclub. And maybe a couple of sets of tennis before the museum. He wonders if she plays, but of course she would.

When you meet the girl who wouldn't et cetera you will tell her that you are slumming, visiting your own six A.M. Lower East Side of the soul on a lark, stepping nimbly between the piles of garbage to the gay marimba rhythms in your head. Well, no, not *gay*. But she will know exactly what you mean.

On the other hand, almost any girl, specifically one with a full head of hair, would help you stave off this creeping sense of mortality. You remember the Bolivian Marching Powder and realize you're not down yet. No way, José. First you have to get rid of this bald girl.

Then . . .

In the bathroom there are no doors on the stalls, which makes it tough to be discreet. But clearly you are not the only person in here to take on fuel. Lots of sniffling going on in the stalls. The windows are blacked over, and for this you are profoundly grateful.

Hup, two, three, four. The soldiers are back on their feet. They are off and running in formation. Some of them are dancing, and you must follow their example.

Just outside the door you spot her: tall, dark and alone, half hidden behind a pillar at the edge of the dance floor. You approach laterally, moving your stuff like a Bad Spade through the slalom of a synthesized conga rhythm. She jumps when you touch her shoulder.

"Dance?"

She looks at you as if you had just suggested instrumental rape. "I do not speak English," she says, when you ask again.

"*Français?*"

She shakes her head. Why is she looking at you that way, as if tarantulas were nesting in your eye sockets?

"You are by any chance from Bolivia? Or Peru?"

She is looking around for help now. Remembering a recent encounter with a young heiress's bodyguard at Danceteria—or was it the Red Parrot?—you back off, hands raised over your head.

The Bolivian Soldiers are still on their feet, but they have stopped singing their marching song. You realize that you are at a crucial juncture vis-à-vis morale. What you need is a good pep talk from Tad Allagash, but he is not to be found. You try to imagine what he would say. *Back on the horse. Now we're really going to have some fun.* Something like that. You suddenly realize that he has already slipped out with some rich Hose Queen. He is back at her place on Fifth Ave., and they are doing some of her off-the-boat-quality drugs. They are scooping it out of tall Ming vases and snorting it off of each other's naked bodies. You hate Tad Allagash.

Go home. Cut your losses.

Stay. Go for it.

You are a republic of voices tonight. Unfortunately, that republic is Italy. All these voices waving their arms and screaming at one another. There's an *ex cathedra* riff coming down from the Vatican: *Repent. Your body is the temple of the Lord and you have defiled it.* It is, after all, Sunday morning, and as long as you have any brain cells left there will be a resonant patriarchal basso echoing down the marble vaults of your churchgoing childhood to remind you that this is the Lord's Day. What you need is another overpriced drink to drown it out. But a search of pockets yields only a dollar bill and change. You paid twenty to get in here. Panic gains.

You spot a girl at the edge of the dance floor who looks like your last chance for earthly salvation. You know for a fact that if you go out into the morning alone, without even your sunglasses—which you have neglected to bring, because who, after all, plans on these travesties?—the harsh, angling light will turn you to flesh and bone. Mortality will pierce you through the retina. But there she is in her pegged pants, a kind of doo-wop Retro ponytail pulled off to the side, as eligible a candidate as you are likely to find this late in the game. The sexual equivalent of fast food.

She shrugs and nods when you ask her to dance. You like the way she moves, the oiled ellipses of her hips and shoulders. After the second song, she says she's tired. She's at the point of bolting when you ask her if she needs a little pick-me-up.

"You've got some blow?" she says.

"Is Stevie Wonder blind?" you say.

She takes your arm and leads you into the Ladies'. A couple of spoons and she seems to like you just fine, and you are feeling very likable yourself. A couple more. This woman is all nose.

"I love drugs," she says, as you march toward the bar.

"It's something we have in common," you say.

"Have you ever noticed how all the good words start with D? D and L."

You try to think about this. You're not quite sure what she's driving at. The Bolivians are singing their marching song, but you can't make out the words.

"You know. Drugs. Delight. Decadence."

"Debauchery," you say, catching the tune now.

"Dexedrine."

"Delectable. Deranged. Debilitated."

"Delinquent."

"Delirium."

"And L," she says. "Lush and luscious."

"Languorous."

"Librium."

"Libidinous."

"What's that?" she says.

"Horny."

"Oh," she says, casting a long, arching look over your shoulder. Her eyes glaze in a way that reminds you precisely of the closing of a sand-blasted glass shower door. You can see that the game is over, although you're not sure which rule you broke. Possibly she finds H words offensive. A purist. She is scanning the dance floor for a man with a compatible vocabulary. You have more: *detumescence*, for instance. *Drowning and depressed; lost* and *lonesome.* It's not that you're really going to miss this girl who thinks that *decadence* and *Dexedrine* are the high points of the language of Kings James and Lear. But the touch of flesh, the sound of another human voice . . . You know there is a special purgatory waiting for you out there in the dawn's surly light, a desperate half sleep which is like a grease fire in the brainpan.

The girl waves as she disappears into the crowd. There is no sign of the other girl, the girl who would not be here. There is no sign of Tad Alla-gash. The Bolivians are mutinous. You can't stop their treacherous voices.

IT IS WORSE even than you expected, stepping out into the morning. The glare is like a mother's reproach. The sidewalk sparkles cruelly. Visibility unlimited. The downtown warehouses look serene and restful in this beveled light. An uptown cab passes and you start to wave, then realize you have no money. The cab stops.

You jog over and lean in the window. "I guess I'll walk after all."

"Asshole." He leaves rubber.

You start north, holding a hand over your eyes. Trucks rumble up Hudson Street, bearing provisions into the sleeping city. You turn east. On Seventh Avenue an old woman with a hive of rollers on her head walks a German shepherd. The dog is rooting in the cracks of the sidewalk, but as you approach he stiffens into a pose of terrible alertness. The woman looks at you as if you were something that had just crawled out of the ocean trailing ooze and slime. An eager, tentative growl ripples the shepherd's throat. "Good Pooky," she says. The dog makes a move but she chokes it back. You give them a wide berth.

On Bleecker Street you catch the scent of the Italian bakery. You stand at the corner of Bleecker and Cornelia and gaze at the windows on the fourth floor of a tenement. Behind those windows is the apartment you shared with Amanda when you first came to New York. It was small and dark, but you liked the imperfectly patched pressed-tin ceiling, the claw-footed bath in the kitchen, the windows that didn't quite fit the frames. You were just starting out. You had the rent covered, you had your favorite restaurant on MacDougal where the waitresses knew your names and you could bring your own bottle of wine. Every morning you woke to the smell of bread from the bakery downstairs. You would go out to buy the paper and maybe pick up a couple of croissants while Amanda made the coffee. This was two years ago, before you got married.

DOWN ON THE West Side Highway, a lone hooker totters on heels and tugs at her skirt as if no one had told her that the commuters won't be coming through the tunnels from Jersey today. Coming closer, you see that she is a man in drag.

You cross under the rusting stanchions of the old elevated highway and walk out to the pier. The easterly light skims across the broad expanse of the Hudson. You step carefully as you approach the end of the rotting pier. You are none too steady and there are holes through which you can see the black, fetid water underneath.

You sit down on a piling and look out over the river. Downriver, the Statue of Liberty shimmers in the haze. Across the water, a huge Colgate sign welcomes you to New Jersey, the Garden State.

You watch the solemn progress of a garbage barge, wreathed in a cloud of screaming gulls, heading out to sea.

Here you are again. All messed up and no place to go.

from

Postcards from the Edge

by Carrie Fisher

Alex

. . . THAT'S IT, I'VE quit. This time I've really quit. I'm not doing cocaine anymore. If someone came up and *offered* me cocaine I wouldn't do it. I doubt that anyone will offer it to me, though. No one offers cocaine anymore. It used to be a way that people got friendly, sharing a few toots, but now everyone hoards their cocaine.

My first party without drugs. Interesting. I mean, when I was a little kid I always went to birthday parties straight, but that was a while ago.

I wonder if anyone here even *has* any cocaine. That guy Steve looks like he might, he usually has some. I *loathe* that guy, but he always has great cocaine . . .

No, I promised myself I would not do any cocaine, because that last time was such a *nightmare* and . . . But it was fun in the beginning. Sometimes it's fun. I don't know, Freud took it, so how bad could it be?

But this is the new me. I'm totally on a health kick. I have not taken any cocaine in four days. I don't even like it anymore. I never really *did* like it, I just did it 'cause it was *around*. And I don't think I was really heavy into it, not like Steve over there. Steve is really, really into cocaine. I would say *he's* got a problem. He can't stop. Well, sometimes he stops for a while, but he can't stay stopped. I really think *I* can. I think I have willpower, I just haven't used it in a while. I've been kind of on a willpower break, but now I feel it's coming back. I really think I can stay with this commitment of not doing cocaine.

Besides, this healthy life is great. I really love this being straight. You know, you see people jogging and you think, "*Yuuucccchh*," but I'm getting on. I'm in my late twenties, and I think taking drugs was all part of being young. I don't think I had a *problem*, I think I was just *young*. And that by definition isn't a problem, it's just a point in your life when it seems *okay* to take a lot of cocaine. And then that point passes.

I don't know, I think it was the bad relationship I was in that really determined my drug intake. And now Joan's left me, and I really feel good about myself. I mean I *want* to. And I went to that juice bar today and bought chlorophyll juice, that green drink. It gave me diarrhea, but I really feel good tonight. And I feel like it's a beginning. You go to a place like that and you buy the chlorophyll juice and the carrot juice, and you're making a statement. And I bought some new sneakers, I'm gonna start running . . . I actually got up at nine thirty this morning and moved my exercise bike right next to my bed, so tomorrow morning I *know* I'm just gonna hop on that cycle. Ten minutes is enough for aerobics, I guess. And then maybe I'll go to that Canyon Ranch health spa. Maybe then I could meet a really great girl. I think if I meet someone who doesn't do drugs, then we won't do them together, obviously, and that'll really help me. I think all of these choices reflect where you're at with *you*.

The only thing that bothers me is the idea of giving it up *completely*. I should be able to celebrate every now and again. Like if I stay straight for a while, I should be able to celebrate by getting loaded. I don't see what's wrong with that. Steve does that, but Steve has a *problem*. I think that once I get this under control, I'll be able to do it. And I really feel like I've made a strong beginning. God, my stomach is upset from that juice, though. I wonder if everything good for you tastes awful. I hope not, because I'm really gonna get into it.

Steve looks kind of loaded now. That looks so awful. You see people and they're loaded and . . . Look how dumb it looks. That looks so *stupid*. I can't believe I ever did it. I feel so good about being on the other side of it now. It really erodes your self-esteem to make a decision like not taking drugs and then taking them. The thing is, I also think you can take a little bit, and not do it to excess. Not *everybody* can — obviously there are some personality types who can't do *anything* a little bit — but I'm not one of those. There are certain areas of my life where I do a very little bit, and I think if I practice, one of those areas could be cocaine.

Well, maybe not cocaine, but maybe I could take a speed pill every so often. I love what speed and coke do to my weight. It's unnatural, I know. I *could* just exercise . . .

God, there's that great feeling right at the beginning. If you get some *good* coke. From now on, I'm just gonna do *good* coke. When I do it, I'm gonna make sure. I'll *never* go to the dealer in Brentwood again. *Never*. I think *that* was the problem. His coke hurts your face, it becomes a *chore* to do it. I'll just do pharmaceutical, that's not hard on the membrane, and I really want to take care of my body. I think I'm unusual, because even during all those years when I was doing drugs, I still sometimes went to the gym. Joan accused me of trying to maintain my body so I could destroy it with chemicals, but I think that's a little harsh. And even if I did, I'm certainly better off than someone like *Steve*, who's just frying himself *and* eating burgers and sugar. I eat no carcinogenic food, I'm drinking some juices now . . . I went overboard today, but . . .

I'm *tired*. Who's that girl? She's attractive . . . Aauugggh, I don't want to get into another relationship thing again. God, I'm so *tired*. I shouldn't be drinking. I shouldn't have started drinking, 'cause I associate the two, alcohol and cocaine. I'm just gonna *not drink* now. Oh, he sees me, he's coming over. I should ignore him so he gets that I'm not interested in doing any —

"Hi, Steve, how ya doin'? Yeah, yeah. I'm fine. No, I feel okay. I don't look *that* bad. I have a stomach thing today. How are you? You seem very *up*. No, I'm . . . I'm not doing any right now. I've quit. Yeah. No, I feel great. No, I'm serious. What do you mean, that's not a great line reading? *I feel great*. I'm absolutely committed to this. No, I don't mean it like a judgment on you. I think it's fine that some people still do coke, you know? I don't think it's weak . . .

"No, I don't think I had a *problem*. It's just that my nose started . . . I don't know. I'll probably end up still doing a little bit every so often, you know. Not right now. Maybe . . . well, like, maybe . . . I don't know, let me just . . . Is there food at this party? All right, maybe like a hit, but *that's* — who is that girl over there? — *that's* it, though. I'm gonna do . . .

No, this is . . . I'm not . . . All right, give me one hit. But don't give me any more even if I ask you to. This is good coke, right? It's not from Brentwood? All right, one hit.

"(*sniff*) Mmmmmhh! (*sniff*) Ooohhhh, *fantastic*. Oh, *great*. Shit, that's great! Mmmmhhhhh! It just burns a little bit. There's not much cut in it, right? Yeah? It's good. No, I really don't need any more. I mean, I can *handle* it, I just think that was it. You know, people come to a party and they do one hit to break the tension, and I think I can really master that now. I can do a little bit.

"God, I feel so . . . I really feel *good* about my commitment to not doing drugs. I mean, just doing a little bit of drugs. Feel my arm. I feel really good. Well, I *know* I don't look that great, but I didn't sleep that much and I drank this bad juice.

"Let's go over and talk to that girl. I wanna go over and talk to that girl. Who is that girl? Lisa what? What is she, an actress or something? I *loathe* actresses. She looks smart, though. Smart people always wear black. Who's the guy she's talking to? *Craig?* I wanna go talk to her. God, he's such a loser. I should talk to her, I'm like a real guy. I have to go talk to her. Give me another hit of that stuff, maybe I'll go talk to her. I *know* what I said, I know what I said. Just give me one more hit. What are you, stingy with the blow now? I'll help pay for it. I'm just gonna do it . . . Like, I'm gonna celebrate not doing it by doing a little bit. (*sniff*) Mmmmhh! (*sniff*) *Yeesssss!*

"I wish there was something like holistic blow, you know what I mean? That there would be some way in nature you could take blow and it would be *good* for you. I wish my doctor would make me take it for some weird ailment. I have. This is *good* coke, though. This is really good. How much did you pay for this? Not bad. That is *not* bad. And who did you get it from? Oh, yeah, I had some once from him that was so great. Remember the night we . . . Give me another hit. Give me one more hit.

"(*sniff*) Aaaahhh! (*sniff*) Ooooww! No, it's not the coke, it's me. I had this cold last week. Actually, I think it was more my sinuses. I have a sinus problem, or I seem to more in the last couple of years. I don't know, I have to go to a doctor at some point.

"Nah, I don't want to talk to that girl anyway. I wanna talk to you. I've missed you. I really feel like I can talk to you, I really feel we have a lot in common. I know we don't see each other much socially, but I've gotta say every time that we've spent time together, I've enjoyed it. Remember the night in Vegas when we met? You weren't actually dealing then, were you? Someone said you were a dealer once, I nearly punched the guy out. You're like a really good guy, man. I really like you.

"Think we can get any more of this stuff? 'Cause, I mean, I'm quitting after tonight anyway because, I don't know, I should start taking care of myself. Whew, my heart is really palpitating. You think if I took one more hit it might calm me down a little bit? I know that sounds like a dumb cocaine question, but I think if you do a certain amount and then taper off, you can *hit that peak* and *really* be buzzing, you know, when you feel like the world is lined up just *exactly right*. God, I sure love life. Can I have another hit?

"I think this is good for me—to test my resistance. I mean, I think it's wimpy to give up cocaine. Master the drug, *that's* the key—the total key to the whole thing. I mean, people who actually have to go and give it up—it just shows they're weak. They go to groups like Cocaine Anonymous and those people, they always fuckin' talk about drugs. You know? It's like all they do is not do drugs. Well, man, I'd rather *do* drugs. Do you have another hit?

"Man, this party's a drag. I don't know, I feel so agitated and, you know, itchy to . . . Can we go to your place? Hey, come over to mine. Well, let's just go outside then, let's walk around. There's nobody here that I like. God, look, they're *eating*. Uuggh, look at that shit, it looks awful. Come on, let's go outside and talk.

"Did I ever tell you I graduated with honors from high school? Yeah, I was a real brainy kid. Very precocious. I don't know, I thought I'd go into writing because it interested me. But I gotta tell you, the environment at the networks is just not that exciting. I'd rather be in music, you know, but I don't play an instrument. Maybe I could learn, though. I feel now like I could learn an instrument. Do you play an instrument? That's interesting, that's very interesting. We both don't play any instruments. But, you know, I feel that you, like me, we have the *spirit* of musicians. You know, sitting around communicating. I think *artists* do that.

"That girl in black, maybe she's an artist. I've always wanted to meet someone who wrote poetry and went to jazz clubs, and she'd draw me into her life and we'd become soulmates. I wonder if I have a soulmate.

"Can I have some more blow? One more hit, 'cause I'm like really cresting now. Maybe we could just buy a little, what the hell? This is a party. I have not been getting loaded. This is a reason to celebrate.

"(*sniff*) Aaaahh! (*sniff*) Ooohhh! There is like an edge on this, though, don't you think? Am I sweating? I look all right, don't I? I don't look paranoid, do I? Sometimes I get paranoid that I look paranoid. I don't want anyone to think I'm paranoid. It's not like I care what people think, but sometimes I do. I admit it. I'm a human being. I've always cared a little bit what people think.

"But anyway, I like it when it's like this, you know, and we're just talking. This is a great conversation, man. We should be taping this. So, what do you do? You're writing? What are you writing about? Articles on stereo equipment. That's fascinating. So should we go buy some more of this blow? He's out? Well, let's go to Brentwood. No, that's true, he *usually* has shitty blow, but it's not that expensive and he's *always* there.

"Are my gums bleeding? It feels like my gums are bleeding. I don't know why, I must have cut myself talking. Maybe we could get a lude, too, because I'm starting to feel very . . . *unhappy*. I don't mean unhappy, literally, but it's like I wanna be somewhere else but I don't know where I wanna be . . . Let's go to Brentwood. Let's just, fuck it, let's go to Brentwood. Leave your car here, I'll drive you back later. How many toots do we have left? Shit, well, let's go to Brentwood.

"God, I wish I hadn't had that wheatgrass juice, I feel *awful*. Shit, they really should give you instructions with health food. Anything taken to excess can be unhealthy, even healthy stuff. But forget about excess, I don't even think it's that good for you in moderation. Nothing *green* can be good for you, can it? Uuugghh! Give me some more. Let's just do the last hit, just so we can get into the car and get to the next stop. (*sniff*) (*sniff*).

"What's the matter with you? You look tense. Are you okay? God, what time is it? Sometimes I get so nervous and I don't know why, you know? I heard this phrase once, 'contentless fear,' and I think that's what I have now. 'Cause there's no reason why I should be this jumpy. I mean, I'm comfortable with you, or I *was* comfortable with you. I'm sorry I'm talking so much. I don't know, it just must be the night. God, what a night.

"*Jesus!* Where did that guy come from, I almost ran him over. *Jesus!* Jesus. Okay, okay, I *am* slowing down. I don't know, somehow it got up to seventy-five. Jesus. Let's do the rest of the blow in case we're stopped. What did you do, *hog* it all?

"God, man. I should never have done this. I should never have done all this blow. I *hate* myself. Why did I do this? Now I have an upset stomach from the wheatgrass juice *and* the fuckin' thing with the blow. I wonder if that girl with the black dress is still at the . . . Here we are, this is his block.

"I feel so dumb now. Why did I *do* that? Well, I didn't do anything dumb. It was probably the blow. That blow *did* burn a little bit. Now we'll get some better blow. I hope he has some *good* blow. I hope he has some *good* blow. Maybe he has a lude, though. You know, if I could . . . Well, now I'm maybe in kind of a two-lude mode . . .

"What do you mean, I'm talking to myself? Well, obviously I'm talking to myself. I can't talk to *you*. What do I have in common with someone who writes articles about stereo equipment? Jesus.

"All right, let's just get inside, we'll get inside. How much cash do I have? Hundred and ten, a hundred and ten bucks, that's good. Maybe he'll take a check, that'd be okay. I don't like to do that, though. What if they . . .

"Alex. It's *Alex!*"

What is this asshole, deaf?

"Hi! Hi, man, how ya doin'? Yeah, yeah, I know it's late. Yeah, well, we were just drivin' around and . . . You know Steve. Yeah. Well, can we come in? Thanks.

"So, do you have any coke? Half a gram? What do you mean? I thought you were a *dealer*. Can you get more?"

Oh, *shit*. Oh, *shit!*

"Well, do you have any ludes or anything? I'm really on edge now, I'm so on edge. Well, yeah, get the half a gram, and see if . . . Whatever you have. Anything you have. I just want *anything* you have. And Steve wants whatever else there is."

Goddamn it, why did I do this? Just give me that half a gram, and then I'll take the half a gram, and then I'll try and decide what to do. I've gotta figure out how I'm gonna get down . . . I don't want to be with these people? Who *are* these people? I *loathe* these people. Look at the *skin* on that guy, God, it's enough to drive anyone *insane*. What is that, a *bug* on the floor? Look at this place. God, what a dive. What a miserable dive.

I hear people. Why do I always hear people? Wait, now, this is the coke, just calm down. What's the big deal? Just *calm down*. I can't believe this, I'm not gonna be able to drive. I feel like digging a hole in the carpet. Oh, Jesus. Oh, Jesus.

Is that the *sun* coming up? No, it's probably just . . . It is, it's the streetlight. I just hope those *birds* don't come out. I'll kill myself, I will, I'll *kill* myself if those fuckin' birds come out. I've gotta have those ludes, gotta have a set of ludes just to get me down. Maybe I should check his medicine cabinet, but he's a dealer so wouldn't he be smart about that? Nah!

"Can I use your bathroom?"

I *loathe* this guy. Let's see, what's he got? Anacin. Afrin. Actifed. Lomotil—sure, 'cause he's got the runs all the time from the baby laxative in his fuckin' blow. Percodan! *Jesus!* Two. Two's not usually enough, but fuck it, I'll take the two. Endo 333, *oooh*, my favorite. I better run the water so they don't hear me close this. Aaahh, that's good, that'll be good. I've taken so much blow, though. Two Percodan on all this blow won't even matter. Maybe I should go get health food . . . Tomorrow I'm really . . .

That's it, man, this is *it*. I'm gonna remember this, I'm *always* gonna remember this. That I'm sitting here in Brentwood with two loser guys that I have nothing in common with, doing drugs and trying to make conversation. I could kill myself. I *loathe* my life.

I'll *never* feel those Percodan. Goddamn it, I hope he's got some ludes. *Please* let him have ludes.

"Oh, man, I feel a little better after going to the john. Hey, listen, man, you wouldn't have any *ludes* or anything? I mean, I know I asked you already, but I had like a very tense day. I had some bad wheatgrass juice and . . . I don't know, maybe it's an astrological thing, but . . .

"Ecstasy? No, but I've heard of it. Yeah, right, who hasn't? Aren't you supposed to be with girls or something? Really? It just puts you in a good mood? Well, great, give me some. A *good* mood? Oh, great. No, no, I'm in a good mood now, I'm just in too *strong* of a mood. No, let's, let's . . . Give me one of those. Sorry, I didn't mean to grab.

"Great! They're big, aren't they? Do you have anything to wash it down? Any tequila or anything? Yeah, beer's fine. Oh, wow. So how long do these take to kick in? No, not since that juice this afternoon. Really? That quick? What's in it, do you know? Somebody said there was heroin in it. Not this stuff? Okay, good, 'cause that's the one thing I don't wanna do. Well, one time I snorted some, but I would *never* do any needles. I really think that makes you a drug addict, and me, I'm like a neck-up person."

I feel a little nauseous all of a sudden. It's probably the juice.

"Hey, this is a nice place. I've never really noticed that you have a nice apartment. It's like, *kind*. I don't know if that's an appropriate way to describe decor, but it seems so . . . friendly. Particularly for a dealer's house. *What* is this music? This is *fantastic* music. Really? I usually *hate* Led Zeppelin. It's so interesting, so interesting. Do you mind if I lie down near the speakers? Do you have a pillow or anything?"

God! I feel like I'm making such a fool of myself. I don't even know these guys and I *love* them. I guess it's gotta be the drug, but it doesn't seem like the drug. Maybe this is the Percodan. I know it's not good to mix so much, but this feels like such a good blend. Maybe this is exactly right. Maybe from now on I should only do a little cocaine, a couple of Percodan maybe, and then that Ecstasy, and listen to Led Zeppelin. And that'll be my recipe. Like when I've been good, like I have for the past whatever. I've been straight . . . I mean, I was drinking, but I don't count that. When I've been straight for this kind of a while and I really get on edge, the way to take it off is to be with *these guys*. I *love* these guys.

I mean, I don't want to have *sex* with them, but that idea is not totally repellent to me, either. Steve, even though he has bad skin, is a great guy, and he's got an ass like a girl. I never noticed that before. Oh, I'm so *happy*. I think I've really turned this experience around.

"Steve. Don't ever leave me. I can't imagine being separated from you people. *Ever*."

I want to bond with them on some level. I want to show them how I feel. Maybe this is too excessive. Yeah, I should just get more into the music.

That girl at the party in black . . . Even the party seems nice now. Maybe we should . . . No, I'd have to move. Maybe I could call the party and tell them to send the girl here. *That* would be perfect.

I just feel at one with everything. I remember the time I took acid, and I took the wrong end of the cardboard and it never came on. Maybe this is like acid. But everything looks the same, it just looks *nicer*. Nicer to be with. Maybe I should decorate *my* apartment like this.

My nose still hurts, though. Maybe I should never take cocaine again.

Yeah, from now on I'll just take Ecstasy every so often. It's probably better *for* me. They only just made it illegal, so how bad could it be? And they haven't even said it's *bad* for you. They just don't really know yet what it does to you.

How could I not have found this before? I'm so happy. Maybe I should just call the party and ask for that girl. What'd he say her name was? No, maybe I'll just . . . Is it rude to jerk off in people's houses? I'll just get up and . . .

"No, no, no, I'm okay, man. I just wanna use your can. What? No, I've snorted heroin, but I would never shoot it. Oh, you would do it *for* me. Well, I suppose that doesn't count, then, right? But I wouldn't have to . . . ? And it'd just be a little bit, right?"

It seems like it would be good. Heroin's like the *natural* drug. I don't know, though. This is so weird.

"You wouldn't do anything bad to me, would you? You have such a great expression on your face right now. All right, sure, I'll trust you. But just give me a little bit. And Steve, you're driving us back, right? Well, maybe I'll just crash here then. That's cool, right? I like Brentwood."

I can't believe this. I'm tying off. This is *so weird*. I never thought I would do this. But I'm just gonna do it once.

"Okay."

Oh, *my God!* Now I understand everything. This is so intensely great. Smack. It sounds like a breakfast cereal. It sure doesn't *feel* like a breakfast cereal. Shit, I *love* this. It's like floating down the Nile in your mind. Deep sea diving in your head. This must be well-being.

Does this make me a drug addict? No, I'm just celebrating tonight. What a great night this is.

I'll never do cocaine again. Uh-uh. Maybe a little Ecstasy, a little heroin, but I'll never do cocaine again. And I'm gonna start working out tomorrow. I'm gonna start an aerobic workout tomorrow on my bike. Maybe tomorrow afternoon. I wish I'd never had that wheatgrass juice, though. I feel sort of nauseous.

"Oops, sorry, man. Let me clean it up."

God, that was the easiest puke I've ever had. I wish I could have always thrown up that way. That felt almost good.

"Sure, take my car. I'll wait here. I'll just . . . be . . . here . . ."

What a nice, kind apartment this is. I think everyone should just love each other. That's what I think.

I don't know when I've felt this rested. I've never truly been relaxed. I'm finally relaxed. I feel like Jesus slipped me in the pocket of his robe, and we're walking over long, long stretches of water.

My parents were so fabulous to have had me. This is just . . . *everything*. My teeth feel so soft. *This* is why people take this. It wouldn't even be so bad to *die* of really good heroin. I wouldn't mind just living two more weeks and dying at the end of it if I could have two more weeks like this. Although it would be better to have years and years. I don't think you can even call this a drug. This is just a response to the conditions we live in.

I wonder what that art student at the party is doing. She had such soft, silky hair. She seemed so invested in everything, like the now was exactly where she wanted to be. And now I know how she feels. This is perfect.

If she were here now, it would be like Adam and Eve. We would make this the Garden of Eden, this apartment. Anywhere we were would be the Garden of Eden. And I could really communicate with my heart. It's just a question of finding the right person. If she were here now, I would just hold her and hold her and hold her, like we were twins waiting to be born out of this apartment in Brentwood.

She's probably my soulmate. What if I met my soulmate and now I'll never see her again? But we met and kissed on the astral plane. We flew in the astral plane, and now I'm flying toward her. If she's my soulmate, and I truly believe she is, we'll meet again. We're always meeting. There is no meeting for soulmates. They're always together and never apart.

We'll have a child, and we'll bring it up on heroin so that it'll have a happy childhood. And I'll buy her lots and lots of black shirts and sweaters. And she'll play the bongo drums in a jazz club in the East Village, while I recite stream-of-consciousness poetry that everyone thinks is brilliant. I am brilliant. I'm everything.

Sometimes I wonder if I really am Jesus, but I just haven't grown into it yet.

I wonder what color Jesus's eyes were. And if he needed glasses.

He had the sweetest face . . .

from

On Writing

by Stephen King

By 1985 I had added drug addiction to my alcohol problem, yet I continued to function, as a good many substance abusers do, on a marginally competent level. I was terrified not to; by then I had no idea of how to live any other life. I hid the drugs I was taking as well as I could, both out of terror—what would happen to me without dope? I had forgotten the trick of being straight—and out of shame. I was wiping my ass with poison ivy again, this time on a daily basis, but I couldn't ask for help. That's not the way you did things in my family. In my family what you did was smoke your cigarettes and dance in the Jell-O and keep yourself to yourself.

Yet the part of me that writes the stories, the deep part knew I was an alcoholic as early as 1975, when I wrote *The Shining*, wouldn't accept that. Silence isn't what that part is about. It began to scream for help in the only way it knew how, through my fiction and through my monsters. In late 1985 and early 1986 I wrote *Misery* (the title quite aptly described my state of mind), in which a writer is held prisoner and tortured by a psychotic nurse. In the spring and summer of 1986 I wrote *The Tommy-knockers*, often working until midnight with my heart running at a hundred and thirty beats a minute and cotton swabs stuck up my nose to stem the coke-induced bleeding.

Tommyknockers is a forties-style science fiction tale in which the writer-heroine discovers an alien spacecraft buried in the ground. The crew is still on board, not dead but only hibernating. These alien creatures got into your head and just started . . . well, tommyknocking around in there. What you got was energy and a kind of superficial intelligence (the writer, Bobbi Anderson, creates a telepathic typewriter and an atomic hot-water heater, among other things). What you gave up in exchange was your soul. It was the best metaphor for drugs and alcohol my tired, overstressed mind could come up with.

Not long after that my wife, finally convinced that I wasn't going to pull out of this ugly downward spiral on my own, stepped in. It couldn't have been easy—by then I was no longer within shouting distance of my right mind—but she did it. She organized an intervention group formed of family and friends, and I was treated to a kind of *This Is Your Life* in hell. Tabby began by dumping a trashbag full of stuff from my office out on the rug: beercans, cigarette butts, cocaine in gram bottles and cocaine in plastic Baggies, coke spoons caked with snot and blood, Valium, Xanax, bottles of Robitussin cough syrup and NyQuil cold medicine, even bottles of mouthwash. A year or so before, observing the rapidity with which huge bottles of Listerine were disappearing from the bathroom, Tabby asked me if I drank the stuff. I responded with self-righteous hauteur that I most certainly did not. Nor did I. I drank the Scope instead. It was tastier, had that hint of mint.

The point of this intervention, which was certainly as unpleasant for my wife and kids and friends as it was for me, was that I was dying in front of them. Tabby said I had I my choice: I could get help at a rehab or I could get the hell out of the house. She said that she and the kids loved me, and for that very reason none of them wanted to witness my suicide.

I bargained, because that's what addicts do. I was charming, because that's what addicts are. In the end I got two weeks to think about it. In retrospect, this seems to summarize all the insanity of that time. Guy is standing on top of a burning building. Helicopter arrives, hovers, drops a rope ladder. *Climb up!* the man leaning out of the helicopter's door shouts. Guy on top of the burning building responds, *Give me two weeks to think about it.*

I did think, though—as well as I could in my addled state—and what finally decided me was Annie Wilkes, the psycho nurse in *Misery.* Annie was coke, Annie was booze, and I decided I was tired of being Annie's pet writer. I was afraid that I wouldn't be able to work anymore if I quit drinking and drugging, but I decided (again, so far as I was able to decide anything in my distraught and depressed state of mind) that I would trade writing for staying married and watching the kids grow up. If it came to that.

It didn't, of course. The idea that creative endeavor and mind-altering substances are entwined is one of the great pop-intellectual myths of our time. The four twentieth-century writers whose work is most responsible for it are probably Hemingway, Fitzgerald, Sherwood Anderson, and the poet Dylan Thomas. They are the writers who largely formed our vision of an existential English-speaking wasteland where people have been cut off from one another and live in an atmosphere of emotional strangulation and despair. These concepts are very familiar to most alcoholics; the common reaction to them is amusement. Substance-abusing writers are just substance abusers—common garden-variety drunks and druggies, in other words. Any claims that the drugs and alcohol are necessary to dull a finer sensibility are just the usual self-serving bullshit. I've heard alcoholic snowplow drivers make the same claim, that they drink to still the demons. It doesn't matter if you're James Jones, John Cheever, or a stewbum snoozing in Penn Station; for an addict, the right to the drink or drug of choice must be preserved at all costs. Hemingway and Fitzgerald didn't drink because they were creative, alienated, or morally weak. They drank because it's what alkies are wired up to do. Creative people probably *do* run a greater risk of alcoholism and addiction than those in some other jobs, but so what? We all look pretty much the same when we're puking in the gutter.

from

Rush

Kim Wozencraft

I AM SO damn good at what I do, I am crawling on the floor, crawling on the fucking floor, wearing the lovely black silk kimono that Jim gave me before he left me in his living room with a quarter ounce of coke and went out on 'business.' Business is what we are about.

I am crawling on the floor, scuffling, looking for one tiny speck of white, hoping for a rock, hoping for one more heart-slamming rush, wanting to get up there where I can smile eye to eye at the Holy Trinity and say, 'Hey, boys, what's happening?' My body wants to go there and my body is crawling on the floor and my brain is trying to keep up, there's a continent between my body and brain, there are light years between my eyes and hands, there is a nanosecond between where I was twenty minutes ago and where I want to be now. One more rock. One speck of white. So tiny. So little. Such a small space between misery and joy. I pick up white pieces from the brown carpet. My knees burn as I crawl. A bit of cotton, pieces of lint, a speck of white paint from the wall. Trash.

I want to watch Jim put the needle in my arm, slide it smoothly into the vein, I love that little piercing pain that comes right before the ocean hits my heart.

I am such a damn good narc.

Jim and I, we could walk into a club cold and come out with three deals set up that same night and four more for the next day. We knew how to buy dope. We knew how to work our snitches, work the streets.

So I pick up a little old jones, so what? We are the good guys. What we do is right.

Right. I am crawling on the floor. There must be more cocaine here. If there isn't more we have to get some. It's evidence. We have to have something to turn in, even four percent will do. There must be more here. Somewhere. Have to find more.

It's like smelling blood, the way it takes over your body, the reactions, the smell everywhere, the pure, clean, smiling smell of cocaine.

Jim stood in the doorway, wearing his own kimono, maroon, with a dragon on the back. I saw his legs, the fine black hairs on his legs.

When there is enough cocaine, too much cocaine, when I am kicking myself just a little bit higher every twenty minutes, watching the clock between shots, pressing my fingers to my neck to count the pulsebeats, waiting for them to come down from one seventy-four, down below ninety so I can do it again, sometimes hair starts to grow out of everything. Leg hair grows right before my eyes, on the pillows, on the walls, out of the carpet. Fine pale hairs or thick black hairs. I close my eyes and hair grows from the insides of my eyelids.

We scored, scored cold a couple of nights ago, or weeks or months or years ago, I don't know, from a scuzzball in a cowboy hat who said he had been the youngest bank robber ever in the history of the whole country. Gave Walker the night off and hit the clubs. When he was a kid, a nine-year-old kid, this cowboy, he helped pull a bank job. And his friend, standing there next to the cowboy, leaning on a pinball machine, got out of Huntsville yesterday and he's got that look in his eyes like he's waiting for somebody in a uniform to come snatch him up and take him back to the joint. Three grams of coke, not even a speck out of the tons that pour in, but we've got some real sorry asses here, some genuine fuckups, and a dope case is just as good as a robbery case when it comes to getting them off the streets. The baby bank robber, the cowboy, he said, 'Hey, man, like we got to know you're cool, man, like here's my rig. Let's get down.' And while he said it he's got his hand wrapped around the pretty walnut grip of a Colt Lawman. So we do it, Jim and I, we run the dope right in front of his squinty red eyes, and it's my first time with cocaine, and what did Willy Red know about a rush, this is a rush, I have never felt anything like it before, not even the heroin. I nod at God and whisper 'It's nice up here,' and Jim is smiling at me because we're both thinking of how this asshole will be screaming in court, 'They shot dope! They fucking shot dope!' and when the prosecutor asks us did we ever take drugs we will say, 'No sir, certainly not, we're police officers,' and we will look so clean and All-American and the jury will just love us for taking armed robbers and dope dealers and fucking third-time recidivists off the streets. For making it safe for children. I find it right somehow, that we beat the sleaze at their own scummy game. I am still capable of appreciating irony.

I am crawling on the floor.

Jim looked down at me, took the rigs from the coffee table and said, 'I guess I'd better clean these up.'

THEY CAME TO our door at any and all hours, staggering, stumbling, looking for sanctuary, a place where they could fix without getting hassled. Sometimes with Walker, sometimes because they'd heard on the streets. They gravitated to the scene, *there's a new kid in town.*

We bought their dope and wrote our reports, paying attention to times and dates and physical descriptions, omitting the details that might make them seem human to a jury: Nadean, a burned-out sixties azalea farmer, who also happened to grow marijuana and who delivered her pounds with a complimentary houseplant and recollections of Woodstock; a guy named Buzz Saw who showed up to sell Quaaludes to his old friend Dice who 'used to live here, I'm sure,' and I, who had six coke deliveries on Dice, calling to tell him Buzz Saw was looking for him and then myself scoring a dozen Quays from Buzz, whom I had never heard of until that moment.

And then there were those like Lester the Mo-lester, who came by one day to show off his brand-new Smith and Wesson .38 Chief Special, which fit so nicely in the pocket of his baggy white pants and which he swore he would break in by shooting 'the first pig that steps across my doorway,' leaving us to wonder whether he was trying to get a message across or just being his usual psychopathic self.

He brought us to his home, come check out the latest merchandise, in

a red '56 Galaxy, bruising down Highway 10 like it was time to die, and
we spilled dopesmoke and vodka all over a Sunday afternoon. We looked
at hot TVs and stolen shotguns while Lester danced around the kitchen
with a loaded syringe in each hand, getting ready to fix his not-so-sweet-
sixteen girlfriend who had pulled jiggers that morning while Lester and
his young brother Douglas broke the back windows of a couple of nice
brick custom homes and went in to see what could be had while the owners were at church. We watched Lester tie Lisa off and inject the meth
and we watched Lisa's eyes get big and heard her gasp when the speed hit
her heart. She made it to the kitchen sink before she puked, but came up
smiling and looked on with fascination while Lester did the deed to
younger brother. They wanted to party, and party we did, and yes I had a
problem, I got the hard rush and smelled the chemical smell and tasted
that burning acid crystal meth taste right there in the back of my throat
even while I was just watching them fix.

TWO DAYS AND how many cases later Jim was in the kitchen, what day
was it, what months was it, how long have we been doing this, holding a
Preludin under the faucet, washing the coating off. Five pink tablets in a
row at the edge of the sink. A test tube, a glass stirring rod, two new
syringes, and a pair of pliers.

He looked up at me, his mouth curled into a question. The medicine
smell rose up the back of my throat, oozed from my tongue, the Preludin
taste, different from coke or meth, and the needles were on the counter,
begging.

And this was what Jim liked, leaning over my arm, watching the blood
mix, stopping to look at my eyes before he pressed the plunger. *I'll take
you there*. It came in slowly, teasing my heart for a single long instant
before it slammed like a head-on collision, standing me up, and I was
coughing, spewing air, too much, he'd given me too much, and everything was red, Jim was red as he bent over his arm, and pink molecules
danced in the room's dead air, and then the burn in my lungs, up the
back of my throat between my legs, and I went to my knees, and my arms
were beneath me, bracing, waiting, my face on the floor, I smelled the
carpet against my cheek, and Jim knelt behind me and grabbed my hips

and it was nothing but fucking, pure and sweat-soaked and desperate, until we screamed, until we lay raw and gasping on the floor.

I STOOD IN front of the bathroom mirror and let my robe fall. The bruises ran from the elbow almost to wrist, big blue-and-yellow blotches on the inside of each arm.

I ran the shower too hot, watched my skin turn pink as I stood under the scalding water. I scrubbed until it felt as though I were taking off, layer by layer, my own skin. I breathed in steam. I tried to understand.

It changes you. You can tell yourself you are doing it because you have to, so you can make the case. Because it's better than sex or it makes sex better. Because you feel like it today. But no matter what you tell yourself, how you explain it, there's only one reason.

You are after the rush.

And no matter how many times you go for it, no matter how many times, you'll never hit it again. Some people look all their lives. They steal for it. Don't know how to give up. Murder for it. Chase after it until it turns on them, roaring. Lumbers onto their backs like a bear, ripping flesh from bone, killing. They've been dead a long time by then.

from

The Story of the Night

Colm Tóibín

As soon as I came in from the airport I went upstairs. I knew immediately that Pablo had left. His clothes were gone; nothing of his was hanging in the wardrobe. He had taken his toothbrush and a special shampoo that he liked. And downstairs there was a note on the kitchen table in his scrawl. It read: 'Things haven't been working out between us recently. I wanted to leave before it became any worse. Maybe I should have stayed and talked about it, but I felt this was the very best way to do it. I want to end our relationship. I also want to thank you for everything. Love, Pablo.'

I walked down to the water and thought about what I should do. I had always believed that things between us would go on for good. Maybe I should have put more effort into it. Maybe I should have travelled less in recent times. I went back up to the house and phoned his parents' place. He answered the phone, and then transferred the call to another room so that he could talk quietly.

'I want to meet you,' I said.

'No, I can't,' he said. 'I made a decision. I'm absolutely sure about it.'

'Thanks,' I said. 'I'm glad that you're so sure. It makes me feel good.'

'That's what I mean, there's no point in us meeting. It's easier just to end it like this.'

'Easier for you,' I said. He said nothing.

'I phoned a few days ago but you were asleep,' I said.

'I've been back two days. I was with Mart just before he died. It was very hard for everyone. Maybe because he was so brave it was hard. It seems unbelievable that he is lying under the ground. I keep feeling that someone could just go to the graveyard and dig him up and talk to him and make him come alive.'

'Pablo, I need to talk to you.'

'No, I can't talk to anybody. I think I'm going to go back to San Francisco, maybe in the next few days. At his funeral he asked that they play "Mad About the Boy" as his coffin was being wheeled down the church. It wasn't funny, like he meant it to be. It was unbearable. I couldn't wait for it to be over. No one is prepared for death. I thought we all were, but we weren't.'

'Can we meet in the city?'

'I'll phone you in a week or two.'

'Are you sure that you're not just upset?'

'Hey, I'm sure, I told you I was sure.'

'I really miss you. I really want to see you.'

'You're going to have to find somebody else.' He put down the receiver.

I was crying as I went to the bathroom. I could not imagine what I was going to do for the rest of the day and the next day. He had left it so that I could not telephone him again. I tried to think what I did before I met him, how I filled my days. I began to brush my teeth, as though that might help in some way. I felt that if I met him I could convince him to come back. I was still crying when I went downstairs.

I lay on the sofa and tried to go to sleep. It was the early evening. As I lay there an idea came to me. I went to my jacket pocket and took out Tom Shaw's address and phone number. I phoned him. He recognized my voice as soon as he picked up the receiver. He laughed.

'I don't know why,' he said, 'but I thought that you might phone.'

'Are you busy this weekend?'

'I would be if you came up here. Otherwise, I'm not.'

'I should be able to make it by the morning. What will I do—just get a taxi from the airport to your address?'

'Yeah, or phone if you're going to be late. Or phone in any case, so I'll be ready for you.'

As soon as I stood up from the sofa I began to have difficulty breathing. I felt a sharp pain in my back but it did not last long. I phoned the airport and got a seat on a night flight to Miami. I did not know when I was going to return. The ticket was expensive, but I reserved it nonetheless. I filled a small bag with clothes and a few books and toilet stuff. I made sure that I had my passport and money and my keys and my address book. I wrote Tom's number and address in the book. And then I drove to the airport. I did not think about Pablo.

I slept as soon as I got on the plane, and I was still groggy and sleepy when we touched down in Miami. I had to walk for what seemed like miles before I found the desk for the connecting flight to New York. I wondered why I had not just got drunk at home and fallen into a sleep. I even thought of turning back and ringing Tom Shaw to say that I would not be able to make it after all. But I got on the plane. I had a window seat and I looked out at the clear blue of the sea and the bright yellow sand of the beaches and then the calm, creamy endless cloud as we made our way north and I was glad that I was alive, and I lay back and thought about Tom Shaw's body, his gleaming smile, his energy, and I thought that everything was all right as I began to doze.

I could not find a working call box which took credit cards in Kennedy Airport; I had no coins. It was eleven thirty in the morning. I took a cab into the city. When I saw myself in the mirror I knew that I should have shaved. I needed a haircut. But I could do all that later. I hoped that Tom had not gone out. The apartment was on east sixty-ninth, and the cab driver wanted to know which streets it was between, but I did not know and this meant that he had to drive around several times to find it. I paid him and stood at the reception desk and asked for Tom Shaw. The porter phoned his apartment, and told me to go to the ninth floor. In the lift I was excited at the idea of seeing him again. He was wearing jeans and a denim shirt and no shoes and socks when he came to the door. He lived in a two-room apartment with a small kitchen and bathroom. The bed was enormous, and one wall of the bedroom was all mirrors.

'Look what the cat brought in,' he said. 'You look like you've been up all night.'

'I've been on a plane all night.'

'Why don't you have a bath and a shave and I'll go out and get stuff for breakfast and then I'll make coffee.'

I could tell that he did not want me to talk about why I had come. Before he went out he opened the bathroom door and left a bathrobe on a hook.

'You can wear that when you dry yourself.'

We had breakfast and then he led me to the bedroom. He had left some cream and condoms conspicuously on the bedside table. He stripped and then made me face the mirror while he removed the bathrobe. I was so tired that I felt the urge to make love, to satisfy myself, much stronger than ever before. There was nothing I would not have done. He left me lying on the bed and came back into the room with a small mirror and what I took to be two lines of cocaine.

'I have never done this before,' I said.

'All the more reason why you'll enjoy it.'

He used a rolled-up ten-dollar bill to snort the cocaine, and then he handed it to me. I snorted it, and I immediately felt a bitter taste on the roof of my mouth and a strange numbness. He pulled the bedclothes back and we got between the clean white sheets.

'We're going to have to make the journey worth your while,' he said.

In the late afternoon, he went out and left me sleeping. When I woke I could not remember where I was. I reached out and could not find the lamp. I got out of bed and found the door and opened it and looked out into the hallway, but still I could not think where I was. There was no one in the living room or the kitchen. I went into the bathroom and began to cough. Each time I coughed I could feel the cocaine at the roof of my mouth. I felt that I had no breath at all. I kept heaving and coughing as I stood there. The clock said seven thirty. I went back into the bedroom and turned on the lamp beside the bed and fell into a light sleep until Tom returned.

He was smiling and cheerful, as though my arrival had provided him with immense amusement. I almost wanted to tell him what had happened, but he seemed to have no curiosity. When I got up and had a shower, he brought me in two huge soft towels which he had heated on the radiator. He said that we were going out to dinner. The good times were just beginning, he said.

We got a cab to take us down the potholed and bumpy streets of Manhattan to Greenwich Village.

'In Buenos Aires,' I said, 'when the streets are in bad condition people really are ashamed.'

'No one around here is ashamed of anything,' Tom said.

For a moment I thought that he was Pablo. I held his hand.

'Don't go all quiet on me,' he said.

'I'm not sure what I'm doing here,' I said.

'Concentrate on the next half-hour, and I've brought some magic powder which will help you along.'

He told the cab driver to stop on a dark street which was crowded with
people.

'Let's get out and walk around,' he said.

I was amazed that the shops selling clothes and books and tapes and
more clothes were still open. People walked the streets with carrier bags.
Each person I saw as we went along would have stood out in the streets of
Buenos Aires. We went to a restaurant on a corner: the ceiling was high
and there were plants everywhere, and the woman who led us to our table
looked even more snobbish than any of the people eating at the tables or
sitting at the bar, and behaved more imperiously.

'You look like a country boy who's just come over the bridge or
through the tunnel,' Tom said.

'Yes, that's what I am.'

'The woman who brought us to our table is probably bridge and tunnel
too, except she has learned not to look like that.'

'And what about you?'

'New Jersey born and bred.'

'Is that so terrible?'

'It means that I couldn't wait to get in here and have a good time.'

'I've never eaten lobster before, maybe it's because I live too near the
sea.'

'Well, now's your chance.'

I ordered lobster with ginger and Tom ordered some sort of chicken.
The waitress did not seem amused when he said we would have Bloody
Marys for starters. Tom still did not know why I was here and when I was
going back. I felt that he wanted to make clear that he had no interest in
getting involved with me. He spoke about the prices of apartments in
New York, how this area used to be cheap, but now everybody wanted to
live here. He would not want to live here himself, he said, there was too
much going on. He liked to take visitors from Argentina down here.

I was still tired and only barely able to concentrate. He noticed this and slipped me a package under the table. He told me to go into the bathroom and have a snort and then I'd feel better. I put the package in my pocket and went to the bathroom and locked myself into a cubicle. It was all here: the powder, the mirror, a tiny plastic spoon to make the line. I rolled up a ten-dollar bill and snorted. Once more, I felt the bitter taste in my mouth and the numbness. I shivered as though the temperature had suddenly gone down. I washed my face in cold water, and stood looking in the mirror.

After dinner we wandered in the streets for a while and had a drink in an old-fashioned hotel where the lights in the bar were so low I could barely see Tom across the table from me. The cocaine was working: I felt alert to everything that moved, I loved the alcohol in my vodka and tonic, I was ready to talk about minor details of the decor, or the barman's uniform and gait, or how good I felt. And this seemed to make Tom happy. He laughed and smiled and showed his shiny white teeth. I was glad I was with him, glad I had come all the way up to New York to experience this.

Later, we got a taxi to a gay bar for older, professional men, as Tom put it. Are you a professional man, he asked me. I said that I was. He laughed. Most of the men there wore suits and ties. The place was full of easy chairs and sofas, and the atmosphere was cheerful. We had several drinks. Tom knew a few people, whom he introduced to me, and we all talked for a while, about Argentina and New York, making vague jokes about sex. It seemed as though these men were tired of hunting for sex on a Saturday night and decided instead to look for company, mild conversation and some laughter. But maybe at a certain time of the night they stiffened and stopped standing around with drinks in their hands talking to people they knew, and they went in search of sex. It was all so casual and civilized, like a gentleman's club. I thought that if I lived in New York I would come here all the time, it would be easier to meet somebody here, it would be easier to grow old here feeling that you were not alone.

'You've gone all dreamy on me again,' Tom said.

'Another drink, maybe,' I said.

He called the waiter and we had two more vodka and tonics.

'I think we should go home soon, now that I've shown you a bit of New York. I think we're going to have a long night.' He put his hand on my crotch. 'In fact, I'm sure of it.'

We walked from the bar to his apartment. It was starting to rain. I still felt elated, full of energy. I could feel the alcohol throbbing in my blood. As soon as he went in the door of the apartment Tom made two more lines of coke and we snorted one each.

'I'll toss a coin,' he said. 'One of us strips, the other keeps his clothes on.'

He won the toss to keep his clothes on. I stripped in the bedroom, dropping my clothes on the floor, and then I walked out into the living room. He put his finger into the bag of cocaine and daubed some on the top of my dick and then on my asshole. We lay on the thick carpet together. He began to bite my nipples and then squeeze them with his thumb and forefinger until it hurt and I tried to stop him, but he carried on as though it were vital to continue. Slowly, a feeling built up inside me that I could endure any pain. He put his finger once more into the bag of cocaine and daubed me with the small white grains. He lay beside me and kissed me, refusing to allow me put my hands inside his clothes. I felt invulnerable, ready for anything.

I woke at about three o'clock and the coughing would not stop. Each time I coughed I felt a sharp pain in my back. I felt hot and sweaty. I lay there trying to stop but I had no control over my breathing. Tom woke up.

'Hey, that cough's becoming a real problem.'

'Maybe it's the cocaine.'

'It sounds serious to me.'

I lay there with my eyes closed trying to breathe calmly. He turned and tried to go back to sleep. Slowly, the cough started again. I felt a burning in my lungs. I was aware that I was disturbing him. He turned on the lamp beside the bed.

'You sound sick,' he said. 'Have you been to a doctor with this?'

'No,' I said. 'I don't know what it is. I think it might be the cocaine.'

'Do you think you're going to cough much more?' he asked.

'I don't know.'

'Because I think I'm going to go out and sleep on a mattress in the living room.'

He stood up and took two pillows with him and rummaged in the built-in cupboard for a mattress, which he dragged across the room. He came back for some sheets and a duvet. He closed the door behind him without saying anything. I began to cough again. I felt as though I were on fire, and I was sorry that I was in a stranger's bedroom and not in my own house. I thought of getting up—it was three thirty—and going out to the airport to catch the next flight home, but I decided to wait and get some rest. I was sweating. I felt helpless.

I must have dozed for a while. I woke with Tom's lamp still on at twenty to five and I decided to go. My bag was in the corner of the bedroom. I checked what I needed — passport, ticket, money, keys — and I put on my clothes. I went into the bathroom and collected my things. I stood in the living room like a long shadow and asked Tom if he was awake. He mumbled something. I told him that I was going to go. He sat up and asked me if I needed anything.

'I'm going to go,' I said.

'Okay.'

'I don't need you to get up.'

'Okay.'

'I'll see you at the next conference.'

'Are you going to Argentina?'

'Yeah, that's where I'm going. I'd better hurry or I'll miss my plane.'

I opened the door and slipped out into the corridor, and I walked quickly to the lift. In the street I hailed a cab and told the driver I wanted to go to Kennedy. I did not know what airline I was going to use to get back, but I told him to drop me at the departure gates of the Argentinian airline. Since it was Sunday, I discovered, there would be no flight to Buenos Aires until the late afternoon, but if I went to LaGuardia, I could catch a flight to Miami and get a connection there. It would cost more money, but I felt I needed to go home. My skin was on fire and I had a terrible thirst. I could barely carry my bag. I paid for my ticket by credit card.

As soon as I got the ticket I felt that I was choking. I walked away and lay down on a bench. I tried desperately to catch my breath, to breathe calmly. People looked at me as I lay there spluttering and coughing. Eventually I managed to stand up and go outside and get a taxi to LaGuardia.

The plane to Miami was almost full. I had a window seat, and I sat back with my eyes closed and my face burning with heat. As soon as the plane took off I started to cough. The woman beside me seemed affronted by this, as though I had been put beside her as a way of annoying her. Each time I coughed she tried to move away from me. I had my head between my knees. It was as though I were trying to cough the cocaine out of my system. I braced myself each time, I knew how sharp the pain was going to be, as though my lungs were going to explode. An air hostess came and stood watching me, and then another. I pretended that they were not there.

'Are you asthmatic?' one of them asked.

I nodded.

'It will be okay,' I said.

'Could I be moved?' the woman beside me asked. The air hostess walked up the aisle and found her a new seat. She moved, muttering and making a great fuss. I lay back and tried to sleep. Every bone in my body was sore, and I felt that I was not going to be able to continue breathing. I wondered if I should stop in Miami and go to a doctor there; maybe they would have more experience of people who were allergic to cocaine. In Buenos Aires I had not been to the doctor for years, not since before my mother died. I knew that doctors had to maintain some sort of confidentiality. I had, in any case, taken the drugs in New York rather than Buenos Aires. Soon, I fell asleep, and when I woke I was coughing once more; at the end of each cough I hit a loud uncontrollable high note which made everyone look around. I desperately wanted to be home.

'Do you want medical attention as soon as we arrive?' one of the air hostesses asked me.

I shook my head. I said I would be okay. I made sure not to say that I was catching a connecting flight to Buenos Aires. I closed my eyes again and she went away. When the plane landed and we collected our hand luggage and made our into the terminal, I tried not to breathe at all. I was afraid that if I did not concentrate, I would double up coughing in the aisle of the aircraft.

As I pushed my trolley along passageways to get to the Buenos Aires plane, I found that I could not continue. I leaned on the trolley coughing, the sound was rasping in the echoing corridors, and I ended up kneeling on the floor not able to take a breath. I did not know what I would do when I got home. It would be late on a Sunday night, I did not suppose that many doctors would be on duty. I wondered if I should not go straight to a hospital, but I did not know what I would tell them.

Slowly, I picked myself up and moved towards the departures gate. I thought about a strong sleeping pill, something that would put me into a deep sleep for the journey home. I wished I had some pills. I thought that this reaction to the cocaine might last some hours and then fade. Once more, I was given a window seat, and as soon as the plane was in the air I began to cough again. As we flew south most people around me fell asleep, but they woke up to the sound of my cough, which seemed louder now on this plane, as though all of my insides were going to come up. The air hostess asked me if I wanted her to see if there was a doctor on board and I said that I did not, but later, when it became worse, and everyone around was awake and listening, I nodded to her. She moved around the plane asking people, but there was no doctor on board. She brought me an extra blanket and a pillow and moved the people around me so that I could stretch out across three seats. As soon as I lay down I knew that I was really sick, and getting sicker, and that maybe it was something else, which the cocaine had merely brought on. I fell asleep, and woke again covered in sweat.

I managed to drive home from the airport. I thought that I was going to die at the wheel, that I would collapse. I knew that I was running a very high temperature. Several times I had to pull in on the highway and cough until I was shivering with exhaustion. It had never occurred to me before that I should be grateful for being well, but now I saw the time when I was not like this as something I wanted to experience again. When I got home, I rang the Juan Fernandez Hospital in the city centre. I had passed it many times and paid it no attention. There was no answer. I checked the phone book again and found an emergency number. I described my symptoms to the woman who answered. I did not mention cocaine. I told her that I had comprehensive health insurance. She told me to come in now to the casualty gate, immediately, and someone would look at me. I phoned a taxi and put the things I thought that I would need into a bag. By this time I believed that they were going to detain me in the hospital overnight.

As soon as I walked in the door marked 'Casualty', I was stopped by a porter. He made me stand while he phoned to see if there was anybody there and I began to cough again. The pain brought tears to my eyes. He turned and looked at me sharply, then dialled another number. He brought me a chair to sit on; he patted my back to reassure me. My skin was still burning and I was short of breath. The journey from New York seemed like some interminable dream. I wanted to lie down on the floor and die.

A nurse came and led me down a corridor and then through double doors down another corridor. When she put me into a curtained-off cubicle with a narrow bed she told me to sit down and pulled back the curtains. She began to ask me questions and wrote the answers down on a chart. I told her about the coughing and about being in New York, but once more I did not mention the cocaine. She took my temperature with a thermometer under my arm and told me it was one hundred and four. She said she would go to get a doctor.

I thought about the difference between now and when I was well. Effortless evenings, having dinner, drinking wine, lying on the sofa, talking to Pablo, going to bed with him and making love, and then sleeping. I realized that my temperature had been high for at least a day, maybe more, and I thought that this was dangerous, or at least not a good sign. After a while, a young doctor came and asked me to remove my jacket and shirt. He asked me to breathe deeply and placed the cold steel of the stethoscope on my back and chest. He put me lying on the bed and came back a few minutes later with an older doctor and a nurse.

The doctor looked at me suspiciously, and then listened to my chest and back through the stethoscope, and said that I had a severe pneumonia. He would need me to fill in forms, and then he would find me a bed and begin treatment. It looks bad, he said. You've let it go too long. He looked down at the chart and wrote something. How bad, I asked. He said that they would have to do tests to find out. I filled in the form, my name, my address, and then my next of kin. I realized that I did not have a next of kin. I did not want them to contact any of my uncles. I wrote down my mother's name, and the address of my apartment. I gave them all the other details they wanted. I thought of them phoning the empty apartment with news about me, and nobody answering the phone.

A porter led me in a wheelchair to a ward. I put my bag on my lap. It was like something from a movie, the long corridors, the strip lighting, the half-glimpses into rooms where people lay in bed, the silence of the night. He wheeled me into a ward with five other beds, all with figures in them lying asleep. A nurse came and pulled the curtains around my bed and told me in whispers to undress here and get into bed. The doctor, she said, would be around shortly. As soon as I began to undress I started coughing again. I lay on the bed with my shoes off until it stopped. I was sure now that I was going to die. Slowly, I took off my clothes and put on the pyjamas I had brought with me. I was too hot for blankets. I waited for the doctor to come. I began to feel thirsty, but when I tried to drink from the jug of water beside the bed, it was impossible to swallow. More time went by and I lay there waiting.

I was half-asleep when a doctor and a nurse came with a trolley of instruments. They turned the light on over my bed. When I saw one of the nurses prepare a needle I felt afraid. I suddenly did not want this. A doctor told me to take down my pyjama-bottoms and turn around. He had the needle in his hand. The nurse daubed cotton wool on the skin of my hip, and the doctor put the needle in. At first I felt nothing, but when the pain came it was sharp and made me tense. The nurse put her hand on my shoulder and told me to relax. The needle went in further now, I could feel it tearing something inside, and then the doctor withdrew it, and the nurse put more cotton wool on the skin. I pulled up my pyjama-bottoms and lay back. Another needle connected to a drip which the nurse set up beside me was put into my arm. The doctor listened to my chest on the stethoscope once more. Neither of them spoke to each other or to me. When they had finished, they walked away as though I did not exist. The nurse who worked on the ward came and pulled back the curtains.

I lay there all night without sleeping, watching everything that moved in the ward and the corridor outside like a baby who has just come into the world and opened its eyes. I watched as the man in the middle bed across the way soiled himself in the night and a couple of nurses came and led him out to the bathroom while they changed the sheets on his bed. I watched the boy in the bed beside me quietly go out to the toilet and come back in again. I watched the man in the bed opposite me wake and sit up and call the nurse and then lie down and go back to sleep. And I watched the dawn, and then the lights coming on in the corridor and the ward, and then breakfast starting. I had not moved all night. A nurse came and took my temperature and my blood pressure. She told me not to take any breakfast as I would be going soon for a bronchoscopy. I asked her what that was; she said it was a test on my lungs. I asked her what my temperature was; she said it was high. She looked at my chart and she could not believe that I had not slept.

About an hour later, I was wheeled down to a sort of operating theatre and left waiting in an ante-room. I wondered if they were going to use needles again. I had a vision of them sticking a needle in my back, all the way into my lungs, and sucking out some liquid which they could test. It only occurred to me when they wheeled me into the theatre that they were going to stick a machine down my throat. I asked the doctor if he could make me unconscious for this. He was a tall man in his fifties. He reacted as though he had not been listening, and then he looked at me and nodded ruefully: if I wanted to be asleep then he was sure he could do something to help. I watched the nurse prepare another needle. But when the doctor came over with the needle he could not find a vein in my left arm. He told me to open and close my hand. Eventually, he stuck the needle in. I gasped and he told me to keep still.

I woke in a small room with a window looking over a lawn. There was a machine beside me with tubes coming from it. One went into my arm, another into my neck. I felt pain in my chest and my back. The room was painted white; there was a window looking onto a corridor. I did not know what time it was, or what day, but I realized that I should send a message to my secretary. Every breath was difficult. I saw two figures at the window looking in at me. I turned and stared at them, but I was too exhausted, and I closed my eyes again and let my head rest on the pillow. It was a moment or two later that I turned and looked again, and by that time I knew that I had seen one of the doctors before; he was the American doctor who had seen Mart. Now he had a chart in his hand and he was looking down at the chart and nodding and then looking in through the window at me.

I suddenly realized that I had AIDS, that's what it was, that's why the American doctor was looking at me. I closed my eyes again. A nurse came to take my temperature. I asked to see the doctor in charge and she told me that the team would be around later. I asked her what time it was. She said it was four o'clock. I gave her my office number and asked her to contact Luisa and get her to call personally at the hospital. I lay back thinking that this would be the end, then, that my body would be covered in a sheet and pushed on a trolley to the morgue, that before then I would spend weeks, maybe months, languishing here or at home, becoming thinner and weaker, waiting for the long ordeal that would result in being alive one minute, alert, with a full memory, and the next minute dead, everything gone. I would fade away. I wondered if there was anything I could do at this stage, if I could begin hoarding sleeping pills, if I could get it all over with easily, now.

No doctor came until late that night. I was half-dozing and when I looked up I saw the American doctor standing over the bed. He was not in a white coat. He was wearing a green pullover and an open-necked shirt. When he spoke in faltering Spanish, I realized that he must have learned it in Colombia or Mexico. He introduced himself as Doctor Cawley; he said that he was in charge of infectious diseases, and he wanted my permission to test me for a few things, including TB and HIV. These were more or less routine tests, he said. I had a serious form of pneumonia, and he needed as much information as he could get.

'Do you think I am HIV positive?' I asked him in English.

'Anything is possible,' he said. 'Anyone in this hospital could be positive.'

'I mean do you think that this pneumonia is part of AIDS?'

'I need to do a test,' he said. 'Otherwise we're just speculating.'

'How long does a test take to do?'

'If I send someone in to draw blood in the morning, I could probably have the results by Friday. The TB test is quicker.'

'Will I still be here on Friday?'

'Yes, it will take quite a while to deal with your pneumonia. It is quite serious.'

'How serious?'

'Only the next few days will tell that. Can I ask you about your sexual history? Are you married?'

'No, I'm gay.'

'Have you been at risk?'

'I don't think so.'

'What do you mean?'

'I mean I have not had unprotected sex since about 1984.'

'And before then?'

I shrugged. He looked down at the chart.

'Can I send in my registrar in the morning?' he asked.

I nodded.

'Is there anything else you want to ask me?'

'Yes, I took a lot of cocaine over the weekend. Do you think that has affected me?'

'No, probably not. I think that the pneumonia has been there for quite some time.'

As he turned to go out he smiled, and I remembered him vividly from that moment when he had accompanied Mart to the side door of the hospital. But then it struck me that it was a different hospital.

'Are you attached to this hospital only?'

'No, I'm involved with infectious diseases overall. I move around.' He smiled again, and then his face became serious and he left the room.

As the young doctor took the blood in the morning, I tried to pray, but I discovered instead that I was talking to my mother and my father and I was asking their help, asking them to make sure that I was okay. For some of the time I was sure that I was infected, and I knew that the results would come back positive, but I found myself going over every phrase the doctor had used, how anyone in the hospital could be HIV positive, how the test was routine. I noticed that since I had been moved into this room, nurses and doctors put on gloves when they came close to me. I wondered if pneumonia was infectious.

When my secretary came, she looked surprised and asked me what was wrong. I told her that I had appendicitis. I said to tell anyone who rang that I was in Comodoro Rivadavia, and I would be back next week. I asked her to call in every day, in case there were messages or important letters. I gave her a list of newspapers, magazines and books I wanted. She wrote everything down. I told her not to come in on Friday.

Every two hours, even in the night, my temperature was taken and my chart was written up and the tubes were checked. Doctors came and went; further blood samples were taken. Sometimes, doctors and nurses spoke about me as though I were not there. I slept and woke and dozed and slept again. I listened to the radio. I felt weak and breathless. I hated the bedpan, trying to shit while lying on my back and calling the nurse when I had finished. I hated injections, the thin needle coming towards me. But mostly, I thought about my blood being tested. I did not know what the testing system looked like, or why it took so long, or what process they used. I thought about my blood lying there in some laboratory in the night, slowly sending out its messages and signals. I concentrated on it, I willed it to be okay. I thought that if it was positive I would try to kill myself, and then I thought that I should ring Pablo and ask him to help me, but I did not think I could do that, and I did not think that I would kill myself. I was reassured by the fact that I had not become thin. There was nothing wrong with my stomach. I was not sweating too much. The fever came from the pneumonia. And anyone could get pneumonia, just as anyone in this hospital could be HIV positive.

I waited all day Thursday, watching the window for Doctor Cawley in case the results came early. I went through the post which Luisa brought me, and tried to read the newspapers, but I was too tired. Two nurses came with soap and hot water to wash me. They dealt with my body as though it were a piece of furniture, as though touching it was of no interest to them. I lay there trying not to be embarrassed.

I woke on Friday thinking that this would be the most important day of my life. If the result was negative, I promised myself that things would change. I would live a better life; I would work out what I must do. Around lunchtime I dozed for a while and when I woke I could not remember what was wrong, and then I realized that I was waiting for the result, someone was going to come and tell me whether I would live or die. I became desperately afraid and anxious, and watched the corridor all the time for signs of the American doctor.

I knew that the HIV virus was mainly passed on by anal intercourse, by letting someone come inside you. I thought back over the times I had done this, but it had been years ago. A nurse arrived to take my temperature; a doctor came to listen to my chest. Another nurse took my chart away. I lay there wanting this to be over. I thought about swimming in warm water, of lying back and floating in the sea. I thought about sex with Pablo when I met him first.

And then, it must have been about five o'clock, the American doctor appeared. I smiled at him and tried to sit up. He did not smile. I thought that he was here to tell me it was negative, but I must be careful in future. I was absolutely sure that it was okay. He closed the door behind him and walked across the room until he was standing with his back to the window.

'It's positive,' he said. 'I've checked it twice and it's positive. I'm very sorry to have to tell you this.'

'This is a nightmare,' I said. I wanted to push back the time, make it one minute earlier, make him cross the room again and tell me that it was okay. He looked calm as he stood there.

'I'm very sorry to have to tell you this,' he said again. 'We were pretty sure when we saw the strain of pneumonia, but obviously we had to do the test.'

'How long have I had it?'

'The virus? It's hard to say, ten years, eight years, six years.'

'Could I have got it in the last two years?'

'I would say not. It's very unlikely.'

'What's the prognosis?'

'We'll work at treating the PCP, which is the type of pneumonia associated with HIV, but it will take time, and, to be frank, there may be other
complications.'

'Like?'

'Your immune system is very weak, and has been considerably weakened by the PCP, and there's very little we can do about that.'

'Do you mean that I don't have much time?'

'I don't know what's around the corner. You can never tell, but at the
moment, well, at the moment, we'll just have to do our best.'

'How long do I have?'

'It always depends on the person. If you were in your twenties, you
would be stronger, but we should concentrate on dealing with what you
have now. I'll come back in the morning and maybe we can talk more
then. Again, I'm really sorry for being the one who had to tell you this.'

'Is there no chance it could be something else?'

'I'll have a second blood test done, but I would say not.'

'Am I going to die then?'

He looked at me and said nothing. He turned and looked out of the
window.

'Things do not look good. I must say that to you. I have a counsellor
outside, and she would like to come in and talk to you now.'

'What will she do?'

'Her job is to deal with all your worries and fears.'

He went to the door and opened it, and looked as though he were
about to say something. He nodded and went out. I lay there trying to
imagine that this had not happened. I kept saying 'I cannot handle this'
over and over to myself.

The counsellor came in and pulled up a chair beside the bed. She
asked me if I wanted someone to ring my mother. I told her that my
mother was dead. She looked at the chart and said, no, her name and
number are here. No, she's dead, I said, she died years ago, and I do not
have anybody else who is close to me and you can ring her if you like but

you will get no reply. The woman held my hand. You must be devastated, she said, you must be devastated. Have you cried yet, she asked. Maybe you should cry. I shook my head and said that I did not want to cry. Did I have any friend whom I would like to see, she asked. No, I did not, I told her. I would be okay, I said, I did not want to see anybody. I might feel differently in the morning, she said. I wanted her to leave me. Had I made a will, she asked. It might put my mind at rest if I made a will. I told her I would think about it and talk to her in the morning. She said that she did not usually come in on Saturdays but she would come to the hospital in the morning in case I needed to talk some more.

I lay there believing that someone would come to talk to me, that someone would give me an injection and make me sleep, that I would have an hour or two away from this, in oblivion somewhere. When it got late I called a nurse and said that I needed a sleeping pill. She said that she would ask the doctor on duty. When she did not return I called her again. She said she had asked the doctor and would ask him again. Later, she came back with a pill in a tiny plastic cup. I took the pill and lay back and tried to sleep. I dreamed that I was dead. I was lying in the hold of a boat at the marina beside my house. I was naked, my body was all white and washed, ready to be taken out to sea, my dick was all slack and my eyes were closed and my mouth was closed, and I could hear the motor starting and the rush of water against the body of the boat. Two men were talking. I lay there, dead, inert. But my mind was still there, and I could feel everything and know everything and remember everything. But I could not move or speak and soon I would be lowered overboard and there would be nothing I could do. When I woke I realized that the dream was real, that being awake was no relief. I watched the lights come on in the corridor outside and the morning begin in the hospital. I thought of the American doctor lying asleep in a bed somewhere in the city, at ease and warm. I lay there repeating to myself the phrase 'I cannot handle this' as though it would save my life.

from

Clockers

by Richard Price

'Do you know that more young men get killed on Thursday nights than any other time of the week?' Rodney drove with a long Vienna Finger sticking out of his mouth. 'This *cop* told me that.'

'Yeah, huh?' Strike watched the cookie shrink under Rodney's mustache.

'Yeah, 'cause it's like the longest time away from the last paycheck, so everybody's all strung out and it's kind of like the beginning of the *weekend, so . . .*'

'Huh.' Strike wasn't really listening. He sat in the shotgun seat with ten dollars on his hip and twenty-odd thousand on his lap, the Toys R Us shopping bag like a lump of radiation as Rodney rolled through the red lights as if they were stop signs.

'So you got Futon running it again?'

'Yeah well, he's the least worst.'

Rodney had left the Cadillac in front of the candy store and taken his van, a hollow rusty hulk with two naked S-frame seats in front, nothing in back except a few loose orange soda cans rolling around on the carpetless floor, the lazy rattling driving Strike crazy.

Strike thought cash and dope exchanges were Erroll Barnes's department. He had wondered and worried about it nonstop since the night before, but now he didn't want to bring it up, preferring to be in the dark than be told to stop and sniff the motherfuckin' roses again. He assumed they were headed over to the O'Brien projects, where Champ held court. Rodney was Champ's lieutenant like Strike was Rodney's lieutenant, and Champ controlled the bottles in Dempsy, buying three kilos a week from New York, stepping on it to make six and distributing the six kis to Rodney and five other lieutenants. The kis cost Champ eighteen grand each for the three, but he sold the stepped-on six for twenty-five grand each to his lieutenants, making a profit of a hundred thousand dollars a week for a few hours' work. Champ had it knocked—no fuss, no muss, no sweating out a million ten-dollar bottle transactions. Champ even had four baby Rottweilers, each one named after a cop in the Fury. That's why he was Champ. Strike just hoped that when they got to O'Brien Rodney would leave him in the car, because he didn't want to know where Champ's dope apartment was. He could live without that information.

Two blocks into JFK Boulevard Rodney got waved over by a pipehead with two shopping bags. Rodney pulled over and peered down, his chin on his arm, the pipehead shiny-eyed, stinking, holding a taped-up box for Rodney's consideration.

'A waterator.' His voice dropped to the lockjaw bass growl that came from hitting the pipe.

Rodney stared at the picture of the water-purifying siphon on the box, clucked his tongue, reached into his pocket and pulled out a fat wad, lots of hundreds. He counted out ten singles, then tossed the box in the back of the van. The basehead mumbled something in the neighborhood of thanks and loped away.

Rodney drove on, saluting his street crews on the boulevard like a general, the clockers dancing in place, absently swinging their arms, smacking fists into open palms, yelling out his name, every once in a while dashing up to the van to ask him something, including one of his other lieutenants, who told Rodney to stop daydreaming and answer his damn beeper, they were down to next to nothing.

Strike didn't really know these clockers. They worked the boulevard lived on the side streets and didn't do nearly as much business as the clockers in the projects—but they also didn't get hassled by the Fury, which only worked public housing. It cost Rodney four to five thousand a week in envelopes to keep the flow going out here. Strike knew that Rodney had worked out something with enough police in various squads and shifts so that as long as the JFK crews were discreet, no one would bust them. But the Fury wouldn't take a dime. Not that they did much more than harass when it came down to it—any night they grabbed as much as two clips was a good night for them. But they were still a pain.

A girl moved along the sidewalk in a mincing half jog, pacing the van, waving for Rodney to stop. The dragging of her high-heeled sandals on the pavement sounded like someone shoveling snow. She was dressed in a red bolero jacket with padded shoulders and a brocade pillbox hat, but Strike saw that she had that sickening gloopy smile of some bitch that'll do anything for a bottle.

Rodney pulled over, and she started in by making small talk and flirting. Then she got down to it.

'Rodney, I got to get this nice sweater I want. This girl sewed it for me, but she says she wants her money tonight.'

Rodney, heavy-eyed, grunted, 'Uh-huh.' The girl worked a gold ring off her finger, its diamond chip a pinhole of light.

'She wants twenty dollar, so you hold this here.' She gave him the ring, pointing out the diamond. 'You know me, you know it's real, see that? I'll come back get it from you tomorrow night, OK?'

Rodney exhaled through his nose, dug out a twenty, held it out between his fingertips, then snatched it away at the last second. 'You don't come back with my twenty tomorrow night, don't bother coming back at all, now. The ring be mine then, you understand?'

The girl looked at her ring, hesitating. 'What if you hold it till Saturday? I'll get you the twenty back Saturday.'

Rodney shook his head and gave her back the ring, the twenty vanishing into his fist. She didn't like that at all, chattering 'OK, OK, OK,' and coaxing the crumpled twenty out of his hand. 'I'll see you tomorrow.'

Rodney drove away from her, studying the ring for a half block, then stuffing it into his pocket.

He made three more stops, once to buy two factory-wrapped horror videotapes from another pipehead with a shopping bag, ten bucks, once to take a leak against the side of a building, some other girl coming up to him as he was pissing, saying, 'Can I talk to you private?' and finally pulling up on a side street in front of a shabby and dark wood-frame house, getting out on the sidewalk and whistling as if for a dog. A scruffed-up pipehead with a ragged beard and a dirty plaid shirt came out of the house onto the porch, a shard of wood sticking out the side of his hair like a chopstick.

'What's up?' Rodney rocked on his heels.

'I almos' finish, man. I tol' you I get it done tonight, right? I got almos' all the downstairs all cleaned up, *boxed* shit, *bagged* shit. You want to see?'

Rodney shook his head. 'You don't leave till you finish, right?'

Seeing no light on inside, Strike wondered how this guy cleaned up in the dark.

Then he saw Rodney take a rubber-band-bound clip of ten purple-stoppered bottles out of his pocket, pluck out five and pass them up to the raggedy guy on the porch. The guy bowed his head and retreated into the house with his bottles. Watching Rodney pass out the dope on the street as if they were cigarettes made Strike sink into his seat with panic: Rodney might as well wear a damn 'Bust Me' sign while he was at it.

Rodney climbed back into the van, pissing and moaning about the house. 'I can get five, six families in there we get it fixed up right, you know? But I can't get a goddamn home improvement loan. 'Cause I do it up front with cash, the IRS is gonna say, Whoa, how you pay for this? Then it's theirs, you know?'

Strike was silent, shaking his head, thinking of the other five bottles still riding in Rodney's pocket.

'You got to have houses,' Rodney said as he pulled into the road. 'I tell you niggers that all the time. This shit's gonna be over someday. Put it in houses, you can get off the street and still make some serious bread. 'Cause I'm getting too old for this shit and I got to make my break, you know? I got me the candy store, the crap house, and I got me four properties now like for rentals. Soon's I get the motherfuckin' improvement loans, I'm off the *street*, I'm in *houses*.' He nodded, tightlipped. 'Give me houses, bawh . . .'

Strike didn't want to hear it: 'What the fuck's *wrong* with you, man, paying that nigger in *bottles*, drivin' aroun' with *bottles*. Let me know up front about that, OK?' Strike rubbed his gut, his face swelling with agitation. 'I mean *goddamn*, Rodney . . . I mean Jesus Christ.'

Rodney smiled. 'I say to the nigger, I give you fifty dollars clean out the ground floor. So it's like this, do I give him five ten-dollar bottles cost me a dollar fifty each? Or do I give him fifty dollars cold cash? What do I do?'

'What you *do*,' Strike said, 'is you don't take a chance on getting caught holding. You pay the nigger his fifty dollars so *this* motherfucker'—he stabbed a finger at the Toys R Us bag—'don't wind up in a goddamn police locker and *this* motherfucker'—he grabbed his own crotch—'don't wind up in no county bullpen. Goddamn, how you get to be *you* anyhow?'

Rodney was still smiling, off somewhere. 'I tell you what happened last week? I got pulled over by this new knocko team. You know that new flyin' squad they got? They got me with a clip. I'm thinking, I don't even *know* these motherfuckers, ho shit, what do I do now, 'cause I got so much violence on my goddamn jacket, they pull me in even with this itty bitty clip, I'm going away three years if a *day*, an' like this flyin' squad supposed to be the goddamn Texas Rangers or the Green Berets, you know? I don't even know what to say, they got me hands up on the car, this little old pink-eyed Santa Claus-looking motherfucker patting me up my legs. He gets up around my chest, you know like *hold*ing me from behind? Starts whisperin' in my ear, "I want a Cadillac." Just like that.' Rodney drove on, smiling. ' "I want a Cadillac.' "

Strike stared at him, waiting for more.

'I had to give him five thousand dollars and I'm supposed to get up another five for him tonight. After that, me and him'll work something out but goddamn, that little ol' clip cost me a thousand a bottle, ain't that some shit?'

'So why you carrying again tonight for?' Strike's voice dropped to a sullen mutter. He was thinking about the cop who had the message for Rodney, the cop working on getting a Caddy for himself.

Rodney just shrugged. 'I'm getting outa this life.'

'Houses.' Strike said it to mock him.

'Houses. You learnin'.'

Strike knew why Rodney was carrying the bottles. He was a damn addict as sure as any other bug-eyed dope fiend out there, hooked on being the *man*. The man? Rodney was more like God because of those bottles. He couldn't drive twenty feet without causing someone to bubble over with hope and joy. He couldn't walk into a room without every lost child in there jerking his way like he was some kind of magnet. All that from bottles: the bottles were the beginning and the end of it. It wasn't the money itself, because no one ever felt that way about a holdup man or some other kind of thief no matter how much they took in.

And Rodney was talking about houses. Strike could just see Rodney giving up his bad-man bottle-king glamour, giving up all that love, to be some landlord chasing down pipeheads for back rent they'd already spent on bottles, giving it to whatever new king had taken over Rodney's throne.

All the kilo men and ounce men around town talked about real estate, about getting out, but Strike knew they were all full of shit. They were all stone junkies like Rodney, hooked on a lifetime of hustling, of making it the outlaw way, hooked on their status as street stars. It was just like Strike's mother said when they'd had their big fight: 'How much is enough? How much money do you have to make to retire? Who do you think you're hustling with that nonsense, me or yourself?'

As Rodney trolled JFK, Strike conjured up his mother's face when she spoke those words, saw again the set of her mouth, the unblinking conviction in her eyes. She had been so sure of her knowledge that she hadn't even raised her voice. Well, now he knew that she was right, knew that he was probably no different from Rodney by now, hooked on the dope of recognition, of adoration. And Strike was just getting started.

THEY DROVE ALONG a miracle mile of strip of Highway I-9, one side of the road lined with carpet outlets, waterbed showrooms and Chinese restaurants, the other by a dark park bordered by a low stone wall. Strike saw the towers of the O'Brien projects about a mile ahead, but long before they got there Rodney slowed down, coming to a full stop on the park side of I-9 behind a Ford Taurus with New York rental plates. There was no one in the car, but Strike saw three Latinos sitting in the shadows on top of the stone wall and listening to a Spanish radio station on a boom box.

'Leave the money in the car.' Rodney grunted, getting out of the van. Strike did as he was told, then slipped onto the sidewalk, feeling jittery and exposed. He didn't know what was happening but would have felt better about it if everybody was indoors.

The Latinos slid off the wall, and the biggest one clasped hands with Rodney, Rodney drawling, 'Papi, my man Papi.' No one looked at Strike, not Papi or the other two, both of them wearing jackets in the warm weather to cover their guns.

'Where you been, brother? I beeped you like three times.' Papi giggled and danced nervously from foot to foot as if he had to pee. He was huge — six three, 230 pounds — wearing an orange Milwaukee Brewers T-shirt over baggy khaki pants. He had calico eyes, a mustardy cat color, the exact tone of his skin. 'I figure my man Rodney's takin' care of some heavy business. Your beeper fucked up, man? I figure maybe you dint recognize the number 'cause I was calling from a *pay* phone.'

'Yeah, I knew it was you.' Rodney's voice was a high singsong. 'Anytime I don't know a number coming in, I know it be Papi.'

Papi exploded into giggles again, tossing his head like a horse. 'Rodney, fuckin' Rodney, man.'

Strike saw tombstones and granite angels in the shadows over the park wall. He looked back at the Latinos' car, and the New York plates made him sick to his stomach: Rodney was getting into something here that might be way out of bounds.

' 'Cause we waitin' like an *hour* here,' Papi said, pushing it. 'I got fuckin' people stacked up like *air*planes, you know? So what was it, like you didn't hear it when the number came in? You like looked down at it later?' Papi smiled, waiting for an explanation.

Strike noticed one of the Latinos studying him. He was a slender, baby-faced teenager, smaller than Strike. A black watch cap pulled down over his hair made his black eyes enormous. The boy looked away, spit a pearl of saliva over the wall into the cemetery.

Rodney gave Papi a backhanded wave. 'Naw, man, I heard it. I heard it every time. It's what you said, I was takin' care of business.'

Papi looked dreamily at Rodney for a beat, as if wondering where to take it. He abruptly reached behind him, elbow high, and Strike's stomach shot a red stream: gun.

But Papi only came up with a beeper that had been clipped to his belt. He pushed a button and it began to vibrate. Papi held it out in his palm to Rodney.

Rodney took it, turning it this way and that. 'Gah-damn, man, what the fuck?'

Strike saw the black-eyed gun boy disappear around the street side of the van.

'Sometime you don't want the beeper noise, that beeper-beep, you know?' Papi beamed.

'Gah-damn, I stick this up some bitch's pussy? She can take a message and get off at the same time, ain't that something?'

The boy rejoined the group holding something between his ribs and his elbow but out of sight under his jacket. Papi was howling at Rodney's comment, staggering as if he was gut shot. The others seemed not to understand English. Rodney handed the vibrating beeper to Strike. Strike made a fast pass at looking intrigued but then didn't know who to give it to. The thing had a powerful, insistent pulse that made it seem alive.

Suddenly the two gun boys became casually alert, turning at the same time and leaning back to look down the dark sidewalk at a lone figure emerging from the shadows, walking toward the group, about a hundred yards off. Papi noticed him too, and his wet laughter subsided into sighs, then just a dewy smile. Rodney winked at Strike, Strike thinking: Ho shit, now what? But as the figure came closer—average height, shoulders hunched as if he was cold, taking small unhurried steps—Strike saw who it was: Erroll Barnes. Everybody made him out at the same time, became relaxed again, but Papi's jokey hysteria was replaced by a sober calm. Strike watched Erroll draw near. He was thirty-five but looked fifty, frail with close-cropped gray hair and beard. His face was deeply furrowed, like a thumb had plowed lines through clay across his forehead and down his cheeks. His mouth was a flat line and his eyes were both furtive and blank. He looked as if he had never uttered a full sentence of conversation in his life.

When Erroll was still a few yards from the group, Rodney raised both hands overhead as if someone had said 'Stick 'em up.'

'Papi,' Rodney barked, hands high, backpedaling to the van. 'Vaya con Dios.'

'Mi amor.' Papi saluted, then turned to Strike. 'My friend . . . ' He smiled expectantly, an open sentence.

Strike nodded goodbye but didn't think that was what the guy was driving at. It took a moment before he realized that Papi was asking for his beeper back.

Strike and Rodney pulled away from the curb just as Erroll reached the group. Reading faces, Strike could tell that Papi had a completely different manner with Rodney gone and Erroll there.

'What you into here?' Strike asked. 'What was that?'

'What was what?' Rodney said, his mouth puckered with secret amuse-
ments.

'I didn't *like* that.' Strike pointedly looked out his side window.

'Didn't like what?' Rodney laughed. 'You just said you dint know what
that was, so how you know you dint like it?'

The gloomy towers of the O'Brien projects were coming up at the next
light and Strike braced himself for the turn. 'Just get the business over
with and take me back to the benches.'

But Rodney flew right by the projects, then drawled out of the side of
his mouth, 'Business *is* over with.'

Startled, Strike sat up, automatically feeling under the seat for the
money. The Toys R Us bag was gone.

'SEE NOW USUALLY I let Erroll do it *all*, you know? Carry the cash
and take the dope, but tonight I figured I do the cash half so's I could
show you the people. Let everybody get a look at everybody for future ref-
erence, just in case I got to ever ask you for some *help*. See what I'm
sayin'?'

Strike was sitting in Rodney's living room on a plastic-slipcovered
turquoise couch, keeping his mouth shut, thinking that as long as he held
his peace he wasn't involved.

He had never been invited to Rodney's house before, never had the
security status of 'house-comfortable,' and he felt both dizzy and alert:
What the fuck was going on? He couldn't stay quiet any longer.

'But y'alls buying from New York people. Champ is gonna *kill* you
man. You can't do that.'

Rodney, nude to the waist, stood by the refrigerator eating a chicken
leg. 'Champ is cool.' He licked his fingers. 'Champ's getting his money.
He got no complaints.'

'You can't *do* that,' Strike said weakly, too freaked to expend a lot of
heat in argument.

Rodney's apartment looked like every other seventy-five-year-old shotgun flat in Dempsy: a small living room going straight back to a same-size
bedroom, continuing back to a kitchen behind which, in a small T, were a
bathroom to one side and a tiny bedroom to the other. There were no doors
to separate the front rooms, just the barest bit of indented molding to define

one area from the next, so that sitting in the living room, Strike found himself staring directly at a pink satin-covered queen-size brass bed twenty feet away and at the kitchen sink fifteen feet beyond that. Rodney had moved in here twenty-two years ago, Strike thinking, Big real estate man.

'You want some?' Rodney extended a Tupperware bowl full of chicken. Strike reflexively touched his stomach as if he was full. Rodney shrugged. 'You go on like this, you ain't gonna have no ass on you at all.'

'I eat.'

'Yeah, you a real pig.' Rodney sighed, then got into it. 'Look, let me tell you about Champ. Champ is on the street, but Papi's about *weight*. It ain't got nothing to do with Champ. What I buy from Papi goes out in ounces and it never see the light of day. I got people coming up from south Jersey, from Pennsylvania—shit, I even got me a customer from Ver*mont*. I don't even know where Vermont *is*. Alls I know is I get me a ki from Papi so good I step on it three times and can still sell a ounce for nine hundred dollars. And the goddamn ki is cheaper up front than the stepped-on shit I buy from Champ.' Rodney belched, hunched over, squinted into the refrigerator. 'Champ is bottles, so don't you worry about Champ.'

Strike dropped his forehead to his palms. 'You can't bring in no dope to Dempsy and sell it. Champ's gonna fuck you up.'

'Who said I sell it here?'

'Well, where you sell it then?'

'Out of town.'

'Where at?'

'I got me a partner.'

Strike gave up. Nobody told nobody nothing save for what they wanted them to know, and even then they were full of shit, just out of habit.

Rodney took a long chef's apron off a hook on the kitchen wall, draped it over his naked chest, fished around the kitchen, reaching into the cabinets, under the sink, then came into the living room holding a big stainless steel wok, a brown jar of lactose, an eggbeater and a fold of cheesecloth.

He sat down across from Strike, placing the paraphernalia on a heavily varnished driftwood coffee table. He rubbed his face with both hands and leaned back, his arms spanning the length of the couch. The matching couches were too big for the tiny front room, but to Strike it seemed that the room itself was too big for the room. Thick blue shag rugs, heavy tan drapes, cutesy statuettes of dentists and drunks and milk-maids everywhere you turned, a fake antique white telephone, three televisions stacked one atop the other, at least two of them looking broken, figurine lamps with suedelike pleated shades sheathed in plastic, graduation pictures, wedding pictures and more diplomas mounted or propped on every flat surface, vivid sunsets painted onto sections of driftwood to match the coffee table, a laminated Jesus holding out his heart from some more driftwood over Rodney's head, a four-foot-high stuffed pink panther like a prize from a carnival standing in a corner of the room—for some reason even that was in a clear plastic bag—and finally a small mini-bar refrigerator, which Strike guessed held dope, booze, money or guns. The whole room made Strike feel like smashing his head through a window just to get some air.

Rodney leaned forward suddenly, looking at his watch. 'You hear what happened to one of my boys on the boulevard?'

Strike was silent, thinking about Newark stickup men, Erroll Barnes, Champ, retribution. Maybe Rodney's new dealings were cool if he kept them out of town. But they seemed dangerously shortsighted, and Strike felt his stutter coming back even though he had nothing to say.

'This old boy like fourteen? He got dumped by a girl so he put some Comet in a glass of milk for hisself, they take him to the hospital and who do he call for, his mother? Hell no, he call for *me*. Ain't that somethin'? Called me first. I got up there like to tear him a new asshole, almost killin' hisself over a thirteen-year-old girl. I tol' him I ain't havin' no business with a fool like that, he better *learn* some things if he wants to continue on with me. Called me first . . . ' Rodney palmed his mouth to mask a satisfied smirk.

'Woo-what you got me up here for, Rodney?' Strike felt as if he was breathing through a pinched straw. 'What's up, like juh-just . . . ' His lips fluttered, then clamped shut, and Strike just let it go. Too much trouble.

There was a soft rap at the door and Rodney lunged to his feet. The apron, untied at the waist, flapped in front of him like a five-foot bib.

Rodney opened the door for Erroll Barnes, who floated into the living room as if he didn't own footsteps. His furrowed face seemed as big as a balloon, and Strike sat frozen, never having been so close or even indoors with him before. Erroll looked at Strike for only a second, then glanced to

Rodney for verification that everything was OK. Rodney shrugged and Erroll took a quart-size Ziploc bag filled with coke out of his jacket, laid it on the coffee table, glanced at Strike one more time and left the house, Rodney saying a soft 'Awright' at the door.

Strike felt as if Erroll was still in the room. He was amazed at how frail the man seemed—more shadow than flesh. And then Strike realized what he'd seen when Erroll was actually standing before him: stuck in Erroll's waistband, right over his belly, was a .38.

Coming back to the table, Rodney stood over the coke, chin on his chest, as he tied the apron strings behind his back. 'Ol' Erroll ain't gonna be aroun' much longer.' He said it softly, as if Erroll had an ear to the wall.

'He goin' up for sentencing?'

Rodney made a quick face. 'He got the Virus.'

'Virus?' Strike's voice fell away. The Virus, for Strike, was something out of the monster closet that struck at the heart of his lifelong dread of others, a ghastly reminder for him to stay true to his instinct for distance. The Virus wasn't a disease; it was a personal message from God or the Devil, and in Strike's imagination the messenger would look something like Erroll Barnes. Erroll's having the Virus was like death squared.

'Yeah, ol' Erroll . . . ' Rodney sat down again. 'The nigger mostly smoke and bluff now, you know, but everybody so scared a him on legend alone, man, that people are gonna be walking tippy-toe two years after he's dead.'

Strike scrambled to remember if he had touched Erroll at all. He imagined he felt something scuttle up his thigh. He slapped at it, then scratched his chest and ran a thumb down his temples. He was sweating.

'Yeah, dint you see that white shit up in his mouth? That the Virus, man. Las' week I had to carry him up a flight of stairs like a baby.' Rodney shook his head sadly as he dumped the contents of the plastic bag into the wok. Then, measuring by eye, he added about two ounces of lactose, draped the cheesecloth over the bowl, slipped the eggbeater through a slit in the cloth and stepped on a quarter kilo as if making whipped cream.

'Erroll give up the needle a little too late, you know? All *proud* a hisself for going on the methadone. Tch-tch. That's why I don't sell that heroin shit anymore. Too disgusting.'

Strike hugged himself, his hands up under his armpits, as he watched Rodney make product. He tilted his chin at the wok. 'That Papi's?'

'Naw, man, this for Champ, this for *bottles*,' Rodney said with contempt. 'Erroll dropped off Papi's shit somewheres else. This for tonight's re-up. You alls gonna help me bottle this, then I'm gonna drop you back by your car.'

Strike didn't know much about Rodney's dealings on the kilo level, mainly the logistics and a little of his marketing strategy. He knew that when Rodney bought his weekly ki from Champ, Erroll picked it up, divided it into quarters and delivered three of the quarters to three old people who held the dope in exchange for having their rent paid, and maybe a little walkaround cash if Rodney had known them from his childhood. Erroll delivered the fourth quarter to Rodney for bottling. Rodney liked to do it himself, converting a loose quarter ki into anywhere from eight hundred to a thousand ten-dollar bottles. Every other day or so, as the bottles started drying up on the street, Erroll brought over another quarter. As a rule, Rodney stepped on alternating re-ups, sending the first bunch of bottles out on the street uncut, getting the pipeheads all excited by the quality, so that by the time the word had gone out and the first batch was sold, the second quarter was out on the street—not as good, but with a built-in market ready to snatch it up. And by the time *that* was all sold and they started complaining that it was weaker, up came the third batch all strong and pure again, the word going out and the ensuing rush to buy spilling over into the last quarter's bottles, which Rodney stepped on again.

All the pipeheads knew Rodney's game, and each day they tried to guess which quarter ki was out there. But even if they wound up with a weaker bottle, they still hung around because tomorrow's bottles would probably be better. Rodney made more money faster than any of the other lieutenants who put a heavier cut on their packages, because half the time his product was the best in town and because, as Rodney had told Strike more than once, 'everybody likes to find out what's behind door number three.'

Finding himself once again lost in a drifting list of all that Rodney had taught him over the last year or so, Strike suddenly remembered who Rodney reminded him of, the long-ago resemblance that had been nibbling at the edges of his consciousness: Wilson Pickett. Strike's father had had an album of Wilson Pickett songs in the house when Strike was a kid, and the singing face on the sky-blue cover was a dead ringer for Rodney's.

Now, sitting on Rodney's couch, Strike recalled that when he was little, when he was five or six and his father was still alive, his father would sometimes throw back a few beers and call his boys into the living room. He would plant them on the green couch opposite the record player and sing for them, accompanying Wilson Pickett on 'International Playboy,' or the Impressions on 'It's All Right.' Strike's father had never been a heavy drinker, and whenever he did get a little messed up he'd never do anything mean or violent. He'd just want to talk about things, like how he could have been a professional singer, how he'd grown up in Jersey City with Kool of Kool and the Gang, and how Kool had wanted him to join the group, but he said no because he didn't want to leave 'you boys' mother' all alone while he went out on tour. He would explain all this to Strike and Victor as they sat on that couch all solemn and quiet, legs swinging, only slightly scared as their father would abruptly kick in on 'Ninety-nine and a Half Just Won't Do' or 'I Found a Love' with a powerful tenor that turned the living room into a church of regret.

Now Rodney removed the cheesecloth, carefully shaking some coke off the folds back into the wok and gently tapping the eggbeater against the side. He pulled out several gray cardboard boxes from under the couch, passed a box to Strike and opened one for himself. Each box contained a gross of glass bottles about two inches high and a half inch in diameter. Next came two plastic bags, each filled with hundreds of tiny purple stoppers. Purple stoppers were Rodney's street brand. If anybody was caught selling any other color in Rodney's territory, whether they worked for Champ or not, Rodney had the right to take away their dope and put them in the hospital—something he had only needed to do once, to some green-stoppered clocker about six months before, in order for everybody in town to get the message.

Strike looked down at all the piecework to come, thinking about how he was the only guy he knew his age who had no interest in or reaction to music, going back in his memory again to hear his father singing in the living room, with the nubby rub of that green couch on the backs of his legs, then snapping out of it as Rodney took a pocketknife out of an end table drawer, dipped the blade into the bowl and silently offered Strike a chunky hit. Strike just stared at him, not in the mood for jokes. Neither of them so much as drank beer, although Rodney had been a heroin addict all through the 1970s.

'Yeah, I got me a partner on the Papi thing,' Rodney drawled as he tilted the coke off the blade back into the wok, took two glass bottles, one in each hand, and dipped them daintily into the mix. Then he tapped them against each other, letting the coke settle, measuring roughly a tenth of a gram by eye. 'He's a real fuck-up, though. I just found out the nigger stealing me blind since the gitty-up.'

'Oh yeah?' Strike hesitated before joining in the bottling operation. It had been his very first job around dope for Rodney and he always hated it, but once he started, his fingers fell to it automatically, and soon he was lost in thought, starting to put the night together a little, figuring that if this other guy was on the way out, Rodney was probably asking him in.

'Greedy, greedy, greedy,' Rodney clucked, eyes on his work. They labored in silence for a few minutes, building up a nice scoop-and-tap rhythm, seesaw style, each one hesitating for a beat as the other one dipped, like two lumberjacks manning a double-handled saw. Between the two of them they were filling two dozen bottles a minute.

'Stealing from you how?' Strike asked flatly.

The door handle rattled. Gently, swiftly, Rodney put the wok between his feet, the cardboard boxes on the floor. The filled bottles vanished into his hands, then under the couch.

The front door opened and Rodney's wife, Clover, came in. She was light-skinned, a bit chunky with a flattened-down face, her hair straight and short, shiny and stiff, curling up on one side like a frozen wave.

Strike stood up awkwardly and bobbed his head. She ignored him, her hands filled with plastic shopping bags, yarn spilling out of one.

'You find something in the kitchen?' she asked Rodney.

'Yeah. I'm good, how're you?'

'The Lord's seein' me through.'

Rodney winked at Strike, and they both watched her move straight through the shotgun flat: first to the bedroom, dumping her bags and her coat on the bed, then into the kitchen, where she ducked into the refrigerator and pulled out a pink bowl covered with plastic wrap, and finally into the back bedroom, the only room that had a door, which she shut behind her.

Rodney pulled out the dope and the bottles again and got back to work. Strike knew that Rodney had been some kind of dope dealer since high school, but he insisted that his wife thought he just ran the candy store. He also insisted that she didn't know anything about the eighteen-month-old boy who was in the store every time she came in to talk to him, or about the constantly changing cast of teenage girls who hung around, including one or two who looked slightly pregnant. His wife was a cashier supervisor for New Jersey Transit, a notary public and an ordained Pente-costal minister. In their own way they got along fine, Rodney and Clover: they'd been tolerating the hell out of each other for more than twenty years.

Strike's back started to knot up from the bottle work. His thoughts returned to Rodney's greedy partner. 'Stealing from you how?'

'Stealing from me hand over fist, that's how.' Rodney turned his head away from the coke and sneezed. 'You know, Erroll won't hurt nobody no more? The nigger killed a TV reporter once—four, no maybe five, six other motherfuckers that *I* know of. I say to him, Yo, Erroll, this boy done stole my money, is *steal*ing my money.'

Rodney hissed in disgust and shook his head, his hands a blur of bottles and stoppers. 'But Erroll's all worried about dyin' now, you know, he's feeling *bad*'n shit about his life, like he's gonna make amends and not do nothing bad no more.' Rodney laughed. 'The motherfucker startin' to sound like my goddamn *wife*.'

Strike nodded. 'Lot of people think heaven is in this bo-bowl, here. That's all the heaven they want.'

'I tell you one thing, bawh.' Rodney passed a finger alongside his nose. 'If God invented anything better'n drugs, he kept it for hisself. That's the *damn* truth.'

Strike rolled his eyes: this was Rodney's second-favorite saying, right behind 'A dime's a dime.'

They went back to working in silence for a while, about two hundred bottles ready to sell, maybe six, seven hundred more still in the bowl.

'Yeah, ol' Erroll . . . Right about now I just pay him to walk around scare the piss out the people with that damn *face* of his.'

Strike held his peace, waiting Rodney out.

'See, people get killed around here 'cause they can't see two minutes in front of they nose. Somethin' feels good *now*, that's all they want to know about. But you know, if you fuck that girl her boyfriend gonna *kill* you. If you get high off that product you supposed to be sellin', if you get greedy, go into business for yourself when you supposed to be out there for the man, well, the *man* gonna kill you.'

Yeah, Strike thought, and that's exactly what Rodney's pulling on Champ. Fucking Rodney should be talking into a mirror right now.

Suddenly Rodney put down the bottles, lifted his hands and let them drop on his kneecaps, as if he was too upset to go on. 'Goddamn greedy motherfucker.'

Strike worked faster as a way of keeping still, sensing that Rodney was finally about to spell it out.

'That boy do nothin' but lay back, pass some baggies, rake in the dough. We clearing two hundred a ounce each, me an him, *sellin'* maybe seventy ounces a week. Nice indoors work, clean, safe, all the dope heading out of town, out of state, Jersey City, New Hampshire. Shit, it almos' legitimate the way we got it set up.'

Allowing for the lying-dope-dealer factor, Strike figured thirty-five ounces at about a hundred each. Strike found himself starting to fume: Are you telling me something or are you asking me something? He didn't know what he would say if it was *ask*.

'We got no hassles with the knockos, no ten dollars here, ten dollars there, no pipeheads all licky-lipped with their greezy little eyes. I tell you, man, it's sweet.'

Strike dreamed his dream: no more bench, no more retail, no more Fury. But right behind it came a newspaper photograph of a maverick dealer who set himself up in Dempsy last year and was found by the police with the brass peephole of his apartment door embedded in his face, courtesy of a shotgun blast from the hallway. Fucking with Champ: Strike was torn between visions of paradise and survival.

'Least it *was* sweet, but the nigger a thief, so like, you know.' Rodney stared at Strike as if looking at someone through blasted black earth. Strike stared back at him, as still as a cat.

Rodney cocked his head and spoke with a terrible softness. 'He got to be got.'

And there it was. Strike had been thinking all along that Rodney was about to offer him something for free, had been debating with himself whether to pass it up, but now Rodney was telling him that it would cost to get in on this partnership and that the cost was high to the point of stupidity. And despite his passion for prudence, Strike suddenly couldn't imagine saying no.

Got to be got. No one had ever challenged him with something like this, but he couldn't think clearly now, couldn't mount any arguments and instead was reduced to blindly searching for something he knew was inside him, an impulse that as yet had no name.

'Yeah, ol' Erroll want to go to heaven, ain't that a bitch? Useless Virus-ass motherfucker—after all I done for him.'

Strike stumbled for a second: maybe Rodney was talking about taking out Erroll all this time. But that didn't make sense. Rodney was just underlining the problem. Well, who was this partner he was talking about? But it didn't make a difference yet. It was a secondary consideration right now.

Strike tried to examine the pros and cons, the Fury versus Champ, the relative jail time for selling bottles versus ounces. But pounding up from under the practical concerns, his heart was quick with colors, brilliant colors that had nothing to do with business, with judgment. He was a virgin in some areas of experience, and somewhere inside his head, inarticulate but powerful, was the understanding that all his life he had it building in him—the stammer, the burning in his gut, the crazed cautiousness, the dicky checks, the minute-to-minute rage and disgust, all begging for an outlet just like the one being offered him right now.

'And you gonna fall *out* when I tell you who I'm talking about too.'

Strike knew that Rodney was trying to tantalize him, draw him in. But there was no need for that now. Strike was so unmanned, so filled with a primitive recognition, that his hands were shaking. 'You sellin' this shit out of town, right?' They were just words.

'Just about,' Rodney said pleasantly. 'Just about.'

'Yeah . . . huh.'

'Say, what the fuck you doin'!' Rodney's voice climbed to a raw squawk.

'What . . . ' Strike jerked as if an alarm had gone off.

'Lookit.' Rodney pointed at the last one hundred bottles Strike had stoppered. He had forgotten to put in the coke.

Strike stared at the empty vials and shook his head. He wondered if this was what it felt like to get high.

AFTER RODNEY DROPPED him off by his car, Strike drove back to the benches, forgetting to perk up at the red lights, forgetting the Newark stickup artists, even flooring it a little on the boulevard.

Strike had been so overwhelmed with his decision to get wet and do this that at first he hadn't given the target more than a passing thought. But when Rodney dropped Darryl Adams' name Strike had almost fallen down, stumbling backwards against the coffee table, and flopped into the easy chair.

Darryl Adams: the hardest-working and least-smiling kid in the history of the grocery business. Strike had worked with him six, seven days a week for an entire year in Rodney's Place, and he had been the only guy who had ever made Strike feel like a frivolous fuck-up.

Darryl Adams. Goddamn Darryl Adams. Strike thought of his mother, spoke to her out loud—'What you think of him *now*?'—even though she didn't know Darryl from the mayor of Dempsy.

Darryl had been selling ounces for Rodney out of Ahab's, the fast-food hole three blocks from Rodney's store. Trying to figure out why the ounces were selling so slowly, Rodney had found out that Darryl had picked up a second supplier, a white guy in Bayonne who had offered him a forty percent commission to Rodney's thirty-five. For the last two months Darryl had been alternating ounces, half the time selling Bayonne weight to Rodney's customers, telling Rodney business was slow and risking his life for an extra five percent cut.

Steamed up, breathing through his nose, Strike drove blind toward the benches. Fucking Rodney, calls me 'my son,' then puts me on the street like some ice cream man, and Darryl's indoors selling ounces like a human being. Well, you get what you sow. Strike conjured up snapshot memories of Darryl: sorting candy bars, stacking Chore Boys, hauling out trash bags.

He spoke to his mother again, to Rodney: 'Yeah? Well, what do you think about him *now*?'

My son. Shoot Rodney too.

Not bothering to stash his car in the old lady's driveway, Strike pulled

up to the curb hard by the semicircle of benches that cupped the
entrance to the central walkway of the Roosevelt projects like a yawning
mouth. It was ten-thirty and the place was rocking now that the Fury was
downing various heart medicines at the Pavonia Tavern. The clockers
had their bottles in bags under benches and in the grass, using tonight's
apartment only to re-up whole clips or more, giving the mule eighty dollars out of the hundred sold to go upstairs and bring down another ten
bottles.

They were selling Redi Rocks this evening, precooked nuggets ready to
smoke, purer than crack and no mystery ingredients like Raid or
formaldehyde. But having the rocks in hand, ready to burn, made some
customers itchy to be high right *now*, and people were piping up on the
street, on the corner, up against a building breezeway, crouched down
between parked cars, their faces flaring up yellow as they fired up the
cocaine.

Futon saw Strike fuming in his car and reluctantly came up to the
window. 'I just sent out for another twenty clips. It feel like somebody
won the *numbers* out here, the way it going.'

Strike counted three pipeheads lighting up in plain sight. 'Look at
that.'

'What?'

'What's wrong with you? Get them motherfuckers out of here.'

Futon stood up straight, curling his hands under the belly of his shirt,
taking in the pipeheads and making a face, clucking his tongue, doing
nothing.

'Get them the fuck out of here.' Strike flicked his hand.

'They ain't doin' nothin'.'

'We got families up and down here. This look like shit, stupid.' To
Strike, selling bottles was clean, no more than a handshake, but piping up
was dangerous to the crew—they might as well put up neon signs. Plus,
he found it disgusting to look at.

'I go look for Hammer.' Futon backed away from the car, glancing
around for the nighttime muscle and security man.

Livid now, Strike jumped out of his car and sprinted toward a
pipehead lighting up while leaning against 8 Weehawken. Strike picked
up speed as he moved, breaking into a dead run the last ten feet, the
pipehead holding a lungful of coke as Strike rammed him in the chest

with both hands. The dope expelled in a white cloud of shock, and the doper went down, Strike kicking him under the armpit, the guy gasping, 'Yo, wait, wait.'

Strike hissed, 'Next time I see you, I will *kill* you.' He marched back past two other startled dopers, one backing away, the other running, and Strike lunged two steps off his march to take a swinging slap at the doper who didn't run, missing him, but the guy got the message and took off. Strike came back to the curb and found Futon and Hammer standing there, blinking, mouths open. Hammer, big but stupid, said, 'What you want me to do?' Strike didn't answer, just got back into his car and drove off, thinking, If I do take care of this other thing about Darryl, Futon'll run this corner into the ground, but then thinking, So what—it won't be my problem if he does.

Strike was pumped up from the beating and didn't want to work the bench tonight, didn't want to see Futon's face. He drove in square circles around the neighborhood for a while before deciding to get out of town altogether, go across the river to the Bronx, see Crystal.

from

Beam Me Up, Scotty

by Michael Guinzburg

MY NAME IS Ed, and I'm a stupid stinking drug addict and alcoholic.

When I landed home, drug-free at last, and saw the apartment empty, no wife or kids, clothes and suitcases gone, the old sickness was upon me, polluting my innards with a poisonous mixture of rage and nausea, like hydrogen peroxide bubbling angry white on an open wound. What had I expected? Happy smiley faces and a cake? A brass band? Michelle in a drum majorette uniform over lacy lingerie? Open arms and forgiveness? The eleven-year-old twin boys turning cartwheels? My senile mother out of the nursing home, clearheaded and young again? My father back from the grave? I don't know. Maybe just a cup of hot chocolate and a hug. Certainly not an abandoned apartment with windows wide open to the winter wind.

Down the stairs. Catbox stink of stale piss and vomit. Dead-soldier crack vials crunching undersneaker. Bare bulbs spilling sour lemon light onto hairy dust balls skittering along the grimy hall like urban tumbleweeds. A bum toilet. A junkie Jiffy Lube. A helluva place to raise a family.

Outside. Intersection of Bowery and Houston. Spindle-shanked winos wiped windshields, begged change.

Just one whiskey, just one whiskey, I thought, to drown this dreary bastard resentment thrashing in my guts.

I walked the Sunday streets. Frozen air chilled my ears, nipped my nose. The city domed by a clear blue sky, the kind of day an Indian dreams of dying on—the sky so clean and crisp and blue the freshly freed soul just sort of zooms to the heavens.

The Lower East Side one huge sprawling drug bazaar. Streets choked with dealers. Junkies and crackheads paced and lounged, guzzling brown-bagged beers, huffing cigarettes. I couldn't escape the eyes. The hard dull eyes. Empty of everything save the deathgreed. Vultures. 'Crack it up!' croaked one. 'Jumbo!' said another. 'How many you need?' As if they knew I'd gone straight. Teasing me, tempting me, mocking the fact that I was clean. They wanted me back with them, down and dirty, strung out, waltz-ing with Lucifer, dying slow and living like a zombie on the streets of Crack City, U.S.A.

I hated them. Jumpy jittery bastards. Ready to pop off at any moment. They'd do anything to keep the glass pipe packed with white rock, to stay wired: lie, cheat, steal, murder—sell their mother's wedding ring, trade their baby sister's virginity, their blind uncle's guide dog and sunglasses. They'd do anything, say anything, anything at all for that next mammoth suck off the Devil's Dick.

I hated what crack did to me. What I did for crack. How low I sank into the slime. The snarling animal I became. For the love of crack. For the hot electric cocaine zap. The raging selfish bastard. How I lost my wife and kids, infected them with my disease. I hated myself for that.

I kicked an empty crack vial. It spun into the gutter.

A long time ago in a galaxy far, far away . . . I was a reporter. A bright fresh face with a bright fresh talent, a bright fresh family, and a bright fresh future. My career had wings. That was B.C. (before crack), before the drugs got me by the short hairs and I took a swan dive into the toilet, a pigeon pecking at scraps. 'You coulda won the Pulitzer,' my friend Ken once mused, cokesmoke billowing from his mouth, passing me the wicked stem. Isn't it pretty to think so?

This, then, is the story of my life after detox (A.D.), where I'd crawled on my knees, moaning and squawking like a cockatoo with a jalapeño pepper jammed up its ass, a prisoner of crack.

I couldn't blame Michelle. I put her through hell. Put them all through hell.

Just one whiskey, just one whiskey, to unravel the pain, make me sane, to uncurdle the sour-milk stink in my heart and brain.

I don't know how long I wandered like that. I smoked a bunch of cigarettes, sucked them down hard, walked until my nose and toes and ears were frozen numb.

A warm smoky East Village church basement crowded with laughing happy people. Clear eyes and clean clothes. After all the years of wildlife it had come to this. Hard Drugs Anonymous. 'When you feel like getting high—and you will feel like getting high—go to a meeting.' That's what the counselor told me back at detox.

I sat on a hard chair and drank black coffee, smoked a cigarette. The speaker up front leading the meeting, blond and pretty, sitting behind a podium on a raised platform facing the crowd, told the story of her life, how a bottle of Boone's Farm apple wine guzzled in a New England graveyard at age fifteen transformed a cheer-leading straight-A student into a pill-popping, vodka-guzzling coke freak who ran off to the big city to make it as an actress, became a junkie-hooker, blew businessmen in cars, got beaten by pimps, stole, turned tricks in stairwells and cars, shot coke and dope time and again until her whole body was freckled with needle tracks, until her veins were clogged, until she was hitting up in the neck, until she hated herself and wanted to die—and now she could sit there, so elegant and serene, so at ease before these laugh-happy strangers, and joke about the horror.

'The disease of addiction is progressive,' she said. 'How could I have known way back when that an innocent bottle of wine would propel this Suzie Creamcheese on a ten-year run that ended in the back seat of a Mercedes when I realized the guy I was going down on was my Uncle Claude? The shame I felt. That's when I hit bottom, got into treatment, and ended up here, in the rooms of HDA. And I keep coming back, because it's the only way I know to work on myself, to feel my feelings instead of stuffing them with drugs and alcohol, to arrest my disease, one day at a time.'

They gave her a nice round of applause, passed the basket, made announcements, then went to a show of hands.

I shot my nicotine-stained mitt into the air. She pointed at me. Must've had a radar for pain.

'My name is Ed, and I'm a stupid stinking drug addict and alcoholic.'

'Hi, Ed!' chorused the joyous recovering boozers and addicts.

'I got out of detox today. My fucking wife has taken off. I thought if I got clean, things would get better. But I feel like fried dogshit on a bun. I want to drink or do some dope or smoke some crack so bad I can taste it. The bitch stole my kids. I'd like to kill her.'

'Thanks for sharing that, Ed,' chirped Miss Happy-face with a shit-eating grin. 'It gets better. Give time time. Keep it simple, stupid. Easy does it. One day at a time. Get a sponsor, someone you can talk with about those feelings. Don't stuff them. Keep coming back. The HDA Center has meetings all day and night. About your wife? Don't beat yourself up about it. Listen to learn and learn to listen.'

I listened. People spilling their guts: pain, hope, doubt, joy, dreams, demons—psychotherapy for the psychotic masses. When the hour was up we all linked hands and prayed. The AC/DC currents of hope and despair flowed through me.

Between meetings the anonymous boozers and junkies welcomed me. 'Thanks for sharing.' 'You're in the right place.' 'Take my phone number.' 'Keep coming back.' 'Don't stuff those feelings.' 'Have some coffee.' Fuckups of all ages, all races, all manner of dress and demeanor, thanked me for my honesty and told me, 'Don't beat yourself up about it.' 'Give time time.' 'Hang in there.' I was overwhelmed. Who the fuck was I? Just some piece of shit scraped off the street. Warm hands pressed mine. An old guy smiled. A beautiful brunette, straight from a girlie magazine, crushed me to her bountiful breast, whispered, 'I know how you feel.' It had been ages since I felt so safe, so warm, so at home. So I stayed, through the afternoon and long into the night, soaking up meetings like a Miami codger takes the sun, studying the faces, downing coffee, smiling at strangers.

'My name is Myron,' said the speaker leading the last meeting of the night, a middle-aged man in a tasteful tweed skirt and a white silk blouse, 'and I'm a grateful recovering alcoholic.'

'Hi, Myron!' we chimed.

'Alcohol is one of the hardest drugs of all, and I let it beat me up for twenty-five years. I've always been a woman inside. I've known that since I was two. I thought like a woman, felt like a woman, had a woman's intuition and emotions, but I lived in a man's body. Now I take hormones and go to therapy to prepare myself for the eventual operation. When I get this silly old troublemaker between my legs chopped off, then I'll be happy and proud to call myself Myra. Of course it will cost a bundle, so I'm saving up, one day at a time.'

Yes, I thought, yes! This is beautiful. A man who feels like a woman and has the balls to do something about it! What a glorious program! It allows people to be who they really are. Yes! And no one is laughing. Not that rough-looking fuck over there with the black hair and the permanent five o'clock shadow who looks like he wouldn't know a feeling if it kicked him in the crackers—he's nodding right along. And those bikers in the front row, they're down with Myron too. And that sweet thang who hugged me earlier—she's crying! And that filthy red-haired guy in the corner who was muttering all through the last meeting—he's quiet now, listening. The old lady; the bald-headed guy with the briefcase; the Native American with his cowboy hat and shitkicker boots; the yuppie couple over there with the matching corduroys and button-down shirts; the black woman with the dreadlocks; the—

'Growing up as Myron was no fun. It felt all wrong. Other boys played ball; I played house. I was different. Little girls teased me. My father beat me. I became withdrawn. I played with my sister's dolls and dressed in my mother's clothes. When I was twelve I was raped. I felt worthless, horrible. That night I discovered alcohol, and it helped the pain. From the beginning I drank to get drunk. I loved the warm glow, the feeling of safety. When I was loaded it was okay to be Myra. With others I had to wear a mask.

'At nineteen I got married. I functioned as a man physically, and yeah, I enjoyed it; but the booze was always there. I was drunk all the time. Had three kids, my own dress shop; but trouble was nipping at my heels. One night my wife came to the shop and found me passed out, wearing a lovely little yellow number from the spring line. Divorce, humiliation: the works. I drank more and more, went over that invisible line and kept on falling deeper and deeper into the abyss. I was so numb I didn't even know I was in pain. My real feelings were stuffed so deep and I was in such denial that if you told me I had a problem I'd laugh in your face. For years I lived on the Bowery in a so-called room. A cage with walls. I drank wine and vodka. Gave blowjobs for cash. Finally I couldn't even do that without throwing up, so I ended up on the street, living in a cardboard box. Couldn't afford vodka or wine, so I drank gasoline. That's right, gas. High-octane, regular, unleaded—I cherished them all. I hung around the pumps and begged. I mixed my gas with ginger ale, called my cardboard box the Gas Chamber. Y'see, I was raised Jewish and I thought that was funny. Ha ha ha. That box was my personal Auschwitz, my prison, my coffin, where I was slowly fucking killing myself. Numerous times the cops picked me up, freezing or puking or bleeding or comatose, and they'd drag me fighting and screaming and complaining to countless emergency rooms to have my stomach pumped out. And every time, I figured it was the ginger ale. I was allergic to ginger ale. Never once did this recovering gasoholic conceive that the problem might just be the gas. Christ. My cousin Bernie was the only member of my family who kept in touch. He'd come by my box and beg me to get help. 'Myron, Myron, what's a nice Jewish boy from the Bronx doing this for? To shame your parents?' He'd give me twenty bucks. I'd buy some panty hose, some lipstick, some vodka, and have plenty left over to keep my motor running for a week . . . '

The feeling of warmth in the room was like an electric blanket. Faces all happy and rapt with attention—even sad-eyed mumblers were grooving to Myron's solo—heads nodding up and down with identification like those little plastic dogs in the rear windows of cars. It didn't take a rocket scientist to figure out that Myron's story was touching them all in some special way. The details were unique, but the emotions that drove him to the Gas Chamber were universal. Feeling different—unloved, rejected, violated, terrorized, hopeless, helpless, despondent—and then the denial that a problem existed. That was a syndrome I knew only too well. The denial. When Michelle badgered me to get help and I'd tell her to get out of my face, that the problem was hers; when I got booted from the newspaper for one too many screw-ups; when I worked as a messenger and crashed the bike into a parked car or some faceless business suit crossing the street and I blamed it on traffic instead of the Lenny Bias-sized hit of crack I'd just sucked down; when I stole the kids' lunch money for a single vial of rock, then came back later that day and pawned their Nintendo box; when I ended up employed as a mopboy in a Times Square peepshow, swabbing semen from the floor for minimum wage, blaming society for my situation—when I did all that and still got sky-high, still kept stoking my head with cokedopeboozeweed and refused to admit that

I was anything but normal, that was the hell of compulsion, the horror of obsession: that was denial. I'd become a dumb junkie, a blackout drinker, a loser.

I'd been on a mission, a long mission, and when I came to, the boys were sobbing and Michelle was yelling. I had no idea what I'd done, so I sat there and smoked a fat joint laced with crack and heroin, guzzled a warm flat beer, tried to block the awful noise of their lamentations out of my ears and piece together the preceding days. I couldn't remember. I was blank and filled with fear. As the substances played pinball in my brain, thrilling and chilling, zipping and zapping, the boys' moans got louder, more horrible, pounding at my weary brain like Muhammad Ali jabs and Joe Frazier hooks. Michelle's voice speared my head like a red-hot knitting needle inserted from ear to ear. I looked into their eyes and saw hate, misery, and fear. My heart ached. God help me, what had I done?

'My name is Ed,' I said when Myron opened the meeting up to the floor, 'and I'm a stupid stinking drug addict and alcoholic.'

'Hi, Ed!'

'My wife is gone. She was right to leave. I was a mess. On the pipe 24/7. A dope-sniffing stemsucking crackerjack. The lowest form of life on the planet. I don't blame her for splitting. But I'm clean and sober now. Why can't it be a Hollywood ending? I don't understand. I miss my boys. I feel like taking some motherfucker by the throat and squeezing till his eyes pop right the fuck out.'

'Listen, Ed.' Myron spoke soothingly, like a mother, like a father, like a mother and father wrapped up in one. 'Don't beat yourself up about it. You weren't in your right mind when you did all those things. The disease transformed you. You weren't responsible for your actions. Everyone in this room has done shit high we're not proud of.' Heads bobbed. 'I myself once siphoned gas from an ambulance on call. I stood there fifty feet away, gassing up on a Mobil martini, watching the paramedics wheel some poor bleeding fish out.' He coughed nervously. 'Ed, they couldn't start the vehicle. The guy maybe died. I don't know. I took off. A sober night doesn't go by I don't think about that man, pray for him, beg God's forgiveness. Look, by working The Program we learn to live with the past. Your wife is angry. With good reason. My own family, all except Cousin Bernie, took years and years to forgive me; six of those years I was clean.

You gotta give time time. Last month my youngest son was married, and I got invited. An Orthodox Jewish wedding, and they let me sit with the women. I wore a secondhand Halston and no one batted an eye-lash. They forgave me, and now they accept me, for who I am, for what I was. You've been wandering in the woods for so long, you expect to find your way out in an instant? Give time time, Ed. Easy does it. Keep coming back. Hang in there. Take the toilet paper out of your ears and listen.'

I listened. I'd been listening for hours. Rich people, poor people ('from Park Avenue to park benches,' 'from Yale to jail'), happy people, sad people ('from pink cloud to black shroud'). People who had conquered fear ('F-E-A-R, the active alcoholic's prime directive: Fuck Everything. And Run'). People who wanted to kill, wanted to commit suicide, wanted to earn fortunes, or were content with nothing. People who lived with AIDS and wanted to die with dignity. People who loved, people whose hearts were breaking, who were jealous, angry, elated, deflated, constipated. Here was the human condition, every emotion and situation imaginable, and people were exulting in it. Living it sober. Sober! A word I once considered the filthiest in the English language. People living sober, people dying sober. It was beautiful, it was heartwarming, it was amazing—it was time for a drink.

Just one whiskey, I thought, as I filed with the penitents out of the church basement into the cold. Just one whiskey.

I felt a tap on the shoulder. Myron.

'It's the first one that gets you drunk.'

'Mind your own business,' I spat back. 'The first will take the edge off. The sixth might get me drunk.'

'Calm down, honey. Listen to me. You take that first drink you'll be back sucking a crackstem in no time. If you don't take that first drink you can't get loaded.'

'Maybe I want to get loaded. It's not every day your wife kidnaps your kids and bolts. I deserve to get shitfaced. I want it. I need it.'

'I don't think so.' He circled my shoulders with his strong arm. 'Why did you come to HDA?'

'Beats me.'

'Drugs beat you. Booze beat you. Used you as a doormat. Walked all over you and wiped streetshit onto your soul. Are you sick and tired of getting beat? Sick and tired of being sick and tired? You want to gain your family's respect? Maybe win them back?'

I nodded through the tears.

'Then come for coffee.'

EIGHT CUPS OF coffee later I had to piss like a racehorse. Myron sure could rap. Made a used car salesman seem downright shy, he was so enthusiastic about The Program. Peppering me with slogans and philosophy, he related the history of Hard Drugs Anonymous, its principles and practices, from the first historic meeting in Painesville, Ohio, back in '34, between Big Jim Williams, the pro wrestler, and Farmer Rob Jones, a simple country boy who'd found he just couldn't get the crop in while zooted on morphine. The two alcoholic addicts had picked up their habits and their friendship in the hospital after being wounded in WWI, and almost two decades of shooting dope later (Farmer Rob was fond of claiming he was 'the only fella in the Midwest who could find a needle in a haystack'), they desperately wanted to get clean. They'd tried every known remedy for addiction, taken all the cures, and still couldn't kick; but there, in that humble Ohio barn, midst a symphony of clucking chickens and oinking pigs, they realized that together—'We can do what I cannot'—through mutual support, one addict helping another, they could scrape the massive monkey off their backs and keep it away forever by just plain talking it to death. So as day stretched into evening, the air perfumed by the sweet country smells of hay and horse manure, they talked. Farmer Rob's wife, Lilly, fetched them coffee and apple pie, and they kept right on talking. They walked through fields of grain under starstudded skies, and talked, sharing their experience, strength, and hope; and by the time the sun nosed red over the horizon and the first rooster crowed, they'd given birth to the Twelve Steps of Hard Drugs Anonymous, the program of recovery that has flourished and spread over the years, mushroomed into a worldwide movement, been adopted by a wide variety of obsessive-compulsives, and provided a second chance, a bridge back to life, for countless millions of sufferers like myself and Myron, who'd managed to make a grade A mess out of things.

It wasn't easy sitting there at Leshko's, holding my water, while Myron, who had agreed to be my sponsor, jabbered away about Program ethics, tossing his bobbed black hair out of his eyes, sipping tea, delicate as a duchess, manicured pinkie finger poking out. My attention kept straying out the window to the street, to Tompkins Park, where the drug world flitted by like some grainy silent movie. Anxious addicts off to cop crack or heroin, then coming back a few minutes later with that buzzed look, that 'don't worry be happy' jaunt to their step. Sure they were the lowest of the low, the slime of the earth, but they were damned happy slime, slime that felt no pain.

'I'm sorry.' I turned to Myron. 'What was that?'

'It's a simple program for complicated people. Remember what Big Jim said to Farmer Rob: "Kiss. K-I-S-S. Keep It Simple, Stupid." The best thing for a newcomer is ninety meetings in ninety days. You'll have a lot of feelings coming up, so don't stuff them. Talk about them. Don't pick up a drink; pick up the phone. Here are my numbers, at home and at work. Call anytime, about anything.'

I was watching a skeletal whitegirl in a ratty old Chevy right outside, hitting from a stem, could see her body stiffen with a huge hit, then relax as she let the smoke pour out her nose and cloud the car. Crackerjack heaven. I was drooling.

'Ed, you have the disease. The AMA recognizes addiction as a disease, a genetic disease. I'll bet a dollar to a doughnut someone in your family suffers from it too.' I thought of my dead father, a real pig drinker, pounding back the 7 and 7's like glasses of water. 'The only way to arrest your disease, one day at a time, is working The Program. So keep coming back to meetings and steer clear of people, places, and things that might bring up urges.'

Yeah, right, and move to Timbukfuckingtu.

'Sure, Myron. It was nice meeting you.'

'Hang in there, Ed. Remember what Farmer Rob said to Big Jim: "The war is over and you lost." Time to surrender. For The Program to work, you have to admit you're powerless over all drugs and alcohol—that your life is out of control. That's Step One.'

His handshake was firm, his smile white. His little breasts budded against the white silk blouse. And you know, maybe if I had listened a little better, taken the toilet paper out of my ears and really listened, if I hadn't been so impressed with what a good-looking woman Myron was for a man his age, maybe if I had drunk less coffee or just simply used the restaurant's bathroom, or ducked around the corner into a bar and banged back a bunch of boilermakers, then maybe, just maybe, the next few days might have broken differently.

'Sure, Myron. And thanks,' I said, trying to figure out his bra size.

I CROSSED INTO the park, past the rows of cardboard-box homes and tents known as Bushville, by blazing garbage-can fires where homeless men and women toasted their hands and guzzled beer, past dreadlocked Rastas hawking reefer, hissing 'Cess! Cess!' like snakes, found a tree and took a steaming whiz, all the while thinking: Just one hit of crack, one delightful delicious lungful of the lip-numbing body-buzzing bubblegum-flavored cokesmoke. I could taste it, smell it, feel it. Then maybe a sniff of heroin, just an itty-bitty one, to get the complete okey-dokey, to forget that Michelle had abducted Mutt and Jeff (Matthew and Jeffrey) and was who-the-fuck-knows-where, probably sitting around her parents' home in Michigan, apple-cheeked Ma Kawalski weeping with relief she'd escaped madman Ed, while Pa K. showed the boys his gun collection and regaled them with bloody WWII stories. Myron had advised me not to call, to leave them be, repeating those phrases I'd already grown to hate: 'Don't beat yourself up about it' and 'Let go and let God.' He was right. Sprinting full tilt into a brick wall would get me nowhere, only hurt, dazed, in further need of medication. To get better I had to consider Hard Drugs Anonymous my salvation, meetings my medicine, had to do ninety in ninety, talk about the pain, take that first baby step: admit I was powerless, that my life was out of control.

Not only was my life out of control, but so were my sneakers. Instead of splitting the park and cruising the few blocks down to Bowery and Houston, I was fast-stepping through the ruins of Alphabet City, what in the Pre-Gentrification Age people called Loisaida, heading for my favorite wholesale crack dealer. Goddammit, my feet were addicted.

I spoke into the intercom. 'It's Ed.' And the basement door buzzed open.

Flaco flopped in the torn leather recliner, so skinny he made Nancy Reagan look like an opera star on a diet of steroids and pizza, his unwashed black hair pulled back in a stylish ponytail. The big-screen TV blared 'Lifestyles of the Rich and Famous.' Flaco slumped mesmerized, the bony face still as freeze-dried death, his crack-bright eyes glittering with the moneylust, on his lap a mean-ass gun. One hand held a crack-stem, the other stroked his dog, a grinning all-white English bull terrier named Natasha, Spuds MacKenzie after a serious weightlifting program. She was chained to the radiator, her ball-peen hammer head oversized and elongated, with huge cruel fangs and prehistoric jaws. If Flaco didn't like you, she didn't hesitate to growl, bark, or strain at her chain. He fed her raw meat and junk food and was fond of bragging that she had once bit a Frenchman's dick in half.

'Yo, Flaco.'

'Crack it up, homeboy. Wha'sup?' His eyes were glued to the tube. 'Wha'sappenin'?'

'How's biz?' I asked, not caring, staring at the eight-inch crackstem growing from his burn-callused fingers, as Natasha nuzzled my crotch.

'Yo bro, what fo' dat bitch like you so much?'

'Maybe 'cause I don't feed her Yodels and Ding Dongs.'

'Say, dude, you French?'

I kneeblocked Natasha's hard-probing slobberpuss. She sighed doggily and waddled back to the radiator.

'Sit you ass down, bro,' he said, fixated on the television. 'Look atta tits on dat broad. Ay, Mommy!'

The top-heavy starlet on-screen cavorted in Ty-D-Bol-blue Bermuda waters, toweled her tush, sipped a fruity rum drink, stuffed her white-toothed pouty-lipped kisser with dripping butter-dipped lobster.

'Oh, man!' moaned Flaco. 'I lick da butta off huh tawpedoes and den I tear huh a new assho'.'

He sure had a way with words. Housekeeping too. Natasha's shit piled stinking on urine-yellow newspapers. Walls and ceiling flaking, spotted with moving cockroaches. Sink overflowing with dishes. Ziploc bags open and full of crack, all in five-dollar vials with red caps, chunks of cokerock flashing bright like diamonds, gleaming white in the blue tube-glow like distant snowy blood-nippled mountains, surrounded by a green fluffy pile of cash.

My heart beat fast, my legs went boiled-spaghetti weak, my palms moist. A trickle of icy sweat raced down my ribs.

'Rock look good, huh Eddieboy?' He grinned. 'Crack it up.'

I swallowed a lump of nerves and grunted, tore my gaze away and sat on the folding chair reserved for customers. The starlet was now riding a motor scooter down a dirt road shaded by palm trees, a road with plenty of potholes so her cleavage did the va-va-voom jiggle.

'Yo, bro, how dat peepshow job be treatin' you an' shit?'

'I got off that ride, man. You don't know how depressing it gets mopping spunk off the floor.'

'Shit, Eddieboy, dat shit sound like fun an' shit. All dose wild chicks an' whatnot.'

Yeah, like an all-expenses-paid vacation to Dante's Inferno.

'I've got an interview for a writing gig at the *Post* tomorrow,' I lied.

'Booshit. You jos' a schemin' dreamin' crackaddick like da res' o' fockin' New York. O'ly way you make it onnada *Pos'* is you try ta rip me off and I gotsta shoot you white ass. Den you be page fockin' one an' shit.' He laughed, displaying yellow rotten choppers splayed about his mouth like ancient bowling pins erupting in a strike.

'We friends or what?' I asked.

Flaco showed even more teeth.

'More like "or what," dude. Business is business. Crack it up, homeboy. How many you need?' He fingered the gun. Nasty-looking piece, a semiautomatic Glock pistol with silencer, lightweight plastic, seventeen shots, long and lethal and quiet as a butterfly's sneeze.

'Yo, Flaco my man, I'm a steady customer. Tonight I just happen to be tapped out. I'm looking to get turned on.'

He found that hilarious. 'You a chump, man. A one-man Comedy Store an' shit. You can smoke an' whatnot, bot I fockin' done los' all respeck an' shit. You pathetic.'

He flicked his Bic, then ritually uttered the crackhead prayer of deliverance. 'Beam me up, Scotty,' he said, and drew orange flame into the crack-packed stem for a good twenty seconds, rotating the snap-cracklepopping tube, sucking hard on the blackening glass, cheeks scrunching, eyes bulging, scrawny chest inflating, temple veins pulsating, smoke trickling from his nose and mouth like a horror-movie skull.

He passed the hot stem and beamer, then exhaled a full cloud of roasted cokesmoke. The sweet bubblegum smell caressed my nostrils, tickled my tonsils. I held the tube, let it cool. The starlet was now doing aerobics, her heavy breasts bouncing in time to dance music.

'Whassamatta, crackhead? You don' wanna sock da Devil's Dick?'

I flicked the Bic. The torch shot six inches high, a neon invitation to hell. I put the stem to my lips, my quivering lips. I was shaking. Just one hit, what would that do? Lose Michelle forever? Fuckit, I thought. She was gone. Might as well get high, forget the pain of loss, smoke that shit and get a good fucking buzz. I made to hit on the stem (and here's where it gets weird — call it God, call it Freud, call it Fate), but it slipped from my jittery sweating fingers, fell to the floor with a crisp clink, the top inch snapping off.

'You clumsy fockin' drog begga!'

'Sorry,' I mumbled.

'Sorry? You a sorry shit whiteboy. Get da fock ou' my house befo' I give you sorry dopefien' ass sumpin' you really be sorry bou'!'

I could feel the hot humiliated flush on my face. I picked the stem up. The jagged edge gleamed bright in the TV's light. I touched it to my arm. A fat droplet of blood pearled on the skin and rolled warm and lazy down my wrist. I licked it and grinned. From the idiot box Robin Leach extolled the virtues of sun-kissed Bermuda, 'where the natives are friendly and life is gentle.'

'You a crazy mothafocka.' Flaco waved the gun.

'Leave my mother out of it, crackerjack.'

'Get the fock ou' or da dog be eatin' white meat fo' a week.'

Natasha growled low from her throat.

'Fuck you and the banana boat you jumped off of,' I said, standing. Then bingo! blackjack! gin! The answer bubbled forth clear as spring water, like a cartoon light bulb flash of inspiration, the solution to my problem with crack, the Final Solution: swift as Bruce Lee, I plunged the sharp seven inches of glass upward into Flaco's left eye hard as I could. A sick scream burbled from his throat, faded into a rattle, as his body did a spastic twitch and a shot of blood spurted through the hollow stem, splashed his surprised face.

He was good and dead before the dog could say 'woof.'

'Bull's-eye,' I said, the sick weight lifting from my soul like night fog burned off by the dawn's early light. 'Crack it up, homeboy.'

'NICE DOG,' MYRON said the next day, Monday, giving the bull terrier a leery look as we walked down lunchtime Broadway past Grace Church.

'Got her last night.' I laughed at the memory of Natasha licking the blood off Flaco's face.

'You sure you're not manic-depressive? This is quite a mood swing. You're like the cat who ate the canary.'

'More like the canary ate the cat.'

'Yesterday you were miserable and heartbroken. Today you're Mr Rogers.'

' "It's a beautiful day in the neighborhood," ' I sang. God, I felt happy, joyous and free, full of purpose and hope. 'Myron, I love being clean and sober.'

'Sounds like you're on the pink cloud. Whatever you're doing, just keep it up.'

Myron looked so serious. In his fake-leopard coat, leopard-print boots, black stockings, and leopard beret, he was ravishing. Fit right in with all the downtown hipster types, the leather jackets and space age haircuts, skinheads, black kids with flattops and fades, hardcore kids with rainbow-colored Mohawks and spiketops flashing bright like exotic fishing lures.

'Here.' I handed him a gift-wrapped package. 'A token of thanks for saving me from demon rum.'

'You shouldn't have,' he said, ripping the wrapping. His eyes gaped. 'Calvin Klein's Obsession! Ed! It's so expensive.'

'Nothing but the best for my sponsor.'

He spritzed his wrist, sniffed, and sighed.

'I love it,' he said, then worry creased his face. 'But can you afford it?'

'I came into some money.'

Natasha scampered, so shiny and beautiful in her new black hair color (compliments of Miss Clairol), happy, smiling, puppylike, breathing the good cold air of winter after months shut up in Flaco's crackerjack hell-hole.

'You really like my dog?'

'No offense, Ed, but she's a fucking land shark.'

'I took her from a crack dealer. He kept her chained up and fed her Twinkies. I liberated her.' Natasha certainly had adjusted well to the change in ownership.

'You got high?'

'Hell no. I'm through with that sucker action. I'm clean and serene.'

'You think I was born yesterday?'

'Myron, I'm telling the truth. As you said last night, this is a program of rigorous honesty.'

'You went to a crack dealer's house and you didn't get high? Ed, you can't bullshit a bullshitter.'

'I wanted to get high—'

'Ah, the truth comes out. As Big Jim said, "Drop by a barbershop, end up with a haircut." That's why you gave me the perfume. Guilty conscience.'

'I swear I didn't get high. Last night I killed a guy.' Myron's eyes bugged in disbelief. 'You got it. I waxed him but good. Dusted the motherfucker. He was a total slime. He tried to victimize me. I ain't no vic. So I took his life. Then I took his dog, his cash, his gun, his ammunition. Today I paid my rent and phone bill, and Jesus, I haven't felt this good in years. And I didn't smoke crack.'

We walked along in silence. Myron shook his head.

'Ed, I don't know what to say.'

'How about, "Don't beat yourself up about it"?'

'Frankly, young man, I don't believe your crazy story. Are you a compulsive liar? As your sponsor, I suggest you go to a lot of meetings and take the toilet paper out of your ears and put it in your mouth. Step Two tells us that a power greater than ourselves can restore our sanity. You're gonna have to get in touch with your Higher Power, Ed.'

I was a little miffed that he had me tabbed as a nutcase mean. I, here he was pushing fifty-five, wearing teeny-bopper outfits. Well, maybe it was safer that way.

'Ed, you're a sick young man. Don't be so defiant. As Big Jim said, "Reliance, not defiance." Have faith. Trust the process. Trust your Higher Power. Stay clean and pray.'

'I haven't prayed since I was a kid.'

'Start praying. But not in a selfish manner. Ask God to show you the way. Say, "Thy will be done." '

'Thy will be done,' I said. 'Hey, that feels pretty good.'

'Of course it does. Turning your will and life over to the care of God is Step Three. The beginning of a new freedom.'

'Speaking of free, Myron, can I buy you lunch?'

'Thanks, but I need to get back to the office. A woman's work is never done.'

'You saving up for that operation?'

'God willing,' he said, looking skyward. Then he giggled. 'A girl's gotta do what a girl's gotta do.'

'Myron, the Obsession smells great on you.'

'I'll pray for you, Ed.'

'Pray for Natasha too.'

New Crack City

by Will Self

A JOURNALIST FRIEND of mine asks me to take her out on the street and show her some crack dealing in action. I can't understand why she needs my help. You only have to stand outside the main entrance to King's Cross for five minutes to start spotting the street people who are involved with drugs. King's Cross has always had a name for prostitution, and where there are brasses there's always smack; and nowadays if you're anywhere in London where there's smack, then there will be crack as well. The two go together like *foie gras* and toast.

Still, I suppose I can understand why my journalist friend needs me. The London street drug scene is as subject to the caste principle as any other part of English society; druggies identify one another by eye contact and little else. As Raymond Chandler once remarked: 'It's difficult to tell a well-controlled doper apart from a vegetarian bookkeeper.' All up and down the promenade outside King's Cross, druggies are making eye contact with one another. There are Italians—they're principally interested in smack—and a contingent of young black men hanging out with white prostitutes. These men are pimps as well as being crack dealers.

We watch the scene: dealers carry rocks of crack or tiny packets of smack wrapped up in silver foil and cling-film inside their cheeks. When a punter scores, he discreetly tucks the money into the dealer's hand, the

er drops the rock or the smack out of his mouth and into the punter's
1. The whole transaction takes only a few seconds. 'Why aren't the
e doing anything?' moans my journalist friend. 'It's all so blatant.'
1d it is. But what can the police do? Snarl up the whole of King's
s in the middle of the rush hour while they try and nab a few street
ers? Supposing they do manage to collar them: the dealers will have
owed their stash. Fear is a fantastic lubricant.
e've seen the street action, and my journalist friend wants to check
crack den: do I know of one? Well, yes, as a matter of fact, I have
friends in the East End who are well-established crack and smack
ers, but they're not the sort of people who accept house calls, espe-
from journalists. What a shame I can't take my voyeuristic friend,
can take you . . .

The day's action is just beginning up at Bob's place. It's about seven in
the evening. Someone has been to see the Cypriot and they're washing
up a quarter ounce of powdered cocaine in the kitchen of Bob's flat.

Bob's flat is situated at the very end of the outside walkway on the top
floor of a thirties council block in Hackney. It's a good position for a drug
dealer. The police have to come up four flights and get through a locked,
bolted and chained door and a barred gate set in the flat's internal passageway before they can gain access. The windows are also barred.

Not that this deters them. To give the constabulary their due, they have
turned Bob's place over several times recently, but they never find anything. Bob keeps his stash up his anus. The police know this but they
can't be bothered to pull him in and fence with his brief while they wait
for it to come out. Bob would have a good brief as well. Bob's family are
well established in this area; this has been their manor for years. Three
generations of the family have been hard men around here, respected
men. Before they got into drugs they were into another kind of blag altogether: armed robbery.

Bob once told me how they made the switch: 'Chance, really. We were
doing a number on this Nigerian bloke. We knew he had something but
we didn't know what. It was six kilos of brown. I got the fucker down on
the floor with my shooter in his ear and said: "You're fucking lucky we're
not the old bill!" '

Bob is a talkative soul: bright, articulate and possessed of a gallows
humour that counts for wit in this society. But Bob is mighty keen on that

rock. Sometimes he'll be up for several days on end rocking it. Not that the crack is his core business—that's still smack.

As William Burroughs so pithily observed, smack is the only commodity that you don't have to sell to people; instead, you sell people to it. And the people who *it* buys come in all shapes and sizes. At Bob's, most of them get dealt with through the bars of the safety gate in the long, dark corridor that runs the length of the flat. The clientele are a really mixed bunch; all the way from shot-to-pieces street junkies, indistinguishable from alcoholics apart from the abscesses on their hands, to the smart end of the carriage trade: a young man, incongruously dressed in a velvet-collared crombie, is buying a rock and a bag of brown when we arrive. He has an accent that would sit more comfortably in St James's than in a Hackney council estate.

Bob doesn't have a pit bull or a Rottweiler; he doesn't need one. The other dealers around here all know who his family are and they respect them. But what about the Yardies? They don't respect man or beast. The word on the scene is that they carry automatic weapons and aren't afraid to use them. They have no respect for the conventions of the London criminal world. I asked Bob about it. 'Yardies?' he snorted. 'They're just another bunch of coons.'

In truth, there are always a lot of black people around at Bob's place. They're heavily involved in the crack scene. Most of them are second- and even third-generation English. They talk like Bob and his family, and a lot of them have done bird together. Bob's current dealing partner, Bruno, is black, and Bob himself has been scoring half ounces of smack through a Yardie.

I'll take you down the dark corridor to the kitchen where Bruno is washing up. Bob's place is always pretty cluttered, so mind the stuff lying around in the hall. Like a lot of professional dealers, Bob is eclectic in his activities. There are always consumer durables lying around the flat that have either been swapped for drugs, or are stolen goods waiting for a buyer. Bob loves gadgets, and he'll often detain an antsy punter and force him to watch while Bob takes the latest lap-top computing device through its paces.

Bruno is holding a whisky miniature over the steam that's spouting from an electric kettle. The little bottle has a solution of acetone, water and powdered cocaine in it. As we watch, Bruno takes a long metal rod

and dips it down the neck of the bottle. A large crystal forms around the rod almost immediately. This is crack cocaine. The fresh rocks have to dry out on a bit of kitchen towel for a while, but then they're ready to smoke.

There are no Coke cans with holes in them round at Bob's. This is a piping household. The pipes are small glass things that look like they belong in the laboratory. The bowl is formed by pressing a piece of gauze down the barrel of a thin Pyrex stem; fragments of crack are sprinkled on top of a bed of ash; the outside of the stem is heated with a blowtorch until the crack begins to deliquesce and melt, then the thick white smoke is drawn off, through the glass body of the pipe and out through a long, flat stem. Smoking a crack pipe properly is an art form.

If you came at the right time, Bob might ask you to join him—if he likes you, that is. And you could while away the evening doing pipe after pipe, with the odd chase of smack in between to stop yourself having a heart attack, or a stroke, or the screaming ad dabs. If you stay, you'll have some amicable conversations with people—one of the Yardies might drop by. The English blacks are also dismissive of them. Bruno says: 'Yardies? They're just down from the trees, man.' It is almost universally agreed that the Yardies overplayed their hand in London. They were easy to spot, too flamboyant for our pinched, *petit bourgeois* drug culture. The Met has managed to have the bulk of them deported, but their influence as a catalyst to the drug scene has gone on working.

But now Bob is expecting his dad, whose flat this is and who is due out on a spot of home leave. It's not that he doesn't want his dad to know that he's dealing out of the flat; far from it. In fact, Bob's dad will expect a commission. It's rather that he won't want to see a lot of low-life punters hanging around the place. So we say our goodbyes:

'Stay safe, man.'

'Yeah, mind yer backs.'

Security is always variable at Bob's; sometimes, when he's especially lucid, it's fantastic. He drills punters to carefully wrap crack and smack and stash the little waterproof bundles, either up their anuses or in their mouths. As Bob says: 'The filth pull a lot of punters as they're leaving here, and they sweat you, so make sure you stash that gear 'cos I don't want to do ten because some dozy prannet had it in his hand.' But at other times, you'll find six or seven addicts scratching outside the door of the flat, waiting for the Man. And there are young black kids running up and down the walkways of the flats, taunting the addicts, especially the white ones.

Even out in the street, Bob's influence is still felt. A tall, young black dude in a BMW CSi notices us coming out of Bob's block and calls us over. 'Have we come from Bob's? And do we want to go somewhere else where we can go on rocking?' Well, of course we do! We have our public to satisfy.

Basie drives us back up towards the Cross. It's dark now. He keeps up a running monologue for our benefit; its sheer braggadocio: 'Yeah, I've bin back to Africa, man. I hung so much paper in Morocco they probably thought I was decorating the place.' He isn't altogether bullshitting. I know from Bob that Basie is both successful at 'hanging paper' (passing false cheques) and at Bob's traditional blag: sprinting into financial institutions with the old sawn-off. I've seen Basie round at Bob's before. Sometimes he'll have a couple of quite classy tarts with him who look vaguely Mayfairy: all caramel tan streaky blonde hair and bright pink lips. If it wasn't for the hungry look and the strained eyes, one might almost take them for PR account handlers.

Up at the Cross, we turn into a backstreet and park the wedge. There's a crack house here that conforms a little more to our public's expectation. It's a squat with smashed windows and no electricity. Once Basie has got us inside, we are confronted with a throng of black faces. Everyone here is either buying, selling or smoking crack. Candles form islands of yellow light around which ivoried faces contort with drawing on the little glass pipes.

The atmosphere here is a lot heavier. Sure, Bob's place isn't exactly a picnic, but at least at his flat there is the sense that there actually *are* rules to be transgressed. Of course, it's bullshit to say there is honour among thieves, but there is a hierarchy of modified trust: 'I think you're a pukkah bloke, and I'll trust you and look out for you until it's slightly more in my favour to do otherwise.' It's an ethic of enlightened self-interest that isn't that dissimilar to any other rapacious free market where young men vie with one another to possess and trade in commodities. And, after all, isn't that what Mrs T wanted us to do? Tool around London in our Peugeot 205s and Golf GTis, cellular phones at the ready, hanging out to cut the competitive mustard.

But, at the crack house in King's Cross, we have no cachet, and we have the feeling here of being very isolated: a wrong move, a word out of place, and these people might get very nasty. The people here are much more 'streety' and they have very little to lose.

We've seen what we wanted to see, we've come full circle: you don't want to stay in the crack zone, do you? No, I didn't think so. Turn the page, get on with the next article, go home.

Evening Standard, September 1991

from

Cocaine

by Phil Strongman

I Live Alone And I Give The Orders

I HAD JUMPED the gun. I had, in fact, been just a bit too hasty. I'd
promised Jerry that a piece about his friend's trip-hop band, the Space
Age Nomads, was definitely going to appear in the next issue of *Groove*
magazine. It wasn't a feature really, more like a re-written press release,
but it still read okay and the Space Agers' single still sounded pretty
good. Good enough to justify me putting them in the mag's Floor-Fillers
chart, anyway. It helped that a few club DJs really had been playing it—
though not enough to justify me charting it—but quality wasn't really
the issue here. The problem was my promise. Although ninety per cent
of what I churned out usually ended up in print, I couldn't guarantee it.
And Jerry, who'd got me into a lig or two over the years, was desperate
that the Space Age Nomads got plugged in the next *Groove*. Not that
plugging was his job. I didn't know *what* Jerry did for a living, come to
think of it, though he always seemed to have money to burn and parties
to go to. Which must have been where I met him, once. Either there or
where we were now, propping up the bar in The Coach & Horses. 'Park
Life' was playing.

'It's not Vee's single, it's just on his label. He's gotta new label,' Jerry

278

said, staring at his glass of Jack Daniel's. I was supposed to know Vee, but I didn't. Vee was something of a big-shot, that much I was aware of.

'Is that sorted? Definite?' Jerry went on, looking around me as he tugged on his designer lapels. It was kind of sorted. Pretty much. I'd seen the next issue at the office, on computer. It was in the bag. But, like I said before, it wasn't definite. His eyes returned to me.

'Oh yeah,' I lied.

'Good,' he went on, ' 'cos he's depending on it. He'll be here in a minute.'

'Who will?'

'The lad hisself. Vee, ma main man.' Jerry must have caught my mental twitch as he spoke because he quickly added, 'Don't worry, you'll love him, he's cherry, he's cool, down with everyone, not heavy at all. Not when you consider what a big noise he is.'

'Yeah?' I said. 'I can't work out why we haven't met before.'

'Well, these big noises always are very quiet, aren't they?' he answered with a cheesy grin. 'Vee's a diamond geezer, though, a diamond geezer. He'll sort you out. With a drink, like.'

'Cheers.'

'Yeah,' Jerry said, accepting my thanks with his usual ligger's catchphrase, 'Put me on the door, put me on the tour . . . '

Before I could ask anything else, Vee walked in. I knew it was him straight away. He was medium-to-tall, dark hair, good looks enhanced by a touch of scar tissue, blue Paul Smith shirt, colourful, undone at the neck. In his late twenties, I guessed. Jerry went over, the perfect courtier, and whispered something to him—about me?—as they approached.

'Hi, Pete. How's it going?' Sarf London accent. Vee's eyes swept around the room, taking it all in—the empty tables, the two lovers necking in a corner, the deserted bar counter. As he did this we shook hands, a move which he used to pass something on to me. I hesitated, then pocketed the plastic packet. A good size bag too.

'What you been doing, Vee?'

'This and that. Caning it . . . Wanna drink?'

'Vodka and it, cheers.'

'Vodka and it, twice,' he said to the Aussie barman. Vee grinned. He was friendly, personable. A London lad. I went to the toilet. Checked the bag—it was white powder, at least a dozen grams. *A dozen grams!* I tasted it and my top gum went numb within seconds. Joy powder, Bolivian marching powder, charlie, coke, cream, gear, terry, tinkle, tink, toot, snoot, sherbet, snow and bu—the latter pronounced like the first two letters of bugle, which was yet another pet name . . . they changed all the time, the names; once one had appeared in the newspapers someone would use another and everyone followed suit. Only the dictionary remained constant: 'Cocaine; a narcotic in the form of an energising powder synthesised from the paste of the South American coca leaf. Seen pre-war as an adult tonic it has been illegal in the United Kingdom since . . . '

I still couldn't believe it though: a dozen grams, what was that worth? The cops would say it's a grand's worth *on the street*—but that would have to be a street in Mayfair. Still, it must have been worth at least six hundred pounds. What to do? Was a dozen grams enough to get the Law casting you as a dealer? Yeah, must be, seven or more grams could do that. I was looking at two years inside, maybe three if I got caught with such an amount. And all of it was on me then. All of it. Guilty as charged and burning a hole in my pocket.

The sensation in the whole top half of my mouth faded fast. The numbness spread though, taking my throat off the list of active organisms. This was strong stuff. Far purer than anything I'd ever taken before—not that I'd taken that much before. How pure was it? Thirty per cent? Thirty-five? Maybe even forty per cent pure? That put its value up to nearer a grand. But getting sentenced to three years inside . . . or would it be four? The paranoia grew, soaring with the high as if it was the high's evil shadow. Every cloud has a tinfoil lining. My heart thumped faster and faster. Shit, I just wanted some humble grass, m'lud, don't jail me . . .

My face was shining so I splashed it with some lukewarm water as I wondered why none of the hot taps ever worked in any London bar. I walked out of the toilet, trying to look legitimate and business-like. The bar was completely deserted now. Even the lovers had gone. And Jerry and Vee were nowhere to be seen, of course. Great, that was all I needed. Maybe they'd just been busted and we were all due to appear on *News at Ten* with blankets over our heads . . . I couldn't help noticing the sunlight as it picked out the lazy dust floating in the air, just like the chalk-dust in a summer class-room as school died.

'Can I get you anything, sir?' The barman returned, grinning blankly, like he knew something. Or someone. I was going to ask where Vee and Jerry had gone but I stopped myself, mid-thought, on the grounds that it might incriminate me. I definitely couldn't give the stuff back now. *Let's just take another dab*, I thought, *and kick the rest under a table, eh?* But what if some plain-clothes copper came in a few seconds later? I could imagine the conversation.

'And who was standing there then, barman?'

'It was a tall bloke, officer—look, that's him outside now!'

The absolute certainty of getting busted was growing on me by the second. Couldn't leave the stuff. Couldn't keep it. Stuck in the middle with you. Great. I should have known better. Always look a gift horse in the mouth.

I had to get out. Get out and get home. I knocked back the dregs of my drink and stumbled outside. Vee and Jerry were not, of course, struggling with a police patrol on the pavement outside. Not that the absence of cops calmed me down. I still felt like I was in the judicial spotlight. *Look inconspicuous!* I silently screamed at myself. I thought about getting a cab, but it was tourist city out there. No chance. A Number 19 bus swung past then got caught at a red light. I jumped on it. Went upstairs. Went to the front. I was unseen. That was good. The vodka I'd taken was combining with the bu now, was kicking in something chronic, so I took another dab, just a little—why not?—as the bus lurched over a bump in the road. *Hey, this soaring nothing feeling is really a great adventure!* I tried to keep it down, tried to feel ironic and distant. I failed.

I was getting careless. Some powder—half a gram, a gram, more!—floated down on to the floor. Shit. I used my boot to grind the powder into the chewing-gum dirt as I bundled the cling-film plastic together again, and thought about getting off the bus. My jaw was buzzing now. Deciding to take a chance, I got off in New Oxford Street and ducked into Denmark Street, which was where I bumped into Chas from the Hot Import record shop. He was there with a couple of baggy rave characters with silly hats—E17 rejects wearing hats with ears. They were all covered with 'Love' logos and acted like they wanted to dish out a good kicking.

'He's back and now he's wack. Just the man I was looking for. Pete here owes me some dosher, doncha now?' said Chas.

'How'd you figure that one?' I fronted it out with a smile.

' 'Cos the last lotta booties you give me was all domestic. Well dodgy.
So you owe me some wonga, doncha?'

Which was true, kind of. Except that he'd ripped me off before, like
every single time he'd ever bought off me, like all buyers in a buyer's market. And it's always a buyer's market. But . . . let's not quibble.

I wasn't a part-time shoe-salesman, by the way. Booties means bootlegs,
for the uninitiated. Illegal recordings that DJs would kill for because all
the turntable wannabes couldn't get hold of them in Woollies. You can
buy them from basements in Covent Garden or Camden. Or even from
Chas if you really want to get ripped off. They're usually from America,
sounds that haven't been or won't be released, rare mixes, mistakes, copyright problems. I was sometimes in possession of one or two . . .

I could have turned on my heel and walked away from Chas and all
that—I might have got a bottle over my head, though I seriously doubted
it—but if I did walk away would I have closed off yet another of my limited outlets? Yes and no.

'Do I? Don't recall that, Chas . . . '

'He don't "recall that". You kill me, man, you kill me, doncha?'

No, I thought, *but I'd like to, right at this minute.*

'No,' I actually said, 'you just did me a favour, didn't you?'

'You,' he shook his head sadly as if this was part of some huge tragedy
which moved him greatly, 'you used to be down with everyone, dincha,
Pete? Way you're going on nah you're gonna end up on the rock'n'roll,
encha?'

Rock'n'roll—dole. Unemployed and unemployable. Yes, it *was* possible. More than possible. I'd never gone to college or anything. I know
that sounds weird, especially now when every other Scout hut has the
word 'university' blue-tacked outside, but that's how it happened. I'd left
school a year before the second Summer of Love (copyright EMI records
1988, all rights reserved) so I joined in that scene instead. University of
life—well, Soho. A full-time course. Running clubs, doing artwork, working for nothing half the time and making thousands the rest. And writing
about it all too, convinced there was some bigger, higher meaning to it all
as we raced the cops to the next rave road-block while screaming
'*Acieeeed! Acieeed!*' It all ended up as big business, of course, being run
by people with double-barrelled names or double-barrelled shotguns. I
should have grovelled my way back into college then, back into the loop,

but I didn't. Too busy partying. I couldn't complain—I'd had a lot of fun—but here I was, a decade on, free of all qualifications, on every credit blacklist going, existing as a freelance music hack. I say 'existing' because it sure as hell wasn't a real living . . .

Chas grunted louder, I'd ignored him too long.

'Said you're gonna end up on the rock'n'roll, encha?' he repeated with emphasis. I shrugged in reply. It seemed the sensible thing to do while he was playing the disillusioned big brother.

'So,' he went on, 'whatcha bin doin' then, boy?' He screwed his eyes up. He wanted an answer. What *had* I been doing? Specifically, what had I been doing to pay him off? Chas and his droogies still looked like they might turn nasty. This was getting crazy, I decided. I couldn't owe him more than a few quid, just peanuts . . . Then again, I've known bouncers that would break your jaw for a twenty. And they knew crackheads who would do it for ten. So what was the deal? I leaned forward, all confidential. *You're in on this too now, Chas baby. Have a favour back.*

'Fancy a dab of something?' I offered.

'What you got? I don't want no speed.'

'No, no. It's faster than that. Only the best for my mate Chas.'

'Sound.'

'Sorted.' The gang chipped in like the idiot chorus they were.

'Solid—'

'Safe—'

'Smooth—'

Chas grinned mirthlessly. We strolled down the tiny alley that separates the guitar shops on Denmark. He took a huge dab, his boys less so, they were lairy of anything that wasn't beer. Chas pulled out a matchbox—this was all so blatant—before he gave me a questioning look, like I was the big boss-man now. And, suddenly, I could see the attraction of dealing gear. Forget the profits, forget the easy access. The biggest bonus was being in demand. Girls suddenly attracted to you. People forming a line at parties. Chas changing moods like the wind. Not that I wanted to become a dealer. I'd spent a few weekends in the cells for various things—usually for being at some pay party that had been raided—and I didn't ever want to extend the experience. But that didn't stop me nodding in reply, granting a favour to Chas as I cleared my debt. He emptied the last few matches from the box and I tipped a gram or so in there and closed the bag. I was probably three grams lighter then, all told—does that make a difference, m'lud? Chas licked his lips. I was forgiven. In fact he now owed me one. I toyed with the idea of giving it all to him, the lot, and forgetting all about it, but something at the back of my brain stopped me. Something definitely stopped me. I dunno what . . . cocaine, probably.

I got a cab home. The ansafone light flickered. It was Jerry's voice.

'Pete baby, this is Jezza. Me an' Vee had to go. Things to do an' that. But you got the stuff, right? That gear is so pukka you can cut it fifty-fifty. You'll make a fortune, my son. Just make sure that feature goes in, eh? Just make sure it's locked. Ring you later.'

That last line made an idea leap from the back of my brain to the front. *Let's be logical*, I thought, *let's be straight ahead logical.* Vee, the coke baron, now expected a feature and/or review. A review of this trip-hop mob. He'd given me nearly a thousand pounds' worth of pure cocaine for just that very purpose. If the feature didn't go in, he'd figure I owed him a grand in return. Maybe much more than a grand, since he probably needed a good review in the next issue far more than he needed the cash. He probably had posters and ads lined up—timing was all.

I didn't just owe Jerry a favour if the review didn't run. If it all went wrong I now owed Vee. I should have checked before I opened my big mouth. I couldn't actually guarantee that the review would go in—a last minute advert paying cash, a mistake at the printers, a rush-release on a Prince album, anything could happen and usually did. As a free-loading freelancer I didn't have that much influence. Any definite was a definite maybe. Nothing was definite unless you were an editor. Or a sub-editor. And sub-editors usually become editors. Although many subs are undoubtedly talented, the main reason for their rapid rise through the ranks is that, like production staff, they are actually in the office all day. Now this is what they are paid for, but the suits in charge of things never seem to quite twig this and think, instead, that this daily attendance shows some extraordinary beyond-the-pale dedication. Freelancers are, with a bit of justification, considered dangerous flakes, and the staff writers, if there are any left, are seen as drunks—and they're always out doing silly things like covering stories—while the very word art, as in art director, is enough to terrify any *bona fide* member of the board. No top spot for them then. So, if you're a magazine writer or freelancer, it always pays to stay in with your subs. Even when they take out, as they usually will, the key paragraph that explains everything—or the punch-line that made others laugh out loud—you can't freak out at 'em because they're more important than you in the grand scheme of things. They were, or would be, in charge. And being in charge was something I most certainly was not.

That was why I'd kept the coke—in case my plug for Vee's mob got spiked and I had to sell some. At least that's what I told myself. I had toyed with the idea of just giving it straight back to Vee, but I knew he wouldn't want the goods back, not now. He'd want their wholesale worth—at least—and in cash. I dialled Jerry's number, thinking that I must find out more about Vee. Jerry's ansafone was on and I decided I wasn't well enough to leave a message.

I took another tiny dab of coke as I sorted through my mail, feeling hyper but strangely confident. Why not be on an upper? The review would probably go in and, even if it didn't, there was always the plug in the Floor-Fillers chart to keep Vee happy. So what was I worrying about? Nothing, as usual . . . The hi-fi automatically flicked through the capital's radio stations. There was Jules Someone playing House on Kiss FM and Capital Radio was playing House and Pete Someone on Radio 1 was playing—guess what?—House . . . The House mafia, live and in full effect on all channels. I figured I was lucky to be alive in such a wonderful age of diversity.

I ripped open the last envelope. There was a lig on. There was always a lig on. This one was at the Happy House. Tonight. My name had been put on the door.

A lig, as you surely know, is a launch party—for some CD or band or book or club or boutique or whatever—wherein copious amounts of free drink are served up to a host of trendies, hacks, paparazzi and various other hangers-on. These party-goers are usually known as liggers. A true ligger won't actually write or photograph anything that will mention the event that he's just ruined—in fact, a true ligger won't even have been officially invited—and this is implicitly understood by most organisers. They pretended to love the product and we pretended we'd write about it—or, at the very least, spread the word.

I hoped Jeff would be there, but it was pretty unlikely. He hated the Happy House—it had been littered with junkies the first time he went and he hadn't been back since. Jeff is my half-brother, a 'top-notch club DJ' as they say in the Sunday supplements. He wasn't ultra-fashionable any more, but he'd still been on air a few times and he still made a living and enjoyed his role. He played whatever he liked, whenever he liked and there weren't that many DJs in clubs who could do that, let alone on the airwaves. As I said, he wasn't that trendy, but trendy had become something of a devalued term. It usually didn't mean trend-*setting* any more. It just meant reading, and getting all your ideas from, certain magazines and/or buying into 'yoof' TV and MTV. And anyone and everyone could buy into that. 'Anastasia only wears grey, has nipple-clamps, a face tattoo of Himmler and her ambition is to date her dad! Big-up respect, yeah! Jungle in the House! And, after the break, we've got some close-ups of a testicle operation!'

No word-of-mouth was required. No special talents. No suss. Therefore everyone was hip. And if everyone was hip, then no one was. So being unhip was hip. And how hip you were depends on how unhip you could be, see? This meant that, in some niteries, the Simon Park Orchestra, the 1910 Fruitgum Company and the cha-cha-cha were the coming thing, while Gilbert O'Sullivan was now the Godfather of Punk. Clever, huh?

Having So Much Fun

THE HAPPY HOUSE entrance lights were too bright, making the scene—a girl in a pink painter's smock being gingerly searched by the security—look like something out of a movie. Thirty seconds after being searched and going on in, she returned, saying to the staff that she'd left her fags in the car and could she please get them and come back in? Please? *Pretty please?* They said yes, of course, though it was really only an old trick that small-time dealers sometimes used, girls especially. They would get frisked, get the all-clear, then nip out and return, loaded down with E's and whizz, and the bouncers would then nod them straight through because, well, they've already been searched, haven't they? Yeah, yeah, yeah . . .

I spied Jerry inside the sunken foyer. He was wearing an oversized powder-blue mac, and I sought him out like an Exocet.

'Jerry, wha' happen, man? What's going on?'

'Everything—come here, I want you to meet some designers.'

That's all I needed. I wanted to find out more about Vee, *vis-à-vis* my chances of being crippled, and Jezza wanted to introduce me to a couple of art students.

'You'll love 'em, they're really fit, cherry man not wack—'

'Great, whatever you want, but we gotta talk about Vee—'

Jerry stopped dead in his tracks, stepping over a sneering girl in a half T-shirt and silver jeans. He licked his lips as he turned slowly and spoke, his eyes everywhere.

'Vee? Is he here?'

'I dunno, Jezza, that's why I'm asking you.'

'Course he's not here,' said Jerry, relaxing and walking on. 'I would know.'

'Thought you said he wasn't heavy . . . '

'He's not, not really.'

'So why d'you look so worried then?'

'Me? Worried? Pete, baby, you're losing it.'

'No, I'm not,' I breezed. 'And you *are* worried. Come on, tell Uncle Pete everything . . . you know what they say, a trouble shared is a rumour started.'

'Nah . . . I jus' owe him a few quid. I was s'posed to give it to him this afternoon, or take it round tonight. But he can wait. He don't mind. Me and Vee are like that.' He showed me his two crossed fingers.

'And which one's on top then?'

'Pete, man, there's no longer any top or bottom,' he philosophised. 'Not anywhere, not with anyone. Now there's just deals. You know? Deals? That's all there is. And the people you trust are the people you deal with, see? And I trust Vee. He's a diamond, man, a fuckin' diamond.'

'So he doesn't knee-cap people then?' I said, my fading paranoia still seeking reassurance.

'Knee-cap? You're crazy, man. You've been caning it too much. Vee might do *someone*, somewhere, maybe, if they pushed their luck. But he'd never do you, 'cos you know me, see? He's gonna be the godfather of me kids. So, lighten up . . . Are you staying out late? What time did you come out tonight?' he asked, trying to change the subject.

'I came out at nine.'

'Still working nine to five then?' He smirked a big, sloppy smirk.

'Why do you always say that?' I asked before he laughed at his own feeble joke.

'Well, I dunno. Why do you always ask me why?'

'Because, Jerry, I'm trying to offer you some solid stability in a ruthless world of change—'

'Bollocks . . . have you seen this?' he said, slapping a magazine into my hands. It was the colour supplement of the *Chronicle*, folded open on a page that featured a big colour splash of the kids' latest heroes, The Scallies, a rock'n'roll band who were fast becoming superstars. One of the hangers-on in the main picture was Jerry, leaning on The Scallies' guitarist.

'Sweet,' I nodded. 'You look good.' And he did look good.

'Yeah, I might be going on their world tour.'

'Friend of the stars, eh?'

'That's it, son,' he said as he slowed to a halt before two girls. 'Pete, meet Desdemona and . . . Georgina, isn't it?'

'Geraldine.' Geraldine, a skinny brunette, corrected Jerry with a tricksy smile. Desdemona was darker, Asian. Both of them *seemed* like sweet young things. They tolerated Jerry and me anyway. A closer look revealed that they had big bright eyes that were flat, and even flatter stomachs with two rings stuck in each belly button. Two. Overkill. You could tell they were designers. They must have been all of eighteen years old. Maybe seventeen. It was no big deal, though. I'd seen girls of fourteen in clubs before now. Geraldine and Desdemona were from Bournemouth, just up for the weekend they said, at which Jerry winked at me. We talked aimlessly about fashion and music, and when things slowed down Jerry showed them the *Chronicle* supplement featuring himself, telling them that I wrote for the *Chronicle*—which was true, I'd get maybe four pieces a year—but the girls were dying to blurt out what they were really after. Jerry, who fancied himself as a remixer that week, was talking about people faking it in music.

'These days,' I mumbled, trying to be profound, 'almost everyone is faking it everywhere.'

'I've never faked it in my life,' pouted Desdemona.

'You haven't been taking the right drugs, then,' giggled Geraldine in a Dorset/London hybrid accent before adding, 'speaking of gear . . . '

Here it was. The pay-off. The inevitable question. *Do you score here often?*

'You boys got any stuff? Any coke?' It was all so predictable that I almost wanted them to go away, but after another ten seconds of contemplating their figures I began to wish I had brought some of my coke with me. I hadn't dated anyone for months, and even my last inglorious one-night-stand had been a week or two ago. Giving these two coke would have been a bit of a bribe, but didn't all relationships involve some kind of bribery? Not that you could call it a relationship.

I shouldn't have worried—Jerry had some charlie on him. Naturally. And that's the way the conversation began to veer. *I'm a journo and he's got more charlie than Chaplin. We can help you, girls, we can help you.* It was sickening, really, but that's the way things were. Twenty seconds later the girls were licking some spilt powder off Jerry's cuff, acting like demented kittens. All four of us were crammed into one cubicle of the gents' toilet, eyes bumping off each other like magnets. They sniffed a line apiece and then it was Jerry's turn. He chopped up his gear on the cistern, sniffed it through a rolled-up tenner and then I took half a line and made a dab at the rest. Jerry finished a third line off as I wondered if my wet finger, just off the cistern lid, was going to give me jaundice later. Jaundice or Hepatitis B. Or both. Or were they the same? I made a mental note to get some vodka—if I swilled it around and gargled it enough it would surely kill all known germs. Either vodka or brandy would do it. A brandy will settle your stomach too. Brandy will settle most things, if you drink enough of it . . .

Things began to go sour when the girls began to act like they were addicts or something. Not that they wouldn't be friendly later, they would probably even put out, but only if we gave them some more toot. If we wanted them. Bittersweet young things that they were.

'There's a party up west. Near the Hangover.' Jerry whispered in my ear when we were back on the stairs.

'Are we taking these two?' I asked as quietly as I could.

'Maybe, if you want to . . . Girls, there's a party on. You up for it?'

Their faces revolved around to ours again. Their big bright eyes were even flatter now, pupils tiny. Germ warfare victims with no emotion. Close up, they'd almost look like aliens. Pretty, but alien. Had I ever looked like that? I might have done once or twice, which was a frightening thought. Maybe they'd scored some coke before they'd even met us.

'Oh yeah, when's it happenin' then? This party?'

'Now. Do you wanna wait outside for us?'

'Outside?' They were genuinely horrified. One minute they were being given Class A drugs in a top London niterie as they hung out with friends of The Scallies, and now they were being asked to wait outside. Outside! Them! Designers! Outside! Them!

'Yeah, just for five minutes, girls, just for five, I gotta get invites y'know. I'll just be five.'

They sulkily strutted up the steps and lingered on the edge of the foyer's pool of light. Jerry said something to the guy with the guest-list and pocketed a couple of crumpled tickets. I looked outside. The designer-clad designer girls outside were chatting to some Essex lads in mod shirts—*we wanna go to Camden!*—as Jerry swept up to me, the mac twirling around his ankles.

'There's someone outside who can give us a lift. We just gotta wait a couple of minutes.'

A few moments later a DJ in duffle-coat and goatee run-walked up to Jerry. Although by then it was jammed tight, we still managed to get through the exit easily enough, but Desdemona and co. were nowhere to be seen. They'd probably had a better offer and taken it. The rest of us piled in a white mini-cab which screamed off like some getaway car. The Yugoslav driver was nineteen or twenty years young and several laws unto himself—he didn't go through a single green light the entire journey—but we were all too high to care. As I glanced back I saw the designer girls outside the club, emerging from behind one of the stone pillars. One of them waved frantically and I nudged Jerry—he had the tickets, after all—but he silently shook his head and the Happy House soon disappeared into the background. They'd find what they were looking for anyway. A trendy-wendy guy with a fuck-off-and-die coke stash. Their knight in shining Armani, some cat with all the cream . . .

'We're running out of toot,' Jerry moaned as the mini-cab neared the West End. By now, I was too much in the swing of things to slow down, so I opened my mouth and gave the game away.

'Make him go via my place. I've got some gear there,' I heard myself saying. The mini-cab radio was blaring out 'Everything Is Gonna Blow' and I thought yeah, that's how I feel.

The party venue was a former restaurant, now a kind of wine-bar-type club with stupid empty picture frames and driftwood thrown on the walls at random. But the floor below almost looked like a night-club when the lights were low. In my hyper state I was totally drug-conscious, aware of all the deals—the tables at the back looked like a hip chess tournament played at high speed. Under flickering lights. Once your eyes—and your mind—had adjusted to the gloom, you saw it all. If you knew what to look for—lots of little hand moves, cash and powder going back and forth over, under and around tables. Amid much back-slapping and side-tapping. As if they were great friends. Young journos and trendies getting loaded. Getting blasted. Almost everyone was, if the truth be known. Virtually every single one of the media crowd was doing something illegal at some point during the week.

There was free booze at the bar to celebrate the launch of some new vodka mixer, so people were knocking back the Russian spirit like there was no tomorrow. Consequently they were all talking more than normal. There were some time-servers from admin, accounting and ad departments present, too, all of them trying to act like real human beings. Top button undone, bri-nylon tie loosened, kissy-kissy! *Love your suit!*

I talked to Eye, Eye being a bottle-blonde PR for Fried Funk records. Eye, as she'd always be the first to tell you, is a good fun person. 'Good fun people' are usually like good fun entertainment, being neither good nor funny, but Eye's actually both. When she's not being miserable, of course. By the time you finish reading this sentence she'll have been promoted or sacked.

That night Eye was the only person there, Jerry aside, that I knew. The rest was a storm of strangers, and Eye was the eye. We talked about today's drug fetish and I repeated what Jeff had said about trip-hop—the discs are okay but you have to be stoned to really love them. Stoned music usually made by stoned people and probably aimed at stoned people. Unlistenable and depressing without chemical stimulants.

'Everyone's on drugs these days,' I said, 'especially the teens, 'cos there's no real jobs for most of 'em and no one thinks they can change anything any more. If you think you can't do anything to *that* out there, you just settle for seriously damaging *this* up here.'

'That's an amazing theory,' Eye said. 'What are you on?'

One of her pals rolled a huge spliff of skunk—liberally sprinkled with Moroccan Black—even as she agreed with me. I took the joint, damned as I was, and inhaled greedily. Even the joint didn't do much to slow me down, my heart was beginning to roar like a lion. Everyone was starting to annoy me by speaking in slow-motion. I'd had too much coke. *And,* I thought, *you are talking too slowly! Far too slowly! Get on with it! Faster! Faster!* Cut to the chase! *Cut to the chase!*

Someone offered me some toffee. *Sweeties and school-age innocence,* I thought, so I took it. And then discovered that by 'toffee' he meant the chewy Manchester thing that's full of speed. I got kicked into overdrive. Double-time. But good. Which was too bad. Everything got very hectic, very fast. I lost Eye—and her pals—and Jerry in the crowd. I found myself with the hostess of the place. She was called Gina. She was an overgrown wild child, a kind of no-nothing twentysomething. She contributed to the *Telegraph*'s fashion pages—or was it *The Times?*—and was operating on the wrong side of twenty-five. Like me. But she also had unlimited credit, and she was supposed to be that week's It person. Unlike me.

'It's all this stupidly fast techno crap that brings me down,' I said as the ruthless soundtrack of bass booms thudded around me.

'If it's too fast, you're too old,' she sniggered. As if she was still seventeen.

'Yeah, yeah, yeah.'

'You're really pre-digital, aren't you?' she lisped sympathetically, her eyes a touch worried as if the dinosaur before her might crumble away before her very eyes. Mind you, the way I felt, total disintegration wasn't a complete impossibility.

'If that stuff can't be about human rhythms, it should at least be about love or hate or Bosnia or something,' I rambled as I felt my left eye start to twitch.

'If you really, really wanna know about love, Pete, you should pop an E—'

'Huh?' I grunted back as my hand desperately smoothed my flickering eye to a standstill. Afterwards I noticed my hand was trembling slightly.

'And as for Bosnia,' she went on, 'we really should leave those ethnic-cleansing things to the government. They do have a plan, you know. A long-term thingy. And I'm *sure* it's clever—'

'Oh yeah, so clever it's fuckin' stupid.'

'No, I really think we should leave it to them—'

'We've done that for years now,' I said, 'and what have you got? TB and rickets are back, the UN's a joke and the Serbs have got away with locking people up in concentration camps and starving 'em—'

'Starving 'em!' she scoffed. 'They should be so bloody lucky! I've been on a diet for months.'

'That's not really that funny, you know? Not really.'

But, I must admit, her idiot views had only been part of my problem with her. Most of it was because she spoke so damned slowly. It felt like time for more vodka—gotta fight that jaundice. Medical paranoia. By 1 a.m., though, it was all even worse. I was seriously worried. I'd only done the odd few lines of coke—was it a few? I couldn't remember—but I was still getting that heart-strain. Pulse flickering! Too fast! Too fast! Too fast! Palpitations. Heart-beat stuttering. That awful *I could die tonight* feeling swirled around me like a shroud. *Maybe I could die now*, I thought gloomily. Cocaine and vodka wasn't an ideal combination, not in large amounts. The bass notes that boomed from the sound system merged into one continuous threatening rumble. The bass drum thumped into my chest, doing a nasty rubber imitation of the heart-beat with the added complication of echoes shooting up into my jaw and reverberating deep down into my stomach. Now it was worse. Non-stop. I hated that feeling. I hated that feeling almost as much as I feared it.

I hit the soft drinks like there was no tomorrow as I hung on to the arm of Marie-Ann, an elfin-looking record company girl. She seemed sweet. She talked sympathetically about the evils of drugs, the many deaths she had known. *Cheer me up, why doncha?* I thought. But even her doomy chat was better than nothing. Marie-Ann was there, after all. She cared, apparently. A witness. But even this port-in-a-storm was doomed.

'Don't leave me. Stay at the bar,' I heard myself plead.

'Don't worry, I'll be back. Are you gonna be here?'

'Yes and no . . . Yes, I mean, I'm not going anywhere.'

'You can say that again.'

'Huh?'

'Well, look at you. A typical music hack! You're off your face . . . doing bad shit. Too much of it. Too much, too soon.'

'I'm trying to chill,' I tried to pacify her, anxious that she should stay. 'You're right. I am in a bad way . . . and I don't mean to be flippant.'

'Okay, I just gotta speak to my boss,' Marie-Ann insisted. 'But don't worry, I'll be back in a second.'

'You will come back?' I sounded like a child pleading. She smiled as she nodded in the affirmative but she then slipped away and didn't look back. The seconds turned into minutes. Of course she wasn't coming back. What kind of fool was I? What was in it for her?

I notice she'd left her business card on the bar. Terrific. Even when you're dying someone's networking you. I drank more orange and mineral water and slowly started to revive. I'd been trying to work a drug evening—going up-down-up-down. Dope then coke then weed then speed then drinks. That way, if you got it right, you could take off while always remaining in control. Unfortunately I'd overdone all the ingredients and my flight had crashed just after take-off. No casualties though, apart from the Captain . . .

After an hour of terror, things started to get better. I hadn't seriously embarrassed myself—I still remembered the whispered giggles that had occurred when the publisher of *Bloated!* magazine had first taken speed. 'Call an ambulance!' she'd screamed over and over again. 'Someone's trying to kill me! Kill me! They are!'

My own feeling of doom started to slink back into its little black box. Maybe I was gonna live—if I could just slow my heart-beat down a little. I blagged my way into the DJ's box and took a few tokes of someone else's joint. Started to feel a little better. Bit by bit. Another joint, another half-pint of mineral water, another inch off the accelerator . . .

At 2.30 a.m. I was definitely alive. I staggered out into the cold night air, all my troubles washed away. Paul, the *Groove* art editor, was outside, leaning on a lamp-post, looking like a French fashion photo—why did he always seem to be in black and white? He was looking for a taxi. I hadn't seen him in there at all—how stoned had I been?

'Hey stranger, long time no see,' he smiled, a little bit wasted, before adding, 'or hear.'

'Well, lad . . . I have phoned a few times.'

'Were you in there?' he jerked a thumb back at the wine-bar club as his eyes sought out a cab.

'I dunno. Probably. Were you?'

'Yeah . . . You should come into the office soon. There's been some changes. The next issue's totally screwed.'

'Screwed?' I felt my voice rising as panic gripped me again. 'Whatcha mean screwed? Are there many changes?'

Paul smiled lazily.

'No. Not many but often.' He thought about what he'd said, smiled at it then laughed. 'Not many but often. No, seriously, there *have* been some problems.'

A cab pulled up at his waved command.

'Problems?' I echoed him weakly like some dying comedian.

'Yeah,' he slammed the cab door behind him and pulled the window down, 'yeah, the dance pages have been halved. We lost the features and the Floor-Fillers. Drop in soon and I'll try and get you some more work.'

The cab sped away before I could ask any more. The dance section was cut in half. The features, the Floor-Fillers chart had gone. I would still get a kill-fee, but kill-fee had taken on an ugly new meaning in the last few hours. And Jerry's reassurances hadn't reassured him, let alone me. *Hey, Vee! Big noise! I didn't get the story in, despite all my promises . . . So there you have it, Mister Master Criminal, I ripped you off—whatcha gonna do about it?*

from

Infinite Jest

David Foster Wallace

UNDER A STREETLAMP on Faneuil St. off W. Beacon, Randy Lenz shares a vulnerable personal thing and tilts his head back to show Bruce Green where his septum used to be.

Randy Lenz reguiles Bruce Green about certain real-estate cults in S. Cal. and the West Coast. Of Delawareans that still believed Virtual-Reality pornography even though it'd been found to cause bleeding from the eye-corners and real-world permanent impotence was still the key to Shrangi-la and believed that some sort of perfect piece of digito-holographic porn was circulating somewhere in the form of a bootleg Write-Protect-notched software diskette and devoted their cultic lives to snuffling around trying to get hold of the virtual kamasupra diskette and getting together in dim Wilmington-area venues and talking very obliquely about rumors of where and just what the software was and how their snufflings for it were going, and watching Virtual fuckfilms and mopping the corner of their eyes, etc. Or of something called Stelliform Cultism that Bruce Green isn't even near ready to hear about, Lenz opines. Or like e.g. of a suicidal Nuck cult of Nucks that worshipped a form of Russian Roulette that involved jumping in front of trains and seeing which Nuck could come the closest to the train's front without getting demapped.

What sounds like Lenz chewing gum is really Lenz trying to talk and grind his teeth together at the same time.

Lenz recalls orally that his stepfather's blue-vested gut had preceded the conductor into rooms by several seconds, fob glinting above the watchpocket's sinister slit. How Lenz's mother back in Fall River had made it a point of utilizing Greyhound for voyages and sojourns, basically to piss her stephusband off.

Lenz discusses how a serious disadvantage to dealing Bing retail is the way customers'll show up pounding on your door at 0300 sporting lint in the terms of resources and putting their arms around your shins and ankles and begging for just a half-gram or tenth of a gram and offering to give Lenz their kids, like Lenz wants to fucking deal with anybody's kids, which these scenes were always constant drags on his spirits.

Green, who's hoovered his share, says cocaine always seemed like it grabbed you by the throat and just didn't let go, and he could relate to why the Boston AAs call Bing the 'Express Elevator To AA.'

In a dumpster-lined easement between Faneuil St. and Brighton Ave., Brighton, right after Green almost steps in what he's pretty sure is human vomit, Lenz proves logically why it's all too likely that Ennet House resident Geoffrey D. is a closet poofta.

Lenz reports how he's been approached in the past to male-model and act, but that the male-model and acting profession is pretty much crawling with your closet pooftas, and it's no kind of work for a man that's confronted the ins and outs of his own character.

Lenz speculates openly on how there are purportaged to be whole packs and herds of feral animals operating in locust-like fashion in the rhythmic lushness of parts of the Great Concavity to the due northeast, descended reputedly from domestic pets and abandoned during the relocational transition to an O.N.A.N.ite map, and how teams of pro researchers and amateur explorers and intrepid hearts and cultists have ventured northeast of Checks-points along the Lucited ATHSCMulated walls and never returned, vanishing in toto from the short-wave E.M. bands, as in like dropping off the radar.

Green turns out to have no conceptions or views on the issues of fauna of the Concavity at all. He literally says he's never given it one thought one way or the other.

Whole NNE cults and stelliform subcults Lenz reports as existing

around belief systems about the metaphysics of the Concavity and annu-
lar fusion and B.S.-1950s-B-cartridge-type-radiation-affected fauna and
overfertilization and verdant forests with periodic oasises of purportaged
desert and whatever east of the former Montpelier VT area of where the
annulated Shawshine River feeds the Charles and tints it the exact same
tint of blue as the blue on boxes of Hefty SteelSaks and the ideas of rava-
cious herds of feral domesticated housepets and oversized insects not
only taking over the abandoned homes of relocated Americans but actually setting up house and keeping them in model repair and impressive
equity, allegedly, and the idea of infants the size of prehistoric beasts
roaming the overfertilized east Concavity quadrants, leaving enormous
scat-piles and keening for the abortive parents who'd left or lost them in
the general geopolitical shuffle of mass migration and really fast packing,
or, as some of your more Limbaugh-era-type cultists sharingly believe,
originating from abortions hastily disposed of in barrels in ditches that got
breached and mixed ghastly contents with other barrels that reanimated
the abortive feti and brought them to a kind of repelsive oversized B-
cartridge life thundering around due north of where yrstruly and Green
strolled through the urban grid. Of one local underground stelliform offshoot from the Bob Hope–worshipping Rastafarians who smoked enormous doobsters and wove their negroid hair into clusters of wet cigars like
the Rastafarians but instead of Rastafarians these post-Rastas worshipped
the Infant and every New Year donned tie-dyed parkas and cardboard
snowshoes and ventured northward, trailing smoke, past the walls and
fans of Checkpoint Pongo into the former areas of VT and NH, seeking
The Infant they called it, as if there were only One, and toting paraphernalia for performing a cultish ritual referred to in oblique tones only as
Propitiating The Infant, whole posses of these stelliform pot-head reggae-
swaying Infant-cultists disappearing forever off the human race's radar
every winter, never heard or smelled again, regarded by fellow cultists as
martyrs and/or lambs, possibly too addled by blimp-sized doobsters to find
their way back out of the Concavity and freezing to death, or enswarmed
by herds of feral pets, or shot by property-value-conscious insects, or . . .
(face plum-colored, finally breathing) worse.

Lenz shudders just at the thought of the raging Powerlessness he'd feel,
he shares, lost and disorientated, wandering in circles in blinding white
frozen points due north of all domesticated men, forget the time not even

knowing what fucking *date* it was, his breath an ice-beard, with just his tinder and wits anf character to live by, armed just with a Browning blade.

Green opines that if Boston AA is a cult that like brainwashes you, he guesses he'd got himself to the point where his brain needed a good brisk washing, which Lenz knows is not an original view, being exactly what big blockheaded Don Gately repeats about once a diem.

14 November
Year of the Depend Adult Undergarment

A DISADVANTAGE OF your nasally ingested cocaine being that at a certain point somewhere past the euphoric crest—if you haven't got the sense left to stop and just ride the crest, and instead keep going, nasally— it takes you into regions of almost interstellar cold and nasal numbness. Randy Lenz's sinuses were frozen against his skull, numb and hung with crystal frost. His legs felt like they ended at the knees. He was trailing two very small-sized Chinese women as they lugged enormous paper shopping bags east on Bishop Allen Dr. under Central. His heart sounded like a shoe in the Ennet House basement's dryer. His heart was beating that loud. The Chinese women scuttled at an amazing rate, given their size and the bags' size. It was c. 2212:30–40h., smack in the middle of the for-mer Interval of Issues-Resolution. The Chinese women didn't walk so much as scuttle with a kind of insectile rapidity, and Lenz was heart-pressed to both keep up and seem to casually saunter, numb from the knee down and the nostril back. They made the turn onto Prospect St. two or a few blocks below Central Square, moving in the direction of Inman Square. Lenz followed ten or thirty paces behind, eyes on the twine handles of the shopping bags. The Chinese women were about the size of fire hydrants and moved like they had more than the normal amount of legs, conversing in their anxious and high-pitched monkey-language. Evolution proved your Orientoid tongues were closer to your primatal languages than not. At first, on the brick sidewalks of the stretch of Mass. Ave. between Harvard and Central, Lenz had thought *they* might be following *him*—he'd been followed a great deal in his time, and like the well-read Geoffrey D. he knew only too well thank you that the most fearsome surveillance got carried out by unlikely-looking people that followed you by walking in front of you with small mirrors in their glasses' temples or elaborate systems of cellular communicators for reporting to the Command Center—or else also by helicopters, also, that flew too high to see, hovering, the tiny chop of their rotors disguised as your own drumming heart. But after he'd had success at successfully shaking the Chinese women twice—the second time so successfully he'd had to tear-ass around through alleys and vault wooden fences to pick them up again a couple blocks north on Bishop Allen Dr., scuttling along, jabbering—he'd settled down in his conviction about who was trailing who, here. As in just who had the controlling discretion over the general situation right here. The ejection from the House, which the ejection had at first seemed like the kiss of a death sentence, had turned out to maybe be just the thing. He'd tried the Straight On Narrow and for his pains had been threatened and dismissively sent off; he'd given it his best, and for the most part impressively; and he had been sent Away, Alone, and at least now could openly hide. R. Lenz lived by his wits out here, deeply disguised, on the amonymous streets of N. Cambridge and Somerville, never sleeping, ever moving, hiding in bright-lit and public plain sight, the last place They would think to find him.

Lenz wore fluorescent-yellow snowpants, the slightly shiny coat to a long-tailed tux, a sombrero with little wooden balls hanging off the brim, oversize tortoise-shell glasses that darkened automatically in response to bright light, and a glossy black mustache promoted from the upper lip of a mannequin at Lechmere's in Cambridgeside—the ensemble the result of bold snatch-and-sprints all up and down the nighttime Charles, when he'd first gone Overground northeast from Enfield several-odd days back. The absolute blackness of the mannequin's mustache—very securely attached with promoted Krazy Glue and made even glossier by the dis-charge from a nose Lenz can't feel running—gives his pallor an almost ghostly aspect in the sombrero's portable shade—another both advantage and disadvantage of nasal cocaine is that eating becomes otiose and optional, and one forgets to for extended periods of time, to eat—in his gaudy pastiche of disguise he passes easily for one of metro Boston's homeless and wandering mad, the walking dead and dying, and is given a wide berth by all comers. The trick, he's found, is to not sleep or eat, to stay up and moving at all times, alert in all six directions at all times, heading for under the cover of T-station or enclosed mall whenever the invisible rotors' cardiac chop betrayed surveillance at altitude.

He'd got quickly familiarized with Little Lisbon's networks of alleys and transoms and back trash-lots, and its (dwindling) population of feral cats and dogs. The area was fertile in overhead clocks of banks and churches, dictating movements. He carried his Browning X444 Serrated in its shoulder-holster strapped inside his one sock just above the spats of the formal footwear he'd taken off the same A Formal Affair, Ltd. sidewalk display as the tux's coat. His lighter was in a fluorescent zip-uppable slash pocket; quality trashbags were plentiful in dumpsters and Land Barges stopped at lights. The *James Principles of the Gifford Lectures*, its razored-out receptacled heart now quite a bit closer to empty than Lenz would be comfortable thinking about directly, he had in his hand tucked up under one formal arm. And the Chinese women scuttled centipedishly abreast, their mammoth shopping bags held in a right hand and left, respective, so the bags were side by side between them. Lenz was closing the gap behind them, but gradually and with no little nonchalant stealth, considering it was hard to walk stealthily when one couldn't feel one's feet, and when one's eyeglasses darkened automatically whenever one went under a streetlight and then took their time lightening up again, after, so that no less than two of Lenz's vital sensory street-senses were disorientated; but he still managed both stealth and nonchalance both. He had no clue how he really looked. Like many of the itinerant mad of metro Boston, he tended to confuse a wide berth with invisibility. The shopping bags looked heavy and impressive, their weight making the Chinese women lean in slightly toward each other. Call it 2214:10h. The Chinese women and then Lenz all passed a gray-faced woman squatting back between two dumpsters, her multiple skirts hiked up. Vehicles were packed bumper-flush all along the curb, with myriad double parking also. The Chinese women passed a man lined up at the curb with a toy bow and arrows, and when the glasses undarkened Lenz could see him as well as he passed also—the guy wore a rat-colored suit and was shooting a suction-cup arrow at the side of a For Lease building and then going up and drawing a miniature chalk circle on the brick around the arrow, and then another circle around that circle, and etc., as in a what's the word. The women paid him no Orientoid mind. The suit's string tie was also brown in tone, unlike a rat's tail. His wall's chalk was more pinkish. One of the women said something high-pitched, like an exclamation to the other. Your monkey-languages' exclamatories have an explosive ricocheting sound to them. As in a component of *boing* to every word. A window up across the street was producing *The Star-Spanned Banner* all this time. The man had a string tie and fingerless little gloves, and he stepped back from the wall to examine his pink circles and almost collided with Lenz, and they both looked at each other and shook their heads like Look at this poor son of an urban bitch I'm on the same street with.

It was universally well known that your basic Orientoid types carried their earthly sum-total of personal wealth with them at all times. As in on their person while they scuttled around. The Orientoid religion prohibited banks, and Lenz had seen mammoth double-width twine-handled shopping bags in too many tiny Chinese women's hands not to have deducted that the Chinese female species of Oriental used shopping bags to carry their personal wealth. He felt the energy required for the snatch-and-sprint increasing now with each stride, drawing nonchalantly closer, able now to distinguish different patterns in the clear like plastic flags they wrapped their little hair in. The Chinese women. His heartrate speedened to a steady warming gallop. He began to feel his feet. Adrenaline about what would shortly occur dried his nose and helped his mouth stop moving around on his face. The Frightful Hog was not and never numb, and now it stirred in the snowpants slightly with excitement of wits and the thrill of the hunt. Far from cutting-edge surveillance: the shoe was on the other foot: the unwitting Oriental women had no idea who they were dealing with, behind them, no idea he was back there surveilling them and closing the nonchalant gap, stumbling only slightly after each streetlight's light. He was in total control of this situation. And they did not even know there was a situation. Bull's-eye. Lenz straightened the mustache with one finger and gave a tiny little Yellow-Brick-Road stutter-skip of pure controlling glee, his adrenaline invisible for all to see.

THERE WERE TWO ways of going, and *Les Assassins des Fauteuils Rollents* were prepared to pursue both these. Less better was the indirect route: surveillance and infiltrating the surviving associates of the Entertainment's *auteur*, its actress and rumored performer, relatives—if necessary, taking them and subjecting them to technical interview, leading with hope to the original *auteur*'s cartridge of the Entertainment. This had risks and exposures and was held *abeyant* until the directer route—to locate and secure a Master copy of the Entertainment on their own—had been exhausted. It was this way that thus they were now still here, in the Antitois' shop of Cambridge, to—*comme on dit*—be turning all the stones.

Sure enough the Chinkette women had been strengthless and lightweight, flew aside like dolls, and their bags were indeed treasure-heavy, hard to heft; but as Lenz cut left down the north-south alley he could hold the bags by their twine handles out slightly before him, so their weight's momentum kind of pulled him along. The cruciform alleys through the blocks between Central and Inman in Little Lisbon were a kind of second city. Lenz ran. His breath came easy and he could feel himself from scalp to sole. Green and green-with-red dumpsters lined both walls and made the going narrow. He vaulted two sitting figures in khaki sharing a can of Sterno on the alley floor. He glided through the foul air above them, untouched by it. The sounds behind him were his footfalls' echo off dumpsters and fire-escapes' iron. His left hand ached nicely from holding both a bag's handle and his large-print volume. A dumpster up ahead had been hitched to an E.W.D. truck and just left to sit: probably quitting time. The Empire guys had an incredible union. In the recess of the hitch's bar a small blue light flickered and died. This was a dozen dumpsters up ahead. Lenz slowed to a brisk walk. His topcoat had slipped slightly off one of his shoulders but he had no free hand to fix it and wasn't going to take time to put a bag down. His left hand felt cramped. It was somewhere vague between 2224 and 2226h. The alley was dark as a pocket. A tiny crash off somewhere south down the network of alleys was actually Poor Tony Krause rolling the steel wastebarrel that tripped up Ruth van Cleve. The tiny blue flame came on, hung still, flickered, moved, hung there, went back out. Its glow was dark blue against the back of the huge E.W.D. truck. Empire trucks were unstrippable, hitches were valuable but locked down with a Kryptonite device thing you needed welding stuff to cut through. From the recess of the hitch there were small sounds. When the lighter lit again Lenz was almost on them, two boys on the hitch and squatting down by the hitch

facing them, four of them, a fire-escape's pull-ladder distended like a
tongue and hanging just above them. None of the boys was over like
twelve. They used a M. Fizzy bottle instead of a pipe, and the smell of
burnt plastic hung mixed with the sicksweet smell of overcarbonated
rock. The boys were all small and slight and either black or spic, greedily
hunching over the flame; they looked ratty. Lenz kept them in peripheral
view as he strode briskly by, carrying his bags, spine straight and extruding
dignified purpose. The lighter went out. The boys on the hitch eyed
Lenz's bags. The squatting boys turned their heads to look. Lenz kept
them in peripheral view. None of them wore watches. One of them wore
a knit cap and watched steadily. He locked eyes with Lenz's left eye,
made a gun of his thin hand, pretended to draw a slow bead. Like performing for the others. Lenz walked by with urban dignity, like he both
saw them and didn't. The smell was intense but real local, of the rock and
bottle. He had to veer out to miss the Empire truck's side mirror on its
steel strut. He heard them say things as the truck's grille fell behind, and
unkind laughter, and then something called out in a minority agnate he
didn't know. He heard the lighter's flint. He thought to himself Assholes.
He was looking for someplace empty and a bit more lit, to go through the
bags. And cleaner than this one north-south alley here, which smelled of
ripe waste and rotting skin. He would separate the bags' valuables from
the nonvaluables and transfer the valuables to a single bag. He would
fence the nonnegotiable valuables in Little Lisbon and refill the recepta-
cle in his medical dictionary, and buy some attractive shoes. The alley
was devroid of cats and rodents both: he did not stop to reflect why. A
rock or bit of brick courtesy of the junior crack-jockeys back there landed
behind him and skittered past and rang out against something, and someone cried out aloud, a sexless figure lying back against a maybe duffel bag
or pack against a dumpster, its hand moving furiously in its groin and its
feet pointed out into the alley and turned out like a dead body's, its shoes
two different shoes, its hair a clotted mass around its face, looking up over
at Lenz going past in the faint start of light from a broader alley's intersection ahead, chanting softly what Lenz could hear as he stepped gingerly over the rot-smelling legs as 'Pretty, pretty, pretty.' Lenz whispered
to himself 'Jesus what a lot of fucked-up ass-eating fucking *losers*.'

from

Weird Like Us

by Ann Powers

WHEN I EMBARKED upon the acid trip whose description starts this book, I had no intention of ever letting my turn-on turn into a drop-out. I was sixteen years old, for God's sake, with everything from sex to college to my first Clash concert ahead of me. The life of a strung-out dope fiend, which I knew about from all those alluringly scary books in the Young Adult section, would not be mine. I believed this not only because I was doing good drugs, but because those drugs made up just one carefully contained corner of my blossoming alternative lifestyle.

Bohemians younger than the baby boom saw the hippie dream of drugs as a "ray of light," as the tripping guru Allen Ginsberg once called them, collapse into darkness. In the 1970s, society itself seemed to overdose, the stoned dreams of a generation dissolving into violence and cynicism. By 1980, when I was sixteen, virtually no one was talking the hippie line about drugs saving the world. Instead, people consumed marijuana and hallucinogens as quietly as possible, afraid of getting busted and uninterested in idealizing their highs. The typical drug-using kid in my high school belonged to the stoner clan: working-class or lower-middle-class arena rockers who lived to party, shoplifted Budweisers from the 7-Eleven to wash down the smoke from their Mexican weed, and tried to pick up underage girls at the roller rink by offering them a toke.

Some stoners may have smoked conscientiously, getting into their Rush albums and having profound thoughts in their bedrooms. But most just wanted to get wasted. Their drug use was an extension of their drinking, dulling the brain instead of expanding it.

I never hung out with the stoners at the back door of the wrestling room after school. Their mindless daily toking seemed like a waste of brain cells. If I was going to fry my synapses, I wanted to feel more than numb. I was influenced by the remnants of the psychedelic countercul-ture as it translated into the free-jazz art-punk of eccentric visionaries like Captain Beefheart, the desert-dwelling abstract artist and musical ranter I learned about from the older kids I'd met following my favorite local bands. Those groups, who dressed in thrift-store rags and went by funny names like Fred and Audio Leter, created dissonant squalls of noise behind free-associating vocals. They took acid, as the hippies had, but in their crayon-colored visions, humor and rawness replaced cosmic mus-ings. They were inventing do-it-yourself psychedelia, created with finger-paint and stuff pulled from trash bins, emphasizing the acid trip's silly, disjointed vision—its playfulness—instead of its spirituality.

In those first drug days, from high school to early college, getting high was part of touching the imagination's frisky underbelly, turning everyday life into an art project without worrying about how we might one day make careers of our experiments. Most of the crowd I ran with played music, and we would all gather in the parking garage beneath the Uni-versity of Washington's main campus thoroughfare—Red Square—hold-ing impromptu jam sessions that continued as long as the spirit (and the chemicals) moved us. To denizens of the 1960s New York art scene, these events probably would have looked like "happenings," those spontaneous art fests organized by people like Allan Kaprow and Al Hansen in store-fronts and private lofts. When I look back on these minicircuses now, their style reminds me more of what would develop into rave culture: the Ecstasy-fueled moving party scene that would slip into abandoned urban spaces and then vanish, physically realizing postmodern theorist Hakim Bey's idea of the "temporary autonomous zone." Psychedelic art-punk was the bridge between the romantic vision of 1960s performance art as an invasion of everyday life, and the 1990s rave scene's reimagining it as a stealth attack.

One trait of the conscientious drug user is that she chooses her poison to suit the personality she either already possesses or is trying to cultivate. We baby art freaks wanted to be fanciful and fun. We floated down University Avenue on clouds of our own whimsicality. Even when our bodies were chemical-free, we remained oblivious to the other punks on the street: the heroin users, slinking around on a jones for cool, and the speed munchers, hyped up on intensity and the drive for whatever came next.

As I drifted along in my own dimension, a future friend of mine was prowling the night vistas of Northern California, hyped up on speedy acid and indulging her own latent tendencies. Cassandra Cole got turned on by her older brother when she was in high school and he'd just started college; they had a band together, and would spend wired nights making music or talking philosophy. "We would sit around for eight to ten hours, tripping," she remembered years later. "We always had things we were supposed to do, but we'd end up sitting in the car for eight hours, talking about social contract theory and Marxism."

Cassandra liked the way drugs unlocked her mind, just like I did, but the hidden compartments she sought to explore held more intellect than id. She also liked cocaine, which got her brain racing, although the payoff was much too limited. "I didn't criticize cocaine until I had speed, and then I was like, Let's talk about this. Coke lasts for twenty minutes and you spend the whole time thinking about how you're going to get more. Speed lasts for twelve hours, and maybe you want a little bit more, but it's not like you're going to freak out if you don't get another line." Cassandra became a speed devotee because it was more practical than coke, but also because it was cheaper, born of the street, more punk.

When I met Cassandra, it was 1985 in San Francisco, and white powder seemed to be falling from the sky. She and her punk buddies were just one gang zipping around under its influence. Far bigger was the crowd I landed in by having a close friend who got a job in a restaurant. Studies have shown that restaurant and bar employees are the largest single group of drug consumers in the nation. It's no wonder, with all that cash making their pockets itch and those weird hours to organize a life around. Other card-carrying members of the service sector—record-store employees, for example—also partake heavily, especially if their place of employ stays open until midnight and their social lives subsequently extend until dawn. Planet Records had its share of tweakers, as serious speed consumers are called. Still, their noses were barely dusted compared to those of the pros at Martin's restaurant.

The itchy-pocket factor, and the fact that many worked second jobs or went to school during the day, made cocaine the powder of choice among the restaurant crowd. It seemed ridiculous to us that coke was getting a rep as a yuppie drug via books like Jay McInerney's *Bright Lights, Big City* and movies like Woody Allen's *Annie Hall*. In the popular culture of the mid-1980s, coke signified the yuppie's endless, empty desire for more, with no concern for what that "more" might be. This portrait of greed-stoned youth reached its nadir in Bret Easton Ellis's deliberately icky *Less Than Zero*, which depicts a pack of zoned-out rich kids slumping around Los Angeles in their parents' expensive cars, draining the meaning out of every landscape they crossed and encounter they had. In the movie version, Robert Downey, Jr., who would one day land in jail for his real-life addictions, played a private-school boy turned male prostitute. This was supposed to be a portrait of my generation.

Except, I didn't know any rich kids who would sell their bodies for blow. I didn't know any rich kids at all, only working people who liked to party after they got done with a shift. Chemicals hit different people unpredictably, heightening one urge in one person and a different urge in another. Those multiple effects translate into multiple cultural meanings. In the 1980s, cocaine signified the impulsive excesses of the yuppie class; distilled into crack, it became the symbol of desperate inner-city life. Both of these extrapolations reflect reality; in the Reagan era, rich fools did suck millions of dollars up their noses while eating tiny portions of overpriced cuisine and blowing their bonuses on luxury co-ops they later couldn't sell. And crack's pressing high has led to much ghetto violence and family tragedy. But the yuppies' greed and the ghetto's violence weren't rooted only in the drugs; other factors, such as the exacerbating effect of Republican economic policies on the gap between rich and poor, mattered more. Focusing on drugs raises a tangible demon for people to chase. I'm not denying that white powder stimulates compulsive tendencies, or that many people fell heavily under its spell. But doing a line or two after work did not mean throwing all the promise of one's life out the window. Especially if that life was a bit of scramble already.

I believed enough of the negative hype about white powder to be very cautious around it. In the days of Martin's restaurant, I limited my intake to the small amounts offered at social gatherings. I can't say I never did anything foolish under its influence—there was a one-night stand I long regretted, and a couple of others that my friends might think I should regret. In each case, though, the drug simply gave me an extra push toward something I wanted to do anyway. The choice to have sex with that darkly brooding bartender in the front seat of his Toyota was my own; I probably would have done it with nothing more in my system than a few shots of tequila. Not only that, but the drug enhanced the experience, made me feel the rush of this gamble through nerve endings that prickled and buzzed. I loved the erotic groove white powder created, the way everyone suddenly seemed fascinating, how nervousness and languor, which sometimes overwhelm my desire to connect with people, just vanished as I danced around the room catching every sparkling eye. It was a blast, hooking up with all those egos. And it certainly wasn't any more meaningless than sitting around by myself watching TV. Since I made it a point to keep my outings recreational, and never kept any speed or coke around the house to tempt me, I had plenty of time for other states of mind.

When I did go out on white powder, I entered an after-hours world I'd never have otherwise discovered. This was the biggest benefit I got from these drugs. Acid had illuminated the city's abandoned corners, as we wandered through silent, luminous parks and labyrinthine parking garages. White powder brought me into another hidden environment: I kept company with the minders of the city's common halls long after the doors had been shut to everyone else. A bar or a restaurant after closing becomes a magical zone; all its shifting elements, the music, the flow of alcohol and food, the mood itself, now fall under your command. As the servers, who make all of those mechanics seem natural during open hours, serve themselves, they open up the long history of secrets such rooms are made of. Playing pool at four in the morning in some Valencia Street dive, I could see every stain and rip in the green felt; fetching myself a drink, I discovered where the joint's ice and baseball bat hid.

I also learned the secrets of the gypsies who spent their lives making these establishments feel like everyone's other home. They often had spotty histories, having escaped from unhappy families and neighborhoods literally or spiritually impoverished, promising them little: they were daughters of Central Valley fruit pickers, Los Angeles liquor-store clerks, Oakland civil servants. Others were college kids uneasy at the prospect of life in middle management. Everybody seemed to have a secret, whether it was a crime, an illegitimate child, or simply a dream with which they hadn't quite reconciled. Most were drifters in one way or another, maybe just for a year or two, maybe for a lifetime. The driftier they were, the more the drugs could prove a problem. Marie, my best friend among them, was a satellite bouncing around, with eyes that never settled, a yen for a new boy every night, and a hunger to be brilliant at something, she just didn't know what. She had a lot of trouble with white powder. Its tendency to drive people can make them reach for their desires, pushing the yuppie to scramble for more dough or the sensualist to look for a hot one-night stand. But Marie had nothing specific on the other end of her want. So the drug pushed her right out of herself.

It was Marie's bad habit that finally led me to swear off white powder. I'd met her when we both worked behind the counter one summer in a North Beach café, making messy sandwiches and feeding our friends for free. Martin's restaurant crowd had dissolved, as these families of run-aways so often do, and I followed Marie into her ragtag clan, which held court at a very scruffy but cool bar in the Mission District. For nights that turned into weeks and months, she and I tripped through that bar and many others like two electric wires, dangerous to touch, touching every-thing we could. We were high on being trouble girls, staying in late in bad places. But we were also high on drugs, and after half a year, when I started to feel sick all the time, I decided that following my nose into the bar's back office every afternoon was stretching my body's limits. And, like most drugs, white powder had only a limited amount to teach. I was getting bored with it.

I tried to tell Marie I needed to take a break. She said, Okay, no prob-lem, just still hang around with me. But it wasn't so much fun anymore; we'd go somewhere, she would fly around the place, I'd be bored, grounded. Eventually Marie stopped bothering to land. People were get-ting mad at her for being there one minute and gone the next. On those rare occasions when she did come down, she plummeted into the nettles of self-hatred. She had abandoned the necessary double consciousness of the conscientious drug user, which keeps you aware that drugs are good and bad at the same time, and that every high is a tightrope over the abyss. "Why can't we stay high all the time?" she asked me once, sitting over lemongrass soup in a Thai restaurant. I didn't know what to say. I felt comfortable in both realities, straight and high, while she had made peace with only one. Like most of the drug abusers I've known, Marie had no problem with being wasted. Her crises began when she got sober. The problems had been there before she'd ever sniffed a line, and she was willing to sacrifice the whole rational world to keep them at bay.

Marie went to the Far East, got even more strung out, and ended up in rehab. She got lucky in there; after many terrified encounters with her own soul, she discovered a self she wanted to hang on to. Now she runs her own boutique in a city far from San Francisco and sticks to red wine. But I lost her for years, and it broke my heart. I know some people will wonder why I don't hate those drugs for what they did to her. Of course I wanted to save Marie when she plunged into the vast emptiness; I felt helpless, furious, betrayed. But it was her emptiness she'd left me for; the drugs just took her there. She would have gone anyway, maybe through sex, or depression, or even suicide. If she'd flung her body from the Golden Gate Bridge, I couldn't have blamed gravity for pulling her down.

So I didn't get mad at drugs. In fact, I came to believe that they deserved a lot more respect than we were giving them. What began to disgust me was the way reckless users (myself included, sometimes) would ingest as if doing so were a normal activity, like drinking a soda. Getting high is never normal. It is profoundly weird—one of the few chances humans have to fully inhabit an alternate sensual reality. Finding the balance between the drug's will and your own is the crucial step in negotiating that reality instead of letting it just crash over you. I learned these lessons by watching people like Marie surrender to a force they'd once controlled. I came to see that drug experiences aren't just about the high. Myriad decisions surround takeoff: how much to ingest, when and how often to do it, what people and places to allow into the trip. I'd grown less meticulous about these things, and too many of my partners in powder didn't pause to consider them at all.

A Eulogy of Sorts

from

Doghouse Roses

by Steve Earle

HAROLD MILLS DIED last night, alone in his $75-a-week room at the Drake Motel, and I'm probably the only motherfucker on Murfreesboro Road that misses him. Hell, I'm the only one that knows he's gone. I just happened to pull up in front of his room just as the EMTs carried him out with a sheet over his face. I had intended to use his place to shoot a couple of pills and cook up an eightball of coke I'd just bought, but I guess I was a little late. On another night he probably would've laid there in the bathroom floor for days until the smell alerted the manager. As it was, the couple next door was interrupted in mid-stroke by a loud bang, which as it turns out, was Harold's big ol' head smashing into the tub as he went down. The crushing blow to the back of his skull alone could've easily killed him, but I'd be willing to bet Harold was dead before he hit the floor.

Junkies die down here everyday. Most of the time nobody notices but other junkies, and they perceive only a brief interruption in the food chain. Nobody down here is really capable of mourning in the normal sense. Oh, we suffer the inconvenience of losing a connection, or a safe place to get high or scam a new set of works or maybe crash for a few hours, but that's about it. As unnerving as life in this neighborhood may appear to the uninitiated, we, the wraiths who inhabit its darkest corners, find each day even more numbingly boring than the one before. But that's cool. We hate surprises. Any break in the tedium makes us uncomfortable. You see, all junkies travel in ever-narrowing concentric circles until the day they find themselves running for their lives with one foot nailed to the floor, as the Beast bears down on them. Grieving over another dope fiend finally, inevitably running out of luck is simply a luxury nobody on the pike can afford, because all of us know that but for the grace of God . . . well hell, there ain't no grace down here. It's just a matter of time.

So when Harold's time finally ran out, I wasn't there. Not that I could've saved him anyway. Harold didn't die of an overdose per se. He most likely had a heart attack that was coming anyway, no matter what the coroner's report says. Ol' Harold merely expedited matters with one long, final pull on his meticulously maintained glass pipe. The pathologist on duty probably never looked any further than the painfully thin, needle-scarred arms before rendering Harold's entire life down into homogeneous statistic.

When I first met Harold Mills he was a real player, the biggest Dilaudid dealer in South Nashville. Dilaudid is the trade name for hydromorphone hydrochloride, a pharmaceutical narcotic typically prescribed only for terminal cancer patients. Nashville, located smack-dab in the middle of the most landlocked state in the Union, has never enjoyed a particularly dependable heroin supply. Then in the seventies two brothers by the name of Mitchell from North Nashville's middle-class black community began to bring in Dilaudid, misappropriated from drug wholesalers in Detroit and Chicago. A good supply of relatively cheap, strong heroin kept the price of the pharmaceutical drug low in major northern cities, but in Nashville the tiny yellow pills brought between forty and sixty dollars each on the street. In a market where an addict could spend nearly that amount on a bag of highly diluted, low-grade Mexican heroin, "D's" were an instant hit. Harold, being related by marriage to the Mitchell brothers, was in on the ground floor.

The first time I saw Harold he was slow draggin' Lewis Street in a sky blue 1978 Cadillac sedan DeVille. He was dressed sharp in an old-school, super-fly, dope-dealer-with-a-heart-of-gold-and-a-tooth-to-match kind of way. He draped his slight six feet two frame across the entire front seat as he leaned across to eye me suspiciously through the passenger-side window. I was being introduced by a coke dealer named Clarence Brown. Make no mistake, South Nashville was *about* cocaine. By this point in my career as a lifelong dope fiend, I had taken to smoking several hundred dollars worth of rock cocaine everyday. Coke was a drug I had never particularly cared for. By this time, however, my tolerance for opiates had become prohibitively high, so I took up the practice of "speedballing," that is, adding a little coke to my frequent injections of Dilaudid for a little extra kick. Exposing myself to cocaine opened the door for freebasing—mixing the deadly white powder with baking soda and cooking it down into smokable "rock" (or "crack" on the East Coast). One hit, crossing my eyes to watch the opaque white smoke billow and expand in the glass bowl and then disappear like a flirtatious genie as I removed my finger from the carburetor and inhaled deeply, and it was a wrap.

No drug had ever grabbed a hold of me as quickly or held me as tightly in its grip. I became conditioned, like some space race laboratory monkey, to keep pushing that button, too far gone to give a fuck whether I received a banana-flavored pellet or a no-volt shock. I'd drive to the projects in East Nashville every morning and buy a pill or two, and as soon as I was straight, head down south to Clarence's to smoke. By five or six in the evening, I was getting sick again, so I'd slide back across the river to cop a few more pills, then back across the bridge and—what did the directions say? Repeat if necessary? Well, it was always necessary as a motherfucker. Clarence had only recently given up on trying to "help" me kick Dilaudid. He saw my other habit as a waste of money I could be spending on coke, his personal drug of choice. When he finally got it through his head that that wasn't ever going to happen, he introduced me to Harold Mills, the only hustler down South who regularly traded in Dilaudid. To Clarence this was simply a means to an end: keeping one of his best customers on his side of the river where he could keep his eye on me. Harold listened while Clarence vouched for me, looked me over one more time and then there was a sudden flash as he bared that big, gold front tooth in an ear-to-ear grin. "I heard about you. I heard you spend money."

He sold me a pill (at $10 less than I was paying for singles out East) and scribbled his beeper number on the dismembered top of a hard pack of Kools, promising to cut me a better price when I bought more than one.

I began seeing Harold twice a day, everyday, once in the morning and once just before dark. I knew better than to try and procure a whole day's supply of dope in one run. That kind of thinking only led to a bigger, even more expensive habit, and God knows I was capable of shooting as many pills at one sitting as I could buy. At first I'd just beep him and he'd meet me somewhere up on the pike. After he got to know me better, he gave me his home number, and I would call to make sure he was home before driving to his apartment in the projects where he lived with his wife Keena and their three boys, ages three, four, and seven. I'd do my wake-up shot right there in Harold's bathroom, and then we'd sit around for a while, watching Oprah and shit on the tube and play with the kids. Harold taught his oldest boy, Courtney, to call me Uncle Honky. He thought that shit was hilarious. In the course of those long dreamlike mornings I found out what I should have already known: Harold sold Dilaudid because Harold shot Dilaudid—lots of it. I was a good customer. Most addicts couldn't afford the kind of volume I bought everyday. Harold was beginning to get "hot" on the street, which meant that every time he rolled out on the pike he ran the risk of being stopped on sight by one of the neighborhood patrol cars or even the vice squad. My business meant Harold could support his own habit without taking so many chances.

We quickly fell into a daily routine of getting high together and solving all the world's problems by the time Keena got home from work. We'd engage in long animated discussions on politics (Harold styled himself a Democrat but he reckoned I was probably a communist), music (we both loved the old Memphis stuff but I knew more about hip-hop than he did, which he didn't care for anymore than "that hillbilly shit ya'll listen to"), even the existence of God (I didn't believe in God, Harold did; he just figured that God didn't mess with junkies one way or the other). Never mind that neither of us had voted, bought records, nor been to church in years. Oh yeah, we knew we were addicts. We even referred to ourselves and each other as "junkies." "You a junkie motherfucker." "Well you a junkie, too." Then we'd laugh our asses off. But god forbid a "citizen" ever calls us that. "Junkie" is a funny word like that. It's kind of like "nigger," I guess.

Harold, like me, was a fairly nontypical dope fiend. He still had a family, a place to live, a car, food to eat. Our common ground, it turned out, was that most of the catastrophes that punctuate "those other" junkies' lives hadn't happened to us . . . yet. You see, we were both smart enough to know our luck couldn't hold out forever, so I guess we had just decided to stick together for a while and wait for the other shoe to drop.

And drop it did. I finally lost touch with Harold a few years later when I migrated to Los Angeles in my never-ending quest for stronger and cheaper dope. In the shape I was in, it didn't take me very long to wear out my welcome in L.A., and eighteen months later, I was back on the pike asking around about Harold Mills. Some folks said he was locked up. "Naw, he out East living with his auntie." There was even a story that Harold had AIDS.

When I finally tracked him down, I immediately saw where the AIDS rumors came from. Harold was always thin, but now he was nothing but sallow, translucent skin, stretched taut over brittle bone. He was wearing a faded, threadbare sweat suit and run-over Kmart sneakers, shit he would never have been caught dead in a year earlier. His usually close-cropped hair was grown out and matted from months of scuffling up and down the pike, hustling for hits. When he recognized me, he smiled, revealing that even the trademark gold tooth was missing along with several of his own. But it wasn't AIDS that had taken Harold down through there. It was rock cocaine.

In all the time I'd known him, I'd never seen Harold Mills touch crack. I use to have to listen to him and Clarence, the coke man, one in one ear and one in the other, like those little guys that sit on a mother-fucker's shoulders in the cartoons, one admonishing him to do the right thing and one leading him astray. Only, in my cartoon they were both devils. Harold used to say, "That shit was sent by Satan his self to finish the dope fiends off." Now the Beast had him by the balls, and he knew it. On top of that, his heart had been weakened by endocarditis, an infection of the bloodstream common to IV drug users. Harold's deterioration in such a short amount of time was especially unsettling to me. After all, he was the same kind of junkie I was. Seeing him like this was too much like looking in a mirror and being confronted by my own death staring back at me through hollow sockets. But after an awkward instant we exchanged dope fiend pleasantries, drove across the river, bought six pills at an exorbitant price, and retired to the Drake Motel to get high. I rented Harold a room there, where he lived for the rest of his life . . . about seven months.

Harold Mills will be buried tomorrow in Greenwood Cemetery in

South Nashville. The funeral will cost his grandmother, who raised him, her entire life savings. She rarely saw Harold the last few years of his life. He'd appear on her doorstep now and then, and she'd give him $20 and watch helplessly as he faded back into the night. Then she'd cry herself to sleep. She never once turned him away, even though she knew what he did with the money. She was just thankful that he loved her enough not to come around too often.

Harold will go down to Greenwood decked out in a new blue suit and surrounded by his wife, his kids, and several relatives, mostly older, who haven't seen him since he was a child. Good, solid, working folks who never knew the hustler, the junkie, the derelict. Never saw him sitting in the backseat of a police car in handcuffs or led into a courtroom dressed in a blaze-orange jumpsuit. Never had to watch in horror, as he mined scar tissue-armored veins for the nearly always empty promise of blood commingling with morphine, just before he pushed it back into his ravaged body and waited for the rush that never quite lived up to that sacred memory of his very first hit.

Most of these folks never knew that Harold Mills. They'll come to Greenwood to bury a husband, a daddy, a grandson, and a little boy who used to ride his tricycle through their flower beds.

I won't be there to say goodbye. None of us, the creatures that knew Harold out here on the pike, will be there, because funerals, they say, are for the living . . . and we're already dead. We're just waiting our turn.

See you when I get there, brother.

from

Cocaine Nights

by J G Ballard

HER CONFIDENCE THAT unknown sins existed, still waiting to be discovered, altogether surprised me. I watched the limousine cross the plaza on its return to Estrella de Mar. Workmen were removing the *Verkauf* and À *Vendre* signs from the untenanted retail units beside the supermarket, but the sports club remained silent. I walked around the empty building, and listened to my feet ring on the polished floor. The Germans lounged by the pool, showing off their physiques to each other. A desultory traffic moved around the plaza, and by noon the Residencia Costasol was already preparing for its afternoon retreat from the sun.

Despite myself, I felt responsible for the club's failure to attract new members, and realized how depressed Frank must have been when he first arrived at the Club Nautico. I stood behind the concierge's counter, watching the waiters pace around the open-air bar and the groundsmen sweep the deserted tennis courts.

I was pointlessly keyboarding the computer, adding up imaginary profits, when I heard the beat of a Porsche's engine thrumming through the sunlight. I reached the glass doors as Bobby Crawford crossed the car park. He sprinted up the steps, bounding on his powerful legs like an acrobat on a trampoline, an arm raised to greet me. He wore his black baseball cap and leather jacket, and carried a large sports bag in one hand. Seeing him, I felt my heart begin to race.

'Charles? Chin up. This isn't the House of Usher.' He took the door from me and stepped into the foyer, eager smile exposing the iceberg whiteness of his polished teeth. 'What's been happening? You look as if you're glad to see me.'

'I am. Nothing's happened—that's the problem. I may be the wrong manager for you.'

'You're tired, Charles. Not a time to get depressed.' Crawford glanced at the pool and tennis courts. 'A lot of hunk in place but no customers. Any new members?'

'Not one. Maybe tennis isn't what the people here need.'

'Everyone needs tennis. The Residencia Costasol may not know it now, but it soon will.'

He turned to face me, beaming warmly and clearly happy to find me waiting for him, and already seeing my grumpy mood as one of the amusing foibles of a family retainer. He had been away for four days, and I was struck by how much more sharply tuned his movements were, as if he had installed a more powerful engine in the Porsche and drawn off part of its huge thrust for his own nervous system. Grimaces and little tics crossed his face as a hundred and one ideas jostled in his mind.

'Things are going to happen here, Charles.' He gripped my shoulder like an older brother, nodding his approval at the cash register. 'Holding the fort isn't easy. Let me tell you, Betty Shand is proud of what you've done.'

'I've done damn-all. Nothing is going to happen here. The Residencia Costasol isn't your sort of place. This isn't Estrella de Mar, it's the valley of the brain-dead. I only wish I could help.'

'You can. By the way, I think I've found a house for you—small swimming pool, tennis court, I'll bring over a tennis machine so you can practise your returns. First I have a few calls to make. We'll take your car—I'd like you to drive. That slow and steady pace of yours soothes my headaches.'

'Of course.' I pointed to the clock in the foyer. 'Do you want to wait? It's two-forty-five. Everything here is in deep sleep.'

'Perfect—it's the most interesting time of day. People are either dreaming or having sex. Perhaps both at the same time . . .'

* * *

AS I STARTED the engine he settled himself into the passenger seat of the Citroën, one arm trailing out of the window and the hold-all between his legs. He nodded approvingly as I fastened my seatbelt.

'Sensible, Charles. I do admire an orderly mind. It's hard to believe, but accidents happen even in the Residencia Costasol.'

'The whole place is an accident. This is where the late twentieth century ran into the buffers. Where do you want to go—the Club Nautico?'

'No, we'll stay here. Drive around, any route you like. I want to see how things are.'

We crossed the plaza and its deserted shopping mall, and then cruised past the marina and its ghost fleet of virtually mothballed yachts. I turned at random into one of the secondary residential avenues in the eastern quadrant of the complex. The detached villas stood in their silent gardens, surrounded by dwarf palms, oleanders and beds of cannas like frozen fire. Sprinklers swayed across the lawns, conjuring rainbows from the overlit air, local deities performing their dances to the sun. Now and then the sea wind threw a faint spray across the swimming pools, and their mirror surfaces clouded like troubled dreams.

'Slow down a little . . . ' Crawford leaned forward, peering up at a large deco house on a corner site. A shared access road ran towards a group of three-storey apartment houses. Awnings flared over the balconies, tethered wings that would never touch the sky. 'Stop here . . . this looks like it.'

'What's the number? For some reason people here refuse to identify themselves.'

'I forget exactly. But this feels right.' He pointed fifty yards beyond the access road, where the fronds of a huge cycad formed a pedestrian shelter. 'Park there and wait for me.'

He unzipped the hold-all and removed what seemed to be a set of golf putters wrapped in an oilcloth. He stepped from the car, face hidden behind his peaked cap and dark glasses, patted the roof and set off in a light stride towards the drive. As I freewheeled down the slope to the cycad, my eyes on the rear-view mirror, I saw him vault the side gate that led to the servants' entrance.

I waited in the car, listening to the faint hiss of sprinklers from the walls and hedges around me. Perhaps the owners of the villa were away on holiday, and a lover was waiting for him in another maid's room. I imagined them playing clock-golf on the carpet, a formal courtship like the mating dance of a bower-bird . . .

'RIGHT, LET'S GO.' Crawford seemed to step from the screen of vegetation around the cycad. Under one arm he carried a video-cassette recorder, cables tied around it to form a black parcel. He placed it on the rear seat and loosened his cap, keeping a careful eye on the access road. 'I'm checking it for them—a couple called Hanley. He's a retired personnel manager from Liverpool. By the way, it looks as if I've recruited two new members.'

'For the sports club? Great stuff. How did you persuade them?'

'Their television set isn't working. Something's wrong with the satellite dish. Besides, they feel that they ought to get out more. Now, let's drive over to the west side of the complex. I need to make a few house calls . . . '

He adjusted the climate-control unit on the instrument panel, sending a stream of cooler air into our faces, and lay back against the head-rest, so relaxed that I could hardly believe that we had embarked on a criminal spree. He stowed the golf putters in the hold-all, deliberately allowing me to see that they were, in fact, a pair of steel jemmies. I had guessed from the moment we left the sports club that he intended to carry out a series of provocative acts, petty burglaries and nuisance raids designed to shake the Residencia Costasol out of its dozing complacency. I assumed that the crimes which the Spanish police had reported to David Hennessy were Crawford's doing, the overture to his campaign of harassment and aggravation.

Twenty minutes later we stopped by the next villa, an imposing mansion in the Moorish style with a speedboat parked in its drive. Almost certainly, the residents would be asleep in the bedrooms upstairs, and the garden and terrace were silent. A slow drip of water from a forgotten hose counted the seconds as Crawford scanned the surveillance cameras, his eyes following the cables that ran from the satellite dish on the roof to the switchbox beside the patio doors.

'Leave the engine running, Charles. We may as well do this in style . . . '

He slipped away, disappearing among the trees that flanked the drive. My hands fretted at the wheel as I waited for him to return, ready to make a quick getaway. I smiled at an elderly couple who passed me in their car, a large spaniel sitting between them, but they seemed unconcerned by the Citroën's presence. Five minutes later Crawford slipped into the passenger seat, casually brushing a few splinters of glass from his jacket.

'More television trouble?' I asked as we set off.

'It looks like it.' Crawford sat straight-faced beside me, now and then taking the wheel from my nervous hands. 'These satellite dishes are very sensitive. They need to be constantly recalibrated.'

'The owners will be grateful. Possible members?'

'Do you know, I think they are. I wouldn't be surprised if they dropped in tomorrow.' Crawford unzipped his jacket and removed an engraved silver cigarette case, which he laid beside the cassette-recorder on the rear seat. 'The husband was a Queen's Club committee member, a keen tennis player. His wife used to be something of an amateur painter.'

'Perhaps she'll take it up again?'

'I think she might . . . '

We continued to make our calls, threading our way through the quiet avenues of the Residencia Costasol like a shuttle weaving a rogue pattern across a sedate tapestry. Crawford pretended to visit the properties at random, but I took for granted that he had selected his victims after carrying out a careful survey, picking those who would send out the largest ripples of alarm. I imagined them dozing through the siesta hours as Crawford moved around the rooms below, sabotaging the satellite systems, stealing a jade horse from a coffee table, a Staffordshire figure from a mantelpiece, rifling the desk drawers as if in search of cash or jewellery, creating the illusion that a gang of skilled house-breakers had taken up residence in the Costasol complex.

While I waited in the car, expecting Inspector Cabrera and the Fuengirola flying squad to seize me on the spot, I wondered why I had allowed Crawford to inveigle me into this criminal romp. As the Citroën's engine trembled against the accelerator pedal I was tempted to drive back to the sports club and tip off Cabrera. But Crawford's arrest would put an end to any hopes of discovering the arsonist who had murdered the Hollingers. Looking up at the hundreds of impassive villas, with their security cameras and mentally embalmed owners, I was sure that Crawford's attempts to transform the complex into another Estrella de Mar would fail. The people of the Residencia had not only travelled to the far side of boredom but had decided that they liked the view. Crawford's failure might well provoke him into a desperate act that would expose his complicity in the Hollinger killings. One fire too many would burn more than his fingers.

Yet his commitment to this bizarre social experiment had a charm all its own. Frank too, I guessed, had been seduced by his gaudy vision, and like Frank I said nothing as the rear seat of the Citroën accumulated its booty. By the sixth villa, one of the older mansions on the north-south radial boulevard, I found a blanket in the trunk and held it ready for Crawford when he emerged from the shrubbery with a waisted Ming vase under one arm, a blackwood stand under the other.

He patted me reassuringly as I draped the blanket over his treasure-trove, pleasantly surprised by the way in which I had held up under pressure.

'They're tokens, Charles—I'll see they find their way back to the owners. Strictly speaking, we don't need to take anything, just convey the sense that a thief has urinated on their Persian carpets and wiped his fingers on the tapestry.'

'And tomorrow the entire Residencia Costasol will feel like a game of tennis? Or decide to take up flower-arranging and needlepoint?'

'Of course not. The inertial forces here are colossal. But one elephant fly can start a stampede if it bites a sensitive spot. You sound sceptical.'

'A little.'

'You don't think it will work?' Crawford pressed my hand to the steering wheel, steeling my resolve. 'I need you, Charles—it's difficult to do this on my own. Betty Shand and Hennessy are only interested in their cash flow. But you can see beyond that to the larger horizon. What happened in Estrella de Mar will happen here, and then move on down the coast. Think of all those pueblos coming to life again. We're freeing people, Charles, returning them to their true selves.'

DID HE BELIEVE his own rhetoric? Half an hour later, as he burgled a small apartment block near the central plaza, I unzipped the hold-all and glanced through its contents. There were jemmies and wirecutters, a selection of lockpicks and perforated entry cards, jump leads and electronic immobilizers. A smaller valise contained several aerosol paint cans, two camcorders and a clutch of fresh video-cassettes. A segmented plastic snake of cocaine sachets wrapped itself around a wallet filled with drug capsules and pills in foil dispensers, packs of syrettes and ribbed condoms.

The aerosols Crawford put to immediate use. Barely bothering to step from the car, he held a can in each hand and sprayed a series of lurid patterns on the garage doors that we passed. After only two hours a lengthy trail of theft and vandalism lay behind us—damaged satellite dishes, graffiti-daubed cars, dog turds left floating in swimming pools, surveillance cameras blinded by jets of paint.

Within earshot of the owners he broke into a silver Aston Martin and freewheeled the car down the gravelled drive. I followed as he drove to a disused builder's yard on the northern perimeter road, and watched him scrape the sides of the car with a jemmy, scratching the paintwork with the care of a chef scoring a side of pork. When he stood back and lit a cigarette I waited for the fire to come. He smiled at the mutilated vehicle, the lighter still flaming in his hand, and I expected him to stuff a rag into the fuel tank.

But Crawford treated the car to a rueful salute, and calmly smoked his cigarette when we drove off, savouring the Turkish fumes.

'I hate doing that, Charles—but sacrifices have to be made.'

'At least it's not your Aston Martin.'

'I was thinking of *our* sacrifices—it's painful medicine for both of us, but we have to swallow it . . . '

We set off along the perimeter road, where the cheaper villas and apartment houses looked out over the Malaga highway. Home-made 'For Sale' signs hung from balconies, and I assumed that the Dutch-German developers had sold the properties at a discount.

'Take that house on the right—the one with the empty pool.' Crawford pointed to a small villa with a faded awning over its patio. A drying frame exposed a selection of gaudy tops and flimsy underwear to the sun. 'I'll be back in ten minutes. They need a little arts counselling . . . '

He reached into the hold-all and removed the valise that contained the camcorders and pharmaceuticals. Waiting for him by the front door were two women in swimsuits who shared the villa. Despite the heat they wore a full maquillage of lipstick, rouge and mascara, as if ready for a session under the film lights, and greeted Crawford with the easy smiles of host-esses at a dubious bar welcoming a regular patron.

The younger of the women was in her twenties, with a pale, English complexion, bony shoulders and eyes that for ever watched the street. I recognized the older woman beside her, the platinum blonde with the over-large breasts and florid face who had played one of the bridesmaids in the porno-film. Glass in hand, she pressed a Slavic cheekbone to Crawford's lips and beckoned him into the house.

I stepped from the car and strolled towards the house, watching them through the patio windows. Together they made their way into the lounge, where a television set played to itself, blinking as the frame-hold lost its grip on an afternoon serial. Crawford opened the valise and took out one of the camcorders and a brace of cassettes. He tore a dozen sachets of cocaine from the plastic snake, which the women tucked into the cups of their swimsuits, and began to demonstrate the camcorder to them. The older woman raised the viewfinder to her eye, snapping at her-self as her long fingernails scratched at the tiny push-buttons. She prac-tised the pan and zoom, while Crawford sat on the sofa with the young Englishwoman. No one exchanged the slightest banter, as if Crawford were a salesman demonstrating a new household appliance.

When he returned to the car the women filmed him from the door, laughing over each other's shoulders.

'Film school?' I asked. 'They look like quick learners.'

'Yes . . . they've always been film buffs.' Crawford waved to them as we pulled away, grinning to himself as if genuinely fond of the women. 'They came here from Estepona to open a beauty parlour, but decided the prospects weren't good enough.'

'So now they'll go into the film business? I imagine they'll find that profitable.'

'I think so. They have an idea for a film.'

'Documentary?'

'More of a nature film, you might call it.'

'The wildlife of the Residencia Costasol.' I savoured the notion. 'Courtship rituals and mating patterns. I think they'll be a success. Who was the platinum blonde? She looks slightly Russian.'

'Raissa Livingston—widow of a Lambeth bookie. She's a tank-trap full of vodka. A great sport. She's done a little acting before, so she'll get things off to a good start.'

Crawford spoke without irony, staring at the roof of the car as if already screening the first day's rushes. He seemed content with his afternoon's work, like a neighbourhood evangelist who had unloaded his stock of biblical tracts. The burglaries and break-ins had left him calm and relaxed, his day's duty done for the benighted people of the Residencia.

When we returned to the sports club he directed me to the service entrance behind the kitchen and boiler room. Here he had parked his Porsche, safely out of sight from any police who might call at the club.

'We'll move the gear to my car.' He threw back the blanket, exposing the booty. 'I don't want Cabrera to catch you redhanded, Charles. You've got that guilty look again.'

'There's a lot of stuff here. Can you remember who owns what?'

'I don't need to. I'll stash it in the builder's yard where we left the Aston Martin and tip off the security people in the gatehouse. They'll put everything on show there and make sure the entire Residencia gets the message.'

'But what is the message? That's something I haven't quite grasped.'

'The message . . . ?' Crawford was lifting a cassette-recorder from the seat, but turned to stare at me. 'I thought you understood everything, Charles.'

'Not exactly. These break-ins, wrecking a few TV sets and painting "Fuck" on a garage door — is that going to change people's lives? If you burgled my house I'd just call the police. I wouldn't join a chess club or take up carol-singing.'

'Absolutely. You'd call the police. So would I. But suppose the police do nothing and I break in again, this time stealing something you really value. You'd start thinking about stronger locks and a security camera.'

'So?' I opened the Porsche's boot and waited as Crawford lowered the cassette-recorder into it. 'We've returned to square one. I go back to my satellite television and my long sleep of the dead.'

'No, Charles.' Crawford spoke patiently. 'You're not asleep. By now you're wide awake, more alert than you've ever been before. The break-ins are like the devout Catholic's wristlet that chafes the skin and sharpens the moral sensibility. The next burglary fills you with anger, even a self-righteous rage. The police are useless, fobbing you off with vague

promises, and that generates a sense of injustice, a feeling that you're surrounded by a world without shame. Everything around you, the paintings
and silverware you've taken for granted, fit into this new moral framework. You're more aware of yourself. Dormant areas of your mind that
you haven't visited for years become important again. You begin to
reassess yourself, as you did, Charles, when that Renault caught fire.'

'Perhaps . . . but I didn't take up t'ai chi or start a new book.'

'Wait—you may do.' Crawford pressed on, keen to convince me. 'The
process takes time. The crime waves continues—someone shits in your
pool, ransacks your bedroom and plays around with your wife's underwear. Now rage and anger are not enough. You're forced to rethink yourself on every level, like primitive man confronting a hostile universe
behind every tree and rock. You're aware of time, chance, the resources of
your own imagination. Then someone mugs the woman next door, so
you team up with the outraged husband. Crime and vandalism are everywhere. You have to rise above these mindless thugs and the oafish world
they inhabit. Insecurity forces you to cherish whatever moral strengths
you have, just as political prisoners memorize Dostoevsky's *House of the
Dead*, the dying play Bach and rediscover their faith, parents mourning a
dead child do voluntary work at a hospice.'

'We realize time is finite and take nothing for granted any more.'

'Exactly.' Crawford patted my arm, happy to welcome me to his flock.
'We form watch committees, elect a local council, take pride in our
neighborhoods, join sports clubs and local history societies, rediscover
the everyday world we once took for granted. We know that it's more
important to be a third-rate painter than to watch a CD-ROM on the
Renaissance. Together we begin to thrive, and at last find our full potential as individuals and as a community.'

'And all this is set off by crime?' I lifted the silver cigarette case from the
rear seat of the Citroën. 'Why that particular trigger? Why not . . . religion
or some kind of political will? They've ruled the world in the past.'

'Not any longer. Politics is over, Charles, it doesn't touch the public
imagination any longer. Religions emerged too early in human evolution—they set up symbols that people took literally, and they're as dead as
a line of totem poles. Religions should have come later, when the human
race begins to near its end. Sadly, crime is the only spur that rouses us.
We're fascinated by that "other world" where everything is possible.'

'Most people would say there's more than enough crime already.'

'But not here!' Crawford gestured with the jade horse at the distant balconies beyond the alley. 'Not in the Residencia Costasol, or the retirement complexes along the coast. The future has landed, Charles, the nightmare is already being dreamed. I believe in people, and know they deserve better.'

'You'll bring them back to life—with amateur porn-films, burglary and cocaine?'

'They're just the means. People are so hung up about sex and property and self-control. I'm not talking about crime in the sense that Cabrera thinks of it. I mean anything that breaks the rules, sidesteps the social taboos.'

'You can't play tennis without observing the rules.'

'But, Charles . . . ' Crawford seemed almost lightheaded as he searched for a retort. 'When your opponent cheats, think how you raise your game.'

We carried the last of the stolen property to the Porsche. I walked back to my car, ready to leave Crawford, but he opened the door and slipped into the passenger seat. The sun shone through the side windows of the Citroën, flushing his face with an almost fevered glow. He had been eager for me to hear him out, but I sensed that he no longer cared if anyone believed him. Despite myself, I felt drawn to him, this small-time healer moving like a mendicant preacher down the coasts of the dead. I knew that his ministry would almost certainly fail and lead to a cell in Zarzuella jail.

'I hope it works,' I told him. 'How did Frank feel about all this? Was it his idea?'

'No, Frank's far too moralistic. I'd thought about it for years, in fact ever since I was a child. My father was a deacon at Ely Cathedral. Unhappy man, never knew how to show affection to me or my mother. What he did like was knocking me around.'

'Nasty—did no one report him?'

'They didn't know, not even my mother. I was hyperactive and always banging into things. But I noticed it made him feel better. After a session with the strap he'd hold me tight and even love me. So I started getting up to all kinds of naughty pranks just to provoke him.'

'Painful medicine. And that gave you the idea?'

'In a way. I found that thieving and little criminal schemes could stir things up. Father knew what was going on and never tried to stop me. At the choir school he'd see me gingering up the boys before an away match, stealing from their lockers and messing up their kit. We always won by six tries to nil. The last time Father used the strap he suggested I take holy orders.'

'Did you?'

'No, but I was tempted. I wasted a couple of years at Cambridge reading anthropology, played a lot of tennis and then joined the army on a short-service commission. The regiment went out to Hong Kong, working with the Kowloon police. A totally demoralized bunch — morale was flat on the floor. They were waiting for the mainland Chinese to take over and send them all to Sinkiang. The villagers in the New Territories were just as bad, already paying cumshaw to the Chinese border guards. They'd lost all heart, letting the paddy fields drain and making a pittance out of smuggling.'

'But you put a stop to that? How, exactly?'

'I livened things up. A spot of thieving here and there, a few gallons of diesel oil in the congs where they stored their rice. Suddenly everyone was sitting up, started rebuilding the dykes and cleaning the canals.'

'And the Kowloon police?'

'Same thing. We had problems with cross-border migrants looking for the good life in Hong Kong. Instead of handing them back we roughed them up a little first. That did the trick with the local police. Believe me, there's nothing like a "war crime" to perk up the soldiery. It's a terrible thing to say, but war crimes do have their positive side. It's a pity I couldn't have stayed on longer, I might have put some backbone into the colony.'

'You had to leave?'

'After a year. The Colonel asked me to resign my commission. One of the Chinese sergeants got over-enthusiastic.'

'He didn't appreciate that he was taking part in a . . . psychological experiment?'

'I don't think he did. But it all stayed in my mind. I started playing a lot of tennis, worked at Rod Laver's club and then came here. The curious thing is that Estrella de Mar and the Residencia Costasol are rather like Kowloon.' He adjusted the rear-view mirror and stared at his reflection, nodding to himself in confirmation. 'I'll leave you, Charles. Take care.'

'Good advice.' As he opened the door I said: 'I assume it was you who tried to strangle me?'

I expected Crawford to be embarrassed, but he turned to stare at me with genuine concern, surprised by the stern note in my voice. 'Charles, that was . . . a gesture of affection. It sounds strange, but I mean it. I wanted to wake you and make you believe in yourself. It's an old interrogation technique, one of the Kowloon inspectors showed me all the pressure points. It's amazingly effective at giving people a clearer perspective on everything. You needed to be roused, Charles. Look at you now, you're almost ready to play tennis with me . . . '

He held my shoulder in a friendly grip, saluted and sprinted back to the Porsche.

LATER THAT EVENING, as I stood on the balcony of Frank's apartment at the Club Nautico, I thought of Bobby Crawford and the Kowloon police. In that world of corrupt border officials and thieving villagers a young English lieutenant with a taste for violence would have fitted in like a pickpocket in a Derby Day crowd. For all his strange idealism, the Residencia Costasol would defeat him. A few bored wives might film themselves having sex with their lovers, but the attractions of t'ai chi, madrigals and volunteer committee work would soon pall. The sports club would remain deserted, leaving Elizabeth Shand to tear up her leases.

I felt the bruises on my neck, and realized that Crawford had been recruiting me when he stepped from the darkness and seized my throat. A laying-on of hands had taken place, as he appointed me to fill Frank's vacant role. By not injuring me he had made the point that the Hollinger murders were irrelevant to the real life of Estrella de Mar and the new social order sustained by his criminal regime.

SOON AFTER MIDNIGHT I was woken by a flash of light across the bedroom ceiling. I stepped on to the balcony and searched for the beacon of the Marbella lighthouse, assuming that an electrical discharge had destroyed the lantern. But the beam continued its soft circuit of the sky.

The flames leapt from the centre of the Costasol marina. A yacht was on fire, its mast glowing like a candlewick. Cut loose from its moorings, it drifted across the open water, a fire-ship searching the darkness for a phantom fleet. But after scarcely a minute the flames seemed to snuff themselves out, and I guessed that the yacht had sunk before Bobby Crawford could rouse the Costasol residents from a slumber even deeper than sleep. Already I suspected that the yacht was the *Halcyon,* and that Crawford had persuaded Andersson to sail the craft from its berth at Estrella de Mar, ready to signal his arrival to the peoples of his ministry.

THE NEXT MORNING, when I passed the marina on my way to the sports club, a police launch circled the debris-strewn water. A small crowd stood on the quay, watching a frogman dive to the submerged sloop. The usually silent yachts and cruisers had begun to stir with activity. A few owners were testing their rigging and engines, while their wives aired the cabins and buffed the brass. Only Andersson sat quietly in the boatyard, face as bleak as ever, smoking a roll-up cigarette as he stared at the rising sails.

I left him to his vigil and drove across the plaza to the club. A car turned through the gates ahead of me and parked by the entrance. Two middle-aged couples, dressed in their crispest tennis whites, stepped nimbly from the car, rackets swinging in their hands.

'Mr. Prentice? Good morning to you.' One of the husbands, a retired dentist I had seen in the wine store, strolled up to me. 'We're not members, but we'd like to join. Can you sign us up?'

'Of course.' I shook his hand and beckoned the party towards the entrance. 'You'll be glad to know that the first year's membership is entirely free.'

Bobby Crawford's first recruits were signing on for duty.

from

Filth

by Irvine Welsh

SO THE EVENING finds me down at the Lodge listening to some referee twat who's a building inspector with the district council. He's holding court and it's not a bad crack. Bladesey's lost. He comes over to join
us sporting his new glesses, but like most English cunts, he kens nowt
about fitba. Ray Lennox appears with a couple of uniformed spastics, who
aren't wearing their uniforms but are still uniformed spastics and always
will be. I nod to him to come over and he's squeezing in beside me. I've
tipped him off before about hanging around with these nonentities. Associate too much with losers and that's exactly what you'll become.

This referee's some cunt. — So there I was at Ibrox and they need the
three points to clinch the title. I mean, they're about thirty points ahead
so it's a foregone conclusion, it's mathematically impossible for them to
be caught. It's a gala day, and the families are all out, the bairns with their
faces painted up, the lads looking forward to celebrating. Coisty's put
them one-nil up with a close-range tap-in at the back post. Ha ha ha. He's
some character. Suspicion of offside but Oswald Beckton's flag stayed
down. Oswald, Lodge 364. You'll ken his face, the ref prompts.

There's a few nods and knowing smiles around the table. — So anyway,
the whole place goes up and it's party-time. Everybody's singing 'we're up
to our knees in fenian blood' and it's a gala atmosphere. But then, with a

couple of minutes left, a long ball gets punted through the middle towards the Rangers goal. This young lad nips inbetween Goughy and McLaren and they bring him down heavily inside the box. Now, it's a blatant penalty, but of course there's no way I'm going to give that and spoil the party. I mean, they'd've had to have gone to Firhill the next week to win it, stuck with a fifteen thousand capacity. How could I spoil it for them to lift the flag at home? They were going to win it anyway! By the length of Argyll Street! No way was yours truly going to be a killjoy. Imagine what the boys in the Lodge at Whitburn would have said! My life wouldnae have been worth living. Spoiling a gala day out! So I waved play on.

—As ye do mate, eh, Councillor Bill Armitage said.

—I had to send off this tube for arguing. The ref's decision is final. This arsehole wouldnae let it go, even after I'd booked him. There's always one, eh!

—Fenian bastard, Bill Armitage scoffed.

—I don't mind telling ye, the ref continues,—that it was a bit embarrassing watching it on Scotball the next day. The boys were great though, they kept the replays to a minimum and avoided any reverse-angle showings. Anyway, I spoke to the SFA observer at the match in the Blue Room afterwards and he understood the situation fully. Turns out that he's in the same Lodge as wee Sammy Kirkwood. You mind of wee Sammy! He says to me.

I nod. Wee Sammy used to get me magazines. Good stuff n all, though not quite as good as Hector The Farmer's. I'll have to bell that auld fucker and see if he's got any new gear.

—Anyway, thank God for the presenter. He said there was no way I could have seen the incident as I wasn't up with play. The guys at the press were great as well, played the whole thing down, didn't let on that the switchboards were jammed with callers. Passed off the odd one or two as token Tim bigots who would say that anyway.

—These cunts are paranoid, Armitage laughs.

—A chief sports writer for one of the dailies told me at the Lodge, he says: normally we'd have made a bit more of a song and dance about it but it does nobody any good to keep running Scottish football down.   •

We then listen to Armitage going on a bit about the new Scottish Parliament.—It'll be a good thing; mair opportunities for our people. Of course we'll have tae deal with the Papes, but there's nothing new there. The party in Scotland's always had that horse-trading between the Catholic mafia and the craft. Ah wouldnae mind gieing them anti-abortion legislation in exchange for some plum chairmanships of working parties or committees . . . particularly licensing, he grins.—It just means that some daft wee hairy that gets knocked up the duff has tae get oan the bus tae Carlisle tae get cleaned oot. Hardly a staggering blow, I would have thought.

—Right enough, Ray nods, then turning to me whispers,—Fancy some coke the night?

I fancied some fucking coke awright, in fact I had some on me. Especially after Toal's news, Drummond heading up the team. Toal. The cunt'll not be happy until he turns me into a fuckin junky.

Me answering to a silly wee lassie?

00000000000000 eating, on and on. 000000000 eating. Perhaps there are others like me. I can certainly conceive of this, the notion that I am not the only one of my kind. Why should I be? Perhaps there are others in here, sharing the parasite role with me. I even fancy that I can feel them in here, twisting and writhing in the Hort's gut with me, but this may be just a response to my melancholic state of mind. I've my Host, my friend who gives me everything I need to survive. But to live, I need much more. I need to feel part of something bigger perhaps something that is part of me. 00000000000000000 0000000000000 it has to be said that this laddie's diet is not that nutritious. This points to my Host coming from, perhaps, a poor disadvantageous starting-out point in this great journey of life. He's eating all sorts of cheap and useless garbage. But on the other hand, the sheer volume consumed goes against this; so maybe we can postulate that the laddie has grown up in a world of privation

Aye, right. I d   ere's a failure on
Toal's part to re   blank and can't
see the possibil   t bit his fucking
useless erse.

I'm up to the   ge business is the
only thing that k   d the rest of the
polis boys again   guys. They tend
tae be a sorry b   ve situation. So
it's me, Lennox   ian Main, Steve
Underwood, Ke   from Aberdeen.

Masonic ritu   pressed sexuality
in that keeps th   the likes of Ray
Lennox and th   e business with
any of them. A   lture within the
masons, but wa   uch further than
any of those cun

In the back   patterns, and a
strobe light wh   ing and shaking
as Coulson cut   hed whine, and
Underwood's o   the tube into the
incision and suc   g the bottle and
it gets auld Gus   out women in a
lusty way, whic   honour, and the

withering loo\ *and although he has been able to accumu-* /x *pas* has been
made. Still, y   *late more resources he has not quite been*   \ auld spastic.
  We get o | *able to shed himself of all those proletarian habits.* |Phillip, as the
dark beers h| *0000000The Host's philosophy of life seems* |ng just about
every cunt's \ *then; more rather than better. 00000000000* |ety. Ray and I
shake off Bladesey after I've pumped the sorry cunt for more information
about Bunty's mental state. Then we abscond back to his flat. Ray's place
is furnished post-Thatcherite nouveau schemie single-shagger style. That
is to say, no real style at all. It's dominated by a red suite, a two-seater vel-
vety love-couch and matching chair. It's like a hoor's room back in the
Dam! I'm no sitting in that couch, Lennox should be so lucky. If it was
fuckin Inglis, he'd be oan it like a shot! No that he would feel anything if
it was Lennox that was up him!

Ray's looking for the mirror, spoon and razor-blade kit I brought him
back from the Dam. He reckons that it gives extra quality tae the chop
and never uses credit cards indoors now. I realise that the set cost me
the equivalent of twenty quid in UK cash and feel a resentment rise up
in my chest. It was a moment of weakness giving Lennox a present,
even if I only gave him it in order to encourage him to sort me out with
posh. I idly press the tip of my fag against his velvet cushion, feeling a
satisfying rush of adrenalin and a lump rise in my chest as it browns and
parts on the first, second, third and fourth contact. Then I admire my
handiwork, before quickly flipping the cushion over to conceal the four
new holes.

Lennox returns and chops out some lines. He's been on D.S. duty and
has nabbed quite a bit of high grade, the lucky bastard. I've divided up
the stuff I brought back from Amsterdam, and thought it pains me to
admit it, Lennox gear's even better. The perks of the job. Okay for some.
What about me? What perks do you get on topped coons? Going round
community groups talking to chip-on-the-shoulder darkies who hate your
guts. And that daft wee lassie Drummond sticking her oar in. Fuck that
for a game of soldiers. Big-time OT on this one mind you, especially with
that docile mutation Toal's breeks full of sludgy, soft shite. Same rules
applying in that case, I kid you not.

— The last sniff I got off these morons I busted, I'm telling you Robbo,
what a total waste ay time. There was so little coke in it, I should've just
left the spastics to it and saved myself the fucking paperwork. They'd have

felt a hell of a lot worse if they had done that rubbish than they did getting a poxy two hundred quid first offence fine.

Lennox is letting his mouser grow a bit.—That's fucking disgusting. Two hundred poxy quid! Who was the magistrate?

—Urquhart. Surprise, Lennox says, not looking up, firmly engrossed in the chopping up of the lines. He's got patience Lennox, he knows that I want that line, but the cunt'll play around until he's got it as fine as fuck.

—Mr fuckin pat-oan-the-heid-and-penny-oot-the-poor-boax, my head's shaking in disgust.

—Conrad fuckin Donaldson defending the cunts as well, Ray scoffs.

I smile at that name. I wonder how his wee lassie's doing. We could handle another gam fae that little sweetheart. I kid you not.

Ray nods at me to come ahead. I'm on the first line, my twenty's already rolled. I close one nostril and snort for Caledonia. It hits me hard. Good gear. Phoah, ya fuckin cunt that ye are. My mouth is instantly numbed and I start gabbing.—Listen Ray you should've heard that cunt Toal on aboot you the other day. It was Ray Lennox this, Ray Lennox that. I said to the cunt, there's an awfay lot ay things getting attributed tae Ray Lennox here. I think Ray Lennox would be baulking at some of the stuff his name's being mentioned in connection with.

—Eh? What's this, Ray asks, looking at me tentatively.

—Between you and me Ray, I wouldnae be surprised if you get drafted into the team on this coon case.

—Like fuck! Ah've been stalking these fucking Sunrise Community hippies on this cannabis bust for months!

—I'm just saying Ray. You know these cunts, same rules apply. One other thing as well . . . this is between you and me likes, I drop my voice canteen-style, even though we're in the privacy of Lennox's gaff.

—What? says Ray, trying to be cool but obviously alarmed.

—Watch Gus.

—Gus Bain?

—Precisely.

—Gus is awright . . . he's been good tae me . . .

—Of course he's awright. He'll have been awright tae you as long as he sees ye as a young laddie, as second fiddle. The thing is Ray, you've earned a lot ay respect in this department, and it's starting tae get tae the auld boy. Ye ken what ah'm saying? I look Lennox in the eye. He's getting the drift I want him to get. — It's the young stag syndrome. Gus is set in his ways. One of the auld school. But he fears the new breed and he can be quite a vindictive old cunt and he's been taking an unhealthy interest in the career progress and extracurricular activities to date of a certain Minister Raymond Lennox.

—You saying that Gus is a squealer?

—Known for it. Watch what you say about cousin charlie when he's around.

—But I never say anything about charlie.

—Aye, well mind and keep it that way.

—Right . . . Lennox nods thoughtfully. — I appreciate this Robbo.

This is all bullshit, but life is one big competition. Ray is a pal, but he's also a potential or actual competitor and the only way to handle competitors is to control their level of uncertainty. That's what life is all about: the management of your opponents' uncertainty levels. We don't want this cunt getting too big for his boots, thinking that he somehow counts.

It's a troubled-looking Ray Lennox who snorts his line. The drug instantly restores that veneer of arrogance, but the seeds of doubt have been planted and the comedown will see the harvest of confusion just ripe for us to reap.

Permissions

About the Editors

Stephen Hyde graduated in film at the University of Westminster, London. He has worked as a researcher and has co-edited the anthologies *Players* and *White Lines* for Thunder's Mouth Press. He lives in Portsmouth, England.

Geno Zanetti is the editor of the acclaimed anthology, *She's a Bad Motorcycle*, which *Jane* magazine described as "super cool" and *Rocky Mountain News* described as "a remarkable collection." He divides his time between Solentsea, England, and New York City.